Statesmanship

Jason Cowley has been widely credited with transforming the fortunes of the *New Statesman*. He is a former editor of *Granta* and has worked on *The Times* and *Observer*. According to the European Press Prize, 'Cowley has succeeded in revitalising the *New Statesman* and re-establishing its position as an influential political and cultural weekly. He has given it an edge and a relevance to current affairs it hasn't had for years.' He is a three-time winner of Editor of the Year (Politics and Current Affairs) at the British Society of Magazine Editors awards. His book of essays and political profiles, *Reaching for Utopia*, was published in 2018.

Statesmanship

The Best of the New Statesman 1913–2020

Edited and introduced by Jason Cowley

WEIDENFELD & NICOLSON

First published in Great Britain in 2019 by Weidenfeld & Nicolson
This paperback edition published in 2021 by Weidenfeld & Nicolson
an imprint of The Orion Publishing Group Ltd
Carmelite House, 50 Victoria Embankment
London EC4Y 0DZ

An Hachette UK Company

1 3 5 7 9 10 8 6 4 2

Anthology © *New Statesman* 2019, 2021
Foreword © Claire Tomalin 2019
Introduction © Jason Cowley 2019, 2021

ISBN (Paperback) 978 1 4746 1927 1
ISBN (eBook) 978 1 4746 1502 0

Typeset by Input Data Services Ltd, Somerset
Printed and bound in Great Britain by Clays Ltd, Elcograf, S.p.A.

www.weidenfeldandnicolson.co.uk
www.orionbooks.co.uk

Contents

The Critical Condition

The Rest of Life

Short Stories

Poems

Foreword

I went to work for the *New Statesman* in 1968, just over 50 years ago, to be deputy literary editor. I felt myself very lucky to be offered the job by the poet Anthony Thwaite and accepted by the editor, Paul Johnson. The NS was to me a great institution, read by just about everyone I knew, family and friends.

It was a three-day-a-week job, perfect for me as I had three daughters of school age – and I liked nothing better than reading. The sight of the big tables covered in parcels of new books, up on the second floor where the back half of the paper was produced, filled me with happiness. The offices were then in a tall, narrow building on Great Turnstile, an alley between Lincoln's Inn Fields and Holborn – to this day I cannot walk along it without a nostalgic pang. Up the steep stairs we had one big room where the critics came to deliver their copy, and a very small room for the literary editor – which I occupied later. Journalism was a gregarious activity in those days, with a lot of talking face to face, in the office – contributors came in to look through the books – in the pub, and over cheap convivial lunches in Red Lion Street and thereabouts.

Richard Crossman succeeded Paul Johnson as editor in 1970 – I was pregnant and he offered me generous maternity leave, during which the poet James Fenton took over my job. Crossman asked me to keep writing for the paper, and a piece I wrote on Mary Wollstonecraft led to my first book. I returned to the *NS* as literary editor in 1974, when Tony Howard was editor. It was a very lively place by then. Francis Hope was the most brilliant of colleagues, as skilful at setting the weekly competition as composing a political essay – tragically he died in a plane crash that year. Christopher Hitchens was working for the front half by then and I brought in Martin Amis and later Julian Barnes.

Picking up the telephone to commission a review from an admired writer, or someone you see as likely to become one, is a very enjoyable way of life: Jonathan Raban, Hilary Spurling, Victoria Glendinning, Marina Warner, Paul Theroux were some who wrote for us. And I was very happy to be able to choose the books I wanted to review myself. In fact working for the *NS* gave me a further education for which I have always been grateful. I don't doubt that it will continue to educate its readers and its staff, and to entertain us all for another century: this amazing anthology shows how consistently it has upheld its high standards.

Claire Tomalin

Introduction

The *New Statesman* was founded in a spirit of optimism as a weekly review of politics and literature on 12 April 1913. Beatrice and Sidney Webb and their friends among the Fabians – George Bernard Shaw contributed a fifth of the £5,000 start-up costs – wanted their own 'newspaper' to propagate their ideas and promote what they hoped would be a scientific socialist transformation of society: the lead editorial in the first issue described the 'world movement towards collectivism'. But Beatrice did not expect the *New Statesman* to endure: 'If I were forced to wager, I should not back our success,' she confided in a diary entry.

Through their efforts – they cofounded the London School of Economics and the young William Beveridge worked for them as a researcher – the Webbs helped lay the foundations of what would become the postwar welfare state. Yet they were a curious couple with eccentric opinions, even for their time. Resolute statists rather than liberals, they were not much interested in individual freedom. They thought the man in Whitehall knew what was best for the working class. They were imperialists and Beatrice, in particular, was a snob. They had an alarming interest in eugenics. And they were fellow-travellers of the Soviet Union, publishing a much-derided book, *Soviet Communism: an Ideal Civilisation?* in 1935. A later, revised edition dropped the qualifying question mark, as one would.

Quite early on, the *New Statesman*, edited in its early years by Clifford Sharp, a Fabian who became an ally of the Asquithian Liberals but who was also a drunk and a spy, began to slip free from the Webbs' influence. In 1931, now under the editorship of Kingsley Martin, a former *Guardian* leader writer, it merged with the *Nation*, the weekly voice of Bloomsbury liberalism. John Maynard Keynes, as chairman of the *Nation*, joined the board of the renamed *New Statesman and Nation*. So these were the early influences that defined and shaped the *New Statesman*: the Fabians, Keynes, Whig radicalism and Bloomsbury bohemianism.

*

Under Martin's editorship (1931-60) the circulation grew rapidly, especially during the Second World War and in spite of paper rationing and a reduction in pagination, and the *New Statesman* achieved greatness. Its literary pages were perhaps the finest in the land and the magazine, as Melvyn Bragg has written of discovering it in the library of Wigton Grammar School, offered for many aspiring readers a 'window on the great world'. The circulation only began to decline in the Seventies and Eighties, when the weekend newspapers launched their own magazines and cultural reviews. The revival of the *New Statesman* has coincided with the rise of the internet and the decline of newspapers.

On 23 November 1957 the philosopher and pacifist Bertrand Russell published an open letter in the paper to two 'Most Potent Sirs', the US president, Dwight Eisenhower, and the first secretary of the Soviet Communist Party, Nikita Khrushchev. In it he wrote passionately about the dangers nuclear weapons posed to the world. Unilateral nuclear disarmament – eventually adopted as official policy by the Labour Party in 1982, and still favoured by the Scottish National Party and Labour's remaining Corbynites – was one of the radical causes Martin championed. The paper became the pulpit from which this passionately committed son of a Nonconformist minister and his colleagues addressed the world.

Russell's open letter had a powerful effect. Shortly before Christmas 1957, a letter from the Soviet embassy arrived at the *New Statesman*'s offices in Great Turnstile Street, London. Because it was written in Russian it was discarded in a wastepaper basket, from where it would be retrieved by either Norman Mackenzie or Paul Johnson, then staff editors (I spoke to both men about the letter and each claimed to have retrieved it). Whoever did so, it was a smart decision; the letter was from Khrushchev, and enclosed with it was his unsolicited reply to Russell, which was published. Early in 1958, the US secretary of state, John Foster Dulles, writing on behalf of Eisenhower, responded to both Khrushchev and Russell.

That cold war nuclear diplomacy was being played out in the pages of the *New Statesman* was testament to its extraordinary influence in the immediate postwar years, when it succeeded in expressing the hopes and aspirations of a generation of progressives who believed that history had purpose and a direction. But it was not only of interest to progressives: the *Statesman* was essential reading for anyone interested in politics and culture, irrespective of their ideological allegiances.

The *New Statesman* was, as I have noted, conceived as a weekly 'review of politics and literature'. Note those two words, 'politics' *and* 'literature'. H. G. Wells and Shaw were among the famous authors who wrote about world affairs (we have included in the book Wells's astonishing and, indeed, deferential 1934 interview with Stalin in Moscow). In the early 1920s, the novelist Arnold Bennett served as chairman and became one of the *New Statesman*'s chief benefactors. From the beginning, it published poetry and fiction, though in later decades it became more narrowly political, and its literary pages were truncated. When I became editor, in the autumn of 2008, I increased the number of pages dedicated to literary reviews, essays and long reads, and re-introduced poetry as well as (more occasionally) fiction.

In 1956, in his celebrated essay on the 'Two cultures', which was first published in the magazine, C. P. Snow articulated the division between science and the humanities. Yet in the *New Statesman* itself there was for too long a decisive separation between the politics and the literature. The *New Statesman* was affectionately caricatured as a 'pantomime horse', with the 'political' front and 'cultural' back halves characterised by different sensibilities. It was as if the demands of politics and literature were in some way antagonistic: that to concentrate too much on the political would be to neglect the literary and to be too literary would be to misunderstand or to be insufficiently serious about politics. I have ignored these artificial divisions, returning the magazine to its founding mission.

The *New Statesman* has been at its best and boldest when it aspired to be much more than a journal of Westminster politics: when it has campaigned and agitated (CND, Charter 88, against appeasement of Hitler, for decolonisation and gender, racial and sexual equality), and when it has been as interested in good literary style as in exposing injustice. Above all, even in the leanest years, when it came close to bankruptcy on several occasions, the *New Statesman* knew what it was against: subordination, privation, unaccountable power, the mystique of hierarchy, social and economic inequalities, racial and sexual discrimination. And it has never ceased publishing some of the finest writers of the age: Keynes, Orwell, Virginia Woolf, J. B. Priestley, V. S. Pritchett, Philip Larkin, John Berger, Christopher Hitchens, Ian McEwan, Clive James, John Gray, Ali Smith. . .

Today, the *New Statesman* is once more in robust health: the print and digital circulation is growing steadily and we have several million unique visitors to our website every month. The number of staff is at its highest ever level. We publish a weekly print magazine, plus newsletters and podcasts, and we have a vibrant and ever-growing website. And the division between the front and back halves has been abolished. We are beholden to no party, and our politics are sceptical and increasingly unpredictable.

This book, *Statesmanship*, showcases the richness and breadth of our archive (which is not yet fully digitised, so no doubt I have missed many great pieces). It has been organised into sections: 'A Radical Century', 'Lives and Letters', 'The Critical Condition' and 'The Rest of Life', with a selection of poetry, and four stand-out stories from the past two decades. I wrote or spoke to previous *New Statesman* editors to ask for their recommendations. Some of the articles have been edited or slightly truncated. Others, such as the letter that led to the creation of Mass Observation, have been included because they are of consequential importance. Some have been chosen because of their prescience or the insights they offer into world-historic figures: Hitler, Stalin, Trotsky ... And others have been chosen because of their intrinsic literary value, such as Virginia Woolf's short piece on Lewis Carroll, in which she explores the mystery and ruthlessness of childhood; the unsigned profile from the 1950s of Jean-Paul Sartre; or V. S. Pritchett's reflection on the death of Orwell. Several pieces were selected simply because they made us laugh – including the actor Hugh Grant's undercover investigation into phone-hacking, Paul Johnson's attack – from the early 1960s – on the cult of the Beatles, and Martin Amis's dismissal of the young David Bowie ('unlikely to last long as a cult'). It's an eclectic selection and, I hope, an enriching one.

In the wonderful long final paragraph of *Homage to Catalonia* (1938), George Orwell describes returning to England from the Spanish civil war, in which he fought for the POUM militia, was shot in the throat and almost died. Orwell had a troubled relationship with the *New Statesman* because of Kingsley Martin's refusal to publish his dispatches from Spain during the civil war. Orwell loathed 'orthodoxy sniffers', of left and right, and totalitarians, and he believed that Martin allowed his personal politics to affect the independence of his editorial judgement.

But back in England, after the torment of his experiences in Catalonia, Orwell discovered the old country was at once reassuringly becalmed and yet complacent:

> 'And then England – southern England, probably the sleekest landscape in the world. It is difficult when you pass that way, especially when you are peacefully recovering from sea-sickness with the plush cushions of a boat-train carriage under your bum, to believe that anything is really happening anywhere. Earthquakes in Japan, famines in China, revolutions in Mexico? Don't worry, the milk will be on the doorstep tomorrow morning, the *New Statesman* will come out on Friday. . .'

Here we are now, in the midst of a global pandemic – and the *New Statesman* is still coming out on a Friday, though in the age of social media the world has changed in ways that even the Webbs, Keynes, Shaw, Orwell and the rest could never have imagined. We consider it our duty to explain and understand this world, without prejudice, with an open mind, and if not in the Webbs' spirit of optimism then in the spirit of sceptical inquiry.

London, September 2020

A Radical
Century

Women's Hidden Discontent

Christabel Pankhurst

Militancy is, as it were, the flowering of the woman's movement for equality. Women's long-existing, hidden discontent with their condition of inferiority, and the patient and law-abiding Woman Suffrage campaign of the last century, were the preparation for militancy.

The non-militant suffrage agitation was of the nineteenth century; the militant agitation is of the twentieth. The anti-militant Suffragism of the present day is, in the opinion of the militant women, an anachronism. Militancy is a political weapon used by women as the only discoverable substitute for the vote. But it is more than that. It is a means of breaking up the false relation of inferior to superior that has existed between men and women, and it is a means of correcting the great faults that have been produced in either sex by the subjection of women.

Subjection had made women unnaturally diffident and unnaturally submissive. Their dominion over women has made men overbearing and vainglorious. Militancy is a sign and an expression of the fact that women have shaken off their diffidence and their servility. Women's militancy is an education to men, because it shows them women not any longer appealing to them – 'coaxing them', as Mr Lloyd George has put it – but, instead, denying their title to withhold the vote.

Anti-militancy involved an admission that men ought to be obeyed and their laws obeyed by women in spite of the disfranchisement of women. Anti-militancy is therefore perilously near to anti-Suffragism. It is, in fact, indistinguishable from the policy of patient Griselda. For Suffragists to be law-abiding at any and every cost is an evil, because this flatters the self-importance of men and disinclines them to concede a demand so meekly made of them. Militancy has not only educated men by proving that there is a limit to women's endurance, but it has roused the best in them. Never since the days of John

3

Stuart Mill, who, with other men of a most exceptional quality, made the Woman Suffrage cause his own, have men so greatly served this cause as during the days of militancy. The spectacle of women fighting for liberty and literally facing death for its sake has more power to rouse men's sense of justice than have any words, however wise and eloquent.

There has been much vague denunciation of militancy, but not a single valid argument has been brought against its use. As a political method it holds the field to the exclusion of every other, save that of voting. It is idle to point to other countries in which women have won the vote by peaceful means. These other countries are not Britain. Politics and political activity do not in any other country hold the same high place in the interest of men as they hold in Britain. Ours is an old country. Prejudice and conservatism in the ugliest sense of the term are entrenched here as they are entrenched nowhere else, unless it be in Turkey. The British man's attitude towards women – above all the British politician's attitude towards women – is a matter of contempt and derision in our Colonies, in America, and in all those enlightened countries where women have the vote. Comparisons between Suffrage conditions in Britain and Suffrage conditions elsewhere are in the highest degree misleading. Besides, it is impossible to ignore the fact that it is since the beginning of British militancy, which has called to attention the whole civilised world, that the greater number of Suffrage victories have occurred. Nothing can be more unprofitable than for a British Suffragist to be daydreaming about the victories won by peaceful methods in countries more enlightened than her own. There is for her no wisdom save in reflection upon the past political history of her own country, in observation of the conditions now existing there, and in the invention of a policy based upon historical knowledge and upon a knowledge of the temperament of her countrymen and the political conditions of her own land. For the British Suffragist militancy is the only way. Militancy will succeed where all other policies will fail.

The virtue of militancy proceeds from the fact that government rests upon the consent of the governed. When the unenfranchised become ungovernable, then is enfranchisement given to them. The only reason why militancy has not long ago resulted in the conquest of votes for women is that not enough women have been militant. The number of militants required to create a situation from which the Government will be driven to escape by granting votes for women is a matter which experiment alone can determine. To those who still doubt the necessity of militancy, the final answer is this. Consider the men who now are at the head of the political parties, consider the men not yet advanced to leadership who are likely to succeed them, and then say whether you believe that the Asquiths, the Lloyd Georges, or the F. E. Smiths, of the present or of the future, are likely to be moved to give votes to women by reasoned and patient appeal – by anything save sheer compulsion!

The case for militancy as a political method is unassailable. Attacks upon militancy have, however, been made chiefly on the score of morality. Militancy, we are told, is wrong, and lawlessness and violence are wrong. The breach of a law, as John Hampden and others have taught by word and by example, is right or wrong according to the nature of the law and the authority possessed by the lawgiver. Bad laws made without due authority ought not to be obeyed, but ought to be resisted by every honest man and woman. It is such laws that militant Suffragists have broken. By marching to Parliament Square they have broken laws which seek to prevent them as voteless citizens from using the only means available to them of claiming the redress of their grievances. But apart from that, all the laws on the Statute book are, as they affect women, bad for want of lawful authority in those who have made them. Women's claim to the vote implies a denial of the validity of any law to which their consent has not been obtained.

Violence is wrong, say the anti-militants. Nothing could be more untrue. Violence has no moral complexion whatsoever. In itself it is neither right nor wrong. Its rightness or wrongness depends entirely upon the circumstances under which it is used. If violence is wrong in itself, then it is wrong to break a breakfast egg, it is wrong to hammer in a nail, it is wrong to pierce a tunnel through the rock, it is wrong to break into a burning house to save the life of a child. Yet, as we know, all these actions are entirely moral. This is because, though violent, they, like militancy, are justified by the motive of those who do them and the object with which they are done. If there are any who still condemn militancy, then they must condemn Nature herself, the Arch-Militant, who to achieve her purposes works so much violence.

The strange fact is that many fervent anti-militants are themselves in favour of militancy – when it is the militancy of men. Some of the foremost amongst them vigorously upheld the South African war, with all its accompaniments of farm-burning and concentration camps. Their souls were thrilled to sympathetic approval when men were militant in Turkey at the time of the revolution, when men were militant during the Chinese revolution, and when men were militant in the Balkan States. Approval of all this militancy was publicly expressed by the leaders of anti-militant Suffragism. Even women they will allow to be militant provided they are not militant in the cause of votes for women. Thus in the official organ of the law-abiding movement we read these words:

> The world is governed by ideas, and force is helpless against them. Not the arms of France, but the faith of Joan of Arc turned the tide of fortune against the English in the Hundred Years' war. Not the arms of William of Orange, but his spirit and the spirit of his people, their patriotism, their religion, wore down the innumerable hosts of Spain.

These words represent precisely the view held by the militants, though they come strangely from the pen of women who condemn militancy. It is the conviction of the militants that their lesser force will overcome the greater force directed against them by the Government. This will happen because of the faith that is in the militants, and because of the spirit of which militancy is the expression. But that does not mean that Suffragists can win without the use of force. If Joan of Arc had relied upon faith without force it is not unlikely that the English would have been in possession of France at the present day. If William of Orange had trusted to spirit, patriotism and religion and nothing more to win his battles, his military successes would have been inconspicuous indeed! The truth is that violence in such cases is itself the expression of the faith, spirit, patriotism and religion of those who employ it. It is then that we have militancy. Violence that is not inspired by spirit and illuminated by faith is not militancy, it is brutality. It is the Suffragettes who are militant, while the Government seek to overcome them by brutality.

People have said as an argument against militancy that it 'rouses the beast in men' – the beast that, as they say, civilisation has put to sleep. If there are men possessed by a familiar spirit so unpleasant as to deserve this name, it is time that that spirit were driven out of them. Better far that well-fed, self-reliant, happy women should undertake the task of luring forth the beast and slaying it than that its victims should be, as now they are, white slaves and other unhappy, exploited women. It would seem that the anti-militants take a less favourable view of the nature of the opposite sex than do the Suffragettes. The Suffragettes pay men the compliment of believing that the brutal is not an essential and unchangeable part of them to be drugged into quiescence, but never to be eradicated.

There are people, again, whose objections to militancy seem to be based on the fact that it involves destruction of property. They would appear to forget that human liberty may, after all, be worth some broken windows or a blaze or two. Whatever may happen, militancy done for the sake of votes for women is not likely to be so destructive to the material interests of the country as was the South African war, waged for the sake of votes for men.

In answering objections to militancy, the Suffragettes have regard to the objections raised by the women rather than to those raised by men. To men critics a sufficient reply is this: 'If you don't like militancy give us the vote, and that quickly!' It ill becomes men to prate of mere property and the Suffragettes' destruction of it, while the nation is being ravaged by venereal disease and innocent women in thousands are being infected by such disease.

The opposition to women's militancy is founded upon prejudice, and upon nothing else. For the very same acts of militancy that militant women commit would, if they were committed by voteless men, be applauded. The moral law which the Suffragettes have defied is not the moral law accepted for themselves by men. It is slave morality that the militant women have denied and defied – slave morality according to which active resistance to tyranny is the greatest crime that a subject class or a subject sex can commit.

A Note on Irish Nationalism

George Bernard Shaw

One of the best-known early contributors to the New Statesman *was the playwright and Fabian activist George Bernard Shaw. His fame helped gain early publicity for Beatrice and Sidney Webb's new weekly review of politics and literature. He also contributed £1,000 of the £5,000 in donations that funded its launch. Shaw's style was theatrical and pugnacious and invariably favoured satire and exaggeration over fact. Here he ridicules his countrymen and women, attempting to offend both Irish nationalists and Ulster loyalists.*

The world seems just now to have made up its mind that selfconsciousness is a very undesirable thing and Nationalism a very fine thing. This is not a very intelligent conclusion; for, obviously, Nationalism is nothing but a mode of self-consciousness, and a very aggressive one at that. It is, I think, altogether to Ireland's credit that she is extremely tired of the subject of herself. Even patriotism, which in England is a drunken jollity when it is not a Jewish rhapsody, is in Ireland like the genius of Jeremiah, a burning fire shut up in the bones, a pain, a protest against shame and defeat, a morbid condition which a healthy man must shake off if he is to keep sane. If you want to bore an Irishman, play him an Irish melody, or introduce him to another Irishman.

Abroad, however, it is a distinction to be an Irishman; and accordingly the Irish in England flaunt their nationality. An Englishman who had married an Irishwoman once came and asked me could I give him the name of any Englishman who had ever done anything. He explained that his wife declared that all England's statesmen, all her warriors, all her musical composers, all her notables of every degree were Irishmen, and that the English could not write their names until the Irish taught them. I suggested Gladstone. 'She says he was an Irishman,' was the reply. After this, it was clear that the man's case was desperate; so I left him to his fate.

From this you may gather that the reaction against the Nationalist variety of selfconsciousness does not mean a reaction against conceit, against ignorance, against insular contempt for foreigners, against bad manners and the other common human weaknesses which sometimes masquerade as patriotism. Ireland produces virulent varieties of all of them; for it is, on the whole, a mistake to suppose that we are a nation of angels. You can always find something better than a good Englishman and something worse than a bad one; but this is not so in Ireland: a bad Irishman is the vilest thing on earth, and a good one is a saint. Thackeray's *Barry Lyndon* is a very accurate sketch of the sort of thoroughpaced scoundrel Ireland can produce, not when she is put to it, but quite wantonly, merely for the fun of being mischievous.

In point of conceit, Ireland, especially northern Ireland, can stagger humanity. The Ulster Unionist is not a shrewd calculator who, on a careful estimate of the pressure of public opinion on any Government which should try to coerce Belfast into submission to a Dublin Parliament, concludes that he can safely bluff Home Rule out of Ulster: he really believes that he can fight and conquer the British Empire, or any other empire that is not Ulster and Protestant. If there were nothing else to be considered except the salvation of the Ulsterman's soul, it would be a positive duty for the British Empire to blow him sky high to convince him that even a Unionist God (and he believes in no other, and therefore does not really believe in God at all) has occasionally to look beyond Down and Antrim.

But these military moral lessons cost more than the souls of the regenerated are worth; and it would, I think, be more sensible to make Ulster an autonomous political lunatic asylum with an expensive fleet and a heavily fortified frontier to hold against the Pope, than to thwart its inclinations in any way. The alternative, if England would stand it, would be to make Ulster a province of England, and have the Education Acts and the Factory Acts applied in the English manner; but I doubt if Ulster would tamely submit to be identified with a country where men touch their hats to a Roman Catholic Duke of Norfolk, and meet him at dinner as if he were their equal.

What will finally settle the Ulster question is just the old-fashioned romantic Nationalism of which the South is so deadly tired. It is clear, as the world is now constituted, that prudent young men should aim at being as unlike Orangemen and as like human beings as possible, even as in the South the young men are discovering that in point of insufferableness there is not a halfpenny to choose between a Nationalist and an Orangeman. Thus, though the Protestant boys will still carry the drum, they will carry it under the green flag, and realise that the harp, the hound, and the round tower are more satisfactory to the imagination than that stupidest of decorative designs, the Union Jack. And the change can be effected without treachery to England; for, if my personal recollection does not deceive me, the Gaelic League began in Bedford Park, London, after a prolonged incubation in Somerset House.

It is not very long since I stood on the coast of Donegal and asked two boys how many languages they had. They had three. One was English, which they spoke much better than it is ever spoken in England. The second was Irish, which they spoke with their parents. The third was the language invented by the Gaelic League, which I cannot speak (being an Irishman), but which I understand to be in its qualities comparable to a blend of Esperanto with fifth-century Latin. Why should not Ulster adopt this strange tongue?

The truth is that all the Nationalist inventions that catch on now are not Irish at all. For instance, the admirable comedies of Synge, who, having escaped from Ireland to France, drew mankind in the manner of Molière, and discreetly assured the public that this was merely the human nature of the Blasket Islands, and that, of course, civilised people never admired boastful criminals nor esteemed them according to the atrocities they pretended to commit. The Playboy's real name was Synge; and the famous libel on Ireland (and who is Ireland that she should not be libeled as other countries are by their great comedians?) was the truth about the world.

PUBLISHED 13 OCTOBER 1934, WRITTEN 1928

A Letter from Germany

D. H. Lawrence

We are going back to Paris tomorrow, so this is the last moment to write a letter from Germany. Only from the fringe of Germany, too.

It is a miserable journey from Paris to Nancy, through that Marne country, where the country still seems to have had the soul blasted out of it, though the dreary fields are ploughed and level, and the pale wire trees stand up. But it is all void and null. And in the villages, the smashed houses in the street rows, like rotten teeth between good teeth. You come to Strasbourg, and the people still talk Alsatian German, as ever, in spite of French shop-signs. The place feels dead. And full of cotton goods, white goods, from Mülhausen, from the factories that once were German. Such cheap white cotton goods, in a glut.

The cathedral front rearing up high and flat and fanciful, a sort of darkness in the dark, with round rose windows and long, long prisons of stone. Queer that men should have ever wanted to put stone upon faithful stone to such a height without having it fall down. The gothic! I was always glad when my card-castle fell but these goths and alemans seemed to have a craze for peaky heights.

The Rhine is still the Rhine, the great divider. You feel it as you cross. The flat, frozen, watery places. Then the cold and curving river. Then the other side, seeming so forsaken. The train stands and steams fiercely. Then it draws through the flat Rhine plain, past frozen pools of flood-water, and frozen fields, in the emptiness of this bit of occupied territory.

Immediately you are over the Rhine, the spirit of place has changed. There is no more attempt at the bluff of geniality. The marshy places are frozen. The fields are vacant. There seems nobody in the world.

It is as if the life had retreated eastwards. As if the Germanic life were slowly ebbing away from contact with western Europe, ebbing to the deserts of the east. And there stand the heavy, ponderous round hills of the Black Forest, black with an inky blackness of Germanic

11

trees, and patched with a whiteness of snow. They are like a series of huge, involved black mounds, obstructing the vision eastwards. You look at them from the Rhine plain, and you know that you stand on an actual border, up against something.

The moment you are in Germany, you know. It feels empty, and, somehow, menacing. So must the Roman soldiers have watched those black, massive round hills: with a certain fear, and with the knowledge that they were at their own limit. A fear of the invisible natives. A fear of the invisible life lurking among the woods. A fear of their own opposite.

So it is with the French: this almost mystic fear. But one should not insult even one's fears. Germany, this bit of Germany, is very different from what it was two and a half years ago, when I was here. Then it was still open to Europe. Then it still looked to western Europe for a reunion, for a sort of reconciliation. Now that is over. The inevitable, mysterious barrier has fallen again, and the great leaning of the Germanic spirit is once more eastwards towards Russia, towards Tartary. The strange vortex of Tartary has become the positive centre again, the positivity of western Europe is broken. The positivity of our civilisation has broken. The influences that come, come invisibly out of Tartary. So that all Germany reads *Men, Beasts and Gods* with a kind of fascination. Returning again to the fascination of the destructive East, that produced Attila.

So it is at night. Baden-Baden is a quiet place. No more Turgenevs or Dostoevskys or Grand Dukes or King Edwards coming to drink the waters. All the outward effect of a world-famous watering-place. But empty now, a mere Black Forest village with the wagon-loads of timber going through, to the French.

The Rentenmark, the new gold Mark of Germany, is abominably dear. Prices are high in England, but English money buys less in Baden than it buys in London, by a long chalk. And there is no work – consequently no money. Nobody buys anything, except absolute necessities. The shopkeepers are in despair. And there is less and less work.

Everybody gives up the telephone – can't afford it. The tramcars don't run, except about three times a day to the station. Up to the Annaberg, the suburb, the lines are rusty, no trams ever go. The people can't afford the ten Pfennigs for the fare. Ten Pfennigs is an important sum now: one penny. It is really a hundred Milliards of Marks.

Money becomes insane, and people with it.

At night the place is almost dark, economising light. Economy, economy, economy – that, too, becomes an insanity. Luckily the government keeps bread fairly cheap.

But at night you feel strange things stirring in the darkness, strange feelings stirring out of this still-unconquered Black Forest. You stiffen your backbone and you listen to the night. There is a sense of danger. It is not the people. They don't seem dangerous. Out of the very air comes a sense of danger, a queer, *bristling* feeling of uncanny danger.

Something has happened. Something has happened which has not yet eventuated. The old spell of the old world has broken, and the old, bristling, savage spirit has set in. The war did not break the old peace-and-production hope of the world, though it gave it a severe wrench. Yet the old peace-and-production hope still governs, at least the consciousness. Even in Germany it has not quite gone.

But it feels as if, virtually, it were gone. The last two years have done it. The hope in peace-and-production is broken. The old flow, the old adherence is ruptured. And a still older flow has set in. Back, back to the savage polarity of Tartary, and away from the polarity of civilised Christian Europe. This, it seems to me, has already happened. And it is a happening of far more profound import than any actual *event*. It is the father of the next phase of events.

And the feeling never relaxes. As you travel up the Rhine valley, still the same latent sense of danger, of silence, of suspension. Not that the people are actually planning or plotting or preparing. I don't believe it for a minute. But something has happened to the human soul, beyond all help. The human soul recoiling now from unison, and making itself strong elsewhere. The ancient spirit of prehistoric Germany coming back, at the end of history.

The same in Heidelberg. Heidelberg full, full, full of people. Students the same, youths with rucksacks the same, boys and maidens in gangs come down from the hills. The same, and not the same. These queer gangs of *Young Socialists*, youths and girls, with their nonmaterialistic professions, their half-mystic assertions, they strike one as strange. Something primitive, like loose, roving gangs of broken, scattered tribes, so they affect one. And the swarms of people somehow produce an impression of silence, of secrecy, of stealth. It is as if everything and everybody recoiled away from the old unison, as barbarians lurking in a wood recoil out of sight. The old habits remain. But the bulk of the people have no money. And the whole stream of feeling is reversed.

So you stand in the woods about the town and see the Neckar flowing green and swift and slippery out of the gulf of Germany, to the Rhine. And the sun sets slow and scarlet into the haze of the Rhine valley. And the old, pinkish stone of the ruined castle across looks sultry, the marshalry is in shadow below, the peaked roofs of old, tight Heidelberg compressed in its river gateway glimmer and glimmer out. There is a blue haze.

And it all looks as if the years were wheeling swiftly backwards, no more onwards. Like a spring that is broken and whirls swiftly back, so time seems to be whirling with mysterious swiftness to a sort of death. Whirling to the ghost of the old Middle Ages of Germany, then to the Roman days, then to the days of the silent forest and the dangerous, lurking barbarians.

Something about the Germanic races is unalterable. White-skinned, elemental, and dangerous. Our civilisation has come from the fusion of the dark-eyed with the blue. The meeting and mixing and mingling of the two races has been the joy of our ages. And the Celt has been there, alien, but necessary as some chemical reagent to the fusion. So the civilisation of Europe rose up. So these cathedrals and these thoughts.

But now the Celt is the disintegrating agent. And the Latin and southern races are falling out of association with the northern races, the northern Germanic impulse is recoiling towards Tartary, the destructive vortex of Tartary.

It is a fate; nobody now can alter it. It is a fate. The very blood changes. Within the last three years, the very constituency of the blood has changed, in European veins. But particularly in Germanic veins. At the same time, we have brought it about ourselves – by a Ruhr occupation, by an English nullity, and by a German false will. We have done it ourselves. But apparently it was not to be helped.

*Quos vult perdere Deus, dementat prius.**

---

* 'Those whom God wishes to destroy, he first drives mad.'

J. M. Keynes

'Primitives'

Paul Robeson

When discriminating racially, popular opinion lays emphasis on the Negro's colour. Science, however, goes deeper than that and bases its arguments on the workings of the Negro mind.

Man, say certain of the scientists, is divided into two varieties – the variety which thinks in concrete symbols, and the variety which thinks in abstract concepts. The Negro belongs to the former and Western man to the latter.

Now the man who thinks in concrete symbols has no abstract conception of such words as 'good', 'brave', 'clever'. They are represented in his mind by symbolic pictures. For instance, 'good' in a concrete mind is often represented as a picture of a woman with a child. The drawing of this picture would be the way of conveying an idea of goodness to a person of the same mentality. Such pictures become conventionalised into a kind of written language. Now to the Western mind this may seem a clumsy way of going about things, but it is a method which has given the world some of the most delicate and richest art, and some of the profoundest and most subtle philosophy that man has ever known.

For it is not only the African Negro, and so-called primitive people, who think in concrete symbols – all the great civilisations of the East (with possibly the exception of India) have been built by people with this type of mind. It is a mentality that has given us giants like Confucius, Mencius, and Lao-tze. More than likely it was this kind of thinking that gave us the understanding and wisdom of a person like Jesus Christ. It has, in fact, given us the full flower of all the highest possibilities in man – with the single exception of applied science. That was left to Western man to achieve and on that he bases his assertion of superiority.

Now I am not going to try to belittle the achievements of science.

Only a fool would deny that the man who holds the secrets of those holds the key position in the world. I am simply going to ask – having found the key, has Western man – Western bourgeois man (the reason for the distinction is made clear later) – sufficient strength left to turn it in the lock? Or is he going to find that in the search he has so exhausted his vitality that he will have to call in the co-operation of his more virile 'inferiors' before he can open the door and enter into his heritage? For the cost of developing the kind of mind by which the discoveries of science were made has been one which now threatens the discoverer's very life.

The reason for this lies in the fact that Western man seems to have gained more and more power of abstraction at the expense of his creative faculties. There is not much doubt that the artistic achievements of Europe have steadily declined. It is true that this decline is partly obscured by an output of self-conscious, uninspired productions, which have a certain artificial grace; but discriminating people have little difficulty in distinguishing these lifeless imitations from the living pulsing thing.

It may be argued that preference for live art over dead imitation may be simply a question of taste and is of no fundamental importance. Neither would it be if the change was something confined to that small minority usually described as artists, but unfortunately what shows amongst these is only a symptom of a sickness that to some extent is affecting almost every stratum of the Western world. The whole problem of living can never be understood until the world recognises that artists are not a race apart. Every man has some element of the artist in him, and if this is pulled up by the roots he becomes suicidal and dies.

In the East this quality has never been damaged – to that is traceable the virility of most Eastern peoples. In the West it remains healthy and active only amongst those sections of the community which have never fully subscribed to Western values – that is, the exploited sections, plus some rebels from the bourgeoisie. The result is, that as Western civilisation advances, its members find themselves in the paradoxical position of being more and more in control of their environment, yet more and more at the mercy of it. The man who accepts Western values absolutely, finds his creative faculties becoming so warped and stunted that he is almost completely dependent on external satisfactions; and the moment he becomes frustrated in his search for these, he begins to develop neurotic symptoms, to feel that life is not worth living, and, in chronic cases, to take his own life.

This is a severe price to pay even for such achievements as those of Western science. Though European thought, in its blind worship of the intellect, has tried to reduce life to a mechanical formula, it has never quite succeeded. Its entire peasantry, large masses of its proletariat, and even a percentage of its middle class have never been really touched. These sections have thrown up a series of rebels who have felt rather than analysed the danger and cried out loudly against it.

Many of these have probably been obscure people but others have been sufficiently articulate to rise above the shoulders of their fellows and voice their protest in forms that have commanded world-wide attention. Of such persons one can mention Blake and D. H. Lawrence. In fact one could say that all the live art which Europe has produced since the Renaissance has been in spite of, and not because of, the new trends of Western thought.

I do not stand alone in this criticism of the Western intellect. Famous critics support me. Walter Raleigh, when discussing Blake, writes: 'The gifts with which he is so plentifully dowered for all they are looked at askance as abnormal and portentous, are the common stuff of human nature, without which life would flag and cease. No man destitute of genius could live for a day. Genius is spontaneity – the life of the soul asserting itself triumphantly in the midst of dead things.'

In the face of all this can anyone echo the once-common cry that the way of progress is the way of the intellectual? If we all took this turning should we not be freeing ourselves from our earthy origins by the too-simple expedient of pulling ourselves up by the roots?

But because one does not want to follow Western thought into this dilemma, one none the less recognises the value of its achievements. It is simply that one recoils from the Western intellectual's idea that, having got himself on to this peak overhanging an abyss, he should want to drag all other people up after him into the same precarious position. That, in a sentence, is my case against Western values. It is not a matter of whether the Negro and other so-called 'primitive' people are incapable of becoming pure intellectuals (actually, in America, many have), it is a matter of whether they are going to be unwise enough to be led down this dangerous by-way.

Perhaps the recognised fact that over-intellectualism tends towards impotence and sterility will result in the natural extinction of that flower of the West that has given us our scientific achievements, and to the rise of the more virile, better-balanced European, till now derided and submerged. Some people think that in the European proletariat this new Western man is already coming to birth. We, however, who are not Europeans, may be forgiven for hoping that the new age will be one in which the teeming 'inferiors' of the East will be permitted to share.

Naturally one does not claim that the Negro must come to the front more than another. One does, however, realise that in the Negro one has a virile people of many millions. That, when he is given a chance, he is capable of holding his own with the best Western Europe can produce is proved by the quality of his folk music both in Africa and the Americas – also by the works of Pushkin, the Russo-African poet; or by Ira Aldrich – the actor who enslaved artistic Europe in the last century. Even a writer like Dumas, though not in the first rank, is a person who could hardly have been fathered by a member of an inferior race. Today there are in existence more Negroes of the first rank than the world cares to recognise.

In reply, it will of course be argued that these are isolated instances. 'It may be true,' people will say, 'that the African thinks as Confucius thought, or as the Aztecs thought; that his language is constructed in the same way as that language which gave us the wonder of Chinese poetry; that he works along the same lines as the Chinese artist; but where are his philosophers, his poets, his artists?'

Even if this were unanswerable, it would not prove that the African's golden age might not lie ahead. It is not unanswerable, however. Africa has produced far more than Western people realise. More than one scientist has been struck by the similarity between certain works by long-dead West African artists and exquisite examples of Chinese, Mexican and Javanese art. Leading European sculptors have found inspiration in the work of the West African. It is now recognised that

African music has subtleties of rhythm far finer than anything achieved by a Western composer.

Such achievements can hardly be the work of a fundamentally inferior people. When the African realises this and builds on his own traditions, borrowing mainly the Westerner's technology, he may develop into a people regarding whom the adjective 'inferior' would be ludicrous rather than appropriate.

Trotsky in Mexico

Kingsley Martin

I went to see Trotsky in the house that Diego Rivera and his wife have lent him in an outlying suburb of Mexico City. He is very well guarded and cannot go out, I am told, without a bodyguard of detectives and armed patrols on motorcycles. Four armed guards were standing at the gate.

Once inside, I thought an exile could scarcely hope to find a lovelier refuge. Trotsky was sitting in a long, cool room looking out on to the patio – a gay and beautiful courtyard, the walls bright blue and the bougainvillea a blazing glory in the sunshine. He was working, he told me, on his new book, *The Crimes of Stalin.*

Pictures of Trotsky are apt to suggest the stage revolutionary in the fuzzy hair and a certain untidy vehemence about the neck. Nothing could be further from the fact. 'Dapper' was the word that came into my head when I first saw him. He looked as if he had just come out of a hot bath, just had his hair cut, his beard trimmed and his suit pressed. His hair and beard are grey and his face is a fresh pink. He looked like a Frenchman, not, I decided after a few minutes, a French politician but, in spite of his neatness, a French artist.

As we talked, I retained the impression of Trotsky as an artist, an intuitive and imaginative man, vain and very able, a man of fierce will and unruly temperament. If I had met him without knowing who he was or what he had done and without having read his books, I should have been impressed; but I doubt if I should have recognised his genius.

Trotsky was charming and friendly. Yes, he was pleased to talk to me because he regarded the *New Statesman and Nation* as one of the few honest and genuinely radical papers. I suppose that he had read a recent article expressing scepticism about the evidence of the Moscow trials.

I told him that I was still puzzled by the confessions. They were difficult to explain on any hypothesis. What possible pressure could be brought on all these experienced revolutionaries that would make them not only confess but stand by their confessions when they had the opportunity of publicly repudiating them in open trial? Trotsky explained that I did not understand the methods of the GPU (the Russian intelligence service). He described how it first got hold of a woman and questioned her until she made a confession that incriminated her husband; how this was used to break down her husband's resistance and how he in turn was induced to incriminate his friends, all of whom were gradually persuaded by pressure of one sort or another to sign what was required.

The GPU knew, he said, how to attack each of its victims in his weakest spot, this man signing from sheer nervous exhaustion, that one because of a threat to his wife and children, and the other in the hope of pardon and release. The preparation of such a case took years and the trials were the climax of a determination that Stalin had taken in 1927 (when the split in the party occurred) completely to eliminate all those who had sympathised with Trotsky and who might in the future swing opinion against Stalin's policy. The GPU would not stage a trial until they were sure of all their men.

I still did not understand why none of the prisoners had repudiated his confession in court. I try to think of myself under such circumstances. I can see myself breaking down and confessing to anything under pressure but the trial was free and open and I think I should have withdrawn an extorted confession when I saw the press correspondents hanging on my words. Russians tell me that this is an English view, that confession is a spontaneous impulse of the Slav soul, 'an old Russian custom', not a peculiar invention of Dostoevsky and the GPU.

However, I put it to Trotsky. It was strange that not one of them should have gone down fighting and have appealed to the public opinion of the world. Most of them knew they were going to die anyway. Trotsky grew very animated. I was wrong. Even after the example of the first trial, these men did not know they were going to die. There was a world of difference between the certainty of death and just that much hope of reprieve – here Trotsky made an expressive gesture with his fingers to indicate even a millimetre of hope. Moreover, in Russia the foreign correspondents were all 'paid prostitutes of Moscow'. He seemed to believe that anyone who had a word to say for Stalin or who hesitates to denounce the whole trial as a frameup must be in the pay of Moscow. He made an exception in the case of the Webbs – they were merely poor, credulous dupes.

Afterwards, turning over this conversation in my mind, I did not find that it had cleared away my perplexity about the Moscow trials. When I wrote that I did not know whether or not to believe in the confessions, I meant exactly what I said. It seemed to me the only honest thing to say. Trotsky, like other people, interpreted my scepticism as a vote against Stalin and he had tried to remove any lingering doubts. Yet I came away from our talk rather less inclined to doubt the possibility of Trotsky's complicity than I had been before, because his judgement appeared to me so unstable and therefore the possibility of his embarking on a crazy plot more credible.

In any case, I shall not let myself become a partisan in this controversy until I have seen what evidence is produced before the inquiry that is now opening in New York and until I have read the facts and arguments that Trotsky is compiling in *The Crimes of Stalin*. But I fear this open-minded attitude will have no effect on Trotsky except to convince him that I, too, am a prostitute in the pay of Moscow.

Anthropology at Home

Tom Harrisson, Humphrey Jennings and Charles Madge

The following letter launched the social research project Mass Observation, aimed at producing an 'anthropology of ourselves'.

Sir—Man is the last subject of scientific investigation. A century ago Darwin focused the camera of thought on to man as a sort of animal whose behaviour and history would be explained by science. In 1847, Marx formulated a scientific study of economic man. In 1865, Tylor defined the new science of anthropology which was to be applied to the 'primitive' and the 'savage'. In 1893, Freud and Breuer published their first paper on hysteria; they began to drag into daylight the unconscious elements in individual 'civilised' man. But neither anthropology nor psychology has yet become more than an instrument in the hands of any individual, which he applies (according to his individuality) to primitives and abnormals.

By 1936 chaos was such that the latent elements were crystallised into a new compound. As so often happens, an idea was being worked out in many separate brains. A letter in the *New Statesman and Nation* from Geoffrey Pyke, arising out of the Simpson crisis, explicitly mentioned the need for an 'anthropology of our own people'. A fortnight later a letter called attention to a group centred in London for the purpose of developing a science of Mass Observation, and this group effected contact with other individuals and with a group working in industrial Lancashire, which had so far concentrated on field work rather than formulation of theory. These interests are now united in the first, necessarily tentative, efforts of Mass Observation.

Mass Observation develops out of anthropology, psychology, and the sciences which study man – but it plans to work with a mass of observers. Already we have fifty observers at work on two sample problems. We are further working out a complete plan of campaign, which will be possible when we have not fifty but 5,000 observers. The following are a few examples of problems that will arise:

- Behaviour of people at war memorials.
- Shouts and gestures of motorists.
- The aspidistra cult.
- Anthropology of football pools.
- Bathroom behaviour.
- Beards, armpits, eyebrows.
- Anti-Semitism.
- Distribution, diffusion and significance of the dirty joke.
- Funerals and undertakers.
- Female taboos about eating.
- The private lives of midwives.

In these examples the anthropological angle is obvious, and the description is primarily of physical behaviour. Other inquiries involve mental phenomena which are unconscious or repressed, so that they can only be traced through mass-fantasy and symbolism as developed and exploited, for example, in the daily press. The outbreak of parturition-images in the press last October may have been seasonal, or may have been caused by some public stimulus: continuous watch on the shifting popular images can only be kept by a multitude of watchers. The observers will also provide the points from which can be plotted weather-maps of public feeling in a crisis.

The subject demands the minimum of prejudice, bias and assumption; the maximum of objectivity. It does not presuppose that there are any inexplicable things. Since it aims at collecting data before interpreting them, it must be allowed to doubt and re-examine the completeness of every existing idea about 'humanity', while it cannot afford to neglect any of them. Equally, all human types can and must assist in this work. The artist and the scientist are at last joining forces and turning back towards the mass from which they had detached themselves.

It does not set out in quest of truth or facts for their own sake but aims at exposing them in simple terms to all observers, so that their environment may be understood, and thus constantly transformed. Whatever the political methods called upon to effect the transformation, the knowledge of what has to be transformed is indispensable. The foisting on the mass of ideals or ideas developed by men apart from it, irrespective of its capacities, causes mass misery, intellectual despair and an international shambles. We hope shortly to produce a pamphlet outlining a programme of action. We welcome criticism and co-operation.

A Magistrate's Figures

··

E. M. Forster

E. M. Forster was 74 when he published this plea for the decriminalisation of homosexuality. Not only did he feel unable to write openly about his sexuality, he was forced to make the case in stark and violent terms. He was right in sensing a shift in public opinion, however. The Wolfenden report followed four years later and became law in 1967. Forster died in 1970.

From time to time one sees a reference in the newspapers to a homosexual case. Two or three cases may be reported in a week, another week may pass without any mention and one is left with the vaguest idea as to how frequent such cases are.

That vagueness has now been dispersed. Last week a Police Court magistrate, a man of wide experience, was dealing with a case of importuning male persons, and he is reported as saying that in his court alone there were over six hundred such cases every year. The figure is so staggering that one suspects a press error, and quotes it subject to correction. But it was evidently large, for the magistrate was greatly concerned, and even expressed the wish that he could send all such offenders to prison. His figure seems to exclude graver charges; they have doubtless come before him, too, and they would further increase the total. And he does not say how many of the charges were brought as a result of a complaint to the police by the person importuned, and how many were the result of police observation. Here, also, figures would be interesting.

If six hundred cases, or a large number of cases, pass through a single police court in a year, what can the figures be for all England? Imagination fails and one is overwhelmed by disgust or by pity. It is terrifying to think of thousands of people – for they must run into thousands – going into the streets for a purpose which they know to be criminal, risking detection and punishment, endangering reputations and incomes and jobs – not to mention the dangers of blackmail. What on earth do they do it for? Some critics will denounce them as infamous. Others will jeer at them for being so daft. Neither criticism goes deep enough. They are impelled by something illogical, by an unusual but existent element in the human make-up. They constitute an extremely small item in society, but an item larger than has been hitherto supposed.

Suggestions for dealing with them, and with the problem generally, are propounded from time to time. Occasionally there is a purity campaign in the press, and a clean-up is eloquently demanded. But where are these people to be cleaned to? Difficulties always arise when we regard human beings as dirt. They can be pushed about from one place to another, but that is all. Prison – that facile solution – is not a remote magical enclave, as it is sometimes supposed. Prison is a place, it is part of society, even when society ignores it, and people who are pushed into it exist just as much as if they had been pushed into the next parish or over the frontier. They can, of course, be pushed right out of the world. That certainly would clean them up, and that has in the past been tried. It is, however, unlikely that the death penalty for homosexuality will be re-established. Civilisation has in this direction become milder. Moreover, holocausts would have to be repeated for each generation periodically.

There is, of course, the remedy of medical treatment, the scope and the methods of which are still controversial. More satisfactory (if it could be achieved) would be an immediate change in the law. If homosexuality between men ceased to be per se criminal – it is not criminal between women – and if homosexual crimes were equated with heterosexual crimes and punished with equal but not with additional severity, much confusion and misery would be averted; there would be less public importuning and less blackmail. But it is unlikely that the law will be changed. Reformers are too optimistic here. In their zeal they do not consider the position of the average MP, through whom the reform must take place. An MP may be sympathetic personally, but he has to face his constituency and justify his vote, and experience has shown how hostile an electorate can be to anything it considers sexually unusual. His enemies will denounce him, his friends will be afraid to defend him, and he may endanger his seat. Change in the law is unlikely until there is a change in public opinion; and this must happen very slowly, for the great majority of people are naturally repelled by the subject and do not want to have to think about it. Even when it does not revolt them it bores them.

Less social stigma under the existing law – that is all that can be hoped for at present, and there are some grounds for hope. Violent and vulgar denunciations do not work as they did, and are apt to recoil on the denouncer. There is more discussion, less emotion, fewer preconceptions. More laymen read modern psychology, which even when it does not satisfy raises salutary doubts. The stigma attaching to the homosexual is becoming more proportioned to the particular facts of each case. Some courts make increasing use of probation.

As a contrast to the magistrate referred to above, one may quote the remarks of a judge, Mr Justice Hallett. Speaking at about the same time as the magistrate, and dealing with an offence far more serious than importuning, the judge is reported as saying: 'It will be a great joy to me and to other judges when some humane method for dealing with homosexual cases is devised, and when something more can be done than simply locking up the offenders.' In such indications as these there is certainly ground for hope.

Britain and the Nuclear Bombs

J. B. Priestley

J. B. Priestley's 'Britain and the Nuclear Bombs' was the essay that led to the creation of the Campaign for Nuclear Disarmament (CND). Not only did Priestley drop his usually comic style, he articulated the fears of a generation and helped to launch a mass movement. The first CND meeting was chaired by the NS *editor, Kingsley Martin, at the end of November 1957.*

Two events of this autumn should compel us to reconsider the question of Britain and the nuclear bombs. The first of these events was Mr Aneurin Bevan's speech at the Labour Party conference, which seemed to many of us to slam a door in our faces. It was not dishonest but it was very much a party conference speech, and its use of terms like 'unilateral' and 'polarisation' lent it a suggestion of the 'Foreign Office spokesman'. Delegates asked not to confuse 'an emotional spasm' with 'statesmanship' might have retorted that the statesmanship of the last ten years has produced little else but emotional spasms. And though it is true, as Mr Bevan argued, that independent action by this country, to ban nuclear bombs, would involve our foreign minister in many difficulties, most of us would rather have a bewildered and overworked Foreign Office than a country about to be turned into a radioactive cemetery. Getting out of the water may be difficult, but it's better than drowning.

The second event was the successful launching of the Soviet satellite, followed by an immediate outbreak of what may fairly be called satellitis, producing a rise in temperature and delirium. In the poker game, where Britain still sits, nervously fingering a few remaining chips, the stakes have been doubled again. Disarmament talks must now take place in an atmosphere properly belonging to boys' papers and science fiction, though already charged with far more hysterical competitiveness. If statesmanship is to see us through, it will have to break the familiar and dubious pattern of the last few years. Perhaps what we need now, before it is too late, is not statesmanship but lifemanship.

One 'ultimate weapon', the final deterrent, succeeds another. After the bombs, the intercontinental rockets; and after the rockets, according to the First Lord of the Admiralty, the guided-missile submarine, which will 'carry a guided missile with a nuclear warhead and appear off the coasts of any country in the world with a capability of penetrating to the centre of any continent'. The prospect now is not one of countries without navies but navies without countries. And we have arrived at an insane regress of ultimate weapons that are not ultimate.

But all this is to the good; and we cannot have too much of it, we are told, because no men in their right minds would let loose such powers of destruction. Here is the realistic view. Any criticism of it is presumed to be based on wild idealism. But surely it is the wildest idealism, at the furthest remove from a sober realism, to assume that men will always behave reasonably and in line with their best interests? Yet this is precisely what we are asked to believe, and to stake our all on it.

For that matter, why should it be assumed that the men who create and control such monstrous devices are in their right minds? They live in an unhealthy mental climate, an atmosphere dangerous to sanity. They are responsible to no large body of ordinary sensible men and women, who pay for these weapons without ever having ordered them, who have never been asked anywhere yet if they wanted them. When and where have these preparations for public warfare ever been put to the test of public opinion? The whole proceedings take place in the stifling secrecy of an expensive lunatic asylum. And as one ultimate weapon after another is added to the pile, the mental climate deteriorates, the atmosphere thickens, and the tension is such that soon something may snap.

The more elaborately involved and hair-triggered the machinery of destruction, the more likely it is that this machinery will be set in motion, if only by accident. Three glasses too many of vodka or bourbon-on-the-rocks, and the wrong button may be pushed. Combine this stock-piling of nuclear weapons with a crazy competitiveness, boastful confidence in public and a mounting fear in private, and what was unthinkable a few years ago now only seems unlikely and very soon may seem inevitable. Then western impatience cries 'Let's get the damned thing over!' and eastern fatalism mutters 'If this has to be, then we must accept it'. And people in general are in a worse position every year, further away from intervention; they have less and less freedom of action; they are deafened and blinded by propaganda and giant headlines; they are robbed of decisions by fear or apathy. It is possible, as some thinkers hold, that our civilisation is bent on self-destruction, hurriedly planning its own doomsday. This may explain the curious and sinister air of somnambulism there is about our major international affairs; the steady drift from bad to worse, the speeches that begin to sound meaningless, the conferences that achieve nothing, all the persons of great consequence who somehow feel like puppets. We have all seen people in whom was sown the final seed of self-destruction. Our individual civilisation, behaving in a similar fashion, may be under the same kind of spell, hell-bent on murdering itself. But it is possible that the spell can be broken. If it can, then it will only be by an immensely decisive gesture, a clear act of will. Instead of endless bargaining for a little of this in exchange for a little of that, while all the time the bargainers are hurried down a road that gets steeper and narrower, somebody will have to say 'I'm through with all of this'.

In plain words: now that Britain has told the world she has the H-bomb she should announce as early as possible that she has done with it, that she proposes to reject, in all circumstances, nuclear warfare. This is not pacifism. There is no suggestion here of abandoning the immediate defence of the island. Indeed, it might be considerably strengthened, reducing the threat of actual invasion, which is the root fear in people's minds, a fear often artfully manipulated for purposes far removed from any defence of hearth and home. No, what should be abandoned is the idea of deterrence by the threat of retaliation. There is no real security in it, no faith, hope, nor charity in it.

But let us take a look at our present policy entirely on its own level. There is no standing still, no stalemates, in this idiot game; one 'ultimate weapon' succeeds another. To stay in the race at all we risk bankruptcy, the disappearance of the Welfare State, a standard of living that might begin to make Communist propaganda sound more attractive than it does at present. We could in fact be so busy defending ourselves against Communism somewhere else, a long way off, that we would wake up one morning to hear it knocking on the back door. Indeed, this is Moscow's old *heads-I-win-tails-you-lose* policy.

Here we might do well to consider western world strategy, first grandiloquently proclaimed by Sir Winston in those speeches he made in America just after the war. The Soviet Union was to be held in leash by nuclear power. We had the bomb and they hadn't. The race would be on but the West had a flying start. But Russia was not without physicists, and some German scientists and highly trained technicians had disappeared somewhere in eastern Europe. For the immediate defence of West Germany, the atom bomb threat no doubt served its turn. But was this really sound long-term strategy? It created the poisonous atmosphere of our present time. It set the Russians galloping in the nuclear race. It freed them from the immense logistic options that must be solved if large armies are to be moved everywhere, and from some very tricky problems of morale that would soon appear once the Red Army was a long way from home. It encouraged the support of so-called peoples' and nationalistic and anti-colonial wars, not big enough to be settled by nuclear weapons. In spite of America's ring of advanced air bases, the race had only to be run a little longer to offer Russia at least an equally good set-up, and, in comparison with Britain alone, clearly an enormously better set-up.

We are like a man in a poker game who never dares cry 'I'll see you'. The Soviet Union came through the last war because it had vast spaces and a large population and a ruthless disregard of losses, human and material. It still has them. If there is one country that should never have gambled in this game, it is Britain. Once the table stakes were being raised, the chips piling up, we were out. And though we may have been fooling ourselves, we have not been fooling anyone else.

This answers any gobbling cries about losing our national prestige. We have none in terms of power. We ended the war high in the world's regard. We could have taken over its moral leadership, spoken and acted for what remained of its conscience; but we chose to act otherwise – with obvious and melancholy consequences both abroad, where in power politics we cut a shabby figure, and at home, where we shrug it all away or go to the theatre to applaud the latest jeers and sneers at Britannia. It has been said we cannot send our ministers naked to the conference table. But the sight of a naked minister might bring to the conference some sense of our human situation. What we do is something much worse: we send them there half-dressed, half-smart, half-tough, half-apologetic, figures inviting contempt. That is why we are so excited and happy when we can send abroad a good-looking young woman in a pretty new dress to represent us, playing the only card we feel can take a trick – the Queen.

It is argued, as it was most vehemently by Mr Bevan at Brighton, that if we walked out of the nuclear arms race then the world would be 'polarised' between America and the Soviet Union, without any hope of mediation between the two fixed and bristling camps. 'Just consider for a moment,' he cried, 'all the little nations running, one here and one there, one running to Russia, one to the US, all once more clustering under the castle wall...' But surely this is one of those 'realistic' arguments that are not based on reality. The idea of the Third Force was rejected by the very party Mr Bevan was addressing. The world was polarised when, without a single protest from all the guardians of our national pride, parts of East Anglia ceased to be under our control and became an American air base. We cannot at one and the same time be an independent power, bargaining on equal terms, and a minor ally or satellite. If there are little nations that do not run for shelter to the walls of the White House or the Kremlin because they are happy to accept Britain as their nuclear umbrella, we hear very little about them. If it is a question of brute power, this argument is unreal.

It is not entirely stupid, however, because something more than brute power is involved. There is nothing unreal in the idea of a third nation, especially one like ours, old and experienced in world affairs, to which other and smaller nations could look while the two new giants mutter and glare at each other. But it all depends what the nation is doing. If it is still in the nuclear gamble, without being able to control or put an end to the game, then that nation is useless to others. And if it is, then we must ask ourselves what course of action on our part might have some hope of changing the world situation. To continue doing what we are doing will not change it. Even during the few weeks since Mr Bevan made his speech the world is becoming more rigidly and dangerously polarised than ever, just because the Russians have sent a metal football circling the globe. What then can Britain do to de-polarise the world?

The only move left that can mean anything is to go into reverse, decisively rejecting nuclear warfare. This gives the world something quite different from the polarised powers: there is now a country that can make H-bombs but decides against them. Had Britain taken this decision years ago the world would be a safer and saner place than it is today. But it is still not too late. And such a move will have to be 'unilateral'; doomsday may arrive before the nuclear powers reach any agreement; and it is only a decisive 'unilateral' move that can achieve the moral force it needs to be effective.

It will be a hard decision to take because all habit is against it. Many persons of consequence and their entourages of experts would have to think fresh thoughts. They would have to risk losing friends and not influencing people. For example, so far as they involve nuclear warfare, our commitments to NATO, SEATO and the rest, and our obligations to the Commonwealth, would have to be sharply adjusted. Anywhere from Brussels to Brisbane, reproaches would be hurled, backs would be turned. But what else have these countries to suggest, what way out, what hope for man? And if, to save our souls and this planet, we are willing to remain here and take certain risks, why should we falter because we might have complaints from Rhodesia and reproaches from Christchurch, NZ?

American official and service opinion would be dead against us, naturally. The unsinkable (but expendable) aircraft carrier would have gone. Certain Soviet bases allotted to British nuclear attack would have to be included among the targets of the American Strategic Air Service. And so on and so forth. But though service chiefs and their staff go on examining and marketing their maps and planning their logistics, having no alternative but resignation, they are as fantastic and unreal in their way as their political and diplomatic colleagues are in theirs. What is fantastic and unreal is their assumption that they are traditionally occupied with their professional duties, attending in advance to the next war, Number Three in the world series. But what will happen – and one wrong report by a sleepy observer may start it off – will not be anything recognisable as war, an affair of victories and defeats, something that one side can win or that you can all call off when you have had enough. It will be universal catastrophe and apocalypse, the crack of doom into which Communism, western democracy, their way of life and our way of life, may disappear for ever. And it is not hard to believe that this is what some of our contemporaries really desire, that behind the photogenic smiles and cheerful patter nothing exists but the death wish.

We live in the thought of this prospect as if we existed in a permanent smog. All sensible men and women – and this excludes most who are in the *VIP-Highest-Security-Top-Secret-Top-People Class*, men now so conditioned by this atmosphere of power politics, intrigue, secrecy, insane invention, that they are more than half-barmy – have no illusions about what is happening to us, and know that those responsible have made two bad miscalculations. First, they have prostituted so much science in their preparations for war and they have completely changed the character of what they are doing, without any equivalent change in the politics of and relations between states. Foreign affairs, still conducted as if the mobilisation of a few divisions might settle something, are now backed with push-button arrangements to let loose earthquakes and pestilences and pronounce the death sentences of continents. This leaves us all in a worse dilemma than the sorcerer's apprentice. The second miscalculation assumed that if the odds were multiplied fast enough, your side would break through because the other side would break down. And because this has not happened, a third illusion is being welcomed, namely, that now, with everything piling up, poker chips flung on the table by the handful, the tension obviously increasing, now at last we are arriving at an acknowledged drawn game, a not-too-stale stalemate, a cosy old balance of power. This could well be the last of our illusions.

The risk of our rejecting nuclear warfare, totally and in all circumstances, is quite clear, all too easy to understand. We lose such bargaining power as we now possess. We have no deterrent to a nuclear threat. We deliberately exchange 'security' for insecurity. (And the fact that some such exchange is recommended by the major religions, in their earlier and non-establishment phases, need not detain us here.) But the risk is clear and the arguments against running it irrefutable, only if we refuse, as from the first too many of us here have refused, to take anything but short-term conventional views, only if we will not follow any thought to its conclusion. Our 'hard-headed realism' is neither hard-headed nor realistic just because it insists on our behaving in a new world as if we were living in an old world.

Britain runs the greatest risk by just mumbling and muddling along, never speaking out, avoiding any decisive creative act. For a world in which our deliberate 'insecurity' would prove to be our undoing is not a world in which real security could be found. As the game gets faster, the competition keener, the unthinkable will turn into the inevitable, the weapons will take command, and the deterrents will not deter. Our bargaining power is slight; the force of our example might be great. The catastrophic antics of our time have behind them men hag-ridden by fear, which explains the irrationality of it all, the crazy disproportion between means and ends. If we openly challenge this fear, then we might break this wicked spell that all but a few uncertified lunatics desperately wish to see broken, we could begin to restore the world to sanity and lift this nation from its recent ignominy to its former grandeur. Alone, we defied Hitler; and alone we can defy this nuclear madness into which the spirit of Hitler seems to have passed, to poison the world. There may be other chain-reactions besides those leading to destruction; and we might start one.

The British of these times, so frequently hiding their decent, kind faces behind masks of sullen apathy or sour, cheap cynicism, often seem to be waiting for something better than party squabbles and appeals to the narrowest self-interest, something great and noble in its intention that would make them feel good again. And this might well be a declaration to the world that after a certain date one power able to engage in nuclear warfare will reject the evil thing for ever.

Open Letter to Eisenhower and Khrushchev

Bertrand Russell

This remarkable correspondence was initiated by the philosopher and pacifist Bertrand Russell. His 'Open Letter' appeared in the New Statesman *in November 1957, and although he may not have expected a reply, two weeks before Christmas the first secretary of the Communist Party, Nikita Khrushchev, sent an unsolicited response, which the NS published on 21 December. Early in 1958 the US secretary of state, John Foster Dulles, wrote in on President Eisenhower's behalf, and nuclear diplomacy was played out in the pages of the NS at the height of the Cold War.*

Most Potent Sirs,

I am addressing you as the respective heads of the two most powerful countries in the world. Those who direct the policies of these countries have a power for good or evil exceeding anything ever possessed before by any man or group of men. Public opinion in your respective countries has been focused upon the points in which your national interests are thought to diverge, but I am convinced that you, as far-seeing and intelligent men, must be aware that the matters in which the interests of Russia and America coincide are much more important than the matters in which they are thought to diverge. I believe that if you two eminent men were jointly to proclaim this fact and to bend the policies of your great countries to agreement with such a proclamation, there would be throughout the world, and not least in your own countries, a shout of joyful agreement which would raise you both to a pinnacle of fame surpassing anything achieved by other statesmen of the past or present. Although you are, of course, both well aware of the points in which the interests of Russia and America are identical, I will, for the sake of explicitness, enumerate some of them.

[1] The supreme concern of men of all ways of thought at the present time must be to ensure the continued existence of the human race. This is already in jeopardy from the hostility between East and West and will, if many minor nations acquire nuclear weapons, be in very much greater jeopardy within a few years from the possibility of irresponsible action by thoughtless fanatics.

Some ignorant militarists, both in the East and in the West, have apparently thought that the danger could be averted by a world war giving victory to their own side. The progress of science and technology has made this an idle dream. A world war would not result in the victory of either side, but in the extermination of both.

The hope of world dominion, either military or ideological, is one which has hovered before many men in the past and has led invariably to disaster. Philip II of Spain made the attempt and reduced his country to the status of a minor power. Louis XIV of France made the attempt and, by exhausting his country, led the way to the French Revolution, which he would have profoundly deplored. Hitler, in our own day, fought for the world-wide supremacy of the Nazi philosophy, and perished miserably. Two great men propounded ideologies which have not yet run their course: I mean the authors of the Declaration of Independence and the Communist Manifesto. There is no reason to expect that either of these ideologies will be more successful in conquering the world than their predecessors, Buddhist, Christian, Moslem, or Nazi. What is new in the present situation is not the impossibility of success, but the magnitude of the disaster which must result from the attempt. We must, therefore, hope that each side will abandon the futile strife and agree to allow to each a sphere proportionate to its present power.

[2] The international anarchy which will inevitably result from the unrestricted diffusion of nuclear weapons is not to the interest of either Russia or America. There was a time when only America had nuclear weapons. This was followed by a time when only Russia and America had such weapons. And now only Russia, America and Britain possess them. It is obvious that, unless steps are taken, France and Germany will shortly manufacture these weapons. It is not likely that China will lag far behind. We must expect that the manufacture of engines of

mass destruction will become cheaper and easier. No doubt Egypt and Israel will then be able to follow the example set by the great powers. So will the states of South America. There is no end to this process until every sovereign state is in a position to say to the whole world: 'You must yield to my demands or you shall die.' If all sovereign states were governed by rulers possessed of even the rudiments of sanity, they would be restrained from such blackmail by the fear that their citizens also would perish. But experience shows that from time to time power in this or that country falls into the hands of rulers who are not sane. Can anyone doubt that Hitler, if he had been able to do so, would have chosen to involve all mankind in his own ruin? For such reasons, it is imperative to put a stop to the diffusion of nuclear weapons. This can easily be done by agreement between Russia and America, since they can jointly refuse military or economic assistance to any country which persists in the manufacture of such weapons. But it cannot be achieved without agreement between the two dominant powers, for, without such agreement, each new force of nuclear weapons will be welcomed by one side or the other as an increase to its own strength.

[3] So long as the fear of world war dominates policy and the only deterrent is the threat of universal death, so long there can be no limit to the diversion of expenditure of funds and human energy into channels of destruction. It is clear that both Russia and America could save nine-tenths of their present expenditure if they concluded an alliance and devoted themselves jointly to the preservation of peace throughout the world. If they do not find means of lessening their present hostility, reciprocal fear will drive them further and further, until, apart from immense armaments, nothing beyond a bare subsistence will be left to the populations of either country. In order to promote efficiency in the preparation of death, education will have to be distorted and stunted. Everything in human achievement that is not inspired by hatred and fear will be squeezed out of the curriculum in schools and universities. Any attempt to preserve the vision of Man as the triumph (so far) of the long ages of evolution, will come to be viewed as treachery, since it will be thought not to minister to the victory of this group or that. Such a prospect is death to the hopes of all who share the aspirations which have inspired human progress since the dawn of history.

[4] I cannot but think that you would both rejoice if a way could be found to disperse the pall of fear which at present dims the hopes of mankind. Never before, since our remote ancestors descended from the trees, has there been valid reason for such fear. Never before has such a sense of futility blighted the visions of youth. Never before has there been reason to feel that the human race was travelling along a road ending only in a bottomless precipice. Individual death we must all face, but collective death has never, hitherto, been a grim possibility.

And all this fear, all this despair, all this waste is utterly unnecessary. One thing only is required to dispel the darkness and enable the world to live again in a noon-day brightness of hope. The one thing necessary is that East and West should recognise their respective rights, admit that each must learn to live with the other and substitute argument for force in the attempt to spread their respective ideologies. It is not necessary that either side should abandon belief in its own creed. It is only necessary that it should abandon the attempt to spread its own creed by force of arms.

I suggest, Sirs, that you should meet in a frank discussion of the conditions of coexistence, endeavouring no longer to secure this or that more or less surreptitious advantage for your own side, but seeking rather for such agreements and such adjustments in the world as will diminish future occasions of strife. I believe that if you were to do this the world would acclaim your action, and the forces of sanity, released from their long bondage, would ensure for the years to come a life of vigour and achievement and joy surpassing anything known in even the happiest eras of the past.

Bertrand Russell

NIKITA KHRUSHCHEV REPLIES TO BERTRAND RUSSELL

Nikita Khrushchev

Dear Lord Russell,

I was extremely interested to read your open letter addressed to the President of the United States and to myself. We, the Soviet people, understand and hold dear the main idea expressed in your letter – to protect mankind from the threat of a war which would be waged with the most terrible weapons of destruction ever known to the world;

to safeguard universal peace and prosperity, on the basis of peaceful co-existence between states; and, above all, through the normalisation of relations between the Soviet Union and the United States.

Everyone is agreed that if a new world war should break out, it would bring untold suffering to the people. For this reason the chief concern of all people, whatsoever their way of thinking, should be to prevent such a tragic turn of events. Man's reason and conscience cannot be reconciled to such a danger, cannot but rise up against the propaganda churned out day after day, propaganda which is accustoming the nations to the idea of the inevitability of atomic war.

The government and Communist Party of the Soviet Union, expressing the wishes of the people of our country, are doing and will do everything possible to prevent the outbreak of a new war. We are convinced that, in the present situation, war is not fatally inevitable, that war can be prevented, if everyone who wants to preserve peace will struggle for it actively and in an organised way.

We were pleased to notice that you support the ending of the arms race which only brings nearer the catastrophe of war. You appeal for an end to the distribution of nuclear weapons, so that the armies of those states which at the present time do not yet possess such weapons will not receive them. Of course, this would be a step forward, especially if you take into account the fact that plans exist for handing over nuclear weapons to – for example – Western Germany, whose government openly stakes its territorial claims in Europe; and the fact that nuclear weapons, brought in from across the ocean, are deployed on the territories of West European member states of NATO. These weapons are imposed on these states under the guise of defence against aggression. In reality, the deployment of nuclear weapons on the territories of those countries is a mortal blow to their security, since, if an aggressor breaks the peace, then, in accordance with the inexorable logic of war, shattering retaliatory attacks on the territories, those countries in which atomic weapon bases are situated, will be inevitable.

You certainly know that the Soviet Union has frequently come out with a proposal that nuclear weapons should not be deployed beyond the state frontiers of those countries which possess them already; and that, in particular, it has also proposed that the US, Britain and the USSR, should reach agreement not to deploy their nuclear weapons in either Western or Eastern Germany. For its part, the government of the German Democratic Republic has proposed to the government of the Federal Republic of Germany that they act together so that there shall be neither German nor foreign nuclear weapons on German territory. The Polish and Czechoslovak governments have announced that if agreement is reached between the Federal Republic of Germany and the German Democratic Republic, then, similarly, neither Poland nor Czechoslovakia would produce nuclear weapons or deploy them on their territory. As you can see, the Socialist states are doing everything in their power to prevent further distribution of nuclear weapons. Unfortunately, this has not yet met with a response from the western powers.

However, even if we succeeded in preventing the further distribution of nuclear weapons in the world, all this would by no means remove the danger of nuclear war. For, even now this danger is very great. The Soviet Union considers that the danger of atomic war will only be removed finally and completely when the manufacture and use of atomic and hydrogen weapons will have been completely prohibited and the stockpiles destroyed. For almost 12 years now the Soviet government has been demanding such a solution of this question and has made quite a few concrete proposals in the UN in support of these aims. If the western powers would express a sincere desire to end the danger of atomic war, then it would be possible – tomorrow, even – to advance along this path, taking, for a start, such steps as the immediate ending of nuclear weapon tests and renunciation of the use of such weapons. But it must be said straight out that, up to the present, unfortunately, we have not had evidence of any such desire by the American, British or French governments. The fact is that those quarters which formulate the policies of those countries wish to preserve war in their arsenal as a means of securing the aims of their foreign policy.

We, the Soviet people, engaged in building Communist society – a social system in which, alongside the achievement of material abundance for all, there will for the first time be the free development of man's spiritual wealth, in all its diversity – understand particularly well your concern over the criminal policy of militarism, which absurdly wastes society's material resources, which corrupts man morally and which leads to people being brought up in the spirit of fear and hate.

It is impossible to be reconciled to such a prospect – all the more so when today the wonderful discoveries of science have given man such immense power over the forces of Nature.

As a philosopher and humanist, deeply concerned at the abnormality of the present international situation, you understand very well along what lines solution of the present situation must be sought. 'The one thing necessary', you write, 'is that East and West should recognise their respective rights, admit that each must learn to live with the other and substitute argument for force in the attempt to spread their respective ideologies. It is not necessary that either side should abandon belief in its own creed. It is only necessary that it should abandon the attempt to spread its own creed by force of arms.'

I am ready to lend my name to those words, since they correspond fully to the conception of peaceful co-existence between states with different social systems, upon which our state has based its foreign policy since the first day of the establishment of Soviet power. There is no need to say how glad I would be to hear that your words had met with similar support from the US government.

In order to 'live with the other' both sides must recognise what politicians call the status quo. The right of each country to develop as the people of that country desire must be recognised. The conduct of 'cold war', engaging in threats, aiming at changing state frontiers and interfering in other countries' domestic affairs with the aim of changing their social structure – these things must not be permitted. 'Cold war' and the arms drive will lead to a new and very bloody war.

You are completely right, of course, when you say that one of the chief reasons for the present state of tension in international relations, and for all that is meant by 'cold war', is the abnormal character of the relations between the Soviet Union and the United States of America. The normalisation of these relations would beyond a doubt lead to a general improvement in the international situation. The Soviet Union has always tried for just such a normalisation of relations with the United States, and it will continue to do so. We have taken quite a few definite steps in this direction. You will probably remember, for example, that in January 1956 the Soviet government proposed to the government of the USA that a treaty of friendship and co-operation be concluded between our two countries. Our proposal still holds. We have tried and will continue to try to re-establish Soviet–American trade relations, which were broken off by the government of the US, and we want to open up cultural, scientific and technical exchanges with the United States.

The Soviet leaders have always believed that personal contacts with government leaders of other countries are of very great importance, as one of the most effective ways of improving international relations. We readily took part in the Geneva four-power conference of heads of government, and, as you are no doubt aware, we have also met the government leaders of many other countries.

I fully support your proposal, Lord Russell, that the leaders of the Soviet Union and the United States should meet and frankly discuss conditions of co-existence. Like you, we are convinced that there are far more questions on which the interests of the Soviet Union and the United States coincide than there are questions on which our interests differ. This, precisely, is why on the Soviet side the opinion has been repeatedly expressed that a high-level meeting between representatives of the USSR and the United States would be most useful for both our countries, as well as for peace among all nations.

N. Krushchev
Moscow, 7 December 1957

MR DULLES REPLIES TO RUSSELL AND KHRUSHCHEV

John Foster Dulles

Sir – On behalf of the President I am replying to Lord Russell's letter to him and to Mr Krushchev published in the 23 November issue of the *New Statesman*. I have also read Mr Krushchev's reply thereto.

Surely if we lived in a world of words, we could relax to the melody of Mr Krushchev's lullaby. The world in which we live is, however, made of stuff sterner than mere words. It is necessary now, as it has always been necessary, to look behind the words of individuals to find from their actions what their true purpose is.

I note that Mr Krushchev directs himself to Lord Russell's statement that as between the East and West, 'It is not necessary that either side should abandon belief in its own creed. It is only necessary that it should abandon the attempt to spread its own creed by the force of arms.' The creed of the United States is based on the tenets of moral law. That creed, as well as the universal conviction of the United States, rejects war except in self-defence. This abhorrence of war, this determination to substitute peaceful negotiation for force in the settlement of international disputes, is founded on the religious convictions that guided our forefathers in writing the documents that marked the birth of America's independence. I do not think that it is possible to find in the history of the United States any occasion when an effort has been made to spread its creed by force of arms. There is, therefore, no need on our side to 'abandon' what Lord Russell condemns. On the contrary, it would be abhorrent that there should be introduced into our creed the concept of its maintenance or extension by methods of violence and compulsion.

Unhappily, it is otherwise with the creed of Communism, or at least that variety of Communism which is espoused by the Soviet Communist Party. Marx, Lenin, and Stalin have all consistently taught the use of force and violence. Marx said 'the proletariat, by means of revolution, makes itself the ruling class'. Lenin taught that the dictatorship of the proletariat means 'unlimited power based on force and not on law'; and Stalin said that the ruling bourgeois classes can 'only be removed by the conscious action of the new classes, by forcible acts of these classes by revolution'. These teachings have never been disavowed by the Soviet Communist Party of which Mr Krushchev is now the First Secretary. On the contrary, as recently as 16 November last, the Communist Parties rededicated themselves in the Moscow declaration to the cause of world revolution directed by the Soviet Communist Party. There are indeed multiple examples of the continuing use of force by the Soviet Communist Party and by other Communists of the same school. A recent illustration is Hungary where, at the behest of the Hungarian Communist Party, the Soviet Communist Party requested the Soviet government to invade with massive military force to repress the people and to assure that they would continue to be subject to a rule dictated by the Hungarian Communist Party.

It is quite improbable that the Soviet Communist Party should now abjure the use of force and violence to maintain the supremacy of its creed where that party, directly or through satellite Communist Parties, is today dominant. The Soviet Communist Party seized power by violence of an intensity and extent that shocked the civilised world. It has extended its power by violence, absorbing one nation after another by force or the threat of force. Within the Soviet Union it has perpetuated its power only by force and violence, the nature of which is usually kept hidden but which is occasionally revealed, as when Mr Krushchev in his speech to the 20th Congress – a speech sought to be kept secret – portrayed the cruel practices employed by Stalin through Beria to maintain his despotism.

Nowhere in the world today does the Communist Party maintain its rule except by forcibly imposing that rule upon the great majority of the people as against their wishes. Although Communist Parties today rule nearly 1,000 million people, comprising what at one time were nearly 20 independent nations, never anywhere have these Communist Parties been willing to have free elections or to limit their rule to peoples whom they persuade by peaceful means. The fact of the matter is that the Communist Parties depend upon force and violence and could not exercise power anywhere in the world today if they should relinquish that. It is equally true that they could not achieve ultimately their announced goal of world domination without involving the same forcible methods which they have consistently used to gain and retain rule where they have it.

That, I feel, is the heart of the problem. That is why those who have freedom must be organised to preserve it. If, indeed, Lord Russell could persuade the Communist Parties of the world to renounce dependence upon force and violence and to exercise power only when this reflected the freely given consent of the governed, then indeed the world would become a happier and safer place in which to live. I earnestly hope that the idealism and persuasiveness of Lord Russell may move the Communist Parties in this direction.

Mr Krushchev's letter deals primarily with a world war which would be a nuclear war. I do not doubt that the Soviet rulers, like all other people who want to go on living, reject that concept. The United States not only rejects that concept, but strives earnestly to do something to remove the danger of nuclear war.

A decade ago, when the United States had a monopoly of atomic weapons and of the knowledge of how to make them, we proposed that we and all others should forgo such destructive weapons and assure that the power of the atom should be used for peaceful purposes. We proposed an international agency to control all use of atomic energy. That proposal was rejected by the Soviet Union, with the consequence that nuclear weapons today exist in vast and growing quantities.

In a further effort to stem the increase of nuclear weapons and their irresponsible spread throughout the world, the United States joined in proposals that fissionable material should no longer be produced for weapons purposes and that existing nuclear weapons stockpiles should be steadily diminished by agreed contributions to peaceful purposes internationally controlled. This proposal, too, has been rejected by the Soviet Union.

Now a new source of danger to humanity looms in the use of outer space for weapons purposes. Both the Soviet Union and the United States are beginning to make such use of outer space. But the United States, in pursuance of its peaceful purposes, proposed that we should not repeat the mistake of ten years ago but should quickly take steps to assure that outer space shall be used only for peaceful purposes. President Eisenhower eloquently pleaded for this peaceful step in his letter of 12 January to Chairman Bulganin. Thus, the Soviet is afforded, now for the third time, a chance to demonstrate that its words of peace mean something more than a mere effort to lull the non-Communist world into a mood of illusory security.

At the moment its propaganda efforts are primarily directed, as was Mr Krushchev's letter, to trying to assure that Western Europe shall be armed only with weapons of the pre-atomic age, while the Soviet Union uninterruptedly develops the most modern weapons of the nuclear age and of the age of outer space. At the recent North Atlantic Council meeting, the heads of the 15 member governments had this to say:

> The Soviet leaders, while preventing a general disarmament agreement, have made it clear that the most modern and destructive weapons, including missiles of all kinds, are being introduced in the Soviet armed forces. In the Soviet view, all European nations except the USSR should, without waiting for general disarmament, renounce nuclear weapons and missiles and rely on arms of the pre-atomic age. As long as the Soviet Union persists in this attitude, we have no alternative but to remain vigilant and to look to our defences.

But also they said:

> We are also prepared to examine any Proposal, from whatever source, for general or partial disarmament, and any proposal enabling agreement to be reached on the controlled reduction of armaments of all types.

While of course nuclear war is the form of war most to be dreaded, particularly if, to nuclear power, is added the use of outer space, it is essential to avoid war of any kind, and to renounce all use of force as a means of subjecting human beings to a ruler to which they do not freely consent. That, I take it, is the heart of what Lord Russell seeks. I can assure you it is also what is sought by the government of the United States and also by all of our people who adhere to the creed of America as it is expressed in the words of the American Declaration of Independence: 'We hold these truths to be self-evident, that all men are created equal, that they are endowed by their Creator with certain inalienable rights, that among these are life, liberty and the pursuit of happiness; that to secure these rights governments are instituted among men, deriving their just powers from the consent of the governed.'

That, I assure you, is the creed of America. It is the creed by which we live and in defence of which many Americans have laid down their lives in a supreme act of fellowship with those of other lands who believe in the dignity of men and men's rights to have governments not imposed upon them but chosen by them. Such a creed cannot be imposed by force because to use force to impose a creed would of itself be a violation of our creed.

I revert again to Lord Russell's statement that 'it is not necessary that either side should abandon belief in its own creed'. Certainly that is true of the United States, whose creed comprehends the renunciation of violence and force to spread its creed. The same, unfortunately, cannot be said of Soviet Communism, whose creed comprehends the use of force and violence. Therefore I believe that it is necessary that at least that part of the Soviet Communist creed should be abandoned in order to achieve the peaceful result which is sought by Lord Russell and all other peace-loving people.

It is the steadfast determination of the United States – you may call it creed – to work in a spirit of conciliation for peaceful solutions based on freedom and justice and the great problems facing the world today.

John Foster Dulles
(Published in the NS *of 8 February 1958)*

The tyranny of the brands

Naomi Klein

What are we to make of the extraordinary scenes in Seattle that brought the twentieth century to a close? A *New York Times* reporter observed that this vibrant mass movement opposed to unregulated globalisation had materialised 'seemingly overnight'. On television, the reliable experts who explain everything couldn't sort out whether the protesters were right-wing nationalists or Marxist globalists. Even the American left seemed surprised to learn that, contrary to previous reports, it did, in fact, still exist.

Despite the seemingly unconnected causes that converged in Seattle that week, there was a common target: the multinational corporation in general and McDonald's, Gap, Microsoft and Starbucks in particular. And what has given the movement against them a new energy and a new urgency is a profound shift in corporate priorities. That shift centres on the idea of corporate branding and the quest to build the most powerful brand image. It will, I believe, be one of the issues that shapes the first decade of the twenty-first century.

Branding seems like a fairly innocuous idea. It is slapping a logo on a product and saying it's the best. And when brands first emerged, that was all it was. At the start of the Industrial Revolution, the market was flooded with nearly identical mass-produced products. Along came Aunt Jemima and Quaker Oats with their happy comforting logos to say: our mass-produced product is of the highest quality.

But the role of branding has been changing, particularly in the past 15 years: rather than serving as a guarantee of value on a product, the brand itself has increasingly become the product – a free-standing idea pasted on to innumerable surfaces. The actual product bearing the brand name has become a medium, like radio or a billboard, to transmit the real message. The message is: It's Nike. It's Disney. It's Microsoft. It's Diesel. It's Caterpillar. The late graphic designer Tibor

Kalman said that a brand used to be a mark of quality; now, it is 'a stylistic badge of courage'.

This shift in the role of the brand is related to a new corporate consensus, which emerged in the late 1980s. It held that corporations were too bloated: they were oversized, they owned too much, they employed too many people, they were weighed down with too many things. Where once the primary concern of every corporation was the production of goods, now production itself began to seem like a clunky liability.

The Nikes and Microsofts, and later the Tommy Hilfigers and Intels, made the bold claim that production was only an incidental part of their operations. What these companies produced primarily were not things, they said, but ideas and images, and their real work lay not in manufacturing, but in building up their brands. Savvy ad agencies began to think of themselves as brand factories, hammering out what is of true value: the idea, the lifestyle, the attitude. Out of this heady time, we learned that Nike was about 'Sport', not shoes; Microsoft about 'Communications', not software; Starbucks about 'Community', not coffee; Virgin about a 'Fun-loving Attitude', not an airline, a record label, a cola, a bridal gown line, a train – or any of the other brand extensions the company has launched. My favourite is Diesel, whose chief executive says he has 'created a movement', not a line of clothes.

The formula for these brand-driven companies is pretty much the same: get rid of your unionised factories in the West and buy your products from Asian or central American contractors and subcontractors. Then, take the money you save and spend it on branding, on advertising, superstores, sponsorships. Based on the success of this formula, virtue in the corporate world has become a sort of race towards weightlessness: the companies which own the least, keep the fewest employees on the payroll and produce the coolest ideas (as opposed to products) win the race.

I have come to think of such companies as transcendent brands because their goal is to escape almost all that is earthbound and to become pure idea, like a spirit ascending. This is a goal that is available not only to companies, but also to people. We have human brands as well as company brands. Bill Gates has quit as chief executive of Microsoft so that he can tend to his true mission: being Bill Gates.

Michael Jordan has stopped playing basketball and has become a pure brand-identity machine. And not only does he now have his own 'Jordan' superstores, he is the first celebrity endorser to get other celebrities endorsing his label. Michael Jordan is no longer an athlete, he is an attitude.

It wasn't until the internet stock explosion that the extent of this shift became apparent. It marks the complete triumph of branding: the ascent of companies, most of which have yet to make a profit, that exist almost purely as ideas of themselves, leaving no real-world trace at all.

This shift to branding explains many of the most fundamental economic and cultural shifts of the past decade. Power, for a brand-driven company, is attained not by collecting assets but by projecting one's brand idea on to as many surfaces of the culture as possible: the wall of a college, a billboard the size of a skyscraper, an ad campaign that waxes philosophic about the future of our global village. Where a previous generation of corporate giants used drills, hammers and cranes to build their empires, these companies need an endless parade of new ideas for brand extensions, continuously rejuvenated imagery for marketing and, most of all, fresh new spaces to disseminate their brand's idea of itself.

In this way, these corporate phantoms become real. If we think of a brand-driven company as an ever-expanding balloon, then public space, new political ideas and avantgarde imagery are the gases that inflate it: it needs to consume cultural space in order to stave off its own deflation. This is a major change. Marketing, in the classic sense, is about association: beautiful girl drinks soda, uses shampoo, drives car; soda/shampoo/car become associated with our aspiration to be beautiful like her.

Branding mania has changed all that: association is no longer good enough. The goal now is for the brands to become real-world, living manifestations of their myths. Brands are about 'meaning', not product attributes. So companies provide their consumers with opportunities not merely to shop but to experience fully the meaning of their brand. The brand-name superstore, for instance, stands as a full expression of the brand's lifestyle in miniature. Many of these stores are so palatial, so interactive, so hi-tech that they lose money hand over fist. But that doesn't mean they aren't working. Their real goal is to act as a 3D manifestation of the brand, so grand that their rather mundane products will carry that grandeur with them like a homing device.

But this is only the beginning. Nike, which used just to sponsor athletes, has taken to buying sporting events outright. Disney, which through its movies and theme parks has sold a bygone version of small-town America, now owns and operates its very own small town, Celebration Florida.

In these branded creations, we see the building blocks of a fully privatised social and cultural infrastructure. These companies are stretching the fabric of their brands in so many directions that they are transformed into enclosures large enough to house any number of core activities, from shopping to entertainment to holidays. The companies are no longer satisfied with having a fling with their consumers, they want to move in together.

These companies are forever on the prowl for new ways to build and strengthen their images. This thirsty quest for meaning and virgin space takes its toll on public institutions such as schools, where, in North America, corporate interests are transforming education, seeking not only to advertise in cafeterias and washrooms but to make brands the uncritical subjects of study. Maths textbooks urge students to calculate the circumference of an Oreo cookie, Channel One broadcasts Burger King ads into 12,000 US schools and a student from Georgia was suspended last year for wearing a Pepsi T-shirt on his school's official 'Coke Day'.

Another effect is to restrict choice. Brands are selfish creatures, driven by the need to eliminate competitors. So Reebok, once it lands a deal to sponsor campus athletics, wants to exclude not only competing brands but also, as was the case at the University of Wisconsin, all disparaging remarks made about Reebok by officials of the university. Such 'non-disparagement' clauses are standard in campus sponsorship deals. Disney, after it bought ABC, decided that it would rather ABC News no longer covered Disney's scandals, and focused instead on promoting its movies in various feats of 'synergy'.

There is another, more tangible, effect of the shift from products to brands: the devaluation of production itself. The belief that economic success lies in branding – production is a distant second – is changing the face of global employment. Building a superbrand is extraordinarily costly: it needs constant managing, tending, replenishing, stretching. The necessity for lavish spending on marketing creates intense resistance to investment in production facilities and labour. Companies that were traditionally satisfied with a 100 per cent mark-up from the cost of factory production to the retail price have spent the decade scouring the globe for factories that can make their products so inexpensively that the mark-up is closer to 400 per cent.

That's where the developing world's 'freetrade zones' (free, that is, of taxes and wage or other labour regulations) come in. In Indonesia, China, Mexico, Vietnam, the Philippines and elsewhere, the export-processing zones (as these areas are also called) are emerging as leading producers of garments, toys, shoes, electronics and cars. There are almost 1,000 zones around the world, spread through 70 countries and employing approximately 27 million workers.

Inside the zones, workers assemble the finished products of our branded world: Nike running shoes, Gap pyjamas, IBM computer screens, Old Navy jeans, or VW Bugs. Yet the zones appear to be the only places left on earth where the superbrands actually keep a low profile. Their names and logos aren't splashed on the façades of the factories. In fact, where a particular branded product is made is often kept secret. And unlike in the brand-segregated superstores, competing labels are often produced side by side in the same factories; glued by the same workers, stitched and soldered on the same machines.

Regardless of where the zones are located, the hours will be long – 14-hour days in Sri Lanka, 12 in Indonesia, 16 in southern China, 12 in the Philippines. The workers are mostly young women; the management, military-style; the wages, sub-subsistence; the work, low-skill and tedious. The factories are owned by contractors or subcontractors from Korea, Taiwan or Hong Kong; the contractors meet orders for companies based in the US, Britain, Japan, Germany and Canada.

These pockets of pure industry are cloaked in a haze of transience: the contracts come and go with little notice (in Guatemala the factories are called 'swallows' because they might take flight at any time); the workers are predominantly migrants; the work itself is short-term, often not renewed. Many factory workers in the Philippines are hired through an employment agency inside the zone walls which collects their cheques and takes a cut.

We tend to think that globalisation moves jobs from one country to another. But in a brand-based economy, the value of the work itself moves to a drastically degraded rung of the corporate hierarchy. What is being abandoned in the relentless quest to reduce the costs of production is the Fordist principle: that labour not only creates products but, by paying workers a decent wage, creates the consumer market for that product and others like it. In Indonesia, the young women factory workers making Nike shoes and Gap jeans live a notch above famine victims and landless peasants.

And so we are left with an odd duality: brands have never been more omnipresent, nor have they ever generated as much wealth. All around us we see these new creations replacing our cultural institutions and our public spaces. And yet, at the same time, these same companies are oddly absent from our lives in the most immediate of ways: as steady employers. Multinationals that once identified strongly with their role as engines of job growth now prefer to identify themselves as engines of 'economic growth'.

The extent of this shift cannot be overstated. Among the total number of working-age adults in the USA, Canada and the UK, those with full-time, permanent jobs working for someone other than themselves are in the minority. Temps, part-timers, the unemployed and those who have opted out of the labour force entirely now make up more than half of the working-age population.

We know that this formula reaps record profits in the short term. It may, however, prove to be a strategic miscalculation. When corporations are perceived as functioning vehicles of wealth distribution – trickling down jobs and tax revenue – they get deep civic loyalty in return. In exchange for steady pay cheques and stable communities, citizens attach themselves to the priorities of the local corporate sector and don't ask too many questions about, say, water pollution. In other words, dependable job creation served as a kind of corporate suit of armour. Only now, without realising it, brand-driven multinationals have been shedding that armour: first came their inability to respect public space, next came their betrayal of the central promise of the information age – the promise of increased choice – and, finally, they severed the bond between employer and employee. They may be big and rich, but suddenly there is nothing to protect them from public rage.

And that is the true significance of Seattle. All around us we are witnessing the early expressions of this anger, of the first, often crudely constructed lines of defence against the rule of the brands. We have, for example, the growth of 'culture-jamming', which adapts a corporation's own advertising to send a message starkly at odds with the one that was intended. So, Apple Computers' 'Think Different' campaign acquires a photograph of Stalin with the slogan 'Think Really Different'. The process forces the company to foot the bill for its own subversion.

The principles of culture-jamming – using the power of brand names against themselves in a kind of brand boomerang – are being imported to much more direct and immediate political struggles. People are beginning to fight the big global economic battles by focusing on one or two brand-name corporations and turning them into largescale political metaphors.

Think of the campaigns that trace the journeys of brand-name goods back to their unbranded points of origin: Nike sneakers back to the sweatshops of Vietnam; Starbucks lattes back to the sun-scorched coffee fields of Guatemala and now East Timor; and virtually every ingredient of a McDonald's hamburger dissected into its bio-engineered beginnings.

There is a clear difference between these campaigns and the corporate boycotts of the past, whether against Nestlé for its baby formula, or against Union Carbide for its infamous toxic accident in Bhopal, India. In those cases, activists had targeted a specific corporation engaged in an anomalously harmful practice. Today's anti-corporate campaigns simply piggyback on the high profile of their brand-name targets as a tactical means of highlighting difficult, even arcane issues. The companies being targeted – Disney, Mattel, Gap and so on – may not always be the worst offenders, but they do tend to be the ones who flash their logos in bright lights on the global marquee. It may seem unfair to single such companies out for their 'success', as some have argued, but it is precisely this success which is becoming an odd sort of liability.

Take McDonald's. In opening more than 23,000 outlets worldwide, the company has done more than spread the gospel of fast, uniform food. It has also, inadvertently, become equated in the public imagination with the 'McJob', 'McDonaldisation' and 'McWorld'. So when activists build a movement around McDonald's, as they did around the McLibel Trial, they are not really going after a fast-food chain, but harnessing the branding might behind the chain as a way to crack open a discussion on the otherwise impenetrable global economy: about labour, the environment and cultural imperialism.

Many superbrands are feeling the backlash. With typical understatement, Shell Oil's chief executive, Mark Moody, states: 'Previously, if you went to your golf club or church and said, "I work for Shell", you'd get a warm glow. In some parts of the world, that has changed a bit.' That change flowed directly from the anticorporate campaign launched against Shell after the hanging of the Nigerian author and activist Ken Saro-Wiwa, who was fighting to get Shell to clean up the environmental devastation left behind when it pumped oil out of the Niger Delta. Had the campaigners focused on the dictatorship alone, the death of the activist could well have been yet another anonymous atrocity in Africa. But because they dared to name names – to name Shell as the economic interest behind the violence – it became an instantly globalised campaign, with protests at petrol stations around the world. The brand was the campaign's best asset.

At the heart of this shift in focus is the recognition that corporations are much more than purveyors of the products we all want; they are also the most powerful political forces of our time, the driving forces behind bodies such as the World Trade Organisation. We've all heard the statistics: how corporations such as Shell and Walmart bask in budgets bigger than the gross domestic products of most nations; how, of the top 100 economies, 51 are multinationals and only 49 are countries. So, although the media often describe campaigns like the one against Nike as 'consumer boycotts', that tells only part of the story. It is more accurate to describe them as political campaigns that use consumer goods as readily accessible targets, as public-relations levers and as popular education tools.

I doubt this current surge of anti-corporate activism would have been possible without the mania for branding. Branding, as we have seen, has taken a fairly straightforward relationship between buyer and seller and – through the quest to turn brands into media providers, art producers, town squares and social philosophers – transformed it into something much more intimate. But the more successful this project is, the more vulnerable these companies become to the brand boomerang. If brands are indeed intimately entangled with our culture, then, when they do wrong, their crimes are not easily dismissed. Instead, many of the people who inhabit these branded worlds feel complicit in their wrongs. And this connection is a volatile one, akin to the relationship of fan and celebrity: emotionally intense but shallow enough to turn on a dime.

Branding, as I have stated, is a balloon economy: it inflates with astonishing rapidity but it is full of hot air. It shouldn't be surprising that this formula has bred armies of pin-wielding critics, anxious to pop the corporate balloon and watch it fall to the ground.

Behind the protests outside Nike Town, behind the pie in Bill Gates's face, behind the shattering of a McDonald's window in Paris, behind the protests in Seattle, there is something too visceral for most conventional measures to track – a bad mood rising. And the corporate hijacking of political power is as responsible for this mood as the brands' cultural looting of public and mental spaces.

All around the world, activists are making liberal use of the tool that has so thoroughly captured the imagination of the corporate world: branding. Brand image, the source of so much corporate wealth, is also, it turns out, the corporate Achilles heel.

India in crisis

Arundhati Roy

The law locks up the hapless felon
Who steals the goose from off the common,
But lets the greater felon loose
Who steals the common from the goose.

Anonymous, England, 1821

In the early morning hours of 2 July 2010, in the remote forests of Adilabad, the Andhra Pradesh State Police fired a bullet into the chest of a man called Cherukuri Rajkumar, known to his comrades as Azad. Azad was a member of the politburo of the banned Communist Party of India (Maoist), and had been nominated by his party as its chief negotiator for the proposed peace talks with the government of India. Why did the police fire at point-blank range and leave those tell-tale burn marks, when they could so easily have covered their tracks? Was it a mistake or was it a message?

They killed a second person that morning – Hem Chandra Pandey, a young journalist who was travelling with Azad when he was apprehended. Why did they kill him? Was it to make sure no eyewitness remained alive to tell the tale? Or was it just whimsy?

In the course of a war, if, in the preliminary stages of a peace negotiation, one side executes the envoy of the other side, it is reasonable to assume that the side that did the killing does not want peace. It looks very much as though Azad was killed because someone decided that the stakes were too high to allow him to remain alive. That decision could turn out to be a serious error of judgement – not just because of who he was, but because of the political climate in India today.

THE TRICKLE-DOWN REVOLUTION

Days after I emerged from the Dandakaranya forest in central India, where I had spent two and a half weeks with the Maoist guerrillas, I found myself charting a weary but familiar course to Jantar Mantar, on Parliament Street in New Delhi. Jantar Mantar is an old observatory built by Maharaja Sawai Jai Singh II of Jaipur between 1727 and 1734. In those days it was a scientific marvel, used to tell the time, predict the weather and study the planets. Today it's a not-so-hot tourist attraction that doubles up as Delhi's little showroom for democracy.

For some years now, protests – unless they're patronised by political parties or religious organisations – have been banned in Delhi. The Boat Club on Rajpath, which has in the past seen huge, historic rallies that sometimes lasted for days, is out of bounds for political activity now, and is available for picnics, balloon-sellers and boat-rides only. As for India Gate, candlelight vigils and boutique protests for middle-class causes – such as 'Justice for Jessica', the model who was killed in a Delhi bar by a thug with political connections – are allowed, but nothing more. Section 144, an old nineteenth-century law that bans the gathering of more than five people – who have 'a common object which is unlawful' – in a public place, has been clamped on the city. The law was passed by the British in 1861 to prevent a repeat of the 1857 Mutiny. It was meant to be an emergency measure, but has become a permanent fixture in many parts of India. Perhaps it was in gratitude for laws like these that our prime minister, while accepting an honorary degree from Oxford, thanked the British for bequeathing us such a rich legacy: 'Our judiciary, our legal system, our bureaucracy and our police are all great institutions, derived from British-Indian administration, and they have served the country well.'

Jantar Mantar is the only place in Delhi where Section 144 applies but is not enforced. People from all over the country, fed up with being ignored by the political establishment and the media, converged there, desperately hoping for a hearing. Some take long train journeys. Some, like the victims of the Bhopal gas leak, have walked for weeks, all the way to Delhi. Though they had to fight each other for the best spot on the burning (or freezing) pavement, until recently protesters were allowed to camp in Jantar Mantar for as long as they liked –

weeks, months, even years. Under the malevolent gaze of the police and the Special Branch, they would put up their faded *shamianas* and banners. From here they declared their faith in democracy by issuing their memorandums, announcing their protest plans and staging their indefinite hunger strikes. From here they tried (but never succeeded) to march on parliament. From here they hoped.

Of late, though, democracy's timings have been changed. It's strictly office hours now, nine to five. No overtime. No sleepovers. No matter from how far people have come, no matter if they have no shelter in the city – if they don't leave by 6 p.m. they are forcibly dispersed, by the police if necessary, with batons and water cannon if things get out of hand. The new timings were ostensibly instituted to make sure that the 2010 Commonwealth Games that New Delhi is hosting go smoothly. But nobody's expecting the old timings back any time soon. Maybe it's in the fitness of things that what's left of our democracy should be traded in for an event that was created to celebrate the British Empire. Perhaps it's only right that 400,000 people should have had their homes demolished and been driven out of the city overnight. Or that hundreds of thousands of roadside vendors should have had their livelihoods snatched away by order of the Supreme Court so city malls could take over their share of business. And that tens of thousands of beggars should have been shipped out of the city while more than a hundred thousand galley slaves were shipped in to build the flyovers, metro tunnels, Olympic-sized swimming pools, warm-up stadiums and luxury housing for athletes. The Old Empire may not exist. But obviously our tradition of servility has become too profitable an enterprise to dismantle.

I was at Jantar Mantar because a thousand pavement dwellers from cities all over the country had come to demand a few fundamental rights: the right to shelter, to food (ration cards), to life (protection from police brutality and criminal extortion by municipal officers).

It was early spring. The sun was sharp, but still civilised. This is a terrible thing to have to say, but it's true – you could smell the protest from a fair distance: it was the accumulated odour of a thousand human bodies that had been dehumanised, denied the basic necessities for human (or even animal) health and hygiene for years, if not a whole lifetime. Bodies that had been marinated in the refuse of our big cities, bodies that had no shelter from the harsh weather, no access to clean water, clean air, sanitation or medical care. No part of this great country, none of the supposedly progressive schemes, no single urban institution has been designed to accommodate them. Not the Jawaharlal Nehru National Urban Renewal Mission, not any other slum development, employment guarantee or welfare scheme. Not even the sewage system – they shit on top of it. They are shadow people, who live in the cracks that run between schemes and institutions. They sleep on the streets, eat on the streets, make love on the streets, give birth on the streets, are raped on the streets, cut their vegetables, wash their clothes, raise their children, live and die on the streets.

If the motion picture were an art form that involved the olfactory senses – in other words, if cinema smelled – then films like *Slumdog Millionaire* would not win Oscars. The stench of that kind of poverty wouldn't blend with the aroma of warm popcorn.

The people at the protest in Jantar Mantar that day were not even slum dogs, they were pavement-dwellers. Who were they? Where had they come from? They were the refugees of India's shining, the people who are being sloshed around like toxic effluent in a manufacturing process that has gone berserk. The representatives of the more than 60 million people who have been displaced, by rural destitution, by slow starvation, by floods and drought (many of them man-made), by mines, steel factories and aluminium smelters, by highways and expressways, by the 3,300 big dams built since independence and now by Special Economic Zones. They're part of the 830 million people of India who live on less than 20 rupees a day, the ones who starve while millions of tonnes of foodgrain are either eaten by rats in government warehouses or burned in bulk (because it's cheaper to burn food than to distribute it to poor people). They're the parents of the tens of millions of malnourished children in our country, of the two million who die every year before they reach the age of five. They're the millions who make up the chain gangs that are transported from city to city to build the New India. Is this what is known as 'enjoying the fruits of modern development'?

What must they think, these people, about a government that sees fit to spend $9bn of public money (2,000 per cent more than the initial estimate) for a two-week-long sports extravaganza which, for fear of terrorism, malaria, dengue and New Delhi's new superbug, many international athletes have refused to attend? Which the Queen of England, titular head of the Commonwealth, would not consider presiding over, not even in her most irresponsible dreams. What must they think of the fact that most of those billions have been stolen and salted away by politicians and Games officials? Not much, I guess. Because for people who live on less than 20 rupees a day, money on that scale must seem like science fiction. It probably doesn't occur to them that it's their money. That's why corrupt politicians in India never have a problem sweeping back into power, using the money they stole to buy elections. (Then they feign outrage and ask, 'Why don't the Maoists stand for elections?')

Standing there, in that dim crowd on that bright day, I thought of all the struggles that are being waged by people in this country – against big dams in the Narmada Valley, Polavaram, Arunachal Pradesh; against mines in Orissa, Chhattisgarh and Jharkhand, against the police by the Adivasis of Lalgarh, against the grabbing of their lands for industries and Special Economic Zones all over the country. How many years (and in how many ways) people have fought to avoid just such a fate. I thought of Maase, Narmada, Roopi, Nity, Mangtu, Madhav, Saroja, Raju, Gudsa Usendi and Comrade Kamla (my young bodyguard during the time I spent with the Maoists in the jungle), with their guns slung over their shoulders. I thought of the great dignity of the forest I had so recently walked in and the rhythm of the Adivasi drums at the Bhumkal celebration in Bastar, like the soundtrack of the quickening pulse of a furious nation.

I thought of Padma, with whom I travelled to Warangal. She's only in her thirties but when she walks up stairs she has to hold the banister and drag her body behind her. She was arrested just a week after she had had an appendix operation. She was beaten until she had an internal haemorrhage and had to have several organs removed. When they cracked her knees, the police explained helpfully that it was to make sure she 'would never walk in the jungle again'. She was released after serving an eight-year sentence. Now she runs the 'Amarula Bandhu Mithrula Sangham', the Committee of Relatives and Friends of Martyrs. It retrieves the bodies of people killed in fake encounters. Padma spends her time criss-crossing northern Andhra Pradesh, in whatever transport she can find, usually a tractor, transporting the corpses of people whose parents or spouses are too poor to make the journey to retrieve the bodies of their loved ones.

The tenacity, the wisdom and the courage of those who have been fighting for years, for decades, to bring change, or even the whisper of justice to their lives, is something extraordinary. Whether people are fighting to overthrow the Indian state, or fighting against big dams, or only fighting a particular steel plant or mine or SEZ, the bottom line is that they are fighting for their dignity, for the right to live and smell like human beings. They're fighting because, as far as they're concerned, 'the fruits of modern development' stink like dead cattle on the highway.

On the 15 August, on the 63rd anniversary of India's independence, Prime Minister Manmohan Singh climbed into his bulletproof soapbox in the Red Fort to deliver a passionless, bone-chillingly banal speech to the nation. Listening to him, who would have guessed that he was addressing a country that, despite having the second-highest economic growth rate in the world, has more poor people in eight states than 26 of Africa's poorest countries put together? 'All of you have contributed to India's success,' he said, 'the hard work of our workers, our artisans, our farmers has brought our country to where it stands today ... We are building a new India in which every citizen would have a stake, an India which would be prosperous and in which all citizens would be able to live a life of honour and dignity in an environment of peace and goodwill. An India in which all problems could be solved through democratic means. An India in which the basic rights of every citizen would be protected.' Some would call this graveyard humour. He might as well have been speaking to people in Finland, or Sweden.

If our prime minister's reputation for 'personal integrity' extended to the text of his speeches, this is what he should have said:

Brothers and sisters, greetings to you on this day on which we remember our glorious past. Things are getting a little expensive, I know, and you keep moaning about food prices. But look at it this way – more than 650 million of you are engaged in and are living off agriculture as farmers and farm labour, but your combined efforts contribute less than 18 per cent of our GDP. So what's the use of you? Look at our IT sector. It employs 0.2 per cent of the population and earns us 34 per cent of our national income. Can you match that? It is true that in our country employment hasn't kept pace with growth, but fortunately 60 per cent of our workforce is self-employed. Ninety per cent of our labour force is employed by the unorganised sector. True, they manage to get work only for a few months in the year, but since we don't have a category called 'underemployed', we just keep that part a little vague. It would not be right to enter them in our books as unemployed.

Coming to the statistics that say we have the highest infant and maternal mortality in the world – we should unite as a nation and ignore bad news for the time being. We can address these problems later, after our Trickle-down Revolution, when the health sector has been completely privatised. Meanwhile, I hope you are all buying medical insurance. As for the fact that the per capita foodgrain availability has actually decreased over the past 20 years – which happens to be the period of our most rapid economic growth – believe me, that's just a coincidence.

My fellow citizens, we are building a new India in which our 100 richest people hold assets worth a full 25 per cent of our GDP. Wealth concentrated in fewer and fewer hands is always more efficient. You have all heard the saying that too many cooks spoil the broth. We want our beloved billionaires, our few hundred millionaires, their near and dear ones and their political and business associates, to be prosperous and to live a life of honour and dignity in an environment of peace and goodwill in which their basic rights are protected.

I am aware that my dreams cannot come true by solely using democratic means. In fact, I have come to believe that real democracy flows through the barrel of a gun. This is why we have deployed the army, the police, the Central Reserve Police Force, the Border Security Force, the Central Industrial Security Force, the Pradeshik Armed Constabulary, the Indo-Tibetan Border Police, the Eastern Frontier Rifles – as well as the Scorpions, Greyhounds and CoBRAs – to crush the misguided insurrections that are erupting in our mineral-rich areas.

Our experiments with democracy began in Nagaland, Manipur and Kashmir. Kashmir, I need not reiterate, is an integral part of India. We have deployed more than half a million soldiers to bring democracy to the people there. The Kashmiri youth who have been risking their lives by defying curfew and throwing stones at the police for the past two months are Lashkar-e-Toiba militants who actually want employment, not *azadi*. Tragically, 60 of them have lost their lives before we could study their job applications. I have instructed the police from now on to shoot to maim rather than kill these misguided youths.

In his seven years in office, Manmohan Singh has allowed himself to be cast as Sonia Gandhi's tentative, mild-mannered underling. It's an excellent disguise for a man who, for the past 20 years, first as finance minister and then as prime minister, has powered through a regime of new economic policies that has brought India into the situation in which it finds itself now. This is not to suggest that Manmohan Singh is not an underling. Only that all his orders don't come from Sonia Gandhi. In his autobiography *A Prattler's Tale*, Ashok Mitra, former finance minister of West Bengal, tells his story of how Manmohan Singh rose to power. In 1991, when India's foreign-exchange reserves were dangerously low, the Narasimha Rao government approached the International Monetary Fund (IMF) for an emergency loan. The IMF agreed on two conditions. The first was structural adjustment and economic reform. The second was the appointment of a finance minister of its choice. That man, says Mitra, was Manmohan Singh.

Over the years he has stacked his cabinet and the bureaucracy with people who are evangelically committed to the corporate takeover of everything – water, electricity, minerals, agriculture, land, telecommunications, education, health – no matter what the consequences.

Sonia Gandhi and her son play an important part in all of this. Their job is to run the Department of Compassion and Charisma, and to win elections. They are allowed make (and also to take credit for) decisions which appear progressive but are actually tactical and symbolic, meant to take the edge off popular anger and allow the big ship to keep on rolling. (The most recent example of this is the 26 August rally that was organised for Rahul Gandhi to claim victory for the cancellation of Vedanta's permission to mine Niyamgiri for bauxite – a battle that the Dongria Kondh tribe and a coalition of activists, local as well as international, have been fighting for years. At the rally, Rahul Gandhi announced that he was a 'soldier for the tribal people'. He didn't mention that the economic policies of his party are predicated on the mass displacement of tribal people. Or that every other bauxite *giri* – hill – in the neighbourhood was having the hell mined out of it while this 'soldier for the tribal people' looked away. Rahul Gandhi may be a decent man. But for him to go around talking about the 'two Indias' – the 'Rich India' and the 'Poor India' – as though the party he represents has nothing to do with it, is an insult to everybody's intelligence, including his own.)

The division of labour between politicians who have a mass base and win elections to keep the charade of democracy going, and those who actually run the country but either do not need to win elections (judges and bureaucrats) or have been freed of the constraint of doing so (like the prime minister), is a brilliant subversion of democratic practice. To imagine that Sonia and Rahul Gandhi are in charge of the government would be a mistake. The real power has passed into the hands of a coven of oligarchs – judges, bureaucrats and politicians. They in turn are run like prize racehorses by the few corporations which more or less own everything in the country. They may belong to different political parties and put up a great show of being political rivals, but that's just subterfuge for public consumption. The only real rivalry is the business rivalry between corporations.

A senior member of the coven is P. Chidambaram, who some say is so popular with the opposition that he may continue to be home minister even if the Congress were to lose the next election. That's probably just as well. He may need a few extra years in office to complete the task he has been assigned. But it doesn't matter if he stays or goes. The die has been rolled.

In a lecture at Harvard, his old university, in October 2007, Chidambaram outlined that task. The lecture was called 'Poor Rich Countries: the Challenges of Development'. He called the three decades after independence the 'lost years', and exulted about the GDP growth rate, which rose from 6.9 per cent in 2001 to 9.4 per cent by 2007. What he said is important enough for me to inflict a chunk of his charmless prose on you:

One would have thought that the challenge of development – in a democracy – will become less formidable as the economy cruises on a high-growth path. The reality is the opposite. Democracy – rather, the institutions of democracy – and the legacy of the socialist era have actually added to the challenge of development. Let me explain with some examples. India's mineral resources include coal – the fourth-largest reserves in the world – iron ore, manganese, mica, bauxite, titanium ore, chromite, diamonds, natural gas, petroleum and limestone. Common sense tells us that we should mine these resources quickly and efficiently. That requires huge capital, efficient organisation and a policy environment that will allow market forces to operate. None of these factors is present today in the mining sector. The laws in this behalf are outdated and parliament has been able only to tinker at the margins.

Our efforts to attract private investment in prospecting and mining have, by and large, failed. Meanwhile, the sector remains virtually captive in the hands of the state governments. Opposing any change in the status quo are groups that espouse – quite legitimately – the cause of the forests or the environment or the tribal population. There are also political parties that regard mining as a natural monopoly of the state and have ideological objections to the entry of the private sector. They garner support from the established trade unions. Behind the unions – either known or unknown to them – stand the trading mafia. The result: actual investment is low, the mining sector grows at a tardy pace and it acts as a drag on the economy.

I shall give you another example. Vast extent of land is required for locating industries. Mineral-based industries such as steel and aluminium require large tracts of land for mining, processing and production. Infrastructure projects like airports, seaports, dams and power stations need very large extents of land so that they can provide road and rail connectivity and the ancillary and support facilities. Hitherto, land was acquired by the governments in exercise of the power of eminent domain. The only issue was payment of adequate compensation. That situation has changed. There are new stakeholders in every project, and their claims have to be recognised. We are now obliged to address issues such as environmental impact assessment, justification for compulsory acquisition, right compensation, solatium, rehabilitation and resettlement of the displaced persons, alternative house sites and farmland, and one job for each affected family ...

Allowing 'market forces' to mine resources 'quickly and efficiently' is what colonisers did to their colonies, what Spain and North America did to South America, what Europe did (and continues to do) in Africa. It's what the apartheid regime did in South Africa. What puppet dictators in small countries do to bleed their people. It's a formula for growth and development, but for someone else. It's an old, old, old, old story – must we really go over that ground again?

Now that mining licences have been issued with the urgency you'd associate with a knock-down distress sale and the scams that are emerging have run into billions of dollars, now that mining companies have polluted rivers, mined away state borders, wrecked ecosystems and unleashed civil war, the consequence of what the coven has set in motion is playing out. Like an ancient lament over ruined landscapes and the bodies of the poor.

Note the regret with which the minister in his lecture talks about democracy and the obligations it entails: 'Democracy – rather, the institutions of democracy – and the legacy of the socialist era have actually added to the challenge of development.' He follows that up with a standard-issue, meaningless clutch of sops about compensation, rehabilitation and jobs. What compensation? What solatium? What rehabilitation? And what 'job for each family'? (Sixty years of industrialisation in India has created employment for 6 per cent of the workforce.) As for being 'obliged' to provide 'justification' for the 'compulsory acquisition' of land, a cabinet minister surely knows that to compulsorily acquire tribal land (which is where most of the minerals are) and turn it over to private mining corporations is illegal and unconstitutional under the Panchayat (Extension to Scheduled Areas) Act. Passed in 1996, PESA is an amendment that attempts to right some of the wrongs done to tribal people by the Indian constitution when it was adopted by parliament in 1950. It overrides all existing laws that may be in conflict with it. It is a law that acknowledges the deepening marginalisation of tribal communities and is meant to radically recast the balance of power. As a piece of legislation, it is unique because it makes the community – the collective – a legal entity and it confers on tribal societies who live in scheduled areas the right to self-governance. Under PESA, 'compulsory acquisition' of tribal land cannot be justified on any count. So, ironically, those who are being called 'Maoists' (which includes everyone who is resisting land acquisition) are actually fighting to uphold the constitution. While the government is doing its best to vandalise it.

Between 2008 and 2009 the ministry of Panchayati Raj commissioned two researchers to write a chapter for a report on the progress of Panchayati Raj in the country. The chapter is called 'PESA, Left-Wing Extremism and Governance: Concerns and Challenges in India's Tribal Districts'; its authors are Ajay Dandekar and Chitrangada Choudhury. Here are some extracts:

The central Land Acquisition Act of 1894 has till date not been amended to bring it in line with the provisions of PESA ... At the moment, this colonial-era law is being widely misused on the ground to forcibly acquire individual and community land for private industry. In several cases, the practice of the state government is to sign high-profile MOUs with corporate houses and then proceed to deploy the Acquisition Act to ostensibly acquire the land for the state industrial corporation. This body then simply leases the land to the private corporation – a complete travesty of the term 'acquisition for a public purpose', as sanctioned by the act.

There are cases where the formal resolutions of *gram sabha* expressing dissent have been destroyed and substituted by forged documents. What is worse, no action has been taken by the state against concerned officials even after the facts got established. The message is clear and ominous. There is collusion in these deals at numerous levels.

The sale of tribal lands to non-tribals in the Schedule Five areas is prohibited in all these states. However, transfers continue to take place and have become more perceptible in the post-liberalisation era. The principal reasons are – transfer through fraudulent means, unrecorded transfers on the basis of oral transactions, transfers by misrepresentation of facts and misstating the purpose, forcible occupation of tribal lands, transfer through illegal marriages, collusive title suites, incorrect recording at the time of the survey, land acquisition process, eviction of encroachments and in the name of exploitation of timber and forest produce and even on the pretext of development of welfarism.

In their concluding section, they say:

> The Memorandums of Understanding signed by the state governments with industrial houses, including mining companies should be re-examined in a public exercise, with *gram sabhas* at the centre of this inquiry.

Here it is, then – not troublesome activists, not the Maoists, but a government report calling for the mining MOUs to be re-examined. What does the government do with this document? How does it respond? On 24 April 2010, at a formal ceremony, the prime minster released the report. Brave of him, you'd think. Except, this chapter wasn't in it. It was dropped.

Half a century ago, just a year before he was killed, Che Guevara wrote: 'When the oppressive forces maintain themselves in power against laws they themselves established, peace must be considered already broken.' Indeed it must. In 2009 Manmohan Singh said in parliament: 'If left-wing extremism continues to flourish in parts which have natural resources of minerals, the climate for investment would certainly be affected.' This was a furtive declaration of war.

(Permit me a small digression here, a moment to tell a very short Tale of Two Sikhs. In his last petition to the Punjab governor, before he was hanged by the British government in 1931, Bhagat Singh, the celebrated Sikh revolutionary – and Marxist – said: 'Let us declare that the state of war does exist and shall exist so long as India's toiling masses and the natural resources are being exploited by a handful of parasites. They may be purely British capitalist or mixed British and Indian or even purely Indian ... All these things make no difference.')

If you pay attention to many of the struggles taking place in India, people are demanding no more than their constitutional rights. But the government of India no longer feels the need to abide by the Indian constitution, which is supposed to be the legal and moral framework on which our democracy rests. As constitutions go, it is an enlightened document, but its enlightenment is not used to protect people. Quite the opposite. It's used as a spiked club to beat down those who are protesting against the growing tide of violence being perpetrated by a state on its people in the name of the 'public good'. In a recent article in *Outlook*, B. G. Verghese, a senior journalist, came out waving that club in defence of the state and big corporations: 'The Maoists will fade away, democratic India and the constitution will prevail, despite the time it takes and the pain involved,' he said. To this, Azad replied (it was the last piece he wrote before he was murdered):

> In which part of India is the constitution prevailing, Mr Verghese? In Dantewada, Bijapur, Kanker, Narayanpur, Rajnandgaon? In Jharkhand, Orissa? In Lalgarh, Jangalmahal? In the Kashmir Valley? Manipur? Where was your constitution hiding for 25 long years after thousands of Sikhs were massacred? When thousands of Muslims were decimated? When lakhs of peasants are compelled to commit suicides? When thousands of people are murdered by state-sponsored Salwa Judum gangs? When Adivasi women are gang-raped? When people are simply abducted by uniformed goons? Your constitution is a piece of paper that does not even have the value of a toilet paper for the vast majority of the Indian people.

After Azad was killed, several media commentators tried to paper over the crime by shamelessly inverting what he said, accusing him of calling the Indian constitution a piece of toilet paper.

If the government won't respect the constitution, perhaps we should push for an amendment to the preamble. 'We, the People of India, having solemnly resolved to constitute India into a Sovereign Socialist Secular Democratic Republic …' could be substituted with 'We, the upper castes and classes of India, having secretly resolved to constitute India into a corporate, Hindu, satellite state …'

The insurrection in the Indian countryside, in particular in the tribal heartland, poses a radical challenge not only to the Indian state, but to resistance movements, too. It questions the accepted ideas of what constitutes progress, development and, indeed, civilisation itself. It questions the ethics as well as the effectiveness of different strategies of resistance. These questions have been asked before, yes. They have been asked persistently, peacefully, year after year in a hundred different ways – by the Chhattisgarh Mukti Morcha, the Koel Karo and Gandhamardhan agitations – and hundreds of other people's movements. It was asked most persuasively and perhaps most visibly by the Narmada Bachao Andolan, the anti-dam movement in the Narmada Valley. The government of India's only answer has been repression, deviousness and the kind of opacity that can only come from a pathological disrespect for ordinary people. Worse, it went ahead and accelerated the process of displacement and dispossession to a point where peoples' anger has built up in ways that cannot be controlled. Today the poorest people in the world have managed to stop some of the richest corporations in their tracks. It's a huge victory.

Those who have risen up are aware that their country is in a state of emergency. They are aware that, like the people of Kashmir, Manipur, Nagaland and Assam, they too have now been stripped of their civil rights by laws such as the Unlawful Activities Prevention Act (UAPA) and the Chhattisgarh Special Public Security Act (CSPSA), which criminalise every kind of dissent – by word, deed and even intent.

When Indira Gandhi declared the Emergency at midnight on 25 June 1975, she did it to crush an incipient revolution. Grim as they were, those were days when people still allowed themselves to dream of bettering their lot, to dream of justice. The Naxalite uprising in Bengal had been more or less decimated. But then millions of people rallied to Jayaprakash Narayan's call for '*Sampoorna Kranti*' (Total Revolution). At the heart of all the unrest was the demand for land to the tiller. (Even back then it was no different – you needed a revolution to implement land redistribution, which is one of the directive principles of the constitution.)

Thirty-five years later, things have changed drastically. Justice, that grand, beautiful idea, has been whittled down to mean human rights. Equality is a utopian fantasy. That word has been more or less evicted from our vocabulary. The poor have been pushed to the wall. From fighting for land for the landless, revolutionary parties and resistance movements have had to lower their sights to fighting for people's rights to hold on to what little land they have. The only kind of land redistribution that seems to be on the cards is land being grabbed from the poor and redistributed to the rich for their land banks which go under the name of Special Economic Zones. The landless (mostly Dalits), the jobless, slum-dwellers and the urban working class are more or less out of the reckoning. In places like Lalgarh in West Bengal, people are only asking the police and the government to leave them alone. The Adivasi organisation called the People's Committee

Against Police Atrocities (PCAPA) began with one simple demand – that the superintendent of police visit Lalgarh and apologise to the people for the atrocities his men had committed on villagers. That was considered preposterous. (How could half-naked savages expect a government officer to apologise to them?) So people barricaded their villages and refused to let the police in. The police stepped up the violence. People responded with fury. Now, two years down the line, and many gruesome rapes, killings and fake encounters later, it's all-out war. The PCAPA has been banned and dubbed a Maoist outfit. Its leaders have been jailed or shot. (A similar fate has befallen the Chasi Mulya Adivasi Sangh in Narayanpatna in Orissa and the Visthappen Virodhi Ekta Manch in Potka in Jharkhand.)

People who once dreamed of justice and equality, and dared to demand land to the tiller, have been reduced to asking for an apology from the police for being beaten and maimed – is this progress?

During the Emergency, the saying goes, when Mrs Gandhi asked the press to bend, it crawled. And yet, in those days, there were instances when national dailies defiantly published blank editorials to protest censorship. (Irony of ironies – one of those defiant editors was B. G. Verghese.) This time around, in the undeclared emergency, there's not much scope for defiance because the media are the government. Nobody, except the corporations which control the media, can tell them what to do. Senior politicians, ministers and officers of the security establishment vie to appear on TV, feebly imploring Arnab Goswami or Barkha Dutt for permission to interrupt the day's sermon.

Several TV channels and newspapers are overtly manning Operation Green Hunt's war room and its disinformation campaign. There was the identically worded story about the '1,500-crore Maoist industry', filed under the byline of different reporters in several different papers. Almost all newspapers and TV channels ran stories blaming the PCAPA (used interchangeably with 'Maoists') for the horrific train derailment at Jhagram in West Bengal in May 2010, in which 140 people died. Two of the main suspects have been shot down by the police in 'encounters', even though the mystery around the train accident is still unravelling. The Press Trust of India put out several untruthful stories, faithfully showcased by the *Indian Express*, including one about Maoists mutilating the bodies of policemen they had killed. (The denial, which came from the police themselves, was published postage-stamp-size, hidden in the middle pages.) There are the several identical interviews, all of them billed as 'exclusive', by the female guerrilla about how she had been 'raped and re-raped' by Maoist leaders. She was supposed to have recently escaped from the forests and the clutches of the Maoists to tell the world her tale. Now it turns out that she has been in police custody for months.

The atrocity-based analyses shouted out at us from our TV screens are designed to smoke up the mirrors and hustle us into thinking, 'Yes, the tribals have been neglected and are having a very bad time; yes, they need development; yes, it's the government's fault, and it's a great pity. But right now there is a crisis. We need to get rid of the Maoists, secure the land, and then we can help the tribals.'

As war closes in, the armed forces have announced (in the way only they can), that they, too, are getting into the business of messing with our heads. In June 2010 they released two 'operational doctrines'. One was a joint doctrine for air-land operations. The other was a doctrine on Military Psychological Operations which 'constitutes a planned process of conveying a message to select target audiences, to promote particular themes that result in desired attitudes and behaviour, which affect the achievement of political and military objectives of the country ... The Doctrine also provides guidelines for activities related to perception management in sub-conventional operations, specially in an internal environment wherein misguided population may have to be brought into the mainstream.' The press release went on to say that 'the Doctrine on Military Psychological Operations is a policy, planning and implementation document that aims to create a conducive environment for the armed forces to operate by using the media available with the Services to their advantage'.

A month later, at a meeting of chief ministers of Naxalite-affected states, a decision was taken to escalate the war. Thirty-six battalions of the India Reserve Force were added to the existing 105 battalions, and 16,000 Special Police Officers (civilians armed and contracted to function as police) were added to the existing 30,000. The home minister promised to hire 175,000 policemen over the next five years. (It's a good model for an employment guarantee scheme: hire half the population to shoot the other half. You can fool around with the ratios if you like.)

Two days later the army chief told his senior officers to be 'mentally prepared to step into the fight against Naxalism ... It might be in six months, or in a year or two, but if we have to maintain our relevance as a tool of the state, we will have to undertake things that the nation wants us to do.'

By August, newspapers were reporting that the on-again-off-again air force was on again: 'The Indian air force [IAF] can fire in self-defence in anti-Maoist operations.' The *Hindustan Times* said, 'The permission has been granted but with strict conditionalities. We cannot use rockets or the integral guns of the helicopters and we can retaliate only if fired upon ... To this end, we have side-mounted machine-guns on our choppers that are operated by our Garuds [IAF commandos].' That's a relief. No integral guns, only side-mounted machine-guns.

Maybe 'six months or in a year or two' is about as long as it will take for the brigade headquarters in Bilaspur and the airbase in Rajnandgaon to be ready. Maybe by then, in a great show of democratic spirit, the government will give in to popular anger and repeal AFSPA, the Armed Forces Special Powers Act (which allows non-commissioned officers to kill on suspicion) in Manipur, Nagaland, Assam and Kashmir. Once the applause subsides and the celebration peters out, AFSPA will be recast, as the home minister has suggested, on the lines of the Jeevan Reddy report (to sound more humane but to be more deadly). Then it can be promulgated all over the country under a new name. Maybe that will give the armed forces the impunity they need to do what 'the nation' wants them to do – to be deployed in the parts of India against the poorest of the poor who are fighting for their very survival.

Maybe that's how Comrade Kamala will die – while she's trying to bring down a helicopter gunship or a military training jet with her pistol. Or maybe by then she will have graduated to an AK-47 or a light machine-gun looted from a government armoury or a murdered policeman. Maybe by then the media 'available to the Services' will have 'managed' the perceptions of those of us who still continue to be 'misguided' to receive the news of her death with equanimity.

So here's the Indian state, in all its democratic glory, willing to loot, starve, lay siege to, and now deploy the air force in 'self-defence' against its poorest citizens.

Self-defence. Ah yes. Operation Green Hunt is being waged in self-defence by a government that is trying to restore land to poor people whose land has been snatched away by Commie Corporations.

When the government uses the offer of peace talks to draw the deep-swimming fish up to the surface and then kill them, do peace talks have a future? Is either side genuinely interested in peace? Are the Maoists really interested in peace or justice, people ask? Is there anything they can be offered within the existing system that will deflect the Maoists from their stated goal of overthrowing the Indian state? The answer to that is: probably not. The Maoists do not believe that the present system can deliver justice. The thing is that an increasing number of people are beginning to agree with them. If we lived in a society with a genuinely democratic impulse, one in which ordinary people felt they could at least hope for justice, then the Maoists would be only be a small, marginalised group of militants with very little popular appeal.

The other contention is that the Maoists want a ceasefire to take the heat off themselves for a while, so that they can use the time to regroup and consolidate their position. Azad, in an interview with *The Hindu* (14 April 2010), was surprisingly candid about this: 'It doesn't need much common sense to understand that both sides will utilise the situation of a ceasefire to strengthen their respective sides.' He went on to explain that a ceasefire, even a temporary one, would give respite to ordinary people who are caught in a war zone.

The government, on the other hand, desperately needs this war. (Read the business papers to see how desperately.) The eyes of the international business community are boring holes into its back. It needs to deliver, and fast. To keep its mask from falling, it must continue to offer talks on the one hand, and undermine them on the other. The elimination of Azad was an important victory because it silenced a voice that had begun to sound dangerously reasonable. For the moment at least, peace talks have been successfully derailed.

There is plenty to be cynical about in the discussion around peace talks. The thing for us ordinary folks to remember is that no peace talks means an escalating war.

Over the past few months, the government has poured tens of thousands of heavily armed paramilitary troops into the forest. The Maoists responded with a series of aggressive attacks and ambushes. More than 200 policemen have been killed. The bodies keep coming out of the forest. Slain policemen wrapped in the national flag, slain Maoists, displayed like hunter's trophies, their wrists and ankles lashed to bamboo poles; bullet-ridden bodies, bodies that don't look human any more, mutilated in ambushes, beheadings and summary executions. Of the bodies being buried in the forest, we have no news. The theatre of war has been cordoned off, closed to activists and journalists. So there are no body counts.

On 6 April 2010, in its biggest strike ever, in Dantewada the Maoists' People's Liberation Guerrilla Army (PLGA) ambushed a Central Reserve Police Force (CRPF) company and killed 76 policemen. The party issued a coldly triumphant statement. Television milked the tragedy for everything it was worth. The nation was called upon to condemn the killing. Many of us were not prepared to – not because we celebrate killing, nor because we are all Maoists, but because we have thorny, knotty views about Operation Green Hunt. For refusing to buy shares in the rapidly growing condemnation industry, we were branded 'terrorist sympathisers' and had our photographs flashed repeatedly on TV like wanted criminals. What was a CRPF contingent doing, patrolling tribal villages with 21 AK-47 rifles, 38 INSAS rifles, seven self-loading rifles, six light machine-guns, one Sten gun and one two-inch mortar? To ask that question almost amounted to an act of treason.

Days after the ambush, I ran into two paramilitary commandos chatting to a bunch of drivers in a Delhi car park. They were waiting for their VIP to emerge from some restaurant or health club or hotel. Their view on what is going on involved neither grief nor patriotism. It was simple accounting. A balance sheet. They were talking about how many lakhs of rupees in bribes it takes for a man to get a job in the paramilitary forces, and how most families incur huge debts to pay that bribe. That debt can never be repaid by the pathetic wages paid to a jawan, for example. The only way to repay it is to do what policemen in India do – blackmail and threaten people, run protection rackets, demand payoffs, do dirty deals. (In the case of Dantewada, loot villagers, steal cash and jewellery.) But if the man dies an untimely death, it leaves the families hugely in debt. The anger of the men in the car park was directed at the government and senior police officers who make fortunes from bribes and then so casually send young men to their death. They knew that the handsome compensation that was announced for the dead in the 6 April attack was just to blunt the impact of the scandal. It was never going to be standard practice for every policeman who dies in this sordid war.

Small wonder then that the news from the war zone is that CRPF men are increasingly reluctant to go on patrol. There are reports of them fudging their daily logbooks, filling them with phantom patrols. Maybe they're beginning to realise that they are only poor khaki trash – cannon fodder in a rich man's war. There are thousands waiting to replace each one of them when they're gone.

On 17 May 2010, in another major attack, the Maoists blew up a bus in Dantewada and killed about 44 people. Sixteen of them were Special Police Officers (SPOs), members of the dreaded government sponsored people's militia, the Salwa Judum. The rest of the dead were, shockingly, ordinary people, mostly Adivasis. The Maoists expressed perfunctory regret for having killed civilians, but they came that much closer to mimicking the state's 'collateral damage' defence.

Last month in Bihar the Maoists kidnapped four policemen and demanded the release of some of their senior leaders. A few days into the hostage drama, they killed one of them, an Adivasi policeman called Lucas Tete. Two days later they released the other three. By killing a prisoner in custody, the Maoists once again harmed their own cause. It was another example of the Janus-faced morality of 'revolutionary violence' that we can expect more of in a war zone, in which tactics trump rectitude and make the world a worse place.

Not many analysts and commentators who were pained by the Maoist killing of civilians in Dantewada pointed out that at exactly the same time as the bus was blown up by the Maoists, in Kalinganagar, Orissa, and in Balitutha and Potko in Jharkhand, the police had surrounded several villages and had fired on thousands of protesters resisting the takeover of their lands by the Tatas, the Jindals and Posco. Even now the siege continues. The wounded cannot be taken to hospital because of the police cordons. Videos uploaded on YouTube show armed riot police massing in the hundreds, being confronted by ordinary villagers, some of whom are armed with bows and arrows.

The one favour Operation Green Hunt has done ordinary people is that it has clarified things to them. Even the children in the villages know that the police work for the 'companies' and that Operation Green Hunt isn't a war against Maoists. It's a war against the poor. There's nothing small about what's going on. We are watching a democracy turning on itself, trying to eat its own limbs. We're watching incredulously as those limbs refuse to be eaten.

Of all the various political formations involved in the current insurrection, none is more controversial than the CPI (Maoist). The most obvious reason is its unapologetic foregrounding of armed struggle as the only path to revolution. Sumanta Banerjee's book *In the Wake of Naxalbari* is one of the most comprehensive accounts of the movement. It documents the early years, the almost harebrained manner in which the Naxalites tried to jump-start the Indian Revolution by 'annihilating the class enemy' and expected the masses to rise up spontaneously. It describes the contortions it had to make in order to remain aligned with China's foreign policy, how it spread from state to state, and how Naxalism was mercilessly crushed.

Buried deep inside the fury that is directed against them by the orthodox left and the liberal intelligentsia is their unease with themselves and a puzzling, almost mystical protectiveness towards the Indian state. It's as though, when they are faced with a situation that has genuine revolutionary potential, they blink. They find reasons to look away. Political parties and individuals who have not in the last 25 years ever lent their support to say, the Narmada Bachao Andolan, or marched in solidarity with any one of the many of peaceful people's movements in the country, have suddenly begun to extol the virtues of non-violence and Gandhian Satyagraha. On the other hand, those who have been actively involved in these struggles may strongly disagree with the Maoists, may be wary, even exasperated, by them, but they do see them as a part of the same resistance.

It's hard to say who dislikes the Maoists more – the Indian state, its army of strategic experts and its instinctively right-wing middle class, or the Communist Party of India (CPI) and Communist Party of India

(Marxist), usually called the CPM, and the several splinter groups that were part of the original Marxist–Leninists or the liberal left. The argument begins with nomenclature. The more orthodox communists do not believe that 'Maoism' is an 'ism' at all. The Maoists in turn call the mainstream communist parties 'social fascists' and accuse them of 'economism' – basically, of gradually bargaining away the prospect of revolution.

Each faction believes itself to be the only genuinely revolutionary Marxist party or political formation. Each believes the other has misinterpreted communist theory and misunderstood history. Anyone who isn't a card-carrying member of one or the other group will be able to see that none of them is entirely wrong or entirely right about what they say. But bitter splits, not unlike those in religious sects, are the natural corollary of the rigid conformity to the party line demanded by all communist parties. So they dip into a pool of insults that dates back to the Russian and Chinese Revolutions, to the great debates between Lenin, Trotsky and Stalin, to Chairman Mao's *Red Book*, and hurl them at each other. They accuse each other of the 'incorrect application' of 'Marxist–Leninist–Mao Zedong Thought', almost as though it's an ointment that's being rubbed in the wrong place. (My earlier essay 'Walking with the Comrades' landed directly in the flight-path of this debate. It got its fair share of entertaining insults, which deserve a pamphlet of their own.)

Other than the debate about whether or not to enter electoral politics, the major disagreement between the various strands of communism in India centres around their reading of whether conditions in the country are ripe for revolution. Is the prairie ready for the fire, as Mao announced in China, or is it still too damp for the single spark to ignite it? The trouble is that India lives in several centuries simultaneously, so perhaps the prairie, that vast stretch of flat grassland, is the wrong analogy for India's social and political landscape. Maybe a 'warren' would be a better one. To arrive at a consensus about the timing of the revolution is probably impossible. So everybody marches to his or her own drumbeat. The CPI and the CPM have more or less postponed the revolution to the afterlife. For Charu Majumdar, founder of the Naxalite movement, it was meant to have happened 30 years ago. According to the Ganapathy, current chief of the Maoists, it's about 50 years away.

Today, 40 years after the Naxalbari uprising, the main charge against the Maoists by the parliamentary left continues to be what it always was. They are accused of suffering from what Lenin called an 'infantile disorder', of substituting mass politics with militarism and of not having worked at building a genuinely revolutionary proletariat. They are seen as having contempt for the urban working class, of being an ideologically ossified force that can only function as a frog-on-the-back of 'innocent' (read primitive) jungle-dwelling tribal people who, according to orthodox Marxists, have no real revolutionary potential. (This is not the place perhaps, to debate a vision that says people have to first become wage-earners, enslaved to a centralised industrial system, before they can be considered revolutionary.)

The charge that the Maoists are irrelevant to urban working-class movements, to the Dalit movement, to the plight of farmers and agricultural workers outside the forests is true. There is no doubt that the Maoist Party's militarised politics makes it almost impossible for it to function in places where there is no forest cover. However, it could equally be argued that the major communist parties have managed to survive in the mainstream only by compromising their ideologies so drastically that it is impossible to tell the difference between them and other bourgeois political parties any more. It could be argued that the smaller factions that have remained relatively uncompromised have managed to do so because they do not pose a threat to anybody.

Whatever their faults or achievements as bourgeois parties, few would associate the word 'revolutionary' with the CPI or CPM any more. (The CPI does play a role in some of the struggles against mining companies in Orissa.) But even in their chosen sphere of influence they cannot claim to have done a great service to the proletariat they say they represent. Apart from their traditional bastions in Kerala and West Bengal, both of which they are losing their grip over, they have very little presence in any other part of the country, urban or rural, forest or plains. They have run their trade unions into the ground. They have not been able to stanch the massive job losses and the virtual disbanding of the formal workforce that mechanisation and the new economic policies have caused. They have not been able to prevent the systematic dismantling of workers' rights. They have managed to alienate themselves almost completely from Adivasi and

Dalit communities. In Kerala many would say that they have done a better job than other political parties, but their 30-year 'rule' in West Bengal has left that state in ruins. The repression they unleashed in Nandigram and Singur, and now against the Adivasis of Jangalmahal, will probably drive them out of power for a few years. (Only for as long as it takes Mamta Banerjee of the Trinamool Congress to prove that she is not the vessel into which people should pour their hopes.) Still, while listing a litany of their sins, it must be said that the demise of the mainstream communist parties is not something to be celebrated. At least not unless it makes way for a new, more vital and genuinely left movement in India.

The Maoists (in their current as well as earlier avatars) have had a different political trajectory. The redistribution of land, by violent means if necessary, was always the centrepiece of their political activity. They have been completely unsuccessful in that endeavour. But their militant interventions, in which thousands of their cadre – as well as ordinary people – paid with their lives, shone a light on the deeply embedded structural injustice of Indian society. If nothing else, from the time of the Telengana movement, which, in some ways, was a precursor to the uprising in Naxalbari, the Naxalite movement, for all its faults, sparked an anger about being exploited and a desire for self-respect in some of the most oppressed communities. In West Bengal it led to Operation Bargadar ('sharecropper') and to a far lesser extent in Andhra Pradesh it shamed the government into carrying out some land reform. Even today, all the talk about 'uneven development' and 'exploitation' of tribal areas by the prime minister, the government's plans to transfer Joint Forest Management funds from the Forest Department directly to the Gram Panchayats, the Planning Commission's announcement that it will allocate Rs14,000 crore for tribal development, has not come from genuine concern, it has come as a strategy to defuse the Maoist 'menace'. If those funds do end up benefiting the Adivasi community, instead of being siphoned away by middlemen, then the 'menace' surely ought to be given some credit. Interestingly, though the Maoists have virtually no political presence outside forested areas, they do have a presence in the popular imagination, an increasingly sympathetic one, as a party that stands up for the poor against the intimidation and bullying of the state. If

Operation Green Hunt becomes an outright war instead of a 'sub-conventional' one, if ordinary Adivasis start dying in huge numbers, that sympathy could ignite in unexpected ways.

Among the most serious charges levelled against the Maoists is that its leaders have a vested interest in keeping people poor and illiterate in order to retain their hold on them. Critics ask why, after working in areas like Dandakaranya for 30 years, they still do not run schools and clinics, why they don't have check dams and advanced agriculture, and why people are still dying of malaria and malnutrition. Good question. But it ignores the reality of what it means to be a banned organisation whose members – even if they are doctors or teachers – are liable to be shot on sight. It would be more useful to direct the same question to the government of India, which has none of these constraints. Why is it that in tribal areas that are not overrun by Maoists there are no schools, no hospitals, no check dams? Why do people in Chhattisgarh suffer from such acute malnutrition that doctors have begun to call it 'nutritional AIDS' because of the effect it has on the human immune system?

In their censored chapter in the ministry of Panchayati Raj report, Ajay Dandekar and Chitrangada Choudhury (no fans of the Maoists – they call the party ideology 'brutal and cynical') write:

> So the Maoists today have a dual effect on the ground in PESA areas. By virtue of the gun they wield, they are able to evoke some fear in the administration at the village/block/district level. They consequently prevent the common villager's powerlessness over the neglect or violation of protective laws like PESA, e.g., warning a *talathi*, who might be demanding bribes in return for fulfilling the duty mandated to him under the Forest Rights Act, a trader who might be paying an exploitative rate for forest produce, or a contractor who is violating the minimum wage. The party has also done an immense amount of rural development work, such as mobilising community labour for farm ponds, rainwater harvesting and land conservation works in the Dandakaranya region, which villagers testified had improved their crops and improved their food security situation.

In their recently published empirical analysis of the working of the National Rural Employment Guarantee Scheme (NREGA) in 200

Maoist-affected districts in Orissa, Chhattisgarh and Jharkhand, which appeared in *The Economic and Political Weekly*, the authors Kaustav Banerjee and Partha Saha say:

> The field survey revealed that the charge that the Maoists have been blocking developmental schemes does not seem to hold much ground. In fact Bastar seems to be doing much better in terms of NREGA than some other areas ... on top of that, the wage struggles, the enforcement of minimum wages can be traced back to the wage struggles led by the Maoists in that area. A clear result that we came across is the doubling of the wage rates for tendu leaf collection in most Maoist areas ... Also, the Maoists have been encouraging the conduct [*sic*] of social audits since this helps in the creation of a new kind of democratic practice hitherto unseen in India.

Implicit in a lot of the debate around Maoists is the old, patronising, tendency to cast 'the masses', the Adivasi people in this case, in the role of the dim-witted horde, completely controlled by a handful of wicked 'outsiders'. One university professor, a well-known Maoist baiter, accused the leaders of the party of being parasites preying on poor Adivasis. To bolster his case, he compared the lack of development in Dandakaranya to the prosperity in Kerala. After suggesting that the non-Adivasi leaders were all cowards 'hiding safely in the forest', he appealed to all Adivasi Maoist guerrillas and village militia to surrender before a panel of middle-class Gandhian activists (hand-picked by him). He called for the non-Adivasi leadership to be tried for war crimes. Why non-Adivasi Gandhians are acceptable, but not non-Adivasi Maoists, he did not say. There is something very disturbing about this inability to credit ordinary people with being capable of weighing the odds and making their own decisions.

In Orissa, for instance, there are a number of diverse struggles being waged by unarmed resistance movements that often have sharp differences with each other. And yet between them all they have managed to temporarily stop some major corporations from being able to proceed with their projects – the Tatas in Kalinganagar, Posco in Jagatsinghpur, Vedanta in Niyamgiri. Unlike in Bastar, where they control territory and are well entrenched, the Maoists tend to use Orissa only as a corridor for their squads to pass through. But as the security forces close in on peaceful movements and ratchet up the repression, local people have to think very seriously about the pros and cons of involving the Maoist Party in their struggles. Will its armed squads stay and fight the state repression that will inevitably follow a Maoist 'action'? Or will they retreat and leave unarmed people to deal with police terror? Activists and ordinary people falsely accused of being Maoists are already being jailed. Many have been killed in cold blood. But a tense, uneasy dance continues between the unarmed resistance and the CPI (Maoist). On occasion, the party has done irresponsible things which have led to horrible consequences for ordinary people. In 2006 at the height of the tension between the Dalit and Adivasi communities in Kandhamal District, the Maoists shot dead Laxmananda Saraswati, leader of the Vishwa Hindu Parishad, a fascist outfit of proselytisers, working among Adivasis to bring them 'back into the Hindu fold'. After the murder, enraged Kandha tribals who had been recently converted to Hinduism were encouraged to go on a rampage. Almost 400 villages were convulsed with anti-Christian violence. Fifty-four Panna Dalit Christians were killed, more than 200 churches burned. Tens of thousands had to flee their homes. Many still live in camps, unable to return. A somewhat different, but equally dangerous situation is brewing in Narayanpatna and Koraput, districts where the Chasi Mulia Adivasi Sangh (which the police say is a Maoist 'front') is fighting to restore land to Adivasis that was illegally appropriated by local moneylenders and liquor dealers (many of them Dalit). These areas are reeling under police terror, with hundreds of Adivasis thrown in Koraput jail and thousands living in the forests, afraid to go home.

People who live in situations like this do not simply take instructions from a handful of ideologues who appear out of nowhere waving guns. Their decisions of what strategies to employ take into account a whole host of considerations: the history of the struggle, the nature of the repression, the urgency of the situation, and quite crucially, the landscape in which their struggle is taking place. The decision of whether to be a Gandhian or a Maoist, militant or peaceful, or a bit of both (like in Nandigram), is not always a moral or ideological one. Quite often it's a tactical one. Gandhian satyagraha, for example, is a kind of political theatre. In order for it to be effective, it needs a sympathetic audience, which villagers deep in the forest do not have. When a posse of 800 policemen lays a cordon around a forest village at night and begins to burn houses and shoot people, will a hunger strike help? (Can starving people go on a hunger strike? And do hunger strikes work when they're not on TV?) Equally, guerrilla warfare is a strategy that villages in the plains, with no cover for tactical retreat, cannot afford. Fortunately people are capable of breaking through ideological categories, and of being Gandhian in Jantar Mantar, militant in the plains and guerrilla fighters in the forest without necessarily suffering from a crisis of identity. The strength of the insurrection in India is its diversity, not uniformity.

Since the government has expanded its definition of 'Maoist' to include anybody who opposes it, it shouldn't come as a surprise that the Maoists have moved to centre stage. However, their doctrinal inflexibility, their reputed inability to countenance dissent, to work with other political formations and, most of all, their single-minded, grim, military imagination makes them too small to fill the giant pair of boots that is currently on offer.

(When I met Comrade Roopi in the forest, the first thing the techie-whiz did after greeting me was to ask about an interview I did soon after the Maoists had attacked Rani Bodili, a girls' school in Dantewada which had been turned into a police camp. More than 50 policemen and SPOs were killed in the attack. 'We were glad that you refused to condemn our Rani Bodili attack, but then in the same interview you said that if the Maoists ever come to power the first person we would hang would probably be you,' he said. 'Why did you say that? Why do you think we're like that?' I was settling into my long answer, but we were distracted. I would probably have started with Stalin's purges – in which millions of ordinary people and almost half of the 75,000 Red Army officers were either jailed or shot, and 98 out of 139 Central Committee members were arrested; gone on to the huge price people paid for China's Great Leap Forward and the Cultural Revolution; and might have ended with the Pedamallapuram incident in Andhra Pradesh, when the Maoists, in their previous avatar People's War, killed the village *sarpanch* and assaulted women activists for refusing to obey their call to boycott elections.)

Coming back to the question: who can fill that giant pair of boots?

Perhaps it cannot, and should not be, a single pair of feet. Sometimes it seems very much as though those who have a radical vision for a newer, better world do not have the steel it takes to resist the military onslaught, and those who have the steel do not have the vision.

Right now the Maoists are the most militant section of a bandwidth of resistance movements fighting an assault on Adivasi homelands by a cartel of mining and infrastructure companies. To deduce from this that the CPI (Maoist) is a party with a new way of thinking about 'development' or the environment might be a little far-fetched. (The one reassuring sign is that it has cautiously said that it is against big dams. If it means what it says, that alone would automatically lead to a radically different development model.) For a political party that is widely seen as opposing the onslaught of corporate mining, the Maoists' policy (and practice) on mining remains pretty woolly. In several places where people are fighting mining companies there is a persistent view that the Maoists are not averse to allowing mining and mining-related infrastructure projects to go ahead as long as they are given protection money. From interviews and statements made by their senior leaders on the subject of mining, what emerges is a sort of 'we'll do a better job' approach. They vaguely promise 'environmentally sustainable' mining, higher royalties, better resettlement for the displaced and higher stakes for the 'stakeholders'. (The present minister for mining and mineral resources, too, thinking along the same lines, stood up in parliament and promised that 26 per cent of the 'profits' from mining would go into 'tribal development'. What a feast that will be for the pigs at the trough!)

But let's take a brief look at the star attraction in the mining belt – the several trillion dollars' worth of bauxite. There is no environmentally sustainable way of mining bauxite and processing it into aluminium. It's a highly toxic process that most western countries have exported out of their own environments. To produce one tonne of aluminium you need about six tonnes of bauxite, more than a thousand tonnes of water and a massive amount of electricity. For that amount of captive water and electricity, you need big dams, which, as we know, come with their own cycle of cataclysmic destruction. Last of all – the big question – what is the aluminium for? Where is it going? Aluminium is the principal ingredient in the weapons industry – for other countries' weapons' industries. Given this, what would a sane, 'sustainable' mining policy be? Suppose, for the sake of argument, the CPI (Maoist) were given control of the so-called Red Corridor, the tribal homeland – with its riches of uranium, bauxite, limestone, dolomite, coal, tin, granite, marble – how would it go about the business of policymaking and governance? Would it mine minerals to put on the market in order to create revenue, build infrastructure and expand its operations? Or would it mine only enough to meet people's basic needs? How would it define 'basic needs'? For instance, would nuclear weapons be a 'basic need' in a Maoist nation state?

Judging from what is happening in Russia and China, and even Vietnam, communist and capitalist societies eventually seem have one thing in common – the DNA of their dreams. After their revolutions, after building socialist societies that millions of workers and peasants paid for with their lives, both countries now have begun to reverse some of the gains of their revolutions and have turned into unbridled capitalist economies. For them, too, the ability to consume has become the yardstick by which progress is measured. For this kind of 'progress' you need industry. To feed the industry you need a steady supply of raw material. For that, you need mines, dams, domination, colonies, war. Old powers are waning, new ones rising. Same story, different characters – rich countries plundering poor ones. Yesterday it was Europe and America, today it's India and China. Maybe tomorrow it will be Africa. Will there be a tomorrow? Perhaps it's too late to ask, but then hope has little to do with reason.

Can we expect that an alternative to what looks like certain death for the planet will come from the imagination that has brought about this crisis in the first place? It seems unlikely. The alternative, if there is one, will emerge from the places and the people who have resisted the hegemonic impulse of capitalism and imperialism instead of being co-opted by it.

Here in India, even in the midst of all the violence and greed, there is still immense hope. If anyone can do it, we can do it. We still have a population that has not yet been completely colonised by that consumerist dream. We have a living tradition of those who have struggled for Gandhi's vision of sustainability and self-reliance, for socialist ideas of egalitarianism and social justice. We have Ambedkar's vision, which challenges the Gandhians as well the socialists in serious ways. We have the most spectacular coalition of resistance movements with experience, understanding and vision.

Most important of all, India has a surviving Adivasi population of almost 100 million. They are the ones who still know the secrets of sustainable living. If they disappear, they will take those secrets with them. Wars like Operation Green Hunt will make them disappear. So, victory for the prosecutors of these wars will contain within itself the seeds of destruction, not just for Adivasis, but, eventually, for the human race. That's why the war in central India is so important. That's why we need a real and urgent conversation between those all those political formations that are resisting this war.

The day capitalism is forced to tolerate non-capitalist societies in its midst and to acknowledge limits in its quest for domination, the day it is forced to recognise that its supply of raw material will not be endless, is the day when change will come. If there is any hope for the world at all, it does not live in climate-change conference rooms or in cities with tall buildings. It lives low down on the ground, with its arms around the people who go to battle every day to protect their forests, their mountains and their rivers, because they know that the forests, the mountains and the rivers protect them.

The first step towards reimagining a world gone terribly wrong would be to stop the annihilation of those who have a different imagination – an imagination that is outside of capitalism as well as communism. An imagination which has an altogether different understanding of what constitutes happiness and fulfilment. To gain this philosophical space, it is necessary to concede some physical space for the survival of those who may look like the keepers of our past, but who may really be the guides to our future. To do this, we have to ask our rulers: Can you leave the water in the rivers? The trees in the forest? Can you leave the bauxite in the mountain? If they say cannot, then perhaps they should stop preaching morality to the victims of their wars.

Bring on the guillotine

Rupert Everett

Dear Russell,
You asked me for some thoughts about revolution and Gay Liberation in my lifetime. Here are some. I am neither a politician nor an intellectual, so I can only draw on my own impressions, my experience.

[the 25 October 2013 issue of the *New Statesman* was guest-edited by comedian and actor Russell Brand]

On 5 February this year, the House of Commons approved the same-sex marriage bill in a landslide vote: 400 to 175. That night I was performing in *The Judas Kiss* by David Hare, a play about the life of Oscar Wilde.

It was an extraordinary evening to be playing Oscar – a man whose life was destroyed because he was a homosexual, with two years of hard labour for gross indecency, followed by three sad years of exile. Oscar died penniless in a cheap hotel in Paris. The dizzy heights from which he fell are hard to imagine for us today, but he was one of the great stars of the times. No party was complete without him, with three hits concurrently playing in the West End at the time of his arrest. Royalty attended his first nights, while later he supped with rent at Willis's.

Like many stars he felt himself above the law. As he waltzed into the fatal lawsuit against the father of his lover, he declared that 'the working classes are behind me – to a boy'. They weren't. Five short years later he was performing for drinks on the Parisian boulevard, with a missing tooth and a shabby suit. His companions were pickpockets and rent boys. He was a ruined man.

Doing the play that cold February night felt like surfing a historical wave. On the street, the *Evening Standard* was full of the news from parliament. The audience converged on the theatre with the same thought. Never was a play more suited to the times than *The Judas Kiss* that night. We were not just a hit show. We were a total eclipse.

The energy in the auditorium was intense. It felt – and I was not on drugs – as if the universe had briefly stopped in its tracks to watch. As I ran on for my first scene as Oscar, into the arms of Lord Alfred Douglas (played by Freddie Fox), I felt like the crest of a wave crashing on to the stage with all the blinding tragedy of gay history in my wake – the drownings, the burials alive, the hangings, the pillorying – all the tortures invented by man in the name of God. The applause was euphoric at the end of the show, as much for the day itself as for the performance. Finally, homosexual relationships were fully and equally accepted in law. We have come a long way. As Oscar predicted, the road to freedom has been long and smeared with the blood of martyrs, and the fight's not over yet.

I was sent away to school in the spring of 1967 at the age of eight. It is strange to think that on 27 July that year the Sexual Offences Bill received royal assent, and to be homosexual was no longer a crime. Technically. Based on the findings of the Wolfenden report of 1957, the Sexual Offences Act decriminalised homosexual acts in private between two men over 21. (The law did not apply, by the way, to the merchant navy or the armed forces, to Scotland or to Northern Ireland. Those countries only decriminalised in the Eighties.) To give one an idea of the national attitude, one has only to listen to Roy Jenkins, the home secretary at the time, during the all-night debate which led up to the vote. He declared that 'those who suffer from this disability carry a great weight of shame all their lives'.

And he was on our side!

The act did little to stop a steady rise in prosecutions, as the police took it upon themselves to raid clubs and bars, parks and bathhouses – anywhere public displays of homosexuality could be found or tricked out.

I can only imagine what my own parents were thinking as they read the *Daily Telegraph* that July morning. Along with most of the country, they were probably horrified at the idea that hordes of 'dirty old men' would suddenly appear to pervert the English youth. Everything bad that happened in the world, from the fall of the Roman empire to the

French Revolution, was the fault of homosexuality in society's eyes. Little did my parents know their youngest son was already 'finding' himself in dormitory frottage sessions after lights out at school.

One had to learn how to act in those days to cover one's tracks. Prep school morphed into public school and sweet little boys in shorts turned vicious and power-hungry with puberty. With no girls around, a boy with homosexual leanings could clean up in the classics room or the bell tower or the monks' cemetery late at night. But it was essential that he learn to act normal the next day at morning prayers or else the very prefect in whose embrace he had languished last night on a woodland tomb could easily turn. This could lead to anything from endless teasing to impromptu lynching sessions with his friends in order to save face.

I attended a Catholic school. We were instructed to turn over and say a Hail Mary if we woke up during a wet dream starring a girl. With the homosexual act we resigned ourselves to hell and no amount of Hail Marys would save us from Satan's ice-cold cock. I sang in the choir, hoping that this would somehow write off some of the heavenly debt engendered by buggery, but I wasn't optimistic, and nor were the priests. It all felt perfectly normal at the time but – looking back – when I escaped from school in 1975 at the age of 15, I was coiled and complicated, with two faces but one aim. To claw my way out of that elephant's graveyard of tweed jackets and chinless wonders and find somewhere I could be myself.

London in the mid-Seventies was still caked in soot, a postwar city of bedsits and mansion flats where the rich (hardly rich by today's standards) and the poor still rubbed shoulders. If you could sing for your supper, you could get by on £4 a week, crashing at other people's houses, eating at greasy spoons and vaulting the barriers at the Underground, with a spot of light grazing at Harrods if provisions were running low. Nobody worried about the future. Nothing was written down, so you found your way about using your nose.

Pretty quickly I sniffed out the forbidden city behind the crumbling façade of respectable Kensington. Following a man down the King's Road one night, I discovered a sex club called the Gigolo. With my heart in my mouth I descended a thin, rickety staircase – not knowing exactly where I was going, but following some interior sat nav, the same one that makes birds fly south, etc – into a writhing cavern of bodies under a naked red light bulb. 'Rocket Man' was on the record player and I felt quite suddenly as if I had disappeared from my own life. There was a sense of complete freedom that I have rarely felt since. There was always the danger of the police and, of course, I had to be there on the night of the famous Gigolo raid. Suddenly the lights snapped on. Elton stopped singing as the needle scratched across the vinyl and the police swarmed down the stairs. There was mayhem as a hundred queens tried to pull their trousers up while being herded on to the street into paddy wagons.

Some attempted to run and were tackled to the ground and dragged back, but I just acted like a passing hooray and managed to squeeze through the crowd and get a lift to the Sombrero, where those of us who had evaded the police went to regroup and embroider the event into the annals of gay history. Being only 16 (the age of consent for homosexuals was still 21), I was living outside the law and I loved it. I felt I was a part of something, and I developed a passive distaste for the status quo, a sort of inverted snobbery, which I have never managed to shake off. The gay world of the late Seventies was a melting pot, classless and ageless. A decrepit duke in leather cruised a young plumber at the Colherne while the smoothie from Sotheby's was the 'sub' of a dangerous felon over the road at the Boltons. We were united just for being there, and sex was good for the fact of doing it. It didn't really matter who it was with.

Yet we were standing on the edge of an abyss.

The Gigolo closed, its owner imprisoned as Thatcher's vision began to take its grip on the country, and I took my first trip to New York. I remember standing on the roof terrace of some rich queen's house in the West Village my first night there, dopey with jet lag, and looking across the rooftops at all those weird water towers perched on houses scribbled over with fire escapes against a backdrop of skyscrapers replete with Twin Towers blinking. The air tasted of metal. A couple of men were copulating on an old mattress on the roof opposite, observed by a half-naked lady riding the banister of her fire escape and stroking her breasts. Two men watched and tweaked each other's nipples in an open window. On another roof further off, a party of men danced on a tiny terrace, and disco music (helium screams over strings and a heartbeat) pulsed through the streets when I left the house. Men loitered on corners, still and tense as lizards, waiting to snatch at a tasty arse swishing by.

I could hardly breathe with the excitement. The whole city seemed poised for the sexual act. At Studio 54 that night I danced with Margaret Trudeau. Well, not exactly. I swished alongside her, off my face, and mingled with the group of sweaty cowboys and Indians fans dancing around her. I walked home to a flat in Tudor City at dawn through the park on Second Avenue. It was crowded with people taking drugs or having sex in the bushes while commuters rushed past like ghosts from another age.

Emboldened by the success of the Stonewall riots of 1969, gay New York in the Seventies was a gritty and lawless jungle of sexual revelry. Queens like Andy Warhol, David Geffen and Steve Rubell ruled the Big Apple. Its constitution had been written at the Factory and on the dance floor at Studio 54, and it was all too good to be true.

But there was a strange feeling, as if one was being followed. Moving secretly through the misty dungeons and discos, the bathhouses and the rotting West Side piers, the invisible vampire was dancing with everyone, killing with a kiss: AIDS hit like a tsunami at the beginning of the Eighties. Many of the club cowboys lost their strut. They turned to skin and bone overnight, a new image of the bankrupt city, colour drained to black and white. They shuffled through the crowds wrapped in oversized scarves against the chill wind or a cold stare, but their glazed eyes and hollow cheeks gave them away. Parents held their children close as these queens limped by. Within our own ranks we became experts overnight. No unexplained rash or dry cough went unnoticed. Old friends meeting scanned one another for signs. Every blemish was a potential lesion, every pound we dropped a signal. Sex became a game of Russian roulette, but still on lonely nights we raised the gun to our head and with a quivering finger pulled the trigger. Each time we promised never to be so reckless again. If only we could dodge the bullet this one last time! There was no cure.

Back in the UK I became a West End star, playing a gay schoolboy groomed for treason in a play by Julian Mitchell called *Another*

Country. I mention this fact not to draw attention to my patchy career but because it was remarkable – a contradiction – that a story about boys falling in love with each other achieved commercial success during such conservative times. This was when I first heard about the Gay Cancer. I turned on the telly one night and a boy's face appeared. He was someone I had been sleeping with on and off for years. In that split second before the sound came up I knew. He was one of the early cases. Nothing would ever be the same.

The next week we went to war.

The *Daily Mail* lit the fire that ended up as Section 28, reporting in 1983 that a book entitled *Jenny Lives With Eric and Martin*, about a little girl who lives with her father and his homosexual lover, was available at a school library run by the Inner London Education Authority. Conservatives roared with indignation at the idea of the 'promotion' of homosexuality, especially since they bluntly considered us a disease trap. But despite the horror of AIDS, the tide was against them and it was not until May 1988 that Section 28 half-heartedly became law. Thatcher had misread the mood of the country. The night before the law was enacted, four lesbians invaded the BBC *Six O'Clock News* studio, one lady managing to chain herself to Sue Lawley's desk, only to be sat on by Lawley's male fellow newscaster.

Around that time two clever queens bought a sandwich shop in Old Compton Street, and suddenly Soho was claimed by the gay community. Gyms changed the gay silhouette and soon we looked much better naked than our heterosexual counterparts. A London club scene exploded at venues with strange names – FF, Queer Nation, Troll (which became Trade), the Daisy Chain. One popular song was called 'Bring on the Guillotine', which always made me laugh. Maybe we were in the middle of a revolution but we just didn't know it. For those of us that had survived the Seventies and were still here, something had definitely shifted. Experience had toughened us. We began to have the same effortless confidence as straights. On the other hand, there was still no cure, but feelings of panic and helplessness were submerged in waves of hedonism that played out against a backdrop of hospital corridors and funeral homes.

In America a doctored poster of Ronald Reagan suddenly appeared all over the country, plastered on walls at night by activists. He seemed to have Kaposi's sarcoma all over his face. It touched a nerve. Reagan had never once uttered the word 'AIDS' in eight years in office. The organisation ACT UP took to the streets and – for the first time since Stonewall – when the police raised their batons the gays fought back. 'Silence equals death' was their mantra. The television images were horrendous and surreal – young men streaming with blood being dragged from the steps of churches by policemen in spacesuits.

Now women joined the fight, outraged by what they saw. Mothers stitched panels on to the AIDS quilt and took it to Washington, DC in a protest for their dead sons. The Princess of Wales walked into a hospital in Harlem and hugged a seven-year-old boy in blue pyjamas – AIDS and all – for the whole world to see.

Perhaps the most incongruous phenomenon to bloom in the wake of this revolution was the American Circuit – the White Party, the Black Party, the Winter Party, from Palm Springs to Montreal, a different city every month. The Circuit Queens travelled in packs, trawling a vast network of virtual friends on the newly invented cellphone, meeting on the dance floor, acting like frat boys on a spring break. It didn't matter that many of them were already in their late thirties. AIDS had stolen their youth. Now they wanted to let off steam while there was still time. They were mostly white, middle-class professionals – their beautiful bodies set off by school clothes, shorts and caps and satchels from Abercrombie & Fitch. Steroids were the new Maltesers and the party drugs got more complicated each year.

Reality was held at bay in the huge convention centres where thousands of half-naked bodies writhed in the mist, in tight clusters, a terrifying white tribe. No fats or fems – unless you were one of the three Ds – dealer, DJ or drag queen. Holiday weekends extended the teeth-grinding to 72-hour marathons, crashing to an end during the working weeks that followed, as the endorphins dried up. All over America, at the front desks of sports studios, in real-estate offices, at sinks in hair salons, and even at trading desks on Wall Street, a fairly butch queen could suddenly snap, bursting into tears at the drop of a hat. 'Another suicide Tuesday!' his colleagues would whisper to each other as he ran to the men's room for an emergency bump.

In 1996 the first 'cocktail' of antiretroviral drugs became available.

Initially it was thought that this 'combination therapy' could only buy time, but it quickly became apparent that the drugs were going to be a major game-changer. If you didn't become 'resistant' and could tolerate them long enough (28 pills a day at various intervals – before food, after food, waking and sleeping) they could even turn around your 'numbers' and – this was the elixir – render you 'undetectable'. For some it came just in time; for others, agonisingly close, but too late. Nevertheless, we were entering a new era tinged with optimism, where AIDS could be managed at least. As if in celebration, the following year, Tony Blair won a landslide victory and I swept to Hollywood for my penultimate reinvention as America's singing and dancing gay best friend.

Today the world has gone full circle. Gay people seem to be doing all the decent things the straights used to do – getting married, having babies and recycling. I feel like an old grandmother, sitting in my rocking chair, writing to you, dear Russell, during a break from my knitting. The past is all twinkling lights in the woods on a snowy night.

Was it revolution? Or were we just crashing up and down on a much deeper wave, as history ploughed on regardless? Did everything change in '67 with the new law? Was Stonewall the defining moment? Were we as free as we felt in the Seventies? Are we as free as we think we are now?

The tragedy of AIDS seems to have become a distant echo. It is impossible to describe to the young what it was like, all the terror, the anguish, the guilt, the utter loneliness of slowly dying as no one dared to touch you. The extraordinary thing is that it made us stronger – and although we didn't see any future at the time, we came through. Something had shifted in the world. Maybe it was a more liberal mood after the war, or maybe it went all the way back to Oscar's day. *Cherchez la femme!* She's in the corner pointing through a door – like the chorus in a Greek tragedy – at the real drama happening offstage. Wilde's wife, Constance, was an amazing character. She never completely abandoned or divorced him after his downfall. When she died she bequeathed him money for the rest of his life.

Women had changed and that changed everything. By the end of the nineteenth century, liberated from thousands of years of de facto slavery, they began to tear up the ancient contract between them and men, causing an earthquake of such magnitude, that we are still stumbling over the shifting landscape two centuries later. I think women must have been the driving force behind gay liberation. We were, after all, liberated from them. After the sexual revolution they danced with us in the gay discos as the men fumed, and offered us their hand in that darkest hour, while the men would probably have been quite happy to see us interned and executed.

So here we are, marriage material at last in one corner of the earth, while in the other we see the whole story repeat itself, in the destructive force of a world controlled by paranoid, petty dictators and so-called religious leaders – all men. It's public school all over again. Russia, Uganda, Greece and God are all putting their best foot forward to trample out the sin of homosexuality, so the revolution is not over, Russell. Maybe it never is.

Long shadows of old wars

David Reynolds

Thiepval didn't make it into the TV version of *Birdsong* starring Eddie Redmayne. But it did feature in the original novel by Sebastian Faulks about Stephen Wraysford, a Great War soldier who survived the Battle of the Somme. To Wraysford's granddaughter in the 1970s, it looks from a distance like a sugar beet refinery; close up, as if the Arc de Triomphe had been 'dumped in a meadow'. And then, as she stands beneath it, like some modernist monstrosity designed by Albert Speer for Hitler's Berlin.

In *Another World* – the novelist Pat Barker's exploration of the haunted mind of a Somme veteran – the grandson of the old man Geordie likens Thiepval to 'a warrior's helmet with no head inside'. 'No,' he adds, 'worse than that: Golgotha, the place of a skull,' celebrating not 'a triumph *over* death but the triumph *of* death'.

For the historian Gavin Stamp, however, Thiepval is simply 'one of the finest works of British architecture of the twentieth century'.

The 140-foot-high war memorial, atop a chalk ridge at the near centre of the Somme battlefield, has always aroused intense and often extreme reactions – as it did again a few weeks ago during televised commemorations of the Somme centenary. Designed by Sir Edwin Lutyens, the architect of the Cenotaph in Whitehall, Thiepval is a red-brick tower of interlocking arches faced in white Portland stone. Carved across every available facing are more than 72,000 names – as if, to quote Faulks again, 'the surface of the sky had been papered in footnotes'.

These names are, indeed, footnotes to the most horrific battle in the annals of the British army. Inaugurated in 1932, Thiepval is officially the Memorial to the Missing of the Somme, commemorating soldiers whose remains were never found. Lutyens and the then Imperial War Graves Commission (IWGC) wished to ensure that at least 'their name liveth for evermore'.

A century on from 1916, it is right to ponder again why we should 'remember them'. The opening day of the Battle of the Somme, 1 July, was the worst in British military history, when 19,240 men were killed and another 37,000 were listed as wounded or missing in action. Yet 1 July 2016 formed the centrepiece of the government's programme of commemorative events for the Great War centenary. So, why do we choose to remember what was, frankly, an utter disaster?

Now that we have moved on from the evocative ceremonies of last month, it is perhaps time to consider this question. It raises challenging questions about the morality of war, the responsibilities of government and, above all, about the special place of the two world wars in Britain's Brexit-shaped national memory. To explore them let's think first about what we are remembering; then about how has it been remembered over time; and finally about why we are still remembering it now.

On the 'what' question the answer is not clear-cut. The Somme offensive was months in the making and remaking. Indeed, that was a central problem. It was originally intended as a joint Franco-British operation to which the French army would commit 40 divisions and the British 25, but the plan changed profoundly when the Germans commenced their all-out assault on the French front further south at Verdun on 21 February. Verdun proved to be a ten-month slugging match, the longest battle of the Great War.

Once Verdun exploded, the British became the senior partners in the Somme operation, with the French demanding that it start as soon as possible to relieve the pressure on them. Field Marshal Douglas Haig, a cavalryman by training, always hankered after a total breakthrough, hoping even to win the war. Haig's principal subordinate, General Henry Rawlinson, commander of the British Fourth Army, was more aware of the tactical difficulties of trench warfare – especially the problem of how to shift rapidly from offence to defence in order to hold initial gains against inevitable counterattacks. Rawlinson favoured a 'bite and hold' strategy on the Somme but Haig rejected this as insufficiently ambitious. The planning for the opening of the battle was, therefore, a messy compromise between Haig and Rawlinson. To quote the Somme historian William Philpott, it was not so much 'bite and hold' as 'rush and hope'.

Compounding the problem was the artillery barrage beforehand – on the face of it, hugely impressive: a week-long, mind-numbing bombardment involving 2.5 million shells in total. But the reality was different. Although Haig employed 1,400 guns, more than the Germans used at the start of Verdun, the firepower was less concentrated because the front was twice as long and many of the shells were 'duds' that failed to explode. The British targeted mainly barbed wire and the enemy front-line trenches, so the German guns in the rear were able to keep blasting Rawlinson's troops. In any case, British artillerymen and their commanders were still only beginning to learn the complex science of the creeping barrage. 'For British gunners,' the military historian Hew Strachan observes, 'the Somme had come a year too soon.'

It was the ordinary Tommies who paid the price for the strategic snafu and the botched barrage. At 07.30 on a beautiful midsummer morning, the shelling ceased and the infantry climbed out of the forward trenches. They were supposed to walk steadily across no-man's-land and through the fragments of the barbed wire and take possession of the German front-line trenches, before pressing on to the second line and maybe beyond. Instead, most were mown down in front of the largely intact wire as the Germans, alerted by the end of shelling, raced up from their fortified dugouts to man their machine guns.

What happened is vividly evoked in two very different new books: Jolyon Fenwick's *Zero Hour*, which presents 14 hauntingly beautiful panoramas of the British front line today on to which are inscribed the lethal data of 1916 ('enemy front line 150 yards', 'machine-gun 240 yards', et cetera), and Hugh Sebag-Montefiore's richly textured account of the battlefield experience, *Somme: Into the Breach*. Some German machine-gunners fired off 20,000 rounds on 1 July, their hands often reduced to lumps of burnt flesh from the red-hot MG 08s. One British survivor never forgot those arcs of bullets, sweeping across the ground to brush away line upon line of Tommies like 'a glistening fan'.

It was the same story along much of the British line. At Beaumont-Hamel, 780 men of the 1st Newfoundland Regiment – mostly fishermen and lumbermen – went into action at 09.15. Less than half an hour later, as Andrew Roberts writes in *Elegy*, another recent book about the first day of the Somme, '89 per cent of the men who went over the top had been either killed or wounded, including all of their

26 officers'. Today a huge bronze Newfoundland caribou, head thrust high in defiance, surveys the memorial park at Beaumont-Hamel, with orientation arrows identifying the battlefield sites. One points dolefully to the rear: 'Newfoundland 2,500 miles'.

A few enterprising British commanders took advantage of the barrage to push their men out into no-man's-land and closer to the barbed wire. As a result, in some cases the Tommies did win the race against the German machine-gunners. The most successful unit was the 36th (Ulster) Division – mostly Protestant loyalists from Belfast – who not only overran the German front line but also reached parts of the second. By the following day, however, virtually isolated, they were driven back to where they had started.

After the war the survivors and the bereaved built the Ulster Tower on Thiepval Ridge – a replica of Helen's Tower on the Clandeboye Estate in County Down, near where they had trained – as a memorial to the 5,500 men, roughly one-third of the division's strength, who ended up killed, wounded or missing on 1–2 July 1916.

Contrary to myth, the First of July was not a total disaster. The Somme front was bisected by the old Roman road from the town of Albert to Bapaume. To the north of the road, the story was grim but to the south the offensive went much better. Much of that sector was in the hands of the French Sixth Army, whose role has been airbrushed out of many centenary accounts. The Sixth Army commander was General Marie Émile Fayolle, who – tellingly – had learned painful lessons from Verdun. 'We have understood that we cannot run around like madmen,' he noted in his diary. 'Doctrine is taking shape.' In particular, the French realised the need to keep the artillery barrage short but sharp to maximise surprise and to redeploy the guns rapidly once the enemy's forward trenches had been captured, so as to target the second line.

But Fayolle could soon see the writing on the wall. 'This battle ...' he noted grimly on 12 July 1916, 'has always been a battle without an objective.' Although apologists for Douglas Haig rightly emphasise that the Somme continued for another 140 days after 1 July, there was little to show for it. Most of the assaults – some 150 in all – were small-scale and poorly co-ordinated. Occasionally, bigger and better-organised offensives did make notable progress but the price was usually high.

The fighting in July and August to secure the village of Pozières on the crest of the Albert-Bapaume road cost the Australians more casualties in six weeks than they had suffered during the whole eight months of the Gallipoli land campaign from April to December 1915. Surveying the devastation from the stump of the Pozières windmill (where a memorial to the 1st Australian Division now stands), their official war historian Charles Bean – the curator of the Anzac myth – wrote of a ridge 'more densely sown with Australian sacrifice than any other place on Earth'.

'Sacrifice' was the operative word – used then and now in an attempt to give meaning to the slaughter. By the time the Battle of the Somme muddied out in mid-November the British had lost 420,000 men killed, wounded or missing, in order to advance at most six miles. The question now was how this 'sacrifice' would be remembered and justified.

In today's world of embedded war reporters and soldier selfies, it needs emphasising how little most British people in 1916 knew about what the Battle of the Somme really was like. The British military were far more secrecy-obsessed than the French or Germans: they kept most journalists well away from the front and had no official photographers until mid-1916. But such was the importance of the Somme (and the expectancy at home about the Big Push) that the army commissioned a special black-and-white, silent movie, with brief intertitles by way of explanation.

Although technically very crude to modern eyes, *The Battle of the Somme* had an immense impact when first screened in August 1916. Twenty million people watched it in the first six weeks. Again and again, reviews extolled the film's 'realism'. Frances Stevenson, David Lloyd George's secretary and then mistress, had lost her brother on the Western Front. After seeing the film she wrote in her diary: 'I have often tried to imagine myself what he went through, but now I know, and I shall never forget.'

In fact the 'realism' was highly contrived: *The Battle of the Somme*'s only footage of combat, showing soldiers climbing out of a trench into no-man's-land, was probably filmed later behind the lines. Yet the image of a wounded man sliding back into a trench was recalled endlessly by viewers as one of the most heart-rending moments in the film. Other scenes, such as the (silent) artillery barrage, the detonation of a huge mine, the recovery of wounded soldiers and shots of ruined villages, all conveyed destruction on a scale far beyond anything previously imagined.

The Battle of the Somme did not dent popular resolve. On the contrary; most people seem to have shared the sentiments expressed in lines from the *London Evening News* that were used in advertisements for the film: 'In this picture the world will obtain some idea of what it costs in human suffering to put down the devil's domination.'

There were dissenters, not only on the radical left, but also at the highest levels of government. In November, as the battle subsided into the mud, Lord Lansdowne, a former foreign secretary and now wartime minister, wrote a memo to his cabinet colleagues imploring them to consider a negotiated peace. 'Generations will have to come and go before the country recovers from the loss which it has sustained in human beings, and from the financial ruin and the destruction of the means of production which are taking place.' Casualties had already topped a million and the war was costing Britain £5m a day. 'All this it is no doubt our duty to bear,' Lansdowne went on, 'but only if it can be shown that the sacrifice will have its reward.'

His pleas, however, were brushed aside. Despite its private doubts, the government closed ranks behind Haig and his belated spin-doctoring of the Somme as part of a carefully planned strategy of attrition. Lloyd George insisted to the press that 'the fight must be to a finish – to a knock-out' because the 'inhumanity and pitilessness' of the current fighting was 'not comparable with the cruelty that would be involved in stopping the war while there remains the possibility of civilisation again being menaced from the same quarter'. And in September he told *The Times*: '"Never again" has become our battle cry.'

Lloyd George's words proved prophetic. After the losses at Verdun and on the Somme, neither France nor Britain could accept a negotiated peace – if that had ever been possible. The body count seemed too high for either side to declare a draw and shake hands; the war 'had' to end in a knockout. But as people in Britain knuckled down for more carnage (in 1917 Passchendaele followed the Somme), they seem also to have found solace in the mantra of 'never again'. The terrible sacrifice might be justified, if the Great War proved to be 'the war that will end war'.

Those words of H. G. Wells, promulgated in 1914 as propaganda, became a statement of faith, or at least hope and love, for millions in the 1920s and 1930s. Although the horrors of trench life were exposed by interwar writers – tongue-in-cheek by Robert Graves, in simple but deadly earnest by R. C. Sherriff – this does not seem to have undermined the widespread conviction that 1914–18 had been a necessary sacrifice in an effort to abolish war. In November 1933 the cover of the *British Legion Journal* depicted a statue of a mother holding the body of her dead son, with the word 'Disarm' on the plinth. Peace, it seemed to millions, would be the sincerest form of remembrance. Hence the passion for appeasement in the 1930s.

That all changed in September 1939. Another conflict against Germany, almost exactly a quarter-century after the first, put 'the war to end war' in a different perspective. The Treaty of Versailles now seemed like a mere armistice – a pause for breath before round two. And this time it was clearly a 'good war' that was fought to the finish, with the knockout blow delivered in the ruins of Berlin as a genocidal dictator took his own life, having taken the lives of millions.

In 1939–45, what's more, Britain's war was waged very differently from that of 1914–18: largely in alliance with the United States and the British Commonwealth after France collapsed in 1940. (There was little mention during the Cold War of those once lauded as 'Our Gallant Russian Allies'.)

During the two decades after 1945 this British-centred narrative was absorbed into popular culture thanks to a cavalcade of war films from British studios, featuring stars such as Jack Hawkins and Richard Todd as stereotypically English males, tough and determined, yet reserved. Recycled on television ever since, these movies have helped to define our cultural memory of the Second World War.

It was only in the mid-1960s, around the fiftieth anniversary of 1914–18, that the British rediscovered the First World War. In the writings of A. J. P. Taylor, Alan Clark and Martin Middlebrook, in the blockbuster BBC television series *The Great War*, with its graphic footage and poignant interviews, and above all in Richard Attenborough's savagely satirical 1969 big-screen version of *Oh! What a Lovely War*, the children and grandchildren of Tommies encountered the Great War almost for the first time.

But this was now a war in which the language of 'sacrifice' had morphed into 'victimhood'. Sniping at Haig and his generals, Clark popularised the tag 'lions led by donkeys'. Middlebrook's bravura oral history-cum-Greek tragedy of the first day of the Somme helped turn the spotlight on a battle previously overshadowed in British memory by the hauntingly named Passchendaele. He and others also rediscovered the battalions of 'Pals' from small towns and cities, who volunteered en masse in 1914, and many of whom went over the top together on 1 July 1916. In the bleak words of the local author John Harris, in his novel about the Sheffield Pals: 'Two years in the making. Ten minutes in the destroying. That was our history'. The First of July 1916, hanging at the mid-point of the middle year of the conflict, had become the crucifixed centre of Britain's Great War.

The 1960s recast the Great War into a mould that is still ours today. Through the cult status in schools of Britain's 'War Poets' (a tiny fraction of the roughly 2,200 men and women who published poetry during the war); through the dark comedy of *Blackadder* and the vivid prose of Pat Barker and Sebastian Faulks; and, at a more domestic level, through the passion for family history – we have become used to seeing the Tommies of 1914–18 as victims. Viewed from this perspective, from the bottom of a trench full of mud, guts and excrement, the Great War looks mindless and meaningless: the appliance of science to the dance of death.

Since the 1990s this '*Blackadder*' view of the conflict has been subjected to counterattack. Revisionist military historians such as Gary Sheffield and William Philpott insist that the first day of the Somme was followed by 140 others in which the German army was irreparably ground down. For them, 1 July 1916 must be seen as the regrettable but necessary start of a 'learning curve' that led slowly but inexorably to what Sheffield calls 'the greatest military victory in British history': Haig's triumphant 'Hundred Days' in the autumn of 1918.

Up to a point, I can see what the revisionists are getting at. Their 'learning curve' argument reminds me of the dictum attributed to

France's Great War hero Marshal Ferdinand Foch: 'It takes 15,000 casualties to train a major general.' In other words, we all learn by our mistakes but for most of us the consequences are merely embarrassing. Soldiers, however, are in the business of death. An officer kills others 'efficiently' only after seeing his own men killed and then absorbing the lessons.

That task gets ever more difficult as one ascends from the circumscribed role of a platoon commander to the complex mysteries of supplying, manoeuvring and deploying thousands of men, and especially so in 1914–18, when a general had only the most rudimentary information with which to penetrate the fog of war. And so a 'fight to the finish' would inevitably entail thousands of casualties for Us as well as Them.

Yet the phrase 'learning curve' sounds clinical and callous. Even if one accepts that Haig and his staff had to learn the craft of generalship at the expense of their countrymen, did such a huge number of British soldiers – 750,000 – have to pay with their lives? Could one ever justify the shambles that occurred on the Somme on 1 July 1916? These questions certainly nagged at the minds of Winston Churchill and Field Marshal Montgomery; together, they managed to end up on the winning side of the second war at roughly half that number of British dead.

In our own time, a similar reluctance to accept what we might call the human cost of educating generals prompted a long campaign to rehabilitate over 300 Tommies of 1914–18 who were executed by firing squad for various capital offences, including murder, but also 'desertion' or 'cowardice'. The Shot at Dawn memorial at the National Arboretum in Staffordshire was unveiled in 2001. Five years later, the Labour defence secretary Des Browne, a human-rights lawyer, offered these men a posthumous group pardon, describing them all as 'victims of war'. For Browne's supporters, it was belated justice; to his critics, an anachronistic rewriting of the past to fit the different moral standards of our own age.

In his recent book *Breakdown* the historian and film-maker Taylor Downing re-creates the mentality of Haig's staff in an era long before modern ideas of post-traumatic stress. He shows how the incidence of so-called shell shock soared in July 1916 with the start of the Somme, amounting to a minimum of 60,000 cases in the second half of the year. The high command saw shell shock as akin to a contagious disease, which, if not contained, might cause the breakdown of the whole army.

A striking example comes from the sad story of the 11th Borders, or 'Lonsdales', a Pals Battalion from what is now Cumbria. The unit lost two-thirds of its officers and men on 1 July. Pulled out of the line, the survivors had to sort out the kit of their dead comrades and bury the decomposing corpses, sleeping in open trenches under heavy artillery fire. Sent back to the front line on 9 July and ordered to take 200 yards of enemy trench in a night attack under even more ferocious shelling, many of the men – shaking and disoriented – baulked at going over the top and the attack had to be aborted. The Lonsdales were court-martialled and ritually humiliated. Stripped of their weapons, the 250 survivors were paraded before the rest of their regimental brigade as a 'disgrace' to themselves and the army.

Today this story seems appalling. Yet, to a high command stuck at the very bottom of its 'learning curve' on the Somme, the epidemic of shell shock that summer posed a crisis as grave as poison gas in 1915. Rejecting one request for clemency for a foot soldier of the Warwickshire Regiment, Haig confirmed the death sentence with almost anguished words: 'How can we ever win if this plea is allowed?'

To recall the 'deserters' and not just the 'heroes' raises a larger question. Again and again today, the words of the poet Laurence Binyon from 1914 are repeated: 'We will remember them.' Yet that simple word, 'remember', needs unpacking. No one now alive in 2016 has direct memories of the war of 1914–18, so this isn't remembering in any normal usage of the word. Our act of remembrance necessarily entails reinterpretation – seeing *their* past through the eyes of *our* present. In other words, anachronism and judgement are almost inescapable. And the verb 'will' also needs interrogating, because remembrance has become an official ritual, orchestrated at selected moments of our national history for reasons that are not always clear.

So, is the Somme a story of victimhood, to adopt the *Blackadder* version? Or are we recalling, as Prime Minister David Cameron declared in 2012, 'the extraordinary sacrifice of a generation' and, in fact, the 'sacrifice they made for us'?

British attitudes to the Great War centenary, it seems to me, quiver uneasily between the two. The language of sacrifice – poignantly meaningful for the survivors and the bereaved in the 1920s and 1930s – comes less naturally to the twenty-first century. On the other hand, it seems equally clear that most veterans of the Great War did not regard themselves as victims. Although appalled by what they had experienced, they continued to believe in the necessity of what they had done and in the rightness of their cause.

Yet it is also worth noting that the language of victimhood is not entirely anachronistic. It lurked in the minds of those who began the remarkable project of war cemeteries for the soldiers of Britain and the empire. Consider three of these men.

Fabian Ware: an educator and journalist, too old to fight, who volunteered to run an ambulance unit in France and was horrified to see the bodies and bones littering the fields. Almost single-handed, he persuaded the British government to establish a proper programme of graves registration and then induced the French government to donate land for the burial of Allied soldiers. The Imperial War Graves Commission received its royal charter in May 1917.

Edwin Lutyens: often dismissed today as the architect of mock-Tudor country houses or the imperial grandiloquence of New Delhi. Yet Lutyens, like several other eminent architects, spent most of the 1920s designing memorials along the Western Front. It proved to be a deeply moving experience. 'I am here doing Graves in France,' he wrote to a client in 1925, 'and the magnitude of that host of boys that lie fearfully still, quickens the sense of unspeakable desolation.' For Lutyens, Thiepval was a work of art, and heart.

And Rudyard Kipling: the bard of empire and the troubadour of war in 1914, who never recovered from the loss of his only son at the Battle of Loos in 1915. This was literally a 'loss', because Jack disappeared without trace. It was Kipling who added words to Ware's vision and Lutyens's monuments. 'Their Name Liveth for Evermore' is taken from Ecclesiasticus and inscribed on the War Stone, designed by Lutyens, that reposes like a secularised altar under the Thiepval arch, and in most cemeteries. And his legend 'Known Unto God' on the headstones of unidentified British soldiers, in striking contrast to the stark 'Inconnu' on the graves of their anonymous French counterparts. One can see the distinction graphically at the little Franco-British cemetery that slips gently away from the Thiepval memorial down the hill towards the old British front line of 1 July 1916.

Ware, Lutyens and Kipling: all men too old to fight, yet haunted by what their generation had inflicted on the next. We catch Kipling's sense of grieving guilt in one of his sardonic 'Epitaphs of the War', first published in 1919:

> *If any question why we died,*
> *Tell them, because our fathers lied.*

For these old men, perhaps, the young Tommies were their victims.

The project of the war cemeteries cost over £8m – roughly the cost of two days' shelling at the end of the war. In other words, burying was a lot cheaper for His Majesty's Treasury than killing. Even so, the work of the Imperial War Graves Commission represented one the biggest government construction projects of the 1920s, eclipsing the building of the modern stations on the London Underground or the network of new telephone exchanges.

It was also a project for the dawning democratic age. 'Tommy' in the trenches and the deserts (and 'Tommy's Sister' in the factories, on farms and in offices on the Home Front) had indeed 'done the state some service'. Their reward was the Representation of the People Act 1918, which gave the vote to nearly all men over 21, propertied or not, and to women over the age of 30 who owned property. The war had in fact changed the terms of political debate. 'What property would any man have in this country if it were not for the soldiers and sailors who are fighting our battles?' asked Sir Edward Carson, the Ulster Unionist leader and former diehard. 'If a man is good enough to fight for you, he is good enough to vote for you.' And even good enough (though this may not have occurred to Carson) for *you* to vote for *him*. The new slogan 'One Gun, One Vote' was rigorous in its logic: the 1918 act denied the franchise to conscientious objectors.

To Ware and his colleagues, the young men who had not lived to vote at least deserved democratic recognition in death. All the headstones were uniform in style: generals just like 'other ranks', the sons of colliers treated no differently from the scions of landed gentry. Rich families were not allowed to repatriate remains to a family plot in some English churchyard. Instead, officers and men would lie together, eternally equal, in 'some corner of a foreign field/That is for ever England'.

Many at home fumed about the 'Prussian' attitude of the IWGC but Ware and his fellow commissioners did not relent. Speaking in their defence, Winston Churchill told the House of Commons in May 1920 that 'there is no reason at all why, in periods as remote from our own as we ourselves are from the Tudors, the graveyards in France of this Great War shall not remain an abiding and supreme memorial to the efforts and the glory of the British army'. He acknowledged 'the mutability of human arrangements', but predicted that 'even if our language, our institutions, and our empire all have faded from the memory of man, these great stones will still preserve the memory of a common purpose pursued by a great nation in the remote past, and will undoubtedly excite the wonder and the reverence of a future age'.

Churchill's rhetoric of 1920, casting forward four centuries, was remarkable: almost a 'Their Finest Hour' oration 20 years before its time. Back in the age of the Tudors only the likes of Henricus Rex, Elisabetha Regina and a happy few aristocrats had their names preserved for posterity. But at Thiepval, the Menin Gate in Ypres and many other war cemeteries and monuments, the names of ordinary soldiers of Britain and the empire live on a century after their death. Through the names their stories live on as well.

The visitors' centre at Thiepval displays a panel of photographs of '600 Missing' whose lives have been painstakingly rescued from oblivion by a Northumbrian couple, Ken and Pam Linge. Their moving book *Missing But Not Forgotten: Men of the Thiepval Memorial, Somme*, tells some of these men's stories.

What is now called the Commonwealth War Graves Commission has carried out Ware's mandate for nearly a century. Under its charter the CWGC's mission is to maintain the graves 'in perpetuity': as Churchill put it, into an era 'as remote from our own as we ourselves are from the Tudors'.

That is a heavy burden. Is it, perhaps, a dead weight? In Britain we are preoccupied – some would say obsessed – with our national memory of the two world wars. The headline slogans of that memory-story are clear. 1914–18: over there in Mud and Blood, sacrificing the

Lost Generation to win only the Lost Peace. 1939–45: over here, Our Finest Hour, Alone in 1940. Then victory, won in tandem with the English-Speaking Peoples. Two wars enshrined in ways that serve to distance us from mainland Europe – even though both narratives are highly selective.

Across the Channel, however, the story is very different. After 1945 the French and Germans, who had been killing each other for three centuries, managed to kick the habit. Not only were they reconciled but they moved on into what the founding father of the European Economic Community, Robert Schuman, called a 'European solution' to the 'German Question'.

Yet European integration has not exerted much attraction in the 'United Kingdom'. As a country we have been at the very most 'reluctant Europeans'; after all, no other member of the EU has held two referendums in four decades on whether to get out. And no one else has actually voted to do so. Of course, both affairs were staged for narrow party-political reasons and the second was a shambolic chapter of accidents from start to … well, not 'finish', but shall we say to 'the end of the beginning', which is where we are now. Yet the referendums also reflect what might be called the 'Channel of the Mind' between Us and Them, a great divide that was deepened by our nationalist narratives of 1914–18 and 1939–45. This, in turn, fed into the Brexit vote of 23 June.

Should we keep clinging to our 'Glorious Dead'? After all, there are no veterans of the First World War still alive. We are now as distant from the men who marched away in 1914 as they were from the Redcoats who fought Napoleon at Waterloo. So maybe it's time to let go of the dead? To allow them to vanish quietly into the past? If we did so, perhaps it might be easier to comprehend the Great War as history?

Part of me, the historian, thinks this way. I worry that when it comes to the Great War we British are still stuck in the trenches and trapped in Poets' Corner. Rather than just evoking myriad individual tragedies on the Western Front, illuminated by a few anguished verses, I would also like us to see 1914–18 as truly a 'world war'; to grasp its impact on eastern Europe, India, China and the Middle East – not to mention on politics and society at home – in ways that still affect us in 2016. In other words, not just to 'remember' but also to understand.

And yet, as a citizen, I keep coming back to Lutyens and Thiepval. To those names. Carved into the stone and thereby etched into the national memory. Reminding us of their mortality – and ours. As the historian G. M. Trevelyan mused softly in 1927: 'The Dead were, and are not. Their place knows them no more, and is ours today. Yet they were once as real as we, and we shall tomorrow be shadows like them.'

Bodiless names that can spring out of the stone shadows – suddenly alive at a glance or even a touch. I still remember being with my son Jim, then ten, when we found his name on the Tyne Cot Memorial, near Ypres. The almost electric shock of encountering a 'James Reynolds' on the wall of the dead.

Or perhaps, dare one say it, of encountering a 'Blair' or a 'Cameron', or even a 'May'. I do not imagine for one moment that any democratic leader lightly sends men (and now women) into battle, knowing that it may be signing their death sentence. This is the moral loneliness of leadership. Power brings with it an inescapable burden of guilt because politicians, no less than generals, learn from their mistakes.

The Somme centenary reminds us of this. So does the excoriating Chilcot report into the Iraq War, published on 6 July. For all the differences of time and place, here are two essentially similar stories. Simplistic assumptions; inept planning; sloppy intelligence; duplicitous spin. It is tragically apt that, having reflected on the first day of the Somme, five days later we were pondering 'Mission Accomplished' in Iraq.

I believe that every political leader should visit the Memorial to the Missing of the Somme. To touch the names and feel the pain. To 'learning-curve' the human cost of going to war. That is why for me, ultimately, Thiepval matters. Why we should not forget 1 July 1916. Why, a century on, and however hard it now may be, we *should* remember them.

Black Death

Gary Younge

I had been spending a fair amount of time reporting from the Caribbean when Hurricane Katrina devastated New Orleans in August 2005. Making my way to the Crescent City from Kingston, Jamaica, I arrived to see US troops stationed outside the Harrah's casino, as mostly black people were plucked from trees and roofs, and bodies floated down main streets and started decomposing in houses.

It wasn't just the levees that had been breached but the facade of a First World nation: one of the United States' most celebrated cities appeared like Port-au-Prince, only with skyscrapers.

The hurricane had not created the inequalities of race and class so evident in the aftermath; it had simply laid them bare. When Katrina struck more than 44 per cent of New Orleans residents were functionally illiterate; close to one in three African Americans in Louisiana lived in poverty; rates of black infant mortality in the state were worse than infant mortality in Sri Lanka, and black male life expectancy was the same as that for men in Kyrgyzstan. African Americans were less likely to leave town before the storm came because they were less likely to have cars or cash. As thousands of people, most of them black, flocked to the convention centre, in search of shelter and sustenance, the head of the Federal Emergency Management Agency, Michael Brown, said, 'We're seeing people that we didn't know exist.'

Witnessing coronavirus disproportionately devastate minority communities, in Britain and elsewhere, feels a lot like being in New Orleans shortly after Katrina. The pandemic is exposing broader inequalities, systemic injustice and official denial.

At the outset the disparities were impressionistic and anecdotal. The roll call of the deceased suggested something more than a pattern. The first ten doctors to die from Covid-19 in the UK were black or Asian.

'At face value, it seems hard to see how this can be random,' the chair of the British Medical Association, Dr Chaand Nagpaul, said on 10 April. 'We have heard the virus does not discriminate between individuals but there's no doubt there appears to be a manifest disproportionate severity of infection in BAME [black, Asian and minority ethnic] people and doctors. This has to be addressed – the government must act now.'

The snapshots appearing in the media merely confirmed what people were experiencing on the ground. Community activist and retired lecturer Hesketh Benoit, who is based in Haringey in north London, recalls chatting to reggae singer Delroy Washington, 67, one morning in late March; by the evening Washington was dead. 'We'd been joking on the phone,' says Benoit. 'He seemed fine. He had high blood pressure. But he'd been a martial arts expert for forty years.'

Washington was the first person to die that Benoit knew. But before long a few others – elders who used to come and 'big him up' while he ran courses for the young; a couple of guys who were security guards – also fell. 'I remember thinking, hang on a minute. Something's going on here.' Today he can count 28 people – all black – he knows of who have perished, of whom five or six were close friends. That's about two a week. The youngest was only 42.

Statisticians and data journalists were soon able to quantify this lived experience. According to the Office for National Statistics (ONS), adjusting for age, black people are more than four times more likely to die from Covid-19 than white people. Pakistanis and Bangladeshis are more than three times as likely, and Indians more than twice as likely. BAME people account for 13.4 per cent of the population and 34 per cent of the patients admitted to intensive care units.

A Guardian data analysis in April revealed that a high proportion of BAME residents was found to be the strongest predictor of a high Covid-19 death rate: for every 10 per cent increase in ethnic minority residents there were 2.9 more Covid-19 deaths per 100,000 people. (British Jews are also over-represented among the dead, although theories as to why that might be – which include religious practices among certain groups and an older-than-average population – are quite different from those relating to racial minorities.)

Carers have it worst. One in five of the NHS's nursing and support staff are BAME, but they comprise two thirds of coronavirus deaths among such workers. In late April, Sky News discovered that 72 per cent of all health and social care staff who have died with Covid-19 were BAME.

Two urgent questions emerge from these grim statistics. The first is: why should this be? At first glance, the answer appears straightforward. Put bluntly, minority communities are more likely to be poor, and poor people are, in a range of ways, more likely to be vulnerable.

For example, the ONS's analysis of English Housing Survey data from between 2014 and 2017 found that Bangladeshi families were 15 times more likely to experience overcrowding than white British households, while Pakistanis were eight times more likely and black people six times more. All three groups were more likely to live in deprived neighbourhoods and to experience higher unemployment, higher poverty and lower incomes than white people.

More than two decades after the 1999 Macpherson report into the Stephen Lawrence case – which found the police to be 'institutionally racist' – minorities remain more likely to fall foul both of the law of the land and the law of probabilities. Wherever there is a pile of deprivation BAME people are over-represented at the bottom of it.

Material deprivation may not be the whole story. The ONS concludes that even when adjusting for deprivation, age and other factors, black people, Pakistanis and Bangladeshis are almost twice as likely to die as white people.

There is speculation that this disparity may be explained genetically. Black people are more likely to suffer from cardiovascular disease and diabetes, which would, it is said, make them more susceptible to succumb to the virus. Scientists at the DataLab at Oxford University have ruled that out. Others claim that a deficiency of vitamin D, common among some BAME communities, could be the cause. Thus far it remains only speculation, though the government started formally recommending vitamin D supplements in late April.

One need not dismiss these claims summarily to see there are sufficient grounds to question their logic. Pakistanis and Bangladeshis are dying at a similarly disproportionate rate to black people but share little in the way of an ethnically related genetic relationship. Meanwhile, Indians, who until relatively recently were part of the same country as Bangladesh and Pakistan, have suffered far lower death rates. The one thing that black people, Pakistanis and Bangladeshis do have in common is that they are the poorest ethnic groups in the country, concentrated in the kind of jobs where you might contract the virus. Indians, meanwhile, tend to be wealthier.

Elsewhere, the picture is similar. In Michigan, African Americans comprise 14 per cent of the population, 33 per cent of the reported infections and 40 per cent of the deaths. In Kansas they are seven times more likely to die of Covid than whites. In New York City Latinos have a higher death rate than African Americans; in Illinois they have a higher infection rate. In Arizona and New Mexico, Native Americans are becoming infected at a far greater rate than Latinos.

African Americans, Native Americans, black Britons, Latinos and British people of Pakistani and Bangladeshi origin do not have culture or ethnically specific genetic material in common. They share a common experience of impoverishment, low pay and poor housing – and all the things that go with that, including ill health – that would make them susceptible to coronavirus.

There are further plausible explanations for the disparity in mortality rates. For historical reasons, related to migration, some groups are more likely to be concentrated in the health service, public transport and care work, while the modern economy has created significant concentrations of certain ethnicities in cleaning, taxi driving and security. For example, about 12.8 per cent of workers from Bangladeshi and Pakistani backgrounds are employed in public-facing transport jobs such as bus, coach and taxi driving, compared with 3.5 per cent of white people. These are all areas where workers are most at risk. Two black employees in London – a taxi driver and one transport worker – have now died after being deliberately spat on by people who, it is believed, had Covid- 19.

Though it adjusted for other factors, the ONS did not weight its findings to take into account the sectors where minorities are over-represented. 'This is something we want to explore further in our next release,' a spokesperson said. 'We see it as a crucial gap in the evidence to fill.'

Then there are a range of experiences that cannot be adjusted for in raw data, but certainly have an effect on behaviour and outcomes. A 2014 report by Roger Kline of Middlesex University for the NHS revealed BAME staff faced discriminatory treatment in recruitment, career development, membership on trust boards and disciplinary action. They were also more victimised if they were whistle-blowers, concluded the report, which was titled 'The "snowy white peaks" of the NHS'.

Other surveys show black and Asian doctors are often treated as 'outsiders' by their bosses and peers. They are significantly more likely than their white colleagues to be referred to the General Medical Council by their NHS employers for an investigation that could damage or end their careers. They are twice as likely not to raise concerns because of fears of recrimination, and complain of often feeling bullied and harassed. Health workers who are migrants may have no recourse to public funds if they are fired, and a disproportionate number are on zero-hours contracts. Add all this together and it becomes clear why they might be more compliant when put on certain shifts and less insistent in demanding personal protective equipment (PPE).

This is what systemic discrimination looks like. Not isolated incidents but a range of processes built on presumption, assumption, confidence, ignorance and exclusory institutional, personal and professional networks all buttressed by the dead weight of privilege.

Race is a construct. 'Marble cake, crazy quilt and tutti-frutti,' the socio-cultural anthropologist Roger Sanjek once wrote, 'are all better metaphors of human physical variability than is the x number of races of humankind.' But racism is real. It's not the virus that discriminates; it is society.

The jury is out on whether more vitamin D would make a difference. But the case on whether more jobs, better pay and better housing would make a difference is closed. Inequality is killing us: being black is a pre-existing condition. 'You already know enough,' wrote the late Sven Lindqvist in his book about European imperialism in Africa, *Exterminate All the Brutes*. 'So do I. It is not knowledge that we lack. What is missing is the courage to understand what we know and to draw conclusions.'

These deaths are the collateral damage of British racism – the indirect consequence of decades of exclusion that have corralled black and Asian people into the kind of jobs, housing and health situations that would make us particularly vulnerable.

And yet, because our lives literally depend on it, we are forced to make the obvious explicit in the hope that some will cease to regard the obscene as inevitable. As recently as December 2019 the rapper Stormzy was asked by an Italian journalist whether Britain was racist. 'Definitely, 100 per cent,' he replied, before going on to explain 'they don't like to admit it'. As if to prove him right his comments were first distorted and then decried.

Less than two years after the Windrush scandal, the then Conservative chancellor Sajid Javid, who had previously said that if his Pakistani father migrated to Britain today he wouldn't let him in, replied on Twitter: '100 per cent wrong. Britain is the most successful multiracial democracy in the world. And one of the most welcoming and tolerant.' So here we are – tolerated while dying for equality.

The police lynching of George Floyd in Minneapolis on 25 May was a clear and brutal manifestation of racial violence. Obscenities such as this, caught on camera, with a clear villain sporting a badge and a number, have become a distressingly familiar occurrence that can distort the vast scope and scale of the racial challenge we all face. It is this incident that has driven tens of thousands to the streets, in occasional violent clashes with the police across the US, and brought people out in solidarity across Europe. But it is not the only thing keeping them there.

Covid-19 has demonstrated how racism can kill in far less dramatic ways and in far greater numbers without offering a morality play that might be shared on social media. When the police and politicians order the protesters to go back to their communities, there seems little recognition that that is where they were dying in such disproportionate numbers: that in the slogan 'I can't breathe' – among George Floyd's last words as the police officer knelt on his neck – there is the connective tissue between the most brazen forms of state violence and the more banal tribulations of the ailing pandemic patient.

'Part of the reason these are systemic inequalities is that they transcend not only party, but time,' Stacey Abrams, an African American politician from Georgia who is being vetted by Joe Biden as a potential vice-presidential running mate [in the event, he appointed Kamala Harris], told the *New York Times*. 'We have to be very intentional about saying this is not about one moment or one murder – but the entire infrastructure of justice.'

One need not crudely transpose the US racial landscape on to Britain's to see how the issues raised by Floyd's killing could pollinate across the Atlantic and find a receptive home here. We do not have the US's levels of gun ownership or its black middle class, its centuries-old black institutions or its degrees of segregation. Our inequalities operate differently. But they are recognisable. And most pertinently, where the virus is concerned, they keep operating. Across the Atlantic, the manner of collecting the data on coronavirus deaths differs – but the racial disparities are, at the very least, comparable. Since we didn't get to this place by accident, we won't get out of it by chance.

The second question is, what can we do about it? In the short term, the answer is fairly straightforward. Just as minorities are disproportionately affected by the disease, they are disproportionately assisted by any efforts to combat it. The more PPE there is for health workers and care workers, the more that people avoid public transport, and the more that testing and tracing is available, the more that racial and ethnic disparities will be reduced. Just as the government's negligence has left us more exposed, government vigilance would make us considerably safer.

Tackling the racial inequalities emerging from the pandemic is not a sectional interest that will just benefit black people, any more than civil rights or community-sensitive policing does; in a public health crisis anything that helps a significant section of the population will help everyone.

It follows that in the medium term there should be a full, independent public inquiry into the racial disparity in the number of deaths. The government's own review simply established what we already knew – the prevalence of ethnic disparities – even if its findings differed substantially from the ONS on which groups were most vulnerable.

The review adjusted the death rate for deprivation, among other things, but made no plans to do anything about it and offered no analysis of why this deprivation might be.

It now plans a further review led by the equalities minister Liz Truss focusing on co-morbidities and obesity. Since conditions such as obesity and hypertension are also related to socio-economic factors the government could be accused of chasing its tail. One need not gainsay Truss' conclusions to see the trajectory in this line of inquiry: to leave the system that produces certain health inequalities unscrutinised while shifting the burden of vulnerability on to the individual – their lifestyle, diet and general health regimen – as though those things existed beyond the influence of race and class.

A proper inquiry would not only seek to establish accountability, where that is appropriate, but also examine the pressures, decisions, contexts and environments that got us to such a calamitous state of affairs. Such an inquiry could do for systemic racism what the Macpherson report of 1999 did for institutional racism – map out the complex and at times invisible relationship between power and discrimination that often traps well-meaning people in oppressive structures and black people in desperate circumstances. A group of BAME public figures have already called on the government to produce a 'Covid-19 race equality strategy'.

None of this will heal the sick or bring back the dead. But it could help us develop a more sophisticated and nuanced understanding of how race is experienced and how racism operates. For the left it would help end the futile attempts to engage race and class separately. They do not exist in silos but are two interdependent forces, among many, and they are either understood in relation to each other or are misunderstood completely.

A public inquiry also offers the opportunity to cement human experience as part of politics, as opposed to something distinct and even antagonistic to it. The effort to relegate race, gender, sexual orientation, disability – the list goes on – to mere 'identity politics' has ramped up of late. The disproportionate number of deaths among minorities, the spike in domestic violence during lockdown, the manner in which disabled people were marginalised at every step – all these factors exemplify the degree to which we have experienced this moment differently in material ways that are not, solely, about class. Acknowledging that doesn't undermine solidarity, it informs it.

We will need this shift in understanding because there's every chance that all of the disparities that made BAME communities so vulnerable are about to get worse. We are barely out of the last economic crisis, which affected black people (particularly women) more heavily, and are about to enter another economic depression.

It does not follow that because the pandemic has illustrated a range of inequalities and inequities, the state will address them. Indeed, if anything the government will desperately try to exploit them to reshape the world in its own ideological image. It wouldn't be the first time we demanded an overhaul of 'the entire infrastructure of justice' and ended up with more injustice.

This is precisely what happened in New Orleans after Katrina. There was a brief acknowledgement of how racism and poverty had shaped the identity of the victims. But before long, the cameras left and the corporate interests and the city establishment applied themselves to the task of reordering the city with great prejudice.

The public schools were auctioned off to private entities and public housing that wasn't even damaged by the hurricane was torn down anyway. More than a third of the black people who left the city never came back. 'We finally cleaned up public housing in New Orleans,' said Republican Congressman Richard Baker only two weeks after the storm. 'We couldn't do it, but God did.'

I returned to New Orleans a year after the hurricane to see how things had progressed. I was driving through the Lower Ninth ward with a resident, Antoinette K-Doe, in the hearse she bought to evacuate the city in. She kept stopping and staring at the dystopian sight of the neighbourhood where she grew up. Whole houses had been washed off their moorings and into the road; cars had been washed into the houses; trees had been blown on to cars. And there they were still. 'We're the richest country in the world,' K-Doe said. 'I don't understand how we can't fix this up.'

Lives
and Letters

Early Recollections of Adolf Hitler

W. W. Crotch

The first time I heard the name of Adolf Hitler mentioned was shortly after the end of the war, when a man named Franz Xavier Huber, a veteran who had a leg shot away before Verdun in 1917, told me the stories of a curious fellow who had been in his regiment at the front. He was a garrulous chap, and, sitting in that same Bürgerbräu Keller in Munich (where in 1923 Hitler took his first plunge into revolutionary activities by firing off his army revolver at the ceiling and declaring the morrow would see him victor or dead – although it saw him neither the one nor the other, but unscathed, a helter-skelter fugitive in the Bavarian hills), he used to tell tales tragic and humorous of his campaign experience.

The thing that had struck him about 'Private Hitler' was his grandiloquence. He was neither popular nor the reverse with his fellows; they just smiled at him and his vague rambling speeches on everything in the world and out of it. He showed distinct talent in avoiding disagreeable tasks, but he knew on which side his bread was buttered. He interested himself particularly in the important question of seeing the officer's washing was done or doing it himself. This secured for him the good graces of the colonel, who removed him from the more constant dangers of the trenches and appointed him runner between regimental headquarters and the front line.

These duties brought him frequently in contact with men and he would sit for hours in a dug-out and hold forth on Socialism, of which it was evident he had only very hazy notions. Old Social Democrats used to laugh at him, but no one debated seriously with him. He could not brook contradiction and used to fly into terrible rages if anyone ventured a word of dissent. Though he got the Iron Cross of the second class, no one in the regiment ever looked upon Hitler as any sort of hero; indeed they rather admired him for the skill with which he avoided hot corners. The regimental records contain not a line concerning an award of the Iron Cross of the first class, though in latter years he has taken to wearing it prominently on his self-constructed uniform.

In those days in Munich I lived in the Thiersh Strasse [sic] and I frequently noticed in the street a man who vaguely reminded me of a militant edition of Charles Chaplin, owing to his characteristic moustache and his bouncing way of walking. He always carried a riding whip in his hand with which he used incessantly to chop off imaginary heads as he walked. He was so funny that I inquired from neighbours who he might be: most of them, owing to his Slav type, took him to be one of those Russian émigrés who abounded in Germany at that time, and they freely talked of his being probably a trifle mentally deranged. But my grocer told me it was a Herr Adolf Hitler from Braunau in Austria, and that he was leader of a tiny political group which called itself the 'German National Socialist Workers Party'. He lived as a boarder in the apartment of a small artisan, wrote articles for an obscure paper called the Völkischer Beobachter, and orated in hole-and-corner meetings before audiences of a dozen or two. Out of curiosity I bought the paper once or twice, and found it a scatterbrained collection of wild anti-Jewish stories and articles interlarded with panegyrics on the Germanic race. My obliging grocer closed his information on Hitler by remarking that he frequently purchased things in his shop and was, despite his eccentric appearance, quite a pleasant fellow, though inclined to talk sixteen to the dozen about anything and everything.

Some time later I became a frequent customer of a little wine saloon in the Schelling Strasse. The public in this inn was mostly composed of Bohemians, artists and art students, members of the staff of *Simplicissimus*, the famous satirical weekly; musicians and poetasters sat around of an evening and listened to Gulbransson or Thöny giving forth on art, politics and the price of a pound of meat. Discussions ensued that lasted far into the night, over tankards of beer and bottles of excellent Chianti. Hitler was an almost daily visitor; he had, I learned, been a house painter in his early days in Vienna, but he was rather sore on the subject, and posed as an artist. He was very fond of airing his views on art and architecture, which, however, were not taken seriously by any of the artists who frequented the place.

Hitler was often accompanied by one or two friends who, I was told, were members of his little political group. The most sensible of the band was a chemist named Gregor Strasser, a very sound fellow with whom I often spoke. Hitler's closest friend at that time, however, seemed to be an ex-army captain named Röhm, who later became chief of the Storm Troops, while his friend, Baldur von Schirach, was entrusted with leadership of the 'Hitler Youth', the boy scout organisation of the National Socialist movement.

One thing that struck me about Hitler was his extreme abstemiousness. He ate every night a dish of vegetables, and mineral water was his only drink. He never smoked. This reminds me of an amusing incident when Hitler became Chancellor. The German vegetarians have a central organ of their league, and this paper came out with flaming headlines:

FIRST GREAT VICTORY OF GERMAN VEGETARIANS. HITLER BECOMES CHANCELLOR.

Sometimes instead of regaling us with chaotic speeches, Hitler would sit for hours on end in front of his mineral water, staring into space, not uttering a word, and apparently quite oblivious of his surroundings. If on these occasions someone suddenly addressed him, he would start as if out of sleep, and stroke his forehead with his hand several times before coming back to reality.

Apart from politics and art, Hitler's chief topics of conversation were Italy and clairvoyance. He had never visited Italy, but he would sometimes talk for half an hour on end about the glories of ancient Rome and the greatness of the Caesars. There was something about his talk that made one think of the prophets of the Old Testament: he spoke as if he believed himself to be inspired. The only thing that dispelled the illusion was his frequent use of words that are not found in the dictionary of a cultivated German.

One day I remember a man came in who, for the price of a plate of soup, read hands and told fortunes. Hitler retired with the soothsayer into a corner and spent a whole hour with him in earnest conference. When he got back among us, he turned with anger upon a student who had made a slighting remark about clairvoyance, and launched out upon an eloquent defence of occultism of every kind, and especially of astrology.

He made a confidant, too, of a Jewish charlatan named Steinschneider who had taken to himself the name of Hanussen, and consulted him frequently. Hanussen, who subsequently founded and ran a weekly newspaper on astrology, devoted to indirect propaganda for Hitler, became for a few weeks after Hitler's accession to power almost as important a factor in Germany as Rasputin had been in Russia. But his end was a tragic one. He was found murdered in a field in the environs of Berlin. The incident does not appear to have shaken Hitler's faith in astrology, and one of Hanussen's chief rivals, a man named Mücke, has been appointed by Hitler 'Federal Commissary for Occultism'. This, I believe, is the first time in modern ages that a state has officially recognised soothsaying and turned it into a government department.

But there is one extraordinary feature about Hitler's faith in the occult which gives rise to intriguing speculation. As everyone knows, he has adopted the Swastika as the emblem of the State. But curiously enough this Swastika is reversed, and anyone acquainted with Eastern beliefs knows that this is to be regarded with positive horror. An inverted Swastika is indicative not of endless life but of the flood and flame of life leading to a violent destruction. Did Hitler know this when he foisted it upon the German nation? Is the reversed Swastika just another sign of the man's half-baked conception of things? Or is this a last vestige of the irony of his political faith?

Hitler was not without devoted adherent in the 'Osteria Bavaria'. Some students became seized with a sort of hero-worship regarding him, and hung on to every word he said with wrapt attention. But his chief admirers were the two waitresses, buxom Bavarian wenches, who listened open-mouthed to him and danced attendance on him in a way that formed the subject of many jokes among the habitués of the place.

Hitler's relations with women indeed are a strange and obscure chapter. I saw a great deal of him at that time, and I can certify that he was in these matters as abstemious as in regard to food and drink. The only woman he seemed to care for at all was the lady to whose villa in the hills he fled after his inglorious collapse in November, 1923.

Latterly he is said to have fallen in love with Winifred Wagner, but I can hardly imagine the Hitler of 1921 in love.

Another thing that struck me was the man's utter incapacity to deal with important details. When he spoke of Italy, or the German race, or occultism, or the Jews, his talk was a succession of vague generalities, couched in attractive if flowery language, but showing in every case either complete ignorance or at least complete contempt for detail.

Though he insisted in season and out of season on the greatness of 'pure Germanism', I never met a German who was so entirely un-German. His speech, his thought, his outlook were far more Slav than Teutonic. He loved everything foreign while he denounced it.

His race theories came from the Frenchman, Gobineau, and the English renegade, Houston Chamberlain. His famous phrase 'the Third Reich' was the invention of the Dutchman, Moeller van den Bruck. The party salute was an Elizabethan stage convention – a subterfuge adopted by actors to imitate the Romans. His regimental standards were a pale imitation of Roman eagles. His uniforms are a sort of cocktail of French, Austrian and English uniforms with most of the bad points to all three.

But I will say this, as the result of those long evenings spent with him: he was, and probably still is, passionately, almost ferociously, sincere in all he says and does, even when it appears hypocritical and insincere.

'It seems to me that I am more to the Left than you, Mr Stalin'

H. G. Wells

In 1934, H. G. Wells arrived in Moscow to meet Soviet writers interested in joining the international PEN Club, of which he was then president. While there, Joseph Stalin granted him an interview. His deferential conversation was criticised by John Maynard Keynes and George Bernard Shaw, among others, in the New Statesman.

Wells: I am very much obliged to you, Mr Stalin, for agreeing to see me. I was in the United States recently. I had a long conversation with President Roosevelt and tried to ascertain what his leading ideas were. Now I have come to ask you what you are doing to change the world . . .

Stalin: Not so very much.

Wells: I wander around the world as a common man and, as a common man, observe what is going on around me.

Stalin: Important public men like yourself are not 'common men'. Of course, history alone can show how important this or that public man has been; at all events, you do not look at the world as a 'common man'.

Wells: I am not pretending humility. What I mean is that I try to see the world through the eyes of the common man, and not as a party politician or a responsible administrator. My visit to the United States excited my mind. The old financial world is collapsing; the economic life of the country is being reorganised on new lines. Lenin said: 'We must learn to do business,' learn this from the capitalists. Today the capitalists have to learn from you, to grasp the spirit of Socialism. It seems to me that what is taking place in the United States is a profound reorganisation, the creation of planned, that is, Socialist, economy. You and Roosevelt begin from two different starting points.

But is there not a relation in ideas, a kinship of ideas, between Moscow and Washington? In Washington I was struck by the same thing I see going on here; they are building offices, they are creating a number of state regulation bodies, they are organising a long-needed civil service. Their need, like yours, is directive ability.

AMERICA AND RUSSIA

Stalin: The United States is pursuing a different aim from that which we are pursuing in the USSR. The aim which the Americans are pursuing arose out of the economic troubles, out of the economic crisis. The Americans want to rid themselves of the crisis on the basis of private capitalist activity, without changing the economic basis. They are trying to reduce to a minimum the ruin, the losses caused by the existing economic system.

Here, however, as you know, in place of the old, destroyed economic basis, an entirely different, a new economic basis has been created. Even if the Americans you mention partly achieve their aim, i.e., reduce these losses to a minimum, they will not destroy the roots of the anarchy which is inherent in the existing capitalist system. They are preserving the economic system which must inevitably lead, and cannot but lead, to anarchy in production. Thus, at best, it will be a matter, not of the reorganisation of society, not of abolishing the old social system which gives rise to anarchy and crises, but of restricting certain of its excesses. Subjectively, perhaps, these Americans think they are reorganising society; objectively, however, they are preserving the present basis of society. That is why, objectively, there will be no reorganisation of society.

Nor will there be planned economy. What is planned economy? What are some of its attributes? Planned economy tries to abolish unemployment. Let us suppose it is possible, while preserving the capitalist system, to reduce unemployment to a certain minimum. But surely, no capitalist would ever agree to the complete abolition of unemployment, to the abolition of the reserve army of unemployed, the purpose of which is to bring pressure on the labour market, to ensure a supply of cheap labour. You will never compel a capitalist to incur loss to himself and agree to a lower rate of profit for the sake of satisfying the needs of the people.

Without getting rid of the capitalists, without abolishing the principle of private property in the means of production, it is impossible to create planned economy.

Wells: I agree with much of what you have said. But I would like to stress the point that if a country as a whole adopts the principle of planned economy, if the government, gradually, step by step, begins consistently to apply this principle, the financial oligarchy will at last be abolished and Socialism, in the Anglo-Saxon meaning of the word, will be brought about. The effect of the ideas of Roosevelt's 'New Deal' is most powerful, and in my opinion they are Socialist ideas. It seems to me that instead of stressing the antagonism between the two worlds, we should, in the present circumstances, strive to establish a common tongue for all the constructive forces.

Stalin: In speaking of the impossibility of realising the principles of planned economy while preserving the economic basis of capitalism, I do not in the least desire to belittle the outstanding personal qualities of Roosevelt, his initiative, courage and determination. Undoubtedly Roosevelt stands out as one of the strongest figures among all the captains of the contemporary capitalist world. That is why I would like once again to emphasise the point that my conviction that planned economy is impossible under the conditions of capitalism does not mean that I have any doubts about the personal abilities, talent and courage of President Roosevelt. But if the circumstances are unfavourable, the most talented captain cannot reach the goal you refer to. Theoretically, of course, the possibility of marching gradually, step by step, under the conditions of capitalism, towards the goal which you call Socialism in the Anglo-Saxon meaning of the word, is not precluded. But what will this 'Socialism' be? At best, bridling to some extent the most unbridled of individual representatives of capitalist profit, some increase in the application of the principle of regulation in national economy. That is all very well. But as soon as Roosevelt, or any other captain in the contemporary bourgeois world, proceeds to undertake something serious against the foundation of capitalism, he will inevitably suffer utter defeat. The banks, the industries, the large enterprises, the large farms are not in Roosevelt's hands. All these are private property. The railroads, the mercantile fleet, all these belong to private owners. And, finally, the army of skilled workers, the engineers, the technicians, these too are not at Roosevelt's command, they are at the command of the private owners; they all work for the private owners. We must not forget the functions of the State in the bourgeois world. The State is an institution that organises the defence of the country, organises the maintenance of 'order'; it is an apparatus for collecting taxes. The capitalist State does not deal much with economy in the strict sense of the word; the latter is not in the hands of the State. On the contrary, the State is in the hands of capitalist economy. That is why I fear that in spite of all his energies and abilities, Roosevelt will not achieve the goal you mention, if indeed that is his goal. Perhaps in the course of several generations it will be possible to approach this goal somewhat; but I personally think that even this is not very probable.

SOCIALISM AND INDIVIDUALISM

Wells: Perhaps I believe more strongly in the economic interpretation of politics than you do. Huge forces striving for better organisation, for the better functioning of the community, that is, for Socialism, have been brought into action by invention and modern science. Organisation, and the regulation of individual action, have become mechanical necessities, irrespective of social theories. If we begin with the State control of the banks and then follow with the control of the heavy industries, of industry in general, of commerce, etc., such an all-embracing control will be equivalent to the State ownership of all branches of national economy. Socialism and Individualism are not opposites like black and white. There are many intermediate stages between them. There is Individualism that borders on brigandage, and there is discipline and organisation that are the equivalent of Socialism. The introduction of planned economy depends, to a large degree, upon the organisers of economy, upon the skilled technical intelligentsia who, step by step, can be converted to the Socialist principles of organisation. And this is the most important thing, because organisation comes before Socialism. It is the more important fact. Without organisation the Socialist idea is a mere idea.

Stalin: There is no, nor should there be, irreconcilable contrast between the individual and the collective, between the interests of the individual person and the interests of the collective. There should be no such contrast, because collectivism, Socialism, does not deny, but combines individual interests with the interests of the collective. Socialism cannot abstract itself from individual interests.

Socialist society alone can most fully satisfy these personal interests. More than that, Socialist society alone can firmly safeguard the interests of the individual. In this sense there is no irreconcilable contrast between Individualism and Socialism. But can we deny the contrast between classes, between the propertied class, the capitalist class, and the toiling class, the proletarian class? On the one hand we have the propertied class which owns the banks, the factories, the mines, transport, the plantations in colonies. These people see nothing but their own interests, their striving after profits. They do not submit to the will of the collective; they strive to subordinate every collective to their will. On the other hand we have the class of the poor, the exploited class, which owns neither factories nor works, nor banks, which is compelled to live by selling its labour power to the capitalists and which lacks the opportunity to satisfy its most elementary requirements. How can such opposite interests and strivings be reconciled? As far as I know, Roosevelt has not succeeded in finding the path of conciliation between these interests. And it is impossible, as experience has shown. Incidentally, you know the situation in the United States better than I do, as I have never been there and I watch American affairs mainly from literature. But I have some experience in fighting for Socialism, and this experience tells me that if Roosevelt makes a real attempt to satisfy the interests of the proletarian class at the expense of the capitalist class, the latter will put another President in his place. The capitalists will say: Presidents come and Presidents go, but we go on for ever; if this or that President does not protect our interests, we shall find another. What can the President oppose to the will of the capitalist class?

Wells: I object to this simplified classification of mankind into poor and rich. Of course there is a category of people which strive only for profit. But are not these people regarded as nuisances in the West just as much as here? Are there not plenty of people in the West for whom profit is not an end, who own a certain amount of wealth, who want to invest and obtain a profit from this investment, but who do not regard this as the main object? They regard investment as an inconvenient necessity. Are there not plenty of capable and devoted engineers, organisers of economy, whose activities are stimulated by something other than profit? In my opinion there is a numerous class of capable people who admit that the present system is unsatisfactory and who are destined to play a great role in future capitalist society. During the past few years I have been much engaged in and have thought of the need for conducting propaganda in favour of Socialism and cosmopolitanism among wide circles of engineers, airmen, military technical people, etc. It is useless to approach these circles with two-track class-war propaganda. These people understand the condition of the world. They understand that it is a bloody muddle, but they regard your simple class-war antagonism as nonsense.

THE CLASS WAR

Stalin: You object to the simplified classification of mankind into rich and poor. Of course there is a middle stratum, there is the technical intelligentsia that you have mentioned and among which there are very good and very honest people. Among them there are also dishonest and wicked people; there are all sorts of people among them. But first of all mankind is divided into rich and poor, into property owners and exploited; and to abstract oneself from this fundamental division and from the antagonism between poor and rich means abstracting oneself from the fundamental fact. I do not deny the existence of intermediate middle strata, which either take the side of one or the other of these two conflicting classes, or else take up a neutral or semi-neutral position in the struggle. But, I repeat, to abstract oneself from this fundamental division in society and from the fundamental struggle between the two main classes means ignoring facts. The struggle is going on and will continue. The outcome will be determined by the proletarian class – the working class.

Wells: But are there not many people who are not poor, but who work and work productively?

Stalin: Of course, there are small landowners, artisans, small traders, but it is not these people who decide the fate of a country, but the toiling masses, who produce all the things society requires.

Wells: But there are very different kinds of capitalists. There are capitalists who only think about profit, about getting rich; but there are also those who are prepared to make sacrifices. Take old [J. P.] Morgan, for example. He only thought about profit; he was a parasite on society, simply, he merely accumulated wealth. But take [John D.] Rockefeller. He is a brilliant organiser; he has set an example of how to organise the delivery of oil that is worthy of emulation. Or take [Henry] Ford. Of course Ford is selfish. But is he not a passionate organiser of rationalised production from whom you take lessons? I would like to emphasise the fact that recently an important change in opinion towards the USSR has taken place in English-speaking countries. The reason for this, first of all, is the position of Japan, and the events in Germany. But there are other reasons besides those arising from international politics. There is a more profound reason, namely, the recognition by many people of the fact that the system based on private profit is breaking down. Under these circumstances, it seems to me, we must not bring to the forefront the antagonism between the two worlds, but should strive to combine all the constructive movements, all the constructive forces in one line as much as possible. It seems to me that I am more to the Left than you, Mr Stalin; I think the old system is nearer to its end than you think.

THE TECHNICIAN CLASS

Stalin: In speaking of the capitalists who strive only for profit, only to get rich, I do not want to say that these are the most worthless people, capable of nothing else. Many of them undoubtedly possess great organising talent, which I do not dream of denying. We Soviet people learn a great deal from the capitalists. And Morgan, whom you characterise so unfavourably, was undoubtedly a good, capable organiser. But if you mean people who are prepared to reconstruct the world, of course, you will not be able to find them in the ranks of those who faithfully serve the cause of profit. We and they stand at opposite poles. You mentioned Ford. Of course, he is a capable organiser of production. But don't you know his attitude towards the working class? Don't you know how many workers he throws on the street? The capitalist is riveted to profit; and no power on earth can tear him away from it. Capitalism will be abolished, not by 'organisers' of production, not by the technical intelligentsia, but by the working class, because the aforementioned strata do not play an independent role. The engineer, the organiser of production does not work as he would like to, but as he is ordered, in such a way as to serve the interests of his employers. There are exceptions of course; there are people in this stratum who have awakened from the intoxication of capitalism. The technical intelligentsia can, under certain conditions, perform miracles and greatly benefit mankind. But it can also cause great harm. We Soviet people have not a little experience of the technical intelligentsia. After the October Revolution, a certain section of the technical intelligentsia refused to take part in the work of constructing the new society; they opposed this work of construction and sabotaged it. We did all we possibly could to bring the technical intelligentsia into this work of construction; we tried this way and that. Not a little time passed before our technical intelligentsia agreed actively to assist the new system. Today the best section of this technical intelligentsia is in the front rank of the builders of Socialist society. Having this experience, we are far from underestimating the good and the bad sides of the technical intelligentsia, and we know that on the one hand it can do harm, and on the other hand it can perform 'miracles'. Of course, things would be different if it were possible, at one stroke, spiritually to tear the technical intelligentsia away from the capitalist world. But that is Utopia. Are there many of the technical intelligentsia who would dare break away from the bourgeois world and set to work reconstructing society? Do you think there are many people of this kind, say, in England or in France? No; there are few who would be willing to break away from their employers and begin reconstructing the world.

ACHIEVEMENT OF POLITICAL POWER

Stalin: Besides, can we lose sight of the fact that in order to transform the world it is necessary to have political power? It seems to me, Mr Wells, that you greatly underestimate the question of political power, that it entirely drops out of your conception. What can those, even with the best intentions in the world, do if they are unable to raise the question of seizing power, and do not possess power? At best they can help the class which takes power, but they cannot change the world themselves. This can only be done by a great class which will take the place of the capitalist class and become the sovereign master as the latter was before. This class is the working class. Of course, the assistance of the technical intelligentsia must be accepted; and the latter, in turn, must be assisted. But it must not be thought that the technical intelligentsia can play an independent historical role. The transformation of the world is a great, complicated and painful process. For this task a great class is required. Big ships go on long voyages.

Wells: Yes, but for long voyages a captain and navigator are required.

Stalin: That is true; but what is first required for a long voyage is a big ship. What is a navigator without a ship? An idle man.

Wells: The big ship is humanity, not a class.

Stalin: You, Mr Wells, evidently start out with the assumption that all men are good. I, however, do not forget that there are many wicked men. I do not believe in the goodness of the bourgeoisie.

Wells: I remember the situation with regard to the technical intelligentsia several decades ago. At that time the technical intelligentsia was numerically small, but there was much to do and every engineer, technician and intellectual found his opportunity. That is why the technical intelligentsia was the least revolutionary class. Now, however, there is a superabundance of technical intellectuals, and their mentality has changed very sharply. The skilled man, who would formerly never listen to revolutionary talk, is now greatly interested in it. Recently I was dining with the Royal Society, our great English scientific society. The President's speech was a speech for social planning and scientific control. Thirty years ago, they would not have listened to what I say to them now. Today, the man at the head of the Royal Society holds revolutionary views, and insists on the scientific reorganisation of human society. Your class-war propaganda has not kept pace with these facts. Mentality changes.

Stalin: Yes, I know this, and this is to be explained by the fact that capitalist society is now in a cul-de-sac. The capitalists are seeking, but cannot find a way out of this cul-de-sac that would be compatible with the dignity of this class, compatible with the interests of this class. They could, to some extent, crawl out of the crisis on their hands and knees, but they cannot find an exit that would enable them to walk out of it with head raised high, a way out that would not fundamentally disturb the interests of capitalism. This, of course, is realised by wide circles of the technical intelligentsia. A large section of it is beginning to realise the community of its interests with those of the class which is capable of pointing the way out of the cul-de-sac.

Wells: You of all people know something about revolutions, Mr Stalin, from the practical side. Do the masses ever rise? Is it not an established truth that all revolutions are made by a minority?

Stalin: To bring about a revolution a leading revolutionary minority is required; but the most talented, devoted and energetic minority would be helpless if it did not rely upon the at least passive support of millions.

Wells: At least passive? Perhaps subconscious?

Stalin: Partly also the semi-instinctive and semi-conscious, but without the support of millions, the best minority is impotent.

THE PLACE OF VIOLENCE

Wells: I watch Communist propaganda in the West, and it seems to me that in modern conditions this propaganda sounds very old-fashioned, because it is insurrectionary propaganda. Propaganda in favour of the violent overthrow of the social system was all very well when it was directed against tyranny. But under modern conditions, when the system is collapsing anyhow, stress should be laid on efficiency, on competence, on productiveness, and not on insurrection. It seems to me that the insurrectionary note is obsolete. The Communist propaganda in the West is a nuisance to constructive-minded people.

Stalin: Of course the old system is breaking down, decaying. That is true. But it is also true that new efforts are being made by other methods, by every means, to protect, to save this dying system. You draw a wrong conclusion from a correct postulate. You rightly state that the old world is breaking down. But you are wrong in thinking that it is breaking down of its own accord. No; the substitution of one social system for another is a complicated and long revolutionary process. It is not simply a spontaneous process, but a struggle; it is a process connected with the clash of classes. Capitalism is decaying, but it must not be compared simply with a tree which has decayed to such an extent that it must fall to the ground of its own accord. No, revolution, the substitution of one social system for another, has always been a struggle, a painful and a cruel struggle, a life-and-death struggle. And every time the people of the new world came into power they had to defend themselves against the attempts of the old world to restore the old power by force; these people of the new world always had to be on the alert, always had to be ready to repel the attacks of the old world upon the new system.

Yes, you are right when you say that the old social system is breaking down; but it is not breaking down of its own accord. Take Fascism for example. Fascism is a reactionary force which is trying to preserve the old system by means of violence. What will you do with the Fascists? Argue with them? Try to convince them? But this will have no effect upon them at all. Communists do not in the least idealise methods of violence. But they, the Communists, do not want to be taken by surprise; they cannot count on the old world voluntarily departing from the stage; they see that the old system is violently defending itself, and that is why the Communists say to the working class: Answer violence with violence; do all you can to prevent the old dying order from crushing you, do not permit it to put manacles on your hands, on the hands with which you will overthrow the old system.

As you see, the Communists regard the substitution of one social system for another, not simply as a spontaneous and peaceful process, but as a complicated, long and violent process. Communists cannot ignore facts.

Wells: But look at what is now going on in the capitalist world. The collapse is not a simple one; it is the outbreak of reactionary violence which is degenerating to gangsterism. And it seems to me that when it comes to a conflict with reactionary and unintelligent violence, Socialists can appeal to the law, and instead of regarding the police as the enemy they should support them in the fight against the reactionaries. I think that it is useless operating with the methods of the old insurrectionary Socialism.

THE LESSONS OF HISTORY

Stalin: The Communists base themselves on rich historical experience which teaches that obsolete classes do not voluntarily abandon the stage of history. Recall the history of England in the seventeenth century. Did not many say that the old social system had decayed? But did it not, nevertheless, require a Cromwell to crush it by force?

Wells: Cromwell acted on the basis of the constitution and in the name of constitutional order.

Stalin: In the name of the constitution he resorted to violence, beheaded the king, dispersed Parliament, arrested some and beheaded others!

Or take an example from our history. Was it not clear for a long time that the Tsarist system was decaying, was breaking down? But how much blood had to be shed in order to overthrow it?

And what about the October Revolution? Were there not plenty of people who knew that we alone, the Bolsheviks, were indicating the only correct way out? Was it not clear that Russian capitalism had decayed? But you know how great was the resistance, how much blood had to be shed in order to defend the October Revolution from all its enemies, internal and external.

Or take France at the end of the eighteenth century. Long before 1789 it was clear to many how rotten the royal power, the feudal system, was. But a popular insurrection, a clash of classes was not, could not be avoided. Why? Because the classes which must abandon the stage of history are the last to become convinced that their role is ended. It is impossible to convince them of this. They think that the fissures in the decaying edifice of the old order can be repaired and saved.

That is why dying classes take to arms and resort to every means to save their existence as a ruling class.

Wells: But were there not a few lawyers at the head of the great French Revolution?

Stalin: I do not deny the role of the intelligentsia in revolutionary movements. Was the great French Revolution a lawyers' revolution and not a popular revolution, which achieved victory by rousing vast masses of the people against feudalism and championed the interests of the Third Estate? And did the lawyers among the leaders of the great French Revolution act in accordance with the laws of the old order? Did they not introduce new, bourgeois-revolutionary law?

The rich experience of history teaches that up to now not a single class has voluntarily made way for another class. There is no such precedent in world history. The Communists have learned this lesson of history. Communists would welcome the voluntary departure of the bourgeoisie. But such a turn of affairs is improbable, that is what experience teaches. That is why the Communists want to be prepared for the worst and call upon the working class to be vigilant, to be prepared for battle.

Who wants a captain who lulls the vigilance of his army, a captain who does not understand that the enemy will not surrender, that he must be crushed? To be such a captain means deceiving, betraying the working class. That is why I think that what seems to you to be old-fashioned is in fact a measure of revolutionary expediency for the working class.

HOW TO MAKE A REVOLUTION

Wells: I do not deny that force has to be used, but I think the forms of the struggle should fit as closely as possible to the opportunities presented by the existing laws, which must be defended against reactionary attacks. There is no need to disorganise the old system because it is disorganising itself enough as it is. That is why it seems to me insurrection against the old order, against the law, is obsolete; old-fashioned. Incidentally, I deliberately exaggerate in order to bring the truth out more clearly. I can formulate my point of view in the following way: first, I am for order; second, I attack the present system in so far as it cannot assure order; third, I think that class war propaganda may detach from Socialism just those educated people whom Socialism needs.

Stalin: In order to achieve a great object, an important social object, there must be a main force, a bulwark, a revolutionary class. Next it is necessary to organise the assistance of an auxiliary force for this main force; in this case this auxiliary force is the party, to which the best forces of the intelligentsia belong. Just now you spoke about 'educated people'. But what educated people did you have in mind? Were there not plenty of educated people on the side of the old order in England in the seventeenth century, in France at the end of the eighteenth century, and in Russia in the epoch of the October Revolution? The old order had in its service many highly educated people who defended the old order, who opposed the new order.

Education is a weapon the effect of which is determined by the hands which wield it, by who is to be struck down. Of course, the proletariat, Socialism, needs highly educated people. Clearly, simpletons cannot help the proletariat to fight for Socialism, to build a new society.

I do not under estimate the role of the intelligentsia; on the contrary, I emphasise it. The question is, however, which intelligentsia are we discussing? Because there are different kinds of intelligentsia.

Wells: There can be no revolution without a radical change in the educational system. It is sufficient to quote two examples – the example of the German Republic, which did not touch the old educational system, and therefore never became a republic; and the example of the British Labour Party, which lacks the determination to insist on a radical change in the educational system.

Stalin: That is a correct observation. Permit me now to reply to your three points. First, the main thing for the revolution is the existence of a social bulwark. This bulwark of the revolution is the working class.

Second, an auxiliary force is required, that which the Communists call a Party. To the Party belong the intelligent workers and those elements of the technical intelligentsia which are closely connected with the working class. The intelligentsia can be strong only if it combines with the working class. If it opposes the working class it becomes a cipher.

Third, political power is required as a lever for change. The new political power creates the new laws, the new order, which is revolutionary order.

I do not stand for any kind of order. I stand for order that corresponds to the interests of the working class. If, however, any of the laws of the old order can be utilised in the interests of the struggle for the new order, the old laws should be utilised. I cannot object to your postulate that the present system should be attacked in so far as it does not ensure the necessary order for the people.

And, finally, you are wrong if you think that the Communists are enamoured of violence. They would be very pleased to drop violent methods if the ruling class agreed to give way to the working class. But the experience of history speaks against such an assumption.

Wells: There was a case in the history of England, however, of a class voluntarily handing over power to another class. In the period between 1830 and 1870, the aristocracy, whose influence was still very considerable at the end of the eighteenth century, voluntarily, without a severe struggle, surrendered power to the bourgeoisie, which serves as a sentimental support of the monarchy. Subsequently, this transference of power led to the establishment of the rule of the financial oligarchy.

Stalin: But you have imperceptibly passed from questions of revolution to questions of reform. This is not the same thing. Don't you think that the Chartist movement played a great role in the reforms in England in the nineteenth century?

Wells: The Chartists did little and disappeared without leaving a trace.

Stalin: I do not agree with you. The Chartists, and the strike movement which they organised, played a great role; they compelled the ruling class to make a number of concessions in regard to the franchise, in regard to abolishing the so-called 'rotten boroughs', and in regard to some of the points of the 'Charter'. Chartism played a not unimportant historical role and compelled a section of the ruling classes to make certain concessions, reforms, in order to avert great shocks. Generally speaking, it must be said that of all the ruling classes, the ruling classes of England, both the aristocracy and the bourgeoisie, proved to be the cleverest, most flexible from the point of view of their class interests, from the point of view of maintaining their power.

Take as an example, say, from modern history, the General Strike in England in 1926. The first thing any other bourgeoisie would have done in the face of such an event, when the General Council of Trade Unions called for a strike, would have been to arrest the trade union leaders. The British bourgeoisie did not do that, and it acted cleverly from the point of view of its own interests. I cannot conceive of such a flexible strategy being employed by the bourgeoisie in the United States, Germany or France. In order to maintain their rule, the ruling classes of Great Britain have never forsworn small concessions, reforms. But it would be a mistake to think that these reforms were revolutionary.

Wells: You have a higher opinion of the ruling classes of my country than I have. But is there a great difference between a small revolution and a great reform?

Is not a reform a small revolution?

Stalin: Owing to pressure from below, the pressure of the masses, the bourgeoisie may sometimes concede certain partial reforms while remaining on the basis of the existing social-economic system. Acting in this way, it calculates that these concessions are necessary in order to preserve its class rule. This is the essence of reform. Revolution, however, means the transference of power from one class to another. That is why it is impossible to describe any reform as revolution.

WHAT RUSSIA IS DOING WRONG

Wells: I am very grateful to you for this talk which has meant a great deal to me. In explaining things to me you probably called to mind how you had to explain the fundamentals of Socialism in the illegal circles before the revolution. At the present time there are only two persons to whose opinion, to whose every word, millions are listening – you and Roosevelt. Others may preach as much as they like; what they say will never be printed or heeded.

I cannot yet appreciate what has been done in your country; I only arrived yesterday. But I have already seen the happy faces of healthy men and women and I know that something very considerable is being done here. The contrast with 1920 is astounding.

Stalin: Much more could have been done had we Bolsheviks been cleverer.

Wells: No, if human beings were cleverer. It would be a good thing to invent a five-year plan for the reconstruction of the human brain, which obviously lacks many things needed for a perfect social order. [*Laughter*]

Stalin: Don't you intend to stay for the Congress of the Soviet Writers' Union?

Wells: Unfortunately, I have various engagements to fulfil and I can stay in the USSR only for a week. I came to see you and I am very satisfied by our talk. But I intend to discuss with such Soviet writers as I can meet the possibility of their affiliating to the PEN Club. The organisation is still weak, but it has branches in many countries, and what is more important, the speeches of the members are widely reported in the press. It insists upon this free expression of opinion – even of opposition opinion. I hope to discuss this point with Gorky. I do not know if you are prepared yet for that much freedom here.

Stalin: We Bolsheviks call it 'self-criticism'. It is widely used in the USSR.

If there is anything I can do to help you I shall be glad to do so.

1 JUNE 1935

We Must Drift:
A Letter from Joseph Conrad

Joseph Conrad

*Joseph Conrad was born Józef Teodor Konrad Korzeniowski in 1857 to
ethnically Polish parents living in western Ukraine. After a time in the British
merchant navy, 'Conrad' became a British citizen in 1886. The following letter
was written the previous year at a time when Conrad had not yet achieved
full fluency in English. The letter, addressed to a Polish friend, remained
unpublished until 1935 when the naval officer and politician Oliver Stillingfleet
Locker-Lampson offered it to the* New Statesman *with the permission of the
addressee's family. H. G. Wells wrote in his 1934 autobiography that Conrad
never quite managed to speak English without a Polish accent but, as this letter
shows, at 28 he was already mastering the language in which he later wrote
novels, short stories and essays. Conrad died in 1924.*

> December 19th, 1885
> Calcutta

My Dear Sir,

I received your kind and welcome letter yesterday, and today being
Sunday, I feel that I could not make better use of my leisure hours
than in answering your missive. By this time, you and the rest of the
'right thinking' have been grievously disappointed by the result of the
General Election. The newly enfranchised idiots have satisfied the
yearnings of Mr Chamberlain's hoard by cooking the national goose
according to his recipe. The next culinary operation will be a 'pretty
kettle of fish' – of an international character! Joy reigns in St Petersburg
– no doubt, and profound disgust in Berlin; the International Socialist
Association are triumphant, and every disreputable *ragamuffin in
Europe feels that the day of universal brotherhood, despoliation and
disorder is coming apace, and nurses day dreams of well plenished
pockets amongst the ruins of all that is respectable, venerable and Holy.*
The great British Empire went over the edge and got on to the inclined

plane of social progress and radical reform! *The downward movement is hardly Preceptible yet and the clever men who started it may flatter themselves with the mistaken and delusive sense of their power to direct the great body in its progress; but they will soon find that the fate of the nation is out of hands now!* The Alpine avalanche rolls quicker and quicker as it nears the abyss – its ultimate destination! Where's the man to stop the crashing avalanche?

Where's the man to stop the rush of social, democratic idiocy? The opportunity and the day have come – and are gone, believe me gone for ever. For the sun is set and the last barrier removed. England was the only barrier to the pressure of infernal doctrines born in continental back-slums. Now there is nothing!

The destiny of this nation and of all nations is to be accomplished in darkness amidst much weeping and gnashing of teeth, to pass through robbery, equality, anarchy and misery under the iron rule of a military despotism. Such is the lesson of history! Such is the lesson of common-sense logic!

Socialism must inevitably end in Cesarism.

Forgive me this long disquistion; but your letter – so earnest on the subject must be my excuse. I understand you perfectly. You wish to apply remedies to quell the dangerous symptoms; you evidently hope yet –. I do so no longer. Truthfully I have ceased to hope a long time ago. We must drift!

The whole herd of idiotic humanity are moving in that direction at the bidding of unscrupulous rascals, and a few sincere and dangerous lunatics. Those things must be. It is a fatality!

I live mostly in the past – and in the future. The present has – you easily understand – few charms for me. I look with the serenity of despair and the indifference of contempt upon passing events. Disestablishment, Land Reform, universal brotherhood are but like milestones on the Road to Ruin. The end will be awful – no doubt! Neither you nor I shall live to see the final crash; although we may both turn in our graves when it comes for we both feel deeply and sincerely. Still there is no earthly remedy. All is vanity...!

This is signed,

Yours very sincerely and faithfully,

K. N. Korzeniowski

The Upside-Down World of Lewis Carroll

Virginia Woolf

The complete works of Lewis Carroll have been issued by the Nonesuch Press in a stout volume of 1,293 pages. So there is no excuse – Lewis Carroll ought once and for all to be complete. We ought to be able to grasp him whole and entire. But we fail – once more we fail. We think we have caught Lewis Carroll; we look again and see an Oxford clergyman. We think we have caught the Rev. C. L. Dodgson – we look again and see a fairy elf. The book breaks in two in our hands. In order to cement it, we turn to the Life.

But the Rev. C. L. Dodgson had no life. He passed through the world so lightly that he left no print. He melted so passively into Oxford that he is invisible. He accepted every convention; he was prudish, pernickety, pious, and jocose. If Oxford dons in the nineteenth century had an essence he was that essence. He was so good that his sisters worshipped him; so pure that his nephew has nothing to say about him. It is just possible, he hints, that 'a shadow of disappointment lay over Lewis Carroll's life'. Mr Dodgson at once denies the shadow. 'My life,' he says, 'is free from all trial and trouble.' But this untinted jelly contained within it a perfectly hard crystal. It contained childhood.

This is very strange, for childhood normally fades slowly. Wisps of childhood persist when the boy or girl is a grown man or woman. Childhood returns sometimes by day, more often by night. But it was not so with Lewis Carroll. For some reason his childhood was sharply severed. It lodged in him whole and entire. And therefore as he grew older this impediment in the centre of his being, this hard block of pure childhood, starved the mature man of nourishment. He slipped through the grown-up world like a shadow, solidifying only on the beach at Eastbourne, with little girls whose frocks he pinned up with safety pins. But since childhood remained in him entire, he could do what no one else has ever been able to do – he could return to that world; he could re-create it, so that we too become children again.

In order to make us into children, he first makes us asleep. 'Down, down, down, would the fall *never* come to an end?' Down, down, down we fall into that terrifying, wildly inconsequent, yet perfectly logical world where time races, then stands still; where space stretches, then contracts. It is the world of sleep; it is also the world of dreams. Without any conscious effort dreams come; the white rabbit, the walrus and the carpenter, one after another, they come skipping and leaping across the mind. It is for this reason that the two Alices are not books for children; they are the only books in which we become children. President Wilson, Queen Victoria, the *Times* leader writer, the late Lord Salisbury – it does not matter how old, how important or how insignificant you are, you become a child again. To become a child is to be very literal; to find everything so strange that nothing is surprising; to be heartless, to be ruthless, yet to be so passionate that a snub or a shadow drapes the world in gloom. It is to be Alice in Wonderland.

It is also to be Alice Through the Looking-Glass. It is to see the world upside down. Many great satirists and moralists have shown us the world upside down, and have made us see it, as grown-up people see it, savagely. Only Lewis Carroll has shown us the world upside down, as a child sees it, and has made us laugh as children laugh, irresponsibly. Down the groves of pure nonsense we whirl laughing, laughing –

> *They sought it with thimbles, they sought it with care*
> *They pursued it with forks and with hope ...*

And then we wake. None of the transitions in Alice in Wonderland is quite so queer. For we wake to find – is it the Rev. C. L. Dodgson? Is it Lewis Carroll? Or is it both combined? This conglomerate object intends to produce an extra-Bowdlerised edition of Shakespeare for the use of British maidens; implores them to think of death when they go to the play; and always, always to realise that 'the true object of life is the development of *character* ...' Is there, then, even in 1,293 pages, any such thing as 'completeness'?

The Wintry Conscience of a Generation

V. S. Pritchett

George Orwell was the wintry conscience of a generation which in the Thirties had heard the call to the rasher assumptions of political faith. He was a kind of saint and, in that character, more likely in politics to chasten his own side than the enemy. His instinctive choice of spiritual and physical discomfort, his habit of going his own way, looked like the crankishness which has often cropped up in the British character; if this were so, it was vagrant rather than puritan. He prided himself on seeing through the rackets, and on conveying the impression of living without the solace or even the need of a single illusion. There can hardly have been a more belligerent and yet more pessimistic Socialist; indeed his Socialism became anarchism. In corrupt and ever worsening years, he always woke up one miserable hour earlier than anyone else and, suspecting something fishy in the site, broke camp and advanced alone to some tougher position in a bleaker place; and it had often happened that he had been the first to detect an unpleasant truth or to refuse a tempting hypocrisy.

Conscience took the Anglo-Indian out of the Burma police, conscience sent the old Etonian among the down and outs in London and Paris, and the degraded victims of the Means Test or slum incompetence in Wigan; it drove him into the Spanish Civil War and, inevitably, into one of its unpopular sects, and there Don Quixote saw the poker face of Communism. His was the guilty conscience of the educated and privileged man, one of that regular supply of brilliant recalcitrant which Eton has given us since the days of Fielding; and this conscience could be allayed only by taking upon itself the pain, the misery, the dinginess and the pathetic but hard vulgarities of a stale and hopeless period.

But all this makes only the severe half of George Orwell's character. There were two George Orwells even in name. I see a tall emaciated man with a face scored by the marks of physical suffering. There is the ironic grin of pain at the ends of kind lips, and an expression in the fine eyes that had something of the exalted and obstructive farsightedness one sees in the blind; an expression that will suddenly become gentle, lazily kind and gleaming with workmanlike humour. He would be jogged into remembering mad, comical and often tender things which his indignation had written off; rather like some military man taking time off from a private struggle with the War Office or society in general.

He was an expert on living on the bare necessities and a keen hand at making them barer. There was a sardonic suggestion that he could do this but you could not. He was a handyman. He liked the idea of a bench. I remember once being advised by him to go in for goat-keeping, partly I think because it was a sure road to trouble and semi-starvation; but as he set out the alluring disadvantages it seemed to dawn on him that he was arguing for some country Arcadia, some Animal Farm, he had once known; goats began to look like escapism and, turning aside as we walked to buy some shag at a struggling Wellsian small trader's shop, he switched the subject sharply to the dangerous Fascist tendencies of the St John's Wood Home Guard who were marching to imaginary battle under the Old School Tie.

As an Old School Tie himself, Orwell had varied one of its traditions and had 'gone native' in his own country. It is often said that he knew nothing about the working classes, and indeed a certain self-righteousness in the respectable working class obviously repelled his independent mind. So many of his contemporaries had 'gone native' in France; he redressed a balance. But he did know that sour, truculent, worrying, vulgar lower-class England of people half 'done down', commercially exploited, culturally degraded, lazy, feckless, mild and kind who had appeared in the novels of Dickens, were to show their heads again in Wells and now stood in danger of having the long Victorian decency knocked out of them by gangster politics. By 'the people' he did not mean what the politicians mean; but he saw, at least in his Socialist pamphlets, that it was they who would give English life of the future a raw, muddy but unmistakable and inescapable flavour. His masochism, indeed, extended to culture.

*

In a way, he deplored this. A classical education had given him a taste for the politician who can quote from Horace; and as was shown in the lovely passages of boyhood reminiscences in *Coming Up for Air*, his imagination was fun only in the kind world he had known before 1914. Growing up turned him not exactly into a misanthrope – he was too good-natured and spirited for that – but into one who felt too painfully the ugly pressure of society upon private virtue and happiness.

His own literary tastes were fixed – with a discernible trailing of the coat – in that boyish period: Bret Harte, Jules Verne, pioneering stuff, Kipling and boys' books. He wrote the best English appreciation of Dickens of our time. *Animal Farm* has become a favourite book for children. His Burmese novels, though poor in character, turn Kipling upside down. As a reporting pamphleteer, his fast, clear, grey prose carries its hard and sweeping satire perfectly.

He has gone: but in one sense, he always made this impression of the passing traveller who meets one on the station, points out that one is waiting for the wrong train and vanishes. His popularity, after *Animal Farm*, must have disturbed such a lone hand. In *Nineteen Eighty-Four*, alas, one can see that deadly pain, which had long been his subject, had seized him completely and obliged him to project a nightmare, as Wells had done in his last days, upon the future.

Last train to nowhere:
The restless spirit of Arthur Koestler

Unsigned

*Like all profiles in the magazine from this period, this profile of Arthur
Koestler was unsigned. Koestler was an occasional contributor to the NS
in the late 1930s and early 1940s, under Kingsley Martin's editorship.
Koestler's masterpiece, the novel* Darkness at Noon, *was reviewed for
the NS in January 1941 by George Orwell, who read it as an 'interpretation'
of the Stalinist show trials of the late Thirties 'by someone with an inner
knowledge of totalitarian methods'.*

When Hardwick built the great arch which leads to Euston Station,
he named it 'the Gateway to the North'. On every great Continental
railway station should have been inscribed: 'The Gateway to Utopia'.
Did not Robert Owen describe his co-operative system as 'the railway
which would take men to universal happiness'? The metaphor had
point: until Iron Curtains descended, railways offered men escape –
from one country, one way of life, to another. And of Hungary, above
all, was this true. Paris and Western civilisation were at one end of
the line; Constantinople and the Orient at the other. Budapest was a
gloried gypsy-encampment; Hungarians never forgot their nomadic
origin. Intellectual life in Budapest was intense but intellectuals had
to be European or nothing; and they took advantage of their railway.
Budapest provided Europe with musicians, film stars, playwrights,
economists – all travellers by train.

Arthur Koestler is the most complete example of this destiny. He
describes his autobiography – the second volume of which has just
been published – as 'the typical case-history of a member of the
Central European educated middle classes, born in the first years of our
century'. He is the man without roots, the man whose mind is his only

fortune, the man who is always in search of perfection. By the middle of the century, he has become the man who knows that perfection can never be found and so concludes that nothing can be found. Here, too, the disillusioned intellectual is typical of his age. We should perhaps quarrel with one word of the description. His case-history is 'typical' only in being extreme. Koestler has gone further than others in quest of Utopia and has been correspondingly more disillusioned. Most men have few roots; Koestler is untypical in that he has none at all. And of course the claim to be typical reveals a false modesty quite out of tune. His transcendent abilities make him far from typical. Many men have had Koestler's experiences, or some of them. No one else could have transformed them into perhaps the most remarkable autobiography since the *Confessions* of Rousseau. Whether we admire or dislike him, learn from him or repudiate his instruction, there is no denying his literary gifts. Koestler is typical only in the way that Bernard Shaw claimed to be normal.

And yet, if we can tear ourselves away from Koestler's magic and look again at the record, we may wonder if his case-history is so representative after all. No doubt many intellectuals ran after Utopias between the wars; and no doubt all were somewhat disappointed. But did any run as hard as Koestler or end up in such complete disillusionment? Indeed, how many ran at all seriously? 'Parlour Bolshevism' was the most popular game of the Thirties; Koestler never played it. His present fate bears witness to this. Other intellectuals have dabbled in Communism at one time or another. They have sloughed it off, and the flirtation might as well never have been. But Koestler is still obsessed by it. Though he may be without roots, he has put out tentacles and now cannot detach them. He himself asks – why do men write autobiographies? and he answers – as a cautionary tale. But this is not always the true answer, certainly not true in his case. Men also write autobiographies in order to relive the past, to experience again their triumphs or, it may be, their failures. The interwar years were, for everyone, years of folly and disaster – for Koestler more than for most. One might imagine that he would like to turn his back on them. On the contrary, he writes of nothing else, just as Dickens could never get the boot-blacking factory out of his mind.

There are, then, two Koestlers – the literary artist who is immersed in the past; the human being who has to make do with the present. All Koestler's writings depict the interwar years. In his private life, he says, he searched always for the perfect woman, the Helen of Troy, and was, as in politics, inevitably disillusioned. Outside, he discovered two Utopias. There was the Zionist Utopia in Palestine, and the Socialist Utopia of the Soviet Union. Both have given him material for novels, for volumes of essays, and now for his autobiography. In each case the material stops in 1940. Thereafter, Koestler implies, the two fraudulent Utopias were just the same, only more so. Both again have another curious characteristic in common – Koestler had lost faith before he set eyes on them, or so he implies nowadays. He knew before he reached Palestine that he could not live the Utopian life of physical labour; this Utopia, even if it had some sort of existence, was not for him. Still more, his entire account of Soviet Russia in the Thirties is shot through with contempt and ridicule. Quite rightly: there has never been a community further removed from Utopia than the Soviet Union of the great famine and the great purge. But did Koestler not observe anything of this at the time? Did he – a mature journalist and political student – fail to notice the starving peasants on the railway platforms? He suggests now that he noticed them only unconsciously or accepted the twaddling excuses of Soviet publicity. Surely there is quite a different explanation. The Soviet fraud – the contrast between Utopia and reality – made Communism all the more attractive for him. It is an old story that the highest form of belief is belief in the impossible; and Koestler shared this emotional satisfaction with the early Christians.

Belief, not a settled way of life, was what Koestler was seeking for in the interwar years. Zionism involved digging. He gave it up. Communism meant for him writing articles, delivering lectures; and he clung to it, by his own account, long after his inner faith had been shaken or destroyed. It never seems to occur to him that Communism may be a way of arranging economic life as well as a system of political tyranny. In Soviet Russia he met propagandists, secret policemen – and beautiful women. He hardly mentions the worried managers of factories or even the engine drivers. The Utopian train is assumed to run itself. The important thing is the discussion in the railway carriage, not the men who somehow make the train go. The Soviet Utopia of

Koestler's dream did not exist. But he does not now see Soviet Russia by the cold light of reality. He has merely turned things upside down; and what was once Utopia has become instead Hell on earth, a place almost equally imaginary.

The political idealist is likely to be disappointed when he comes into contact with life. Koestler was certainly disappointed; and in this he was 'a typical case-history'. In the harsh years before 1939 the idealist might expect to end in prison; here, too, Koestler was typical – no man has been in more. But the sorts of prisons he fell into were not at all typical. Siberia and Nazi concentration camps were the typical prisons of the 1930s, crammed with political idealists. Koestler never entered either except in imagination. His prisons were in Spain, in France, finally at Pentonville. Experience of these is less common, and less representative. Koestler has 'green fingers' so far as prisons are concerned. He can hardly go anywhere without finding himself in jail. But they are jails of an old-fashioned type, clumsy, brutal, careless, but not the jails of the new totalitarian tyrannies. It would be unfair to say that Koestler was happy only in prison. But it is not unfair to say that only there did he find inner peace. He describes the rest of the spirit which came to him at the prison window, the mystical experience which revealed to him 'the invisible writing'. At last the train had brought him somewhere. In prison Koestler had arrived.

But in Western Europe life does not end in prison. The prison gates open; and life has to begin. It is a stroke of profound symbolism that Koestler's autobiography closes when he left Pentonville. No more Utopias; no more prisons, except as a casual touch of luck. Instead, one would suppose, drab reality. Life brought to Koestler success as an author, material rewards which satisfied his 'hedonism', and a comfortable house in Knightsbridge. He could be admired, respected, at ease. But this was not what he wanted. Where previously he had been embittered at failure, now he must be embittered at success. He claims to have grown roots in England; but the way he displays it is to describe England as 'a kind of Davos for internally bruised veterans of the totalitarian age'. He is exasperated with English softness, exasperated with the low sales of his books here, exasperated that English people do not bestir themselves against Communist tyranny. In England, he writes, 'I am only read by highbrows, and even by them only as a penance'; and he refers to the English gift 'of looking at reality through a soothing filter'.

Perhaps Koestler is not a reliable or penetrating judge of English ways. Perhaps 'their lotus-eating disposition' covers a deeper understanding of reality than he supposes. Englishmen are aware of the concentration camps and the gas chambers, but do not regard them as a profitable topic of conversation – or even of literature.

Why should we go on talking about things that are both absurd and repellent? There is no 'Communist tyranny' in England: few vote Communist here. Besides, to quote Koestler, even English Communists are 'certainly closer to the Pickwick Club than to the Comintern'. He condemns, or perhaps praises, them for indulging 'in humour and eccentricity – dangerous diversions from the class struggle'. Dangerous diversions, we might add, from the anti-Communist struggle also.

Koestler's new fervour sets out to be as fierce as his old. Only he now denounces what he once idealised. He condemns himself for being blind and ignorant. But it is difficult to believe that his new judgements are any more reliable. A political authority who took as long as Koestler did in facing the evil side of Soviet Communism has surely disqualified himself as a guide for the future. Instead of beating a new and bigger drum even more loudly than before, he had better retire from the band. And this is what Koestler has really done, though he is unwilling to admit it. The greatest virtues of his autobiography are not political penetration or religious mysticism; they are 'humour and eccentricity'. *Struwwelpeter* was written as a warning tale; but it has brought entertainment to countless nurseries. Koestler would like us to see in him the fanatic of anti-Communism, the martyr in search of a stake; and we do our best. But he preaches with such gusto, describes his sufferings with such gaiety, that we pay him the greatest of compliments. We refuse to take him seriously. He has qualified as an honorary member of the Pickwick Club.

Jean-Paul Sartre: The Far Side of Despair

Unsigned

In our age, there is one besetting moral problem: what attitude to adopt towards Communism. There is, therefore, a unique and universal significance in the ratiocinations of a man whose formidable intellectual energy has been devoted exclusively to its solution. Jean-Paul Sartre is a playwright of genius, an incisive pamphleteer and controversialist, a writer of ideological novels, a schematic philosopher, an anti-Freudian psychologist, a brilliant teacher and editor, and a professional Left Bank *mandarin*. But through each and all of these activities runs a unifying thread: the search for an intellectual reconciliation with the dominant material and political force of our times.

Nobody else has made the attempt in such a systematic and determined manner, or been so ruthless in eliminating extraneous considerations. The Koestlers and Silones have surrendered to rigid moral imperatives, the Kanapas and Aragons have embraced dogmatism. But Sartre, with his fanatical – almost irrational – belief in reason, has marched doggedly on into the dark tunnel. Somewhere within the mind of this dwarflike sage, behind the thick spectacles, the angry eyes, the fleshy facial mask with its wide and sensual mouth, the decisive intellectual battle of our century is being fought in microcosm.

Yet, despite the single-mindedness of Sartre's aim and the logical symmetry of his intellectual development, no great thinker has been more misunderstood and provoked such violent and conflicting reactions. Sartre has been denounced as 'unfathomably obscure' (Raymond Aron) and as 'a deliberate vulgariser' (Merleau-Ponty). *L'Être et le Néant* was once called 'the most difficult philosophical work ever written'; yet *L'Existentialisme Est Un Humanisme* has sold more copies (150,000) than any other volume of modern philosophy. The Vatican has placed his works on the Index; yet Gabriel Marcel, himself a militant Catholic, regarded him as the greatest of French thinkers.

The State Department found his novels subversive; but *Les Mains Sales* was the most effective counter-revolutionary play of the entire Cold War. Sartre has been vilified by the Communists in Paris and fêted by them in Vienna. No great philosopher ever had fewer disciples; but no other could claim the intellectual conquest of an entire generation.

Amid the bitter hatreds and controversies of which Sartre has been the centre, his principal objective – and the logical concentration with which he has pursued it – has tended to become obscured. Around the man has grown a myth; and around the myth, foggy, concentric rings of intellectual prejudice. When we strip the layers, however, we find that increasingly rare – indeed, today, unique – phenomenon: a complete philosophical system, an interlocking chain of speculation which unites truth, literature and politics in one gigantic equation.

In the late Thirties, Sartre was a young, underpaid, over-educated philosophy teacher in a smart Paris school, a member – and a typical one – of the most discontented, numerically inflated and socially dangerous group in the world: the French bourgeois intellectuals. He had studied Heidegger and Kierkegaard in Germany; he taught Descartes in France. Like all intellectuals, he asked himself the question: had his knowledge any relevance to the problems of his day? The Fascists were at the gates of Madrid; what was he supposed to do about it? Why had Blum failed? Did it matter that Stalin had seen fit to murder the Old Guard of the Bolsheviks? Why was capitalism in ruins, Hitler triumphant, the democracies afraid?

It is typical of Sartre that he began his search for the answers to these problems by reformulating them at an abstract level. *La Nausée* (1938), his first major work, is an imaginative inquiry into the problems of existence. Roquentin, its autobiographical and solitary hero, discovers that the bourgeois world in which he lives is senseless and incoherent. His past no longer exists, his future is unknown, his present unrelated; life has no pattern. Through Roquentin's introspective reveries, Sartre presents his fundamental metaphysical image: a loathing for the incompleteness of existence in the world as he finds it, a longing for completeness which is both intelligible and creative. If Kafka's *The Trial* epitomises the nightmare of the ordinary man in a hostile and incomprehensible world, *La Nausée* is the nightmare of the philosopher, in which physical fear is replaced by intellectual disgust.

*

Under the impact of the war, Sartre's view of existence acquired firmer outline and greater depth. By 1943 he had completed, in *L'Être et le Néant*, a full exposition of his Existentialist philosophy, which concluded his exploration of the problem at an abstract level. In it, he succeeded in isolating the fundamental dilemma. Like Wittgenstein, he bluntly denied the existence of value ('In the world everything is as it is and happens as it does happen. In it there is no value'), and concluded that meaning and purpose do not reside as objective facts in the world of things. Man's sense of value – which he defined as essentially a sense of incompleteness – could never, therefore, be satisfied, and value itself – stable, lived totality – could never be achieved. Yet man is a creature who requires value, 'a being who aspires to be God'. Despite the impossibility of his task, he continues to pursue his desire for completeness. Hence his agony, because his life is a vain quest: *'L'Homme est une passion inutile.'* Could the dilemma be solved? Sartre asked. And, if so, how? By self-destruction? By social organisation? Was there an intellectual Third Force between the extremes of resignation and despair?

Inevitably, Sartre was intellectually drawn into the world, and into its highest organisational manifestation: politics. In his plays and, above all, in his long novel-cycle, *Les Chemins de la Liberté*, he began to reformulate his problem at a concrete level. In abstract terms, he had calculated that the dilemma was insoluble, and that a Third Force was not viable. As the postwar years unfolded, he saw his calculations – like Einstein's – proved correct by empirical observation. The world polarised into the capitalist and Communist extremes. His own political group proved a noisy failure. The Socialists were prised apart from the Communists and imprisoned on the right. Sartre could not accept the intellectual limitations of Communism: 'Marxist doctrine,' he wrote, 'has been withering away; for want of internal controversy it has been degraded to a stupid determinism.' Yet neither could he accept the world as he found it. What, then, was he to do? Already, by 1948, when he wrote *What Is Literature?*, he was conscious of the impotence and isolation of his own position. 'We bourgeois,' he wrote, 'who have broken with our class but who remain bourgeois in our moral values, separated from the proletariat by the Communist screen, remain up in the air; our good will serves no one, not even ourselves ... we are writing against the current.' As the Cold War progressed, Sartre found his position more and more intolerable. He slowly came round to the view that the Communist Party, despite its bad faith and intellectual sterility, was the objective personification of the workers, and this led him to the agonising conclusion, which he puts into the mouth of one of his characters: 'If the party is right, I am more lonely than a madman; if the party is wrong, the world is done for.' Could he remain intellectually neutral? And, if so, for how long? By 1952, when the Cold War seemed to be moving irresistibly towards the ultimate catastrophe, Sartre had decided to take sides. After all, he reasoned, in Marxism, as in Existentialism, the search for truth in action is the central, reconciling feature. The Marxist vision of the world is completeness; the system it has created is evil only in so far as it is fallible. If we presuppose that the system is perfectible, any of its aspects to which we object – for non-philosophical reasons, for instance – can simply be dismissed as imperfections. By this time, Sartre was willing to make the decisive presupposition. His conversion was a piece of philosophical legerdemain – a case of the intellectual end justifying the intellectual means. But it brought his mind four-square with his moral conscience, because it satisfied his basic moral compulsion to be at one with the working class.

Even so, Sartre took sides in a characteristically complicated manner. He refused to join the party: on his own premises, he could not organically ally himself with a system which demanded, of necessity, absolute mental discipline and which, though perfectible, was not yet perfect. But, at the same time, he accepted the consequences of his choice in the spirit in which he had made it. Of all the fellow-travellers, he became the most impeccable. He repudiated his anti-Communist writings and disowned a new production of *Les Mains Sales*. His latest play, *Nekrassov*, is the pure, strong milk of Communist satire: the little bits of Existentialism which refused to fit into the mould were pummelled either into Marxism or out of sight.

His slavish orthodoxy, in fact, has led him into grave embarrassments. A philosophical certainty made him join forces with the Communists; but a geographical accident placed him under the intellectual suzerainty of the French Communist Party. He thus became a spokesman of the party which, above and beyond all the rest, has always been, and remains, the most Stalinist. When, therefore, the 20th Party Congress in Moscow signalised the liberating event for which Sartre, along with so many others, had waited for so long, he was placed in an impossible quandary. He, of all people, could not observe the surly silence of *L'Humanité*. But if he chose to comment, he would inevitably be forced to acclaim the news from Moscow in terms which could objectively be construed as criticism of his local hierarchs. His position was made even more difficult by the fact that a leading Communist intellectual, Pierre Hervé, had chosen to jump the gun and had been promptly expelled for his pains. Sartre should, from an intellectual – even from a doctrinal – point of view, have applauded Hervé's gesture. But his position as a French fellow-traveller – and therefore as a faithful ally of the top brass of the French CP – made such a move, from a political point of view, impossible. Nevertheless, everyone expected Sartre to comment on Hervé's book, and comment he dutifully did, struggling manfully to reconcile the irreconcilable. It was not a very happy performance, and in the weeks that have followed, the *mandarins* of the non-Communist Left have used Sartre as an easy target for some intellectual firing-practice. 'Sartre,' one of them commented, 'is now merely a figure of fun.'

Their contempt, even their pity, is understandable. For Sartre made his choice between two irreconcilable systems just before the 20th Congress made that kind of choice obsolete. Convinced that the march towards Communism could not be halted, Sartre set out to guide other intellectuals who, he believed, must follow him in seeking a reconciliation between their philosophical beliefs and the harsher realities of life under Stalin-style Communism. Rationalising his own commitment, his own misjudgement, he went over to the Communists because he thought, as Oreste remarks in *Les Mouches*, that 'it is on the far side of despair that life begins.'

Here lies the tragedy of his choice. In the Communist countries, the intellectuals are now seeking the road back from the far side of despair, and of all living thinkers none is so well qualified by intellect, and sympathy, to aid them as Jean-Paul Sartre. Unhappily he too has to find his way back.

The Man We Trusted

John Freeman

The most grievous assassination in modern history has transformed John Kennedy from an embattled president, deadlocked with a hostile and suspicious Congress, into the brightest legend of our time. It was inevitable. The shock and the grief are universal and so great. Emotions have poured out – and they have gilded the truth. Yet that too may be misleading, for the emotions were part of the truth; and if Kennedy is remembered, as I think he may be, along with Lincoln and FDR as one of the great presidents, it will be more because he captured the imagination of a whole generation in almost every corner of the world than because he succeeded in fulfilling the purposes to which he dedicated his presidency.

His great achievement, for which the world outside America chiefly honours him this week, was his leadership of the western alliance. When he took over, we walked in the shadow of nuclear war. Two years and 10 months later, the dialogue between the White House and the Kremlin has proceeded so far that no one can doubt the genuineness of Krushchev's dismay at the young President's death. Yet he wrought this change without any surrender of vital interest, by strength and not by weakness. He persuaded Krushchev that negotiations were practicable, because he was himself clear about what could be negotiated – and firm about what could not. The test-ban treaty and the hotline are the visible signs of a business relation between the Soviet bloc and the West, in which each side recognises the power of the other and the suicidal folly of pressing points of difference to the brink of war.

Kennedy's achievement in all this was not one-sided. Nuclear war would be as deadly to Russia as to the West, and Krushchev has played his part. But few would deny that the initiative has lain most of the time with the White House or that Kennedy's own qualities have been decisive. The three personal gifts which lifted him into the realm of international statesmanship were intellect, steadiness of nerve and the capacity to take decisions. Indeed, this week's inevitable anxiety about the future is based not on half-baked guesses about President Johnson's capacity or intelligence as a politician, but on the fact that the decision-making machine – largely extra-governmental – which Kennedy created to meet his own needs proved so uniquely well-suited to the strategic demands of the Cold War. The doubt must exist whether President Johnson, operating through more normal political channels, will be able to match the speed, logic and certainty of his predecessor. For Kennedy's decisions were his own. The professors, the soldiers, the computers, seldom the professional politicians, were detailed to provide the data and rehearse the arguments. The President listened, reflected, balanced the equation and, fortified by all that intellect and calculation could bring to bear, finally took the decision.

Naturally this method of government was unpopular on Capitol Hill, and the unpopularity was reflected in Kennedy's inability to secure from Congress either the money or the legislation he needed to implement his domestic policies. And this inability amounted to something like failure. Whether it stemmed fundamentally from a lack of profound conviction about liberal causes with which he was saddled by his 1960 campaign-managers, or from the intellectual's contempt for the log-rolling of the workaday politicians, or from over-caution about the electoral consequences of controversy, or from a constitutional inadequacy of Congress to live with the speed of modern decision-making will long be argued by American historians. What we can say this week is that, despite his visible achievement in foreign affairs, the quality of Kennedy's presidency as a whole – apart from the noble and historic decision to stake the whole prestige of the presidency on his civil rights legislation – is arguable.

His quality as a man is to me beyond argument. He brought to public life not only the hard assets of leadership which determined his actions, but the rarest capacity to illuminate ideas by the grace of his personality and the clarity of his speech. One can only guess, for instance, at the legislative outcome of his battle with Congress and his own party over civil rights. But one can be sure that individual

American opinion about the cause of justice for the Negroes has been touched, as never since Lincoln, by the words he spoke.

Perhaps his greatest achievement in the end was to turn the gaze of his own people towards some of the more distant goals of political action and to infuse his pragmatic programmes with the radiant light of tolerance, idealism and purpose. If so, the glossy wrappings of the New Frontier may be remembered as a permanent landmark in the evolution of American democracy.

'And so, my fellow Americans: ask not what your country can do for you – ask what you can do for your country. My fellow citizens of the world: ask not what America will do for you, but what together we can do for the freedom of man.' Those words struck the keynote of his inaugural address; they form a message which evokes a response in every radical heart. However limited his social achievement, his approach to politics was fundamentally a challenge to conservatism everywhere. That is why, with all our reservations about where his ultimate convictions lay – they certainly did not lie with the ideological left – and with all our disappointment at his comparative failure to make good the promise of 1960, the left in Britain admired and, when the chips were down, trusted him. He was the golden boy of the postwar world, and we mourn him as a friend.

A Fallen Woman

Claire Tomalin

Two o'clock – My dear love, after making my arrangements for our snug dinner today, I have been taken by storm, and obliged to promise to dine, at an early hour, with the Miss —s, the *only* day they had intended to pass here. I shall however leave the key in the door, and hope to find you at my fireside when I return, about eight o'clock. Will you not wait for poor Joan? – whom you will find better, and till then think very affectionately of her.

How many novels start as well as this? It is a love letter, written in a city in revolution, from an eminent bluestocking lady of 34 to a captain in the American army. The date is 1793, the town Paris, the woman Mary Wollstonecraft; for all her professed allegiance to Reason, her letters speak of spontaneity, warmth, clinging affection and a sensibility that makes Marianne Dashwood seem a model of prudence and steadiness in comparison. As someone who has 'always been half in love' with J. J. Rousseau, Mary gives free rein to her feelings and her expression of them.

The letters are extraordinary; they describe, directly and fluently, the sensations and emotions of love and longing, and of pregnancy and motherhood, with a frankness not equalled again in England until the twentieth century. Mary possessed a melancholy temperament and her love affair was mostly a matter of separations and disappointments (hence the abundance of letters); but she could be spirited and happy, especially when talking of her baby or imagining good days ahead. Here and there she adopts a highflown manner, usually when she begins to preach to her errant lover; much more often she writes, as the best letter writers do, with the appearance of being off her guard: 'when my heart is warm, pop come the expressions of my childhood into my head'; 'I do not want to be loved like a goddess; but I wish to be necessary to you'; 'If you do not return soon ... I will throw your slippers out at window, and be off – nobody knows where.' Missing him, she 'makes the most of the comfort of the pillow', turning to the side of the bed where he lay. She meets friends who observe she is with child: 'let them stare! ... all the world may know it for aught I care! – Yet I wish to avoid —'s coarse jokes.' She feels the 'little twitcher' move inside her, speculates whether it sleeps and wakes, grows anxious when it is still: 'I sat down in an agony till I felt those said twitches again.'

The letters tell their own story, but it is as well to fill in the background. Mary, fresh from the success of her *Vindication of the Rights of Woman*, but suffering from an unreciprocated passion for the artist Fuseli, decided to visit Paris in December 1792. The French admired her and at first she admired the revolution. Her circle included Tom Paine and the Helen Maria Williams to whom Wordsworth addressed a sonnet. In the spring of 1793 she met, at the house of an English friend, Gilbert Imlay, an American who had fought in the War of Independence [and] written a still readable book on the topography of Kentucky and Ohio as well as an overblown novel, *The Emigrants*, aimed at reforming English divorce law and proclaiming the idyllic possibilities of life in the American wilderness.

Imlay has been roughly handled by Mary's biographers for his treatment of her, but I find it impossible not to have some sympathy for him; clearly he got himself into a false position; he had neither the nature to settle into matrimony nor the strength of mind to break off the affair which seemed so sacred and binding to her. Probably he was bowled over by her fame, her charm and her unusual sexual forwardness; the wooing was very swift. An early meeting place was at the Neuilly tollgate, known to them as the 'barrier' (*la barrière*); the child, conceived there, was often referred to as the 'barrier-girl' and Imlay's good moods as his 'barrier-face'.

They went through no marriage ceremony, but Mary registered herself with the American ambassador under the name Imlay (probably as a protection against imprisonment, to which English subjects became liable when war was declared). Both lovers at times referred to her as a wife, but Mary spoke cheerfully about not having 'clogged' her soul by promising obedience; their arrangement was of that semi-formal variety most difficult to manage smoothly. In spite of a grumble or two, she was delighted with her pregnancy, having strong theoretical views about maternity; but already Imlay was called away on business, the first of many separations that indicate the rapid cooling of his attachment.

At least they provided us with Mary's letters: her love, her reproaches, her self-chastisement for doubting him, her joy in the child. She followed Imlay to Le Havre, where Fanny was born in May 1794, under the care of an admiring midwife. 'Nothing could be more natural or easy than my labour,' she wrote to a woman friend. She was out walking eight days after the birth, and suckled her child: 'My little Girl begins to suck so Manfully that her father reckons saucily on her writing the second part of the R—ts of Woman.'

Soon Imlay was off again, and the story grows sadder and sadder as she travels with the baby to Paris, London, and then, on Imlay's business, to Scandinavia. His infidelities drove her to desperation and she twice projected suicide, the second time saturating her clothes before walking into the Thames (Mirah's method in *Daniel Deronda*; Charles Kegan Paul suggested that George Eliot was inspired by Mary). She was rescued by friends and Imlay tried to behave 'kindly' towards her; but kindness, when one looks for love, is the worst torture:

> I never wanted but your heart – That gone, you have nothing more to give. Had I only poverty to fear, I should not shrink from life. – Forgive me then, if I say, that I shall consider any direct or indirect attempt to supply my necessities, as an insult which I have not merited. I have been hurt by indirect enquiries, which appear to me not to be dictated by any tenderness to me. –You ask 'If I am well or tranquil' – They who think me so, must want a heart to estimate my feelings by.

But Mary's behaviour could be trying; on one occasion she rushed into a room where Imlay was sitting with some friends and thrust the two-year-old Fanny on to his lap. This was typical of one aspect of her – the impulsive, dramatising side – but equally she knew how to pull herself together again. The most important and affecting aspect of the letters is their picture of a woman refusing to accept that she is 'ruined', a resourceless victim of seduction and abandonment; she goes down into the depths of misery again and again, but repeatedly determines to be rational and independent, to learn to cope with her situation both emotionally and financially and to give up her lover, in the end, without bitterness or demands. It was not easy for her, jealous, passionate, agonised for her child: 'my little darling is calling papa, and adding her parrot word – Come, come!' There is something heroic in her final words to Imlay: 'I part with you in peace.'

The story of the publication of the letters provides a tragi-comic epilogue. Few love letters survive, and those that do generally remain unpublished for decades; but Imlay preserved these and returned them at Mary's request. In 1797 she married William Godwin and died within a few months in childbirth; whereupon this odd man, as an act of devoted homage, published her impassioned letters to her former lover. Deeply mistrustful of violent emotion at first hand, he seems to have been fascinated by the evidence of it at one remove; at any rate, though he tried to calm the Wollstonecraft temperament in Mary and later her daughters (Fanny and Mary, who married Shelley), he greatly admired it in her words to another man. Perhaps he felt safer thus. His preface begins: 'The following letters may possibly be found to contain the finest examples of the language of sentiment and passion ever presented to the world.' Godwin's action in publishing them called down the satirical contempt of his opponents. Even Mary's supporters thought he had done her a disservice; an anonymous defender writing in 1803 attacked Godwin for his failure to protect her reputation by silence about her personal life. He was probably right; the eclipse of Mary Wollstonecraft in the nineteenth century can be partly attributed to Godwin's revelations, which shocked middle and upper classes alike: a revolutionary thinker and unchaste to boot!

Godwin expunged Imlay's name from his edition, but it was generally known: he was ill regarded and disappeared from the scene, never (as far as we know) taking any interest in Fanny; he is thought to have died in Jersey in 1828. Fanny was kindly brought up by Godwin; her step-sisters Mary and Claire Clairmont were lively girls, but she was melancholic and committed suicide, alone in a Swansea inn to which she had travelled for the purpose, in October 1816; a sadly effective repetition of her mother's efforts.

Mary's letters were reprinted in 1879 by Charles Kegan Paul and again in 1908 by Roger Ingpen. Both editors felt obliged to explain away and apologise for some of her behaviour and freedom of speech, and Ingpen quaintly dismissed Imlay as a 'typical American', always dashing about on business. The only good modern biography is a long and meticulously scholarly one by another American, Ralph Wardle. Mary Wollstonecraft is not much known in this age when we are able to be more understanding of her behaviour and also of her lover's. Perhaps it is time for a new edition of her letters.

6 JULY 1973

David Bowie: 'A Mild Fad'

Martin Amis

When Glam-Rock superstar David Bowie flounced on to the Hammersmith Odeon stage last Monday night, recognisably male and not even partially naked, it seemed that we would be denied the phenomenon-of-our-times spectacle which your reporter was banking on. The preludial ambience, too, was discouragingly humdrum: behind me in the audience upper-class slummers boomingly voiced their fears of having to endure a 'really grotty' supporting band; in front of me teenage couples snogged with old-fashioned – not to say reactionary – zeal; beside me a joint was lit and furtively extinguished; and on stage, prior to curtain-up, a fat old teddy-boy appeared, asked Hammersmith if it was feeling good, wanted a louder answer, got one, and left us with a lie about the anticipated time lapse before Mr Bowie's arrival. Once under way, admittedly, that musician went through various stages of déshabillé – now in orange rompers, now a miniskirt, now in hot-pants, now a leotard – but we never got to see the famous silver catsuit and pink jockstrap. Bowie did, it's true, have a habit of turning away from the audience and sulkily twitching his backside at it before floating off to arouse each aisle in turn with his silky gaze – but there was no sign of the celebrated sodomistic routine involving lead guitarist Mick Ronson, no acts of stylised masturbation and fellatio with microphone and mikestand. Perhaps Mr Bowie just wasn't feeling up to it that evening, or perhaps Mr Bowie was just a mild fad hystericised by 'the media', an entrepreneur of camp who knew how little, as well as how much, he could get away with.

But despite these austerities the superstar's dinky weapon of a torso remained the centrepiece of the concert. When Bowie entered, half the audience rushed the stage and the other half got to its feet; during the interval, the fat teddy-boy lumbered on to coax and cajole everyone back to their places; when Bowie re-entered, half the audience rushed the stage and the other half got to its feet – or its knees. Interestingly, this physical presence was exerted with none of the Grand-Guignol goonery of an Alice Cooper (black leather and bull-whips) or a Gary Glitter (moronic foot-stomping), and without any of the sincere, and therefore quite charmless, exhibitionism of the beefy Mr Ronson. For all his preening and swanking Bowie often seemed a frail, almost waiflike figure, curiously dwarfed by the electric aura of knowing sexiness and modish violence on which his act depends – panicky strobes, dizzying light effects, a *Clockwork Orange*-theme *ritornello*, and SS lightning-flashes.

This incongruity may be responsible for Bowie's appeal and for what (if anything) is sinister about it. Among certain more affluent hippies Bowie is apparently the symbol of a kind of thrilling extremism, a life-style (the word is for once permissible) characterised by sexual omnivorousness, lavish use of stimulants – particularly cocaine, very much an elitist drug, being both expensive and galvanising – self-parodied narcissism, and a glamorously early death. To dignify this unhappy outlook with such a term as 'nihilist' would, of course, be absurd; but Bowie does appear to be a new focus for the vague, predatory, escapist reveries of the alienated young. Although Bowie himself is unlikely to last long as a cult, it is hard to believe that the feelings he has aroused or aggravated will vanish along with the fashion built round him.

Why Allende Had to Die

Gabriel García Márquez

Almost fifty years have passed since the Chilean president Salvador Allende died at La Moneda Palace in Santiago, attempting to defend himself with an AK-47 he had been given by Fidel Castro. Here, in a piece from the New Statesman *published in 1974, the Nobel Prize-winning novelist Gabriel García Márquez explores Allende's record in Chile, his rivals' dealings with the United States and the rise of his successor – the army general Augusto Pinochet.*

It was towards the end of 1969 that three generals from the Pentagon dined with five Chilean military officers in a house in the suburbs of Washington. The host was Lieutenant Colonel Gerardo López Angulo, assistant air attaché of the Chilean Military Mission to the United States, and the Chilean guests were his colleagues from the other branches of service. The dinner was in honour of the new director of the Chilean Air Force Academy, General Carlos Toro Mazote, who had arrived the day before on a study mission. The eight officers dined on fruit salad, roast veal and peas and drank the warm-hearted wines of their distant homeland to the south, where birds glittered on the beaches while Washington wallowed in snow, and they talked mostly in English about the only thing that seemed to interest Chileans in those days: the approaching presidential elections of the following September. Over dessert, one of the Pentagon generals asked what the Chilean army would do if the candidate of the left, someone like Salvador Allende, were elected. General Toro Mazote replied: 'We'll take Moneda Palace in half an hour, even if we have to burn it down.'

One of the guests was General Ernesto Baeza, now director of national security in Chile, the one who led the attack on the presidential palace during the coup last September and gave the order to burn it. Two of his subordinates in those earlier days were to become famous in the same operation: General Augusto Pinochet, president of the military junta, and General Javier Palacios. Also at the table was Air Force Brigadier General Sergio Figueroa Gutiérrez, now minister of public works and the intimate friend of another member of the military junta, Air Force General Gustavo Leigh, who ordered the rocket bombing of the presidential palace. The last guest was Admiral Arturo Troncoso, now naval governor of Valparaíso, who carried out the bloody purge of progressive naval officers and was one of those who launched the military uprising of 11 September.

That dinner proved to be a historic meeting between the Pentagon and high-ranking officers of the Chilean military services. On other successive meetings, in Washington and Santiago, a contingency plan was agreed upon, according to which those Chilean military men who were bound most closely, heart and soul, to US interests would seize power in the event of Allende's Popular Unity coalition victory in the elections.

The plan was conceived cold-bloodedly, as a simple military operation, and was not a consequence of pressure brought to bear by International Telephone and Telegraph. It was spawned by much deeper reasons of world politics. On the North American side, the organisation set in motion was the Defence Intelligence Agency of the Pentagon but the one in actual charge was the naval intelligence agency, under the higher political direction of the CIA, and the National Security Council. It was quite the normal thing to put the navy and not the army in charge of the project, for the Chilean coup was to coincide with Operation Unitas, which was the name given to the joint manoeuvres of American and Chilean naval units in the Pacific. Those manoeuvres were held at the end of each September, the same month as the elections, and the appearance on land and in the skies of Chile of all manner of war equipment and men well trained in the arts and sciences of death was natural.

During that period, Henry Kissinger had said in private to a group of Chileans: 'I am not interested in, nor do I know anything about, the southern portion of the world from the Pyrenees on down.' By that time, the contingency plan had been completed to its smallest details and it is impossible to suppose that Kissinger or President Nixon himself was not aware of it.

Chile is a narrow country, some 2,660 miles long and an average of 119 wide, and with ten million exuberant inhabitants, almost three million of whom live in the metropolitan area of Santiago, the capital. The country's greatness is derived not from the number of virtues it possesses but, rather, from its many singularities. The only thing it produces with any absolute seriousness is copper ore but that ore is the best in the world and its volume of production is surpassed only by that of the United States and the Soviet Union. It also produces wine as good as the European varieties but not much of it is exported. Its per capita income of $650 ranks among the highest in Latin America but, traditionally, almost half the gross national product has been accounted for by fewer than 300,000 people.

In 1932, Chile became the first socialist republic in the Americas and, with the enthusiastic support of the workers, the government attempted the nationalisation of copper and coal. The experiment lasted only for 13 days. Chile has an earth tremor on average once every two days and a devastating earthquake every presidential term. The least apocalyptic of geologists think of Chile not as a country of the mainland but as a cornice of the Andes in a misty sea and believe that the whole of its national territory is condemned to disappear in some future cataclysm.

Chileans are very much like their country in a certain way. They are the most pleasant people on the continent, they like being alive and they know how to live in the best way possible and even a little more; but they have a dangerous tendency toward scepticism and intellectual speculation. A Chilean once told me on a Monday, 'No Chilean believes tomorrow is Tuesday,' and he didn't believe it, either. Still, even with that deep-seated incredulity – or thanks to it, perhaps – the Chileans have attained a degree of natural civilisation, a political maturity and a level of culture, that sets them apart from the rest of the region. Of the three Nobel Prizes in Literature that Latin America has won, two have gone to Chileans, one of whom, Pablo Neruda, was the greatest poet of this century.

Kissinger may have known this when he said that he knew nothing about the southern part of the world. In any case, US intelligence agencies knew a great deal more. In 1965, without Chile's permission, the nation became the staging centre and a recruiting locale for a fantastic social and political espionage operation: Project Camelot. This was to have been a secret investigation that would have precise questionnaires put to people of all social levels, all professions and trades, even in the furthest reaches of a number of Latin American nations, in order to establish in a scientific way the degree of political development and the social tendencies of various social groups. The questionnaire destined for the military contained the same question that the Chilean officers would hear again at the dinner in Washington: what will their position be if communism comes to power? It was a wild query.

Chile had long been a favoured area for research by North American social scientists. The age and strength of its popular movement, the tenacity and intelligence of its leaders and the economic and social conditions themselves afforded a glimpse of the country's destiny. One didn't require the findings of a Project Camelot to venture the belief that Chile was a prime candidate to be the second socialist republic in Latin America after Cuba. The aim of the United States, therefore, was not simply to prevent the government of Allende from coming to power in order to protect American investments. The larger aim was to repeat the most fruitful operation that imperialism has ever helped bring off in Latin America: Brazil.

On 4 September 1970, as had been foreseen, the socialist and Freemason physician Allende was elected president of the republic. The contingency plan was not put into effect, however. The most widespread explanation is also the most ludicrous: someone made a mistake in the Pentagon and requested 200 visas for a purported navy chorus, which, in reality, was to be made up of specialists in government overthrow; however, there were several admirals among them who couldn't sing a single note. That gaffe, it is to be supposed, determined the postponement of the adventure. The truth is that the project had been evaluated in depth: other American agencies, particularly the CIA, and the American ambassador to Chile felt that the contingency plan was too strictly a military operation and did not take current political and social conditions in Chile into account. Indeed, the Popular Unity victory did not bring on the social panic US intelligence had expected. On the contrary, the new government's independence in international affairs and its decisiveness in economic matters immediately created an atmosphere of social celebration.

During the first year, 47 industrial firms were nationalised, along with most of the banking system. Agrarian reform saw the expropriation and incorporation into communal property of six million acres of land formerly held by the large landowners. The inflationary process was slowed, full employment was attained and wages received a cash rise of 30 per cent.

ALL COPPER NATIONALISED

The previous government, headed by the Christian Democrat Eduardo Frei, had begun steps towards nationalising copper, though he called it 'Chileanisation'. All the plan did was to buy up 51 per cent of US-held mining properties and for the mine of El Teniente alone it paid a sum greater than the total book value of that facility.

Popular Unity, with a single legal act supported in Congress by all of the nation's popular parties, recovered for the nation all copper deposits worked by the subsidiaries of the American companies Anaconda and Kennecott. Without indemnification: the government having calculated that the two companies had made a profit in excess of $800m over 15 years.

The petite bourgeoisie and the middle class, the two great social forces that might have supported a military coup at that moment, were beginning to enjoy unforeseen advantages and not at the expense of the proletariat, as had always been the case, but, rather, at the expense of the financial oligarchy and foreign capital. The armed forces, as a social group, have the same origins and ambitions as the middle class, so they had no motive, not even an alibi, to back the tiny group of coup-minded officers. Aware of that reality, the Christian Democrats not only did not support the barracks plot at that time but resolutely opposed it, for they knew it was unpopular among their own rank and file.

Their objective was something else again: to use any means possible to impair the good health of the government so as to win two-thirds of the seats in Congress in the March 1973 elections. With such a majority, they could vote for the constitutional removal of the president of the republic.

The Christian Democrats make up a huge organisation cutting across class lines, with an authentic popular base among the modern industrial proletariat, the small and middle-sized rural landowners and the petite bourgeoisie and middle class of the cities. Popular Unity, while also inter-class in its make-up, was the expression of workers of the less-favoured proletariat – the agricultural proletariat – and the lower middle class of the cities. The Christian Democrats, allied with the extreme right-wing National Party, controlled the Congress and the courts; Popular Unity controlled the executive. The polarisation of these two parties was to be, in effect, the polarisation of the country. Curiously, the Catholic Frei, who doesn't believe in Marxism, was the one who took the best advantage of the class struggle, the one who stimulated it and brought it to a head, with an aim to unhinge the government and plunge the country into the abyss of demoralisation and economic disaster.

The economic blockade by the United States, because of expropriation without indemnification, did the rest. All kinds of goods are manufactured in Chile, from automobiles to toothpaste, but this industrial base has a false identity: in the 160 most important firms, 60 per cent of the capital was foreign and 80 per cent of the basic materials came from abroad. In addition, the country needed $300m a year in order to import consumer goods and another $450m to pay the interest on its foreign debt.

But Chile's urgent needs were extraordinary and went much deeper. The jolly ladies of the bourgeoisie, under the pretext of protesting rationing, galloping inflation and the demands made by the poor, took to the streets, beating their empty pots and pans.

It wasn't by chance, quite the contrary; it was very significant that that street spectacle of silver foxes and flowered hats took place on the same afternoon that Fidel Castro was ending a 30-day visit that had brought an earthquake of social mobilisation of government supporters.

SEED OF DESTRUCTION

President Allende understood then – and he said so – that the people held the government but they did not hold the power. The phrase was more bitter than it seemed and also more alarming, for inside himself Allende carried a legalist germ that held the seed of his own destruction: a man who fought to the death in defence of legality, he would have been capable of walking out of La Moneda Palace with his head held high if the Congress had removed him from office within the bounds of the constitution.

The Italian journalist and politician Rossana Rossanda, who visited Allende during that period, found him aged, tense and full of gloomy premonitions as he talked to her from the yellow cretonne couch where, seven months later, his riddled body was to lie, the face crushed in by a rifle butt. Then, on the eve of the March 1973 elections, in which his destiny was at stake, he would have been content with 36 per cent of the vote for Popular Unity. And yet, in spite of runaway inflation, stern rationing and the pot-and-pan concert of the merry wives of the upper-class districts, he received 44 per cent. It was such a spectacular and decisive victory that when Allende was alone in his office with his friend and confidant, the journalist Augusto Olivares, he closed the door and danced a *cueca* all by himself.

For the Christian Democrats, it was proof that the process of social justice set in motion by the Popular Unity coalition could not be turned back by legal means but they lacked the vision to measure the consequences of the actions they then undertook. For the United States, the election was a much more serious warning and went beyond the simple interests of expropriated firms. It was an inadmissible precedent for peaceful progress and social change for the peoples of the world, particularly those in France and Italy, where present conditions make an attempt at an experiment along the lines of Chile possible. All forces of internal and external reaction came together to form a compact bloc.

CIA-FINANCED FINAL BLOW

The truck owners' strike was the final blow. Because of the wild geography of the country, the Chilean economy is at the mercy of its transport. To paralyse trucking is to paralyse the country. It was easy for the opposition to co-ordinate the strike, for the truckers' guild was one of the groups most affected by the scarcity of replacement parts and, in addition, it found itself threatened by the government's small pilot programme for providing adequate state trucking services in the extreme south of the nation. The stoppage lasted until the very end without a single moment of relief because it was financed with cash from outside. 'The CIA flooded the country with dollars to support the strike by the bosses and ... foreign capital found its way down into the formation of a black market,' Pablo Neruda wrote to a friend in Europe. One week before the coup, oil, milk and bread had run out.

During the last days of Popular Unity, with the economy unhinged and the country on the verge of civil war, the manoeuvring of the government and the opposition centred on the hope of changing the balance of power in the armed forces in favour of one or the other. The final move was hallucinatory in its perfection: 48 hours before the coup, the opposition managed to disqualify all high-ranking officers supporting Allende and to promote in their places, one by one, in a series of inconceivable gambits, all of the officers who had been present at the dinner in Washington.

At that moment, however, the political chess game had got out of the control of its players. Dragged along by an irreversible dialectic, they themselves ended up as pawns in a much larger game of chess, one much more complex and politically more important than any mere scheme hatched in conjunction by imperialism and the reaction against the government of the people. It was a terrifying class confrontation that was slipping out of the hands of the very people who had provoked it, a cruel and fierce scramble by counterposed interests, and the final outcome had to be a social cataclysm without precedent in the history of the Americas.

A military coup under those conditions would not be bloodless. Allende knew it.

The Chilean armed forces, contrary to what we have been led to believe, have intervened in politics every time that their class interests have seemed threatened and they have done so with an inordinately repressive ferocity. The two constitutions that the country has had in the past 100 years were imposed by force of arms and the recent military coup has been the sixth uprising in a period of 50 years.

The bloodlust of the Chilean army is part of its birthright, coming from that terrible school of hand-to-hand combat against the Araucanian Indians, a struggle that lasted 300 years. One of its forerunners boasted in 1620 of having killed more than 2,000 people with his own hands in a single action. Joaquín Edwards Bello relates in his chronicles that during an epidemic of exanthematic typhus the army dragged sick people out of their houses and killed them in a poison bath in order to put an end to the plague. During a seven-month civil war in 1891, 10,000 died in a series of gory encounters. The Peruvians assert that during the occupation of Lima in the war of the Pacific, Chilean soldiers sacked the library of Don Ricardo Palma, taking the books not for reading but for wiping their backsides.

HISTORY OF BRUTALITY

Popular movements have been suppressed with the same brutality. After the Valparaíso earthquake of 1906, naval forces wiped out the longshoremen's organisation of 8,000 workers. In Iquique, at the beginning of the century, demonstrating strikers tried to take refuge from the troops and were machine-gunned: within ten minutes, there were 2,000 dead. On 2 April 1957, the army broke up a civil disturbance in the commercial area of Santiago and the number of victims was never established because the government sneaked the bodies away. During a strike at the El Salvador mine during the government of Eduardo Frei, a military patrol opened fire on a demonstration to break it up and killed six people, among them some children and a pregnant woman. The post commander was an obscure 52-year-old general, the father of five children, a geography teacher and the author of several books on military subjects: Augusto Pinochet.

The myth of the legalism and the gentleness of that brutal army was invented by the Chilean bourgeoisie in their own interest. Popular Unity kept it alive with the hope of changing the class make-up of the higher cadres in its favour. But Allende felt more secure among the Carabineros, an armed force that was popular and peasant in its origins and that was under the direct command of the president of the republic. Indeed, the junta had to go six places down the seniority list of the force before it found a senior officer who would support the coup. The younger officers dug themselves in at the junior officers' school in Santiago and held out for four days until they were wiped out.

That was the best-known battle of the secret war that broke out inside military posts on the eve of the coup. Officers who refused to support the coup and those who failed to carry out the orders for repression were murdered without pity by the instigators. Entire regiments mutinied, both in Santiago and in the provinces, and they were suppressed without mercy, with their leaders massacred as a lesson for the troops.

The commandant of the armoured units in Viña del Mar, Colonel Cantuarias, was machine-gunned by his subordinates. A long time will pass before the number of victims of that internal butchery will ever be known, for the bodies were removed from military posts in garbage trucks and buried secretly. All in all, only some 50 senior officers could be trusted to head troops that had been purged beforehand.

FOREIGN AGENTS' ROLE

The story of the intrigue has to be pasted together from many sources, some reliable, some not. Any number of foreign agents seem to have taken part in the coup. Clandestine sources in Chile tell us that the bombing of La Moneda Palace – the technical precision of which startled the experts – was actually carried out by a team of American aerial acrobats who had entered the country under the screen of Operation Unitas to perform in a flying circus on the coming 18 September, Chile's national independence day. There is also evidence that numerous members of secret police forces from neighbouring countries were infiltrated across the Bolivian border and remained in hiding until the day of the coup, when they unleashed their bloody persecution of political refugees from other countries of Latin America.

Brazil, the homeland of the head gorillas, had taken charge of those services. Two years earlier, she had brought off the reactionary coup in Bolivia, which meant the loss of substantial support for Chile and facilitated the infiltration of all manner and means of subversion. Part of the loans made to Brazil by the United States was secretly transferred to Bolivia to finance subversion in Chile. In 1972, a US military advisory group made a trip to La Paz, the aim of which has not been revealed. Perhaps it was only coincidental, however, that a short time after that visit, movements of troops and equipment took place on the frontier with Chile, giving the Chilean military yet another opportunity to bolster their internal position and carry out transfer of personnel and promotions in the chain of command that were favourable to the imminent coup.

Finally, on 11 September, while Operation Unitas was going forward, the original plan drawn up at the dinner in Washington was carried out, three years behind schedule but precisely as it had been conceived: not as a conventional barracks coup but as a devastating operation of war.

It had to be that way, for it was not simply a matter of overthrowing a regime but one of implanting the Hell-dark seeds brought from Brazil, until in Chile there would be no trace of the political and social structure that had made Popular Unity possible. The harshest phase, unfortunately, had only just begun. In that final battle, with the country at the mercy of uncontrolled and unforeseen forces of subversion, Allende was still bound by legality. The most dramatic contradiction of his life was being at the same time the congenital foe of violence and a passionate revolutionary. He believed that he had resolved the contradiction with the hypothesis that conditions in Chile would permit a peaceful evolution toward socialism under bourgeois legality. Experience taught him too late that a system cannot be changed by a government without power.

That belated disillusionment must have been the force that impelled him to resist to the death, defending the flaming ruins of a house that was not his own, a sombre mansion that an Italian architect had built to be a mint and that ended up as a refuge for presidents without power. He resisted for six hours with a sub-machine gun that Castro had given him and was the first weapon that Allende had ever fired.

Around four o'clock in the afternoon, Major General Javier Palacios managed to reach the second floor with his adjutant, Captain Gallardo, and a group of officers. There, in the midst of the fake Louis XV chairs, the Chinese dragon vases and the Rugendas paintings in the red parlour, Allende was waiting for them. He was in shirtsleeves, wearing a miner's helmet and no tie, his clothing stained with blood. He was holding the sub-machine gun but he had run low on ammunition.

Allende knew General Palacios well. A few days before, he had told Augusto Olivares that this was a dangerous man with close connections to the American embassy. As soon as he saw him appear on the stairs, Allende shouted at him: 'Traitor!' and shot him in the hand.

FOUGHT TO THE END

According to the story of a witness who asked me not to give his name, the president died in an exchange of shots with that gang. Then all the other officers, in a caste-bound ritual, fired on the body. Finally, a non-commissioned officer smashed in his face with the butt of his rifle.

A photograph exists: Juan Enrique Lira, a photographer for the newspaper *El Mercurio* took it. He was the only one allowed to photograph the body. It was so disfigured that when they showed the body in its coffin to Señora Hortensia Allende, his wife, they would not let her uncover the face.

He would have been 64 years old next July. His greatest virtue was following through but fate could grant him only that rare and tragic greatness of dying in armed defence of an anachronistic booby of bourgeois law, defending a Supreme Court of Justice that had repudiated him but would legitimise his murderers, defending a miserable Congress that had declared him illegitimate but which was to bend complacently before the will of the usurpers, defending the freedom of opposition parties that had sold their souls to fascism, defending the whole moth-eaten paraphernalia of a shitty system that he had proposed abolishing but without a shot being fired.

The drama took place in Chile, to the greater woe of the Chileans, but it will pass into history as something that has happened to us all, children of this age, and it will remain in our lives for ever.

Do you dare like this book?

Ian McEwan

In the current public debate on freedom of expression there is something not altogether free. One writer told an editor last week that she feared for her life if she spoke out for *The Satanic Verses*. Another said he felt strongly about the right to publish but if he made his views public he would only make things 'worse' for Salman Rushdie. Muslims who have spoken out against book burning or banning or author murdering have been threatened by those of more straightforward convictions. Muslims of all shades of opinion have been threatened by white racists.

The poison of intimidation is infecting the free exchange of ideas. The stain of one crazed edict is spreading. What follows from intimidation is fear. Going to bed with fear, and waking up (if you've managed to sleep) with fear is hardly any life at all. But what follows from fear has direr consequences. I am talking of self-censorship. It is an invisible process, even to the one who is doing the censoring. No Muslim, Christian, atheist or whatever should feel obliged to make public statements in an atmosphere of threat. The right to silence is inalienable from the right to free expression. But fear needs to be fingered. If we name it, then we can see it. If we can see it, we might be able to do something about it.

But let's not be solemn. Since I am feeling a little fearful myself today, I think I would rather talk about Voltaire. The famous attributed remark, 'I might disapprove of what you say, but I will defend to the death your right to say it,' has had many airings recently. It is a fine sentiment. But just lately the remark has seemed somewhat abused. There are, after all, more difficult positions to take. Suppose I actually approve of what you say, of what you've written? Then not only might I die for your right, I might even have read your book and engaged with its ideas.

And what is it you are saying? Is Christianity the subject? It might as well be, what with the phone ringing again, and someone talking to me from a public call box. What has always puzzled me is the distance you might travel in, say, 1,500 years. You start with a man, a very special man, who claims a direct relationship with his God. His teachings are a unique blend of tolerance and compassion, forgiveness and love, and they hold out the prospect of great joy in the afterlife. After his death, his followers continue his work. The life and teachings are written down.

But then, 15 centuries or so later, what do we have? A vast, hierarchical bureaucracy, certain members of which are aware of God's intentions and accordingly issue their edicts, fiats, decrees, canons, encyclicals, bulls and whathaveyou. How the major fourth is the devil's interval and must never be heard in church, how women are weak and unclean and less in reason, how the sun goes round the earth. *Rules about every damn thing.*

From the vision of one man, to a total thought-system, impatient with dissent and ready to kill to keep the small print intact, ready to slaughter the inhabitants of Albi, or the followers of Luther, or risk the wine-dark seas to kill the infidel Muslims. And the dissenters, the Reformers, they don't seem so shy of slaughter for their cause either. The faithful are ready to kill or die bravely for their particular spin on doctrine. They hear each sound of their own Word of God, they all get their instructions direct. *From the beginning, men used to justify the unjustifiable.*

But, coming back to Voltaire, perhaps it is Stalinism we are talking about. You are asking me to fight to the end for your right to talk about that? Well, yes, there's another long hard road to travel, from an initial impulse to lift from the majority of mankind its heavy burden of hard work and ignorance, to the ministrations of Uncle Joe. Another full-nelson on thought, a total system, as happy devouring its friends as its enemies. Mock it if you dare – *It's his Word against mine.*

Or again, are we talking about the space between Danton and Robespierre? Or is this all too harsh? Am I really offering myself up to your right to talk about *any* closed system of thought, any monopoly on truth? Scientific method, Freudian analysis, structuralism, voodooism, sociology, Thatcherism, journalism? They all have their high priests with their direct line to the Highest Authority.

Have you heard, the Ayatollah has announced that his Edict, this pronouncement on your Headandballs, is not something dreamed up in the bath. It was God's Word in his ear. His Word against yours. God told the Ayatollah, and the Ayatollah told us. God made Viking publish your novel to demonstrate the international conspiracy against Iran. *You brought us the Devil himself, so that we could witness the workings of the Evil One, and his overthrow by the Right.*

But back to Voltaire. I'm getting the idea now, it's the monotheistic you want to shake your stick at. What you're wanting to hammer to the door of this here church is hardly a reasoned argument at all. It's a fairground, a carnival, a riot. It's a *novel*. You are a trouble maker.

And Ohmigod! You want to include Islam, you want me to fight to the death for your right to treat Islam as if it were only one more thought-system, one more authority, one more idea. That's a helluvalot to ask, brother. That's a wrathful world religion you're talking about there. Christ, Socrates, Buddha, Lao Tse, but not this one, baby. I'll only make things worse for you and (da!) here's the phone ringing again. It's that racist Peter Sellers imitation in the call box, so (hello? hello?) I think I'd better (you'll do what?) stop right here.

All italicised quotations are from Salman Rushdie's *Satanic Verses*.

Terry Pratchett, science and story telling

A. S. Byatt

Terry Pratchett's first *Discworld* novel was published in 1983. As a wartime child in the 1940s I was already puzzling over an image of a domed world poised on the backs of three elephants that stood on a monstrous turtle. This discworld had a small temple on top of it, and the clawed feet of the turtle rested on the coils of a huge serpent, which also stretched to encircle the world, with the point of its tail in its mouth. It was reproduced in my favourite book, *Asgard and the Gods*, a scholarly German work on Norse myths, which my mother had used at Cambridge.

This image, and this book, provoked my earliest thinking about the nature of belief and its relation to storytelling. Where on earth did the idea of the turtle and the elephants come from? Did people really believe in them? These questions were related to the kind of embarrassed pain with which I contemplated the stories of origins I was expected to believe in, the Bible with its heaven and hell, the tale of judgement to come.

Pratchett's new book, *The Science of Discworld IV*, co-written with the mathematician Ian Stewart and the biologist Jack Cohen, discusses ideas about origins and endings, cosmology and astrobiology, entropy and genetics. The idea of storytelling is not just an embroidered way of including a tale of the discussion of the 'Roundworld' taking place on the Discworld. Human beings are defined as *pan narrans*, the storytelling ape, who exists in a dimension known as the 'narrativium'. We look for causes because we think in linear sequences of words. We look for origins because we arrange our world into narrative strings with beginning, middle and end. Stewart, Cohen and Pratchett set out to puzzle us and make us think differently.

Central to their approach is the distinction made by the physicist and science-fiction author Gregory Benford between human-centred thinking and universe-centred thinking. Human-centred thinking comes naturally to human beings. 'In this world-view, rain exists in order to make crops grow and to provide fresh water for us to drink. The sun is there because it warms our bodies.' From human-centred thinking comes the idea of a ruler of the universe, as well as the idea that the earth and the creatures, the sea and the oil and the forests are somehow there for our benefit. Universe-centred thinking, on the other hand, sees human beings as 'just one tiny feature of a vast cosmos, most of which does not function on a human scale or take any notice of what we want'. The universe-centred thinker must have what Keats called 'negative capability' – the capacity to be in uncertainties, mysteries, doubts, without any irritable reaching after fact and reason. This is hard and invigorating.

The writers discuss creation myths – including a number of myths about cosmic turtles and scientific ideas about origins, including the Big Bang. They discuss the evolution of ideas about evolution, recent thoughts about the relation of RNA to DNA and the idea of the curvature of space. They also consider neural networks and decision theory, and the strong and weak anthropic principles – ideas about how the physical universe is uniquely suited to the existence of human beings.

Pratchett and co also explore the psychology of belief and disbelief. They describe one way of coming to conclusions – the brain taking in new evidence, and fitting it to the knowledge and beliefs it already holds. This is what they call 'System 1', and it includes scientific thinkers as well as people with inherited religious beliefs. There are, they say, scientists who 'know' that DNA is the most important part of the system, physicists who 'know' that the world is moving towards entropy. 'System 2', on the other hand, is steadily analytical and sceptical – 'trying, not always successfully, to ignore inbuilt prejudices'. Karl Popper's system of 'critical rationalism' held that a theory could be considered scientific if, and only if, it was capable of falsification. Stewart and Cohen claim that 'scientists actively try to disprove the things they would like to be true'. They use the example of a believer in UFOs who sees disbelief in UFOs as another form of belief. 'Zero belief in UFOs', they point out, is not the same as 100 per cent belief in the non-existence of UFOs. 'Zero belief is an absence of belief, not an opposed form of belief.' What they aspire towards and desire is 'a disbelief system'. This is exhilarating.

I remember being on a platform where various poets and writers discussed the ways in which the arts could figure the world of the scientist. That blunt sceptic Lewis Wolpert, sitting in the audience, rose to inform the assembled artists that we would not understand any of his work were we to find ourselves in his laboratory. Some of us were indignant but I believe he was right. People like me can read what is written by those scientists who try to tell us about neurons, genes, the shape of the brain, the shape of space and time. We can respond to those descriptions but we are responding to stories, at second hand.

One of the most pleasing things about Pratchett, Stewart and Cohen's book is the way the authors demonstrate that we don't understand even what we think we understand. I realised, reading their account of the complex relations between RNA and DNA, that I had been guilty of holding a belief. I was very excited in the late 1970s by ideas about the 'selfish gene', and particularly by the points made by John Maynard Smith about the immutable nature of the inherited and eternal germ cell. Now the *New Scientist* is full of articles about newly discovered 'orphan DNA'. Stewart and Cohen write:

> Darwin's tree of life, a beautiful idea that derives from a sketch in *The Origin of Species* and has become iconic, gets very scrambled around in its roots because of a process called horizontal gene transfer. Bacteria, archaea and viruses swap genes with gay abandon, and they can also insert them into the genomes of higher animals, or cut them out. So a gene in one type of bacterium might have come from another type of bacterium altogether, or from an archaean, or even from an animal or a plant.

The story I believed in has to be modified and rethought. When I read this, I think in a human way with a series of images, in the grammar of a story. I should not be able to recognise any gene, let alone think intelligently about it. Stewart and Cohen are very good at illustrating our incapacity to understand. They do so with images and stories. My favourite is the one they tell to make us think about the difference between complicated chemistry and the 'organised complexity' of the ribosome. It is a story about caramel.

Every cook knows that heating sugar with fats, two fairly simple chemical substances, produces caramel … Caramel is enormously complicated on a chemical level. It includes innumerable different molecules, each of which has thousands of atoms. The molecular structure of caramel is far more complicated than most of the molecules you're using to read this page.

But the complexity of caramel, or other complicated polymers, doesn't produce organised complexity, as ribosomes do. Wolpert would rightly tell me that I still don't know anything about the ribosomes. But I am at least able now to think about the problem. And the juxtaposition of caramel and brain is unforgettable. There are delights like this on most pages of this book.

In a chapter entitled 'Where did that come from?' we are invited to reflect on how we can't think about things like the origin of an oak tree, or a child, or even a thunderstorm. They make the reader imagine thinking about clouds, the constituents of the atmosphere, static electricity, physics and physical chemistry. Most of us, they say, 'will not have come across one or more phrases such as 'saturated solution' or 'particle carries a tiny electrical charge'. These phrases are themselves simplifications of concepts with many more associations, and more intellectual depth, than anyone can be expected to generate for themselves.' Human beings tend to retreat from uncertainty or difficulty into belief stories, like the American Republican candidate who opposed any regulation of the markets on the grounds that this was 'interfering with God's plan for the American economy'.

Pratchett, Stewart and Cohen use their method of complicating descriptions and explanations to examine several problems with things I have trouble with believing myself, because they feel to me like human stories that tidy up our relation to the universe – the Big Bang, the existence of dark matter, entropy and the 'anthropic principle'. They discuss conflicting views of the expanding universe and the steady state and cast doubt on the existence of dark matter. They are not propounding or supporting any particular theory of the shape and origins of the universe, but are rather considering evidence that complicates the explanations we have become used to. They are good at picking out the operations of what they call our 'very parochial' minds, which use ideas of space and time that evolved with us. 'Our view of the universe may be just as parochial as the world-bearing animals of ancient cultures were. Future scientists may view both the Big Bang and four elephants riding on a turtle as conceptual errors of a very similar kind.'

In Richard Feynman's *The Character of Physical Law*, they find a tendency evident in 'too many physicists' to consider physical reality to be all of reality. Feynman, they write, states that 'the same kind of atoms appear to be in living creatures as in non-living creatures [sic]; frogs are made of the same "goup" as rocks only in different arrangements.' Things in the biological world are the results of the behaviour of physical and chemical phenomena with no 'extra something.' Stewart and Cohen agree about the 'no extra something' but think that a bleak view of the world of particles and elements misses out the complexity of living things, and the things they make and use and learn from.

Entropy may not be our destiny – they see Feynman rather as Pratchett sees his undifferentiated auditors, who want to tidy everything up into packets of particles. Life, say Stewart and Cohen, has 'lifted itself up into a story.' That is a metaphor – and an attractive one. It feels right, and should therefore be regarded with the necessary doubt and suspicion. They also take a mocking run at the idea of 'fine-tuning', the idea that the world has evolved as the only possible world in which humans could exist – just the right amount of carbon and water, and so on.

This 'anthropic principle', in both its strong and its weak forms, has always horrified me because it is so clearly a function of the human mind thinking in a human-centred way. Isn't it amazing, say the Discworld scientists, that our legs are just long enough to reach the ground? Isn't it amazing that there was a hole exactly the right size to contain that puddle? And what about a sulphur-centred form of thought?

There was one chapter I found hard to understand – on the curvature of space, round worlds and disc worlds. This was where I wished the book had illustrations – I read pages about the doughnut-shaped torus, and then had the sense to consult Wikipedia, where I could see what was being discussed. And I also needed to see the geometry of the wonderful Escher image of angels and demons.

I have become rather sad about surviving into the anthropocene age of human history, where everything is controlled and constructed by and for what the King of Brobdingnag called 'the most pernicious race of little odious vermin that Nature ever suffered to crawl upon the surface of the earth'. But, paradoxically, both Pratchett's storytelling and the resolutely universe-centred perspective of the scientists make me happier to be human. I look forward to the next volume.

King Arthur: Our once and future king

Rowan Williams

Does anyone now read the historical novels of Henry Treece? A minor poet associated with the postwar 'New Apocalyptic' group, he produced in the 1950s and 1960s a steady stream of fiction for the adult and young adult market, set mostly in early Britain and in the Viking age. The books are characterised by vivid, simple and sometimes repetitive plotting, ample bloodshed, a well-judged mixture of the cynical and the romantic, and plenty of gloomy Celtic and Nordic atmospherics. Several of the novels feature an 'historical' King Arthur – a sixth-century warlord, co-ordinating resistance to the invading Saxons. Treece portrays with some skill the ways in which such a figure might have manipulated vague memories of Roman power and cultural identity to shore up his dominance in a chaotic post-Roman Britain.

The picture Treece outlines (a picture that can be found in rather less highly coloured narratives by writers such as Rosemary Sutcliff and Meriol Trevor) is in fact not too far away from what a substantial number of professional historians of the mid-twentieth century had come to take for granted. The withdrawal of Roman military presence from Britain in the first quarter of the fifth century must have left the native population at the mercy of rapidly increasing swarms of settlers from north-western Europe, who pushed across lowland Britain, sacking Roman settlements and killing a substantial proportion of the population. Archaeology seemed to support this picture: Roman towns had been ruined and abandoned, British hill settlements were reoccupied and refortified. There appeared to be a bit of a hiatus in 'Saxon' settlement in the first half of the sixth century, however, and some historians saw this as the result of a concerted campaign of British resistance.

There was an obvious gap for an 'Arthurian' figure to fill, a military leader with nationwide authority, leaving a legacy in popular memory strong enough ultimately to generate the familiar legends of a great British hero and king. We are on our way to the Round Table and the Holy Grail and all the other riches of the 'Matter of Britain', as the medieval authors called the jungle of legendary traditions that grew around the name of Arthur.

Unfortunately, this satisfying historical reconstruction had one fatal weakness: the earliest clear reference to an Arthur fighting the Saxons comes from 300 years after the alleged date of the events, in a chronicle that shows very little sign of having dependable earlier sources. What's more, archaeology has moved on dramatically since the 1970s: sites that were once assumed to be Roman towns sacked by marauding barbarians can be much more convincingly interpreted as having been deserted well before the fourth century, as part of a general drift away from urban living. And the analysis of genetic patterns in the British population, along with evidence from burial sites and other important sources of information about daily life in the post-Roman period, suggests a very slow penetration of Britain by the Germanic settlers, and, in many areas, no substantial change of population at all: ruling elites might change – or simply change their cultural habits – but there was no wholesale genocidal replacement of one ethnic group by another.

All this leaves no room for an 'Age of Arthur', to borrow the title of one influential but very speculative book. Professor Nicholas Higham is a leading historian of the early Middle Ages who has devoted a great deal of scholarly labour over the years to dismantling the historical-King-Arthur industry. 'Industry' is not an inappropriate word: dozens of books have appeared in the past half-century purporting to identify the 'real' Arthur, and a couple of colourful and historically preposterous films have claimed to tell the true story behind the legend.

Higham approaches all this with the not-quite-controlled impatience of a Shakespearean expert dealing with Baconians, or a theologian or medievalist dissecting The Da Vinci Code. Indeed, the parallels here are instructive. It is always possible to find some neglected bit of documentary or archaeological record that can be magnified into a long-sought solution to a supposed historical riddle. But so often this process displays a complete disregard for the ordinary laws of historical evidence. In this demi-monde of scholarship, it is easy enough to attract popular headlines; but this is no substitute for genuinely moving a subject forward.

The first few chapters of Higham's book deal with the wilder reaches of Arthurian speculation. It is fairly likely that the name 'Arthur', not all that common in Celtic sources, derives from the Latin 'Artorius' (though this itself may reflect an older Celtic form, 'Artorigos' or 'bear-king'). Scholars have known for decades about the memorial in Croatia to a blamelessly dull military bureaucrat named Artorius Castus, who seems to have served briefly in Britain, probably in the late second century; and (appropriately) heroic attempts have been made to argue that he must be the origin of the stories. Piquant as it is to think of the original Arthur as more like Captain Mainwaring than Conan the Barbarian, there is nothing substantial to support this idea. It is not clear even that Castus ever took part in any actual campaigning in Britain, and we are left with no explanation whatever of why an obscure administrator in the Roman army should have been remembered.

But the theory has opened up a further startling claim. Castus may have had in his command some auxiliary troops from what are now Hungary and Romania, 'Sarmatians' in the terminology of the day; and there were at least some Sarmatians serving in Roman Britain at some point. Enthusiasts have identified a couple of elements in the Arthurian legends with folkloric themes from the ancient homelands of the Sarmatians. But once again, the connection is vanishingly thin; and the legendary elements are all from very late strands of the Arthurian tradition.

A valiant attempt to link Arthur with legends around the star Arcturus in Greek legendary texts is no more convincing; and neither is the extraordinary proposal that some of the narratives are related to Caucasian tales about a race of ancient supernatural tribespeople called the Narts (a chapter entitled 'King Arthur and the Narts' sounds irresistibly like a lost competitor to Noggin the Nog).

More serious is the material that was once appealed to in order to justify the Henry Treece picture. But Higham relentlessly brings us back to the central obstinate fact that there is not a trace of con-temporary corroboration. The only text that has any claim to be a contemporary record of British-Saxon conflict (an elaborate tirade from the mid-sixth century by a dyspeptic cleric called Gildas) names several British rulers and leaders of the period, but no one called Arthur. The ninth-century chronicle that first mentions Arthur was written, as Higham shows, with the aim of salvaging the reputation of the indigenous British at a time when a new dynasty in north Wales badly needed positive publicity; the often-cited passage listing Arthur's great battles against the Saxons is probably a rather randomly assembled catalogue of military encounters spanning a century or more. It is simply meant as the portrait of a native military hero, whose story, Higham argues, is deliberately shaped as a pendant to the stories in the same chronicle about St Patrick as a great ecclesiastical hero of Britain.

Higham's book features an interesting discussion of the factors that might have inclined mid-twentieth century historians to take this Arthurian pseudo-history more seriously than it deserved. Fighting off Germanic invaders was a resonant theme between 1940 and 1950, and the notion of a resilient indigenous British culture, independent of both Roman imperial and imported European identities, will have had some traction in Britain's first post-imperial phase. But historically speaking, the 'Age of Arthur' has had its day.

Does anything remain? Higham is determined to take no prisoners in his scepticism. But, as he somewhat grudgingly allows, the tradition doesn't quite come from nowhere. There may well have been folk tales about a British hero named Arthur – a figure very like Fionn MacCumhaill in Irish legend, the leader of a band of heroes engaged in feuds and quests and supernatural conflicts, with no exact historical or geographical setting – and that these stories fused with vague records of a historical ruler remembered as a formidable fighter.

We know of such a figure, Artur Mac-Aedan, son of a king of the Irish settlers in western Scotland, who died in battle against the Picts in the late sixth century. His father was certainly remembered in Welsh tradition, and there seems to have been intermarriage between his family and the neighbouring British kingdoms in the Scottish Lowlands and the Borders. The family were close to St Columba (the saint is said to have foretold Artur's death) and this may have helped to consolidate the later chronicle's depiction of Arthur as a devout Christian. The dates are several decades later than our ninth-century chronicle implies – but its writer is notoriously bad at chronology.

A figure like this Artur, with a strong but local reputation, could without too much difficulty melt into the much older tradition of a mythical hero-king (the sort of personage who appears in the earliest Welsh sources, in which there is no trace at all of any campaigning against Saxons), as memories of the 'Old North' – the British states that flourished for a time around Carlisle and Glasgow and Edinburgh – drifted south towards Wales between 600 and 800.

The truth is that the whole context of British-Saxon struggle needs rethinking, despite the melodramatic account of Saxon slaughter presented by Gildas. It suits his purpose to underline the brutality and aggression of the settlers so as to make it plain that the British are being punished by God for their evil-doing. On closer inspection, though, the narrative of a co-ordinated 'invasion' begins to fade, as does the assumption of consistent ethnic conflict.

There are telling pieces of evidence to support the idea that, in the early stages of the Germanic settlements in lowland Britain, indigenous British groups and settlers from the eastern shores of the North Sea – the 'English' – alternated between rivalry and co-operation. It is not wholly unlike the early stages of more modern patterns of settlement, where the first generation of colonialists, still insecure in a new and often menacing environment, were happier than their descendants to intermarry and make alliances (North America and South Africa in the early years of European intrusion come to mind). And it is sadly not surprising in this light that within a century or so of its foundation, almost certainly as a joint British-Saxon venture, the Kingdom of Wessex had instituted a form of apartheid-style discrimination against the indigenous British.

But the interesting point is that, in accounts of the Saxon settlement by foreign settlers and native British alike, myths of timeless, clearly defined racial division and conflict are being projected back on to much more confused and diverse social situations. The 'historical' Arthur of the scholars and novelists of the last century is in fact the reflection of a particular style of nationalist storytelling; and the dismantling of this dramatic but misleading model by historians such as Higham enables us to see more clearly the racial and cultural fluidity of Britain in the century and a half after the end of direct Roman rule. Ethnic identities have a history; they do not drop from Heaven.

Curiously enough, Arthur was never just a hero for indigenous British ethnicity, as if the fluidity of the age in which he was supposed to have lived kept a larger space open for him. The 'real' King Arthur is like the 'real' King Lear – a figure that has been used to aid thought within a huge diversity of settings across the centuries. In the case of Arthur, this has ranged from thinking about Norman imperial ambitions in the twelfth century to reflecting on the balance of military valour and courtly eros in the thirteenth and fourteenth centuries, or on the tensions between grace and fallen human nature in the Grail legends, or about the tragic collisions of public responsibility with private passion and loyalty in the unsurpassed narratives in the later books of Malory's Morte d'Arthur.

And this is more abidingly valuable than even the most ingenious reconstruction of the career of a sixth-century chieftain. It seems to have proved difficult to turn the Arthurian legacy simply into a matter of ethnic self-glorification (though the Tudors had a good try). By the end of the Middle Ages, it was a vehicle for depicting both the fragility of grand moral projects in political history (Camelot is doomed from the first because of hidden personal sins and errors) and the stubborn courage and fidelity that makes these projects worth celebrating, even when they are tied up with the stories of very flawed individuals.

It is not easy to hold on to a belief in the value of a morally ambitious political or social vision at the same time as recognising the human frailties involved and the need for forgiveness and the patience to start again. Political programmes painted in more primary colours – heroic leadership, ethnic glory and triumphant innocence – look more attractive to a substantial percentage of humanity, however lethal they prove themselves over and over again. It is because of all this that Arthur – 'historical' or not – is a national hero worth having.

The queen of 'quiet storm'

Tracey Thorn

Like many people I was excited to hear that film director Ava DuVernay had persuaded Sade to record a new original song, her first in eight years, for the forthcoming movie *A Wrinkle in Time*. Announcing the news on Twitter, DuVernay wrote, 'I never thought she'd say yes, but asked anyway. She was kind and giving. A goddess.'

It's how we all think of Sade. A goddess, a queen. Yet of course, behind all that she's a real person: Helen Folasade Adu, born in Nigeria in 1959, to a Nigerian academic and an English nurse. When her parents separated she moved back to England with her mother and brother, growing up in Essex listening to Curtis Mayfield, Donny Hathaway and Bill Withers. As a teenager she saw the Jackson Five at the Rainbow Theatre in Finsbury Park, where she worked behind the bar: 'I was more fascinated by the audience... They'd attracted kids, mothers with children, old people, white, black. I was really moved. That's the audience I've always aimed for.'

Before becoming a singer, she studied fashion, and modelled a bit, but was no mere model-turned-singer. Instead she had put in three years of touring, from 1981 to 1984, with London soul band Pride, until their standout song, which she'd co-written, 'Smooth Operator', came to the attention of record companies. Refusing to abandon her bandmates, she only signed to Epic once they'd agreed to take Stuart, Andrew and Paul as well – and together they became the band Sade.

This was the period in the wake of post-punk when a Soho scene grew up around the Wag Club, which started in 1982, and attracted a crowd who dressed in zoot suits and danced to a mixture of Latin jazz, northern soul, funk and hip hop, as opposed to the chart hits being played in other West End clubs. Where punks had revelled in being guttersnipes, the new soul or new jazz aficionados, like the New Romantics, were more inspired by the Oscar Wilde line: 'We are all in the gutter, but some of us are looking at the stars.'

The first Sade album, *Diamond Life* (1984), embodied much of that scene, and was a sophisticated record made by strugglers and underdogs. 'We're hungry for a life we can't afford', she sang, 'we're hungry but we won't give in.' There's a song about the Salvation Army picking up the pieces for the casualties of uncaring 1980s capitalism – 'doing our dirty work' – and a cover of Timmy Thomas's 'Why Can't We Live Together', a plea for racial and social integration ('no matter, no matter what colour, you are still my brother'). Set against these is 'Smooth Operator', which I've always thought of as a Roxy Music type of lyric about urban sleaze and corrupt glamour: 'He move in space with minimum waste and maximum joy/City lights and business nights/When you require streetcar desire for higher heights.'

As with the fashion, there was a vintage element to the sound, a kind of classic soul/jazz vibe, produced by Robin Millar (who also produced the first two Everything But the Girl albums). In love with simplicity and acoustic instruments, his skill was in arrangement – 'congas in on the second verse' as we used to joke with him. With Sade this was enormously successful and right from the start the band created a signature sound that they have barely deviated from their entire career.

We'd bump into them at Power Plant Studios, and while their fashion sense and style could make them seem a little dazzling or intimidating, they were also warm and friendly. Sade once told me that my singing reminded her of Chet Baker's trumpet playing – not his *singing*, she was at pains to point out, but his playing, which she felt was a greater compliment. I took it as such, and admired the specificity. This was clearly someone who cared about detail.

As a singer, Sade sounds like no one else. There's a plangent tone to her voice, a liking for the long-held note, almost vibrato-free. A precision of diction. No melisma, no swooping octave leaps. And there are two very distinct tones – softness with just a slight husk in the bottom range, and above that, a more strident note, bringing a hardness which is vital, adding the only sharp edge.

But of course you can't talk about Sade without talking about what she looks like. It wasn't just her beauty, it was how she carried herself: always, to go back to that first band name, with pride. Her style and poise was a legacy from the fashion school days. She always knew exactly which Levis were correct. She could make a trench coat look edgy. She could make huge hoop earrings look like the crown jewels.

The style of the times meant that women in pop tended to wear more clothes than they do now. Bananarama were considered sexy in their dungarees, and Annie Lennox was androgynously cool in a man's suit. Soul singers – even the girls – wore peg-top trousers, crisp tucked-in shirts, bolero jackets, bow ties and felt hats. Yet given Sade's beauty, it is striking how little she used her sexuality. On the cover of *Love Deluxe* (1992) she appears uncharacteristically naked – though with arms folded so nothing can be seen, the shot more stylised than erotic, more about art than sex. She holds herself, eyes closed, and it is clear you'd get nowhere near her.

If she often looked unreachable and untouchable, what more powerful statement could there be from a young black woman? Belonging to nobody, beholden to nobody but herself, she held the male gaze at bay, deflecting it, controlling it. The band carried *her* name, and behind that reserve that appeared a mixture of shyness and strength, a core of steel held everything together.

It grates on me how, given their huge international success, the band gets overlooked when the history and triumphs of British music are recounted. In the US, her legacy is clear – artists such as Rakim, Kanye West and Beyoncé express their respect and love for her work. In the Eighties she ruled over the 'quiet storm' radio stations, which specialised in a genre of smooth soul – music to have sex to, rather than march to.

But Sade herself often smuggled politics into the songs. You won't find lyrics about yachts or champagne or limos. As a writer she is a product of Eighties social realism. She sang about Jezebel, who 'wasn't born with a silver spoon in her mouth' but was another struggler, a survivor – 'every winter was a war, she said, I want to get what's mine'. Both 'Slave Song' and 'Immigrant' explicitly address racism: 'He didn't know what it was to be black/'Till they gave him his change/But didn't want to touch his hand.'

Sade's whole career tells a story of precision and minimalism, from the scraped-back hair to the fact that there are only six albums in 26 years. She has remained incredibly private, rarely gives interviews, and avoids the chat-show sofa. She does, however, go on tour with every new album, feeling that the songs come alive on stage. For this, she's called reclusive, though what this means is that she is still playing no one's game, and living no one's life but her own.

The Critical
Condition

Why Picasso?

John Berger

Why is Picasso the most famous living artist in the world? Why does everything he does have such news value? Why do even those of us who are more seriously interested than the sensational press, go to a new Picasso exhibition hoping to be surprised? And why do we never come away disappointed?

Take the present Picasso show at the Lefèvre. It contains two jokes cast in bronze. One is an ape with a toy model car for a head, a vase for a belly and a piece of an iron bracket for a tail. The other is a bird with a head and plume made from a gas-tap, a tail from the blade of a small shovel and legs and feet from two kitchen forks. The fifteen paintings include some recent (1953) sketches of women's heads in which profile and full-face are dislocated and re-assembled together, a flippant canvas of a dog and a woman wrestling hammer and tongs on the floor, and two small pictures from the tragic series of women in hats painted during the German occupation – their faces brutally wrenched into shapes reminiscent of gas masks. There are no important works in the show. Yet it remains intensely memorable. Why?

The easy answer is to say: because Picasso is a great artist – because he can set a model car in clay and somehow make it convincing as a head of an ape – because he can draw a goat's skull (No. 20) with such finesse that one can feel every twist and turn worn away by the muscles. But to answer like that is to beg the question. It doesn't explain why the scrappiest work by Picasso is so disproportionately compelling, or why all his work is so much more immediately arresting than that of, say, Matisse or Léger who in the long run will probably be seen to possess equal or even greater genius as painters. Those who petulantly and sceptically say 'You only admire it because it's been done by Picasso,' are in a way quite right. In front of Picasso's work one pays tribute above all to his personal spirit. The old argument about his political opinions on one hand and his art on the other is quite false. As Picasso himself admits, he has, as an artist, discovered nothing. What makes him great are not his individual works but his existence, his personality. That may sound obscure and perverse, but less so, I think, if one inquires further into the nature of his personality.

Picasso is essentially an improviser. And if the word improvisation conjures up amongst other things, associations of the clown and the mimic – they also apply. Living through a period of colossal confusion in which so many values both human and cultural have disintegrated, Picasso has seized upon the bits, the fragments, the smithereens, and with magnificent defiance and vitality made something of them to amuse us, shock us, but primarily to demonstrate to us by the example of his spirit that within the confusion, out of the debris, new ideas, new values, new ways of looking at the world can and will develop.

His achievement is not that he himself has developed these things, but that he has always been irrepressible, has never been at a loss. The romanticism of Toulouse Lautrec, the classicism of Ingres, the crude energy of Negro sculpture, the heart searchings of Cézanne towards the truth about structure, the exposures of Freud – all these he has recognised, welcomed, pushed to bizarre conclusions, improvised on, sung through, in order to make us recognise our contemporary environment, in order (and here his role is very much like that of a clown) to make us recognise ourselves in the parody of a distorting mirror. In *Guernica* the parody was tragic; there, angrily and passionately, he improvised with the bits left over from a massacre: as in other paintings, also tragically, he improvises with features and limbs dislocated and made fragmentary by the dilemmas of our time. But the process, the way he works – not by sustained creative research but by picking up whatever is in front of him and turning it to account, the account of human ingenuity – is always the same. Even when as now he makes a bird from the scrap metal found in some cupboard.

Obviously this shorthand view of Picasso oversimplifies, but it does, I think, answer the questions I began by asking. And also goes some way to explaining other facts about him: the element of caricature in all his work; the extraordinary confidence behind every mark he makes – it is the confidence of the born performer; the failure of all his disciples

– if he were a profoundly constructive artist this would not be so; the amazing multiplicity of his styles; the sense that, by comparison with any other great artist, any single work by Picasso seems unfinished; the truth behind many of his enigmatic statements: 'In my opinion to search means nothing in painting. To find is the thing.' 'To me there is no past or future in art. If a work of art cannot live always in the present it must not be considered at all.' Or, 'when I have found something to express, I have done it without thinking of the past or the future.'

The conclusions one can draw are these: that it is Picasso's simple and incredible vitality that is his secret – and here it is significant that of all his works it is those that deal with animals that are most complete and profound in sympathy; that to future generations our estimate of Picasso, judged on the evidence of his works themselves, will seem exaggerated; and that we are absolutely right to hold this exaggerated view because it is the present existence of this spirit that we celebrate.

The Royal Soap Opera

Malcolm Muggeridge

There probably are quite a lot of people – more than might be supposed – who, like myself, feel that another newspaper photograph of a member of the royal family will be more than they can bear. Even Princess Anne, a doubtless estimable child, becomes abhorrent by constant repetition. Already she has that curious characteristic gesture of limply holding up her hand to acknowledge applause. The Queen Mother, the Duke of Edinburgh, Nanny Lightbody, Group Captain Townsend – the whole show is utterly out of hand, and there is a much graver danger than might superficially appear that a strong reaction against it may be produced.

This attitude of adulatory curiosity towards the royal family is, of course, something quite new. *Punch* in the nineteenth century made full use, for instance, of the rich vein of satirical material provided by the Royal Dukes, and in our own time Max Beerbohm found the reigning monarch a natural subject, along with all the eminent, for caricature. All this was very healthy. It presupposed a respect for the institution of monarchy, and a sense that the incumbents were, like us all, mortal men and women. Let us beware lest, in adulating the incumbents, in insulating them from the normal hazards of public life, we jeopardise the institution. It is, of course, true that the present royal family are much more respectable than most of their Hanoverian ancestors, and therefore lend themselves less to satire. But to put them above laughter, above criticism, above the workaday world, is, ultimately, to dehumanise them and risk the monarchy dying of acute anaemia.

It may be argued that it is the general public who require this adulation of the royal family, and that the newspapers, magazines and the BBC, in catering for it, are merely meeting the public's requirement in this, as they do in any other field. Undoubtedly it is true that a picture in colour of the Queen or Princess Margaret is a circulation-builder.

Equally undoubtedly it is true that the unspeakable Crawfie, and all the other dredgers up of unconsidered trifles in the lives of members of the royal family, down to and including Godfrey Winn, provide popular features. It may even be true (though there is no means of proving this) that those portentous, unctuous BBC announcements, with 'the Queen and the Duke of Edinburgh' rolled off the tongue like a toastmaster at a particularly awesome Guildhall banquet – that even these are liked by listeners. Personally, I came to feel, during the recent royal tour, that it was better to sacrifice the news than endure them.

The fact remains that tedious adulation of the royal family is bad for them, for the public, and ultimately for the monarchical institution itself. Is there anything that can be done to check it? One step would be for the royal family to provide themselves with an efficient public relations set-up in place of the rather ludicrous courtiers who now function as such. This would enable information and photographs to be channelled out in a controlled, instead of haphazard, manner. It would also, if astutely conducted, check some of the worst abuses in the way of invasion of privacy and sheer impertinence. An experienced public relations operator knows how to distribute and withhold favours in such a manner as to maintain some measure of control over those with whom he deals. Also, he knows how to advise those on whose behalf he acts. When, for instance, this Townsend business first started it would have been his duty to convince the royal family that it was essential to make some sort of statement at once, frankly explaining the situation. Otherwise, he would have urged, there was bound to be an orgy of vulgar and sentimental speculation which could not but, in the long run, damage the whole standing and status of everyone concerned. After all, if we are to accept that the Crown is useful constitutionally even though deprived of all real power, it must be maintained with some dignity. A Lord Chancellor who was constantly providing material for the commoner sort of magazine and newspaper feature would soon be considered unsuitable for his high office. Likewise a Speaker of the House of Commons or a Lord Chamberlain. How much more, then, is this true of the royal family?

Of course it is not their fault, though I suspect that they develop a taste for the publicity, which, in theory, they find so repugnant. This is merely human. Even a tiny television notoriety is liable to please, or at any rate excite, when all one's conscious being finds it vulgar and odious. At the same time, the royal family ought to be properly advised on how to prevent their lives from becoming a sort of royal soap opera.

Nothing is more difficult than to maintain the prestige of an institution which is accorded the respect and accoutrements of power without the reality. The tendency for such an institution to peter out in pure fantasy is very great. It is like the king in chess. If he ventures into the middle of the board the game is lost. He has to be kept in the background and ringed round with pieces more powerful than himself. Indeed, in a sense it could be said that popularity is fatal to monarchy. The Russian monarchy was never so popular, or treated to such scenes of insensate adulation as in 1914; and even for Farouk's wedding the streets of Cairo were crammed with cheering Egyptians. Yet when, a few years later, the Tsar and his family were cruelly shot down in a cellar no one seemed to care much, and most, if not all, eyes were dry in Egypt when Farouk made off. Extremes of public emotion are always socially dangerous. Cromwell remarked to Fairfax when they were riding through cheering crowds that the same people would have turned out as eagerly to see him hanged. It was the very fatuity of adulation and sycophancy to which King Edward VIII, as Prince of Wales, was subjected which made the reaction so much the greater when the soap opera took, from the point of view of those set in authority over us, an ugly turn. The whole question of the King's relations with Mrs Simpson might have been handled sensibly if sense had prevailed before. You cannot graft a Henry James denouement on to an Elinor Glyn novel.

The probability is, I suppose, that the monarchy has become a kind of *ersatz* religion. Chesterton once remarked that when people cease to believe in God, they do not then believe in nothing, but in anything. Among other solaces, like Johnnie Ray and dreams of winning a football pool, is royalty. The people one sees staring through the railings of Buckingham Palace even when the Queen is not in residence are like forlorn worshippers at one of those shrines, whether Christian or Hindu or Buddhist, which depend on some obviously bogus miraculous happening. As a religion, monarchy has always been a failure; the god-king invariably gets eaten. Men can only remain sane by esteeming what is mortal for its mortality. I dare say what really drove the Gadarene swine mad was the thought that Group Captain Townsend was at the bottom of the cliff.

The normal middle-class attitude is to blame the press, and, heaven knows, it has excelled itself in vulgarity in dealing with the Townsend story. Yet the provocation has been very great. Has even the Foreign Office ever devised a more inept communiqué than the one about no statement of Princess Margaret's future being contemplated at present? If the intention had been to give the story another shot in the arm no more effective device could have been adopted.

This sort of thing is expected of Rita Hayworth, but the application of film-star techniques to the royal family is liable to have, in the long run, disastrous consequences. The film-star soon passes into oblivion. She has her moment and then it is all over. And even her moment depends on being able to do superlatively well whatever the public expects of her. Members of the royal family are in an entirely different situation. Their role is to symbolise the unity of a nation; to provide an element of continuity in a necessarily changing society. This is history, not *The Archers*, and their affairs ought to be treated as such.

If there were a republican party, as in Joseph Chamberlain's time, it might get quite a few recruits. A lot of the old arguments which pointed to the great advantages of a monarchical over an elective presidential system no longer apply. The simple fact is that the United States' Presidency today is a far more dignified institution than the British monarchy. It is accepted that the President must be 'put over' by all the vast and diverse apparatus of mass communications. If the result lacks elegance, at least the impression created is of efficiency and forethought. Just imagine if Princess Margaret and Group Captain Townsend, instead of being trailed about the country (which the procedure imposed on them actually encouraged, just as T. E. Lawrence's avoidance of publicity necessarily brought reporters scurrying after him) and thereby, incidentally, occupying a great many police sorely needed elsewhere, had called a press conference and explained simply and in their own words just how matters stood. What a relief for us all! What a saving of acres of newsprint! The objection, no doubt, would be that such a press conference would be undignified.

In fact, it wouldn't be nearly as undignified as what has happened. The royal family and their advisers have really got to make up their minds – do they want to be part of the mystique of the century of the common man or to be an institutional monarchy; to ride, as it were, in a glass coach or on bicycles; to provide the tabloids with a running serial or to live simply and unaffectedly among their subjects like the Dutch and Scandinavian royal families. What they cannot do is to have it both ways.

6 OCTOBER 1956

The Two Cultures

C. P. Snow

....

The scientist and novelist C. P. Snow first articulated his 'Two Cultures'
thesis in an essay for the New Statesman. *He later developed the idea*
to compose the celebrated Rede Lecture of the same title. His contention
that we need to bridge the gulf between the scientific and the 'traditional',
'mainly literary' cultures resonates today; but arguably it is now science and
technology that have gained the upper hand.

'It's rather odd,' said G. H. Hardy, one afternoon in the early Thirties,
'but when we hear about 'intellectuals' nowadays, it doesn't include
people like me and J. J. Thomson and Rutherford.' Hardy was the first
mathematician of his generation, J. J. Thomson the first physicist of
his; as for Rutherford, he was one of the greatest scientists who have
ever lived. Some bright young literary person putting them outside
the enclosure reserved for intellectuals seemed to Hardy the best
joke for some time. It does not seem quite such a good joke now. The
separation between the two cultures has been getting deeper under
our eyes; there is now precious little communication between them,
little but different kinds of incomprehension and dislike.

The traditional culture, which is, of course, mainly literary, is behaving
like a state whose power is rapidly declining – standing on its precarious
dignity, spending far too much energy on Alexandrine intricacies,
occasionally letting fly in fits of aggressive pique quite beyond its
means, too much on the defensive to show any generous imagination
to the forces which must inevitably reshape it. Whereas the scientific
culture is expansive, not restrictive, confident at the roots, the more
confident after its bout of Oppenheimerian self-criticism, certain
that history is on its side, impatient, intolerant, creative rather than
critical, goodnatured and brash. Neither culture knows the virtues

of the other; often it seems they deliberately do not want to know. The resentment which the traditional culture feels for the scientific is shaded with fear; from the other side, the resentment is not shaded so much as brimming with irritation. When scientists are faced with an expression of the traditional culture, it tends (to borrow Mr William Cooper's eloquent phrase) to make their feet ache.

It does not need saying that generalisations of this kind are bound to look silly at the edges. There are a good many scientists indistinguishable from literary persons, and vice versa. Even the stereotype generalisations about scientists are misleading without some sort of detail – e.g. the generalisations that scientists as a group stand on the political Left. This is only partly true. A very high proportion of engineers is almost as conservative as doctors; of pure scientists, the same would apply to chemists. It is only among physicists and biologists that one finds the Left in strength. If one compared the whole body of scientists with their opposite numbers of the traditional culture (writers, academics, and so on), the total result might be a few per cent more towards the Left wing. Nevertheless, as a first approximation, the scientific culture is real enough and so is its difference from the traditional. For anyone like myself, by education a scientist, by calling a writer, at one time moving between groups of scientists and writers in the same evening, the difference has seemed dramatic.

The first thing, impossible to miss, is that scientists are on the up and up; they have the strength of a social force behind them. If they are English, they share the experience common to us all – of being in a country sliding economically downhill – but in addition (and to many of them it seems psychologically more important) they belong to something more than a profession, to something more like a directing class of a new society. In a sense oddly divorced from politics, they are the new men. Even the staidest and most politically conservative of scientific veterans have some kind of link with the world to come. They do not hate it as their colleagues do; part of their mind is open to it; almost against their will, there is a residual glimmer of kinship there. The young English scientists may and do curse their luck; increasingly they fret about the rigidities of their universities; they violently envy their Russian counterparts who have money and equipment without discernible limit, who have the whole field wide open. But still they stay pretty resilient: they are swept on by the same social force. Harwell and Windscale have just as much spirit as Los Alamos and Chalk River: they are symbols, frontier towns.

There is a touch of the frontier qualities, in fact, about the whole scientific culture. Its tone is, for example, steadily heterosexual. The difference in social manners between Harwell and Hampstead, or as far as that goes between Los Alamos and Greenwich Village, would make an anthropologist blink. About the whole scientific culture, there is an absence – surprising to outsiders – of the feline and oblique. Sometimes it seems that scientists relish speaking the truth, especially when it is unpleasant. The climate of personal relations is singularly bracing, not to say harsh: it strikes bleakly on those unused to it who suddenly find that the scientists' way of deciding on action is by a full-dress argument, with no regard for sensibilities and no holds barred. No body of people ever believed more in dialectic as the primary method of attaining sense; and if you want a picture of scientists in their off-moments it could be just one of a knock-about argument. Under the argument there glitter egotisms as rapacious as any of ours: but, unlike ours, the egotisms are driven by a common purpose.

How much of the traditional culture gets through to them? The answer is not simple. A good many scientists, including some of the most gifted, have the tastes of literary persons, read the same things, and read as much. Broadly, though, the infiltration is much less. History gets across to a certain extent, in particular social history: the sheer mechanics of living, how men ate, built, travelled, worked, touches a good many scientific imaginations. Philosophy the scientific culture views with indifference, especially metaphysics. As Rutherford said cheerfully to Samuel Alexander: 'When you think of all the years you've been talking about those things, Alexander, and what does it all add up to? *Hot air*, nothing but *hot air*.' A bit less exuberantly, that is what contemporary scientists would say. They regard it as a major intellectual virtue to know what not to think about. They might touch their hats to linguistic analysis, as a relatively honourable way of wasting time; not so to existentialism.

The arts? The only one which is cultivated among scientists is music. It goes both wide and deep; there may possibly be a greater density of musical appreciation than in the traditional culture. In comparison, the graphic arts (except architecture) score little, and poetry not at all. Some novels work their way through, but not as a rule the novels which literary persons set most value on. The two cultures have so few points of contact that the diffusion of novels shows the same sort of delay, and exhibits the same oddities, as though they were getting into translation in a foreign country. It is only fairly recently, for instance, that Graham Greene and Evelyn Waugh have become more than names. And, just as it is rather startling to find that in Italy Bruce Marshall is by a long shot the best-known British novelist, so it jolts one to hear scientists talking with attention of the works of Nevil Shute. In fact, there is a good reason for that: Mr Shute was himself a high-class engineer.

Incidentally, there are benefits to be gained from listening to intelligent men, utterly removed from the literary scene and unconcerned as to who's in and who's out. One can pick up such a comment as a scientist once made, that it looked to him as though the current preoccupations of the New Criticism, the extreme concentration on a tiny passage, had made us curiously insensitive to the total flavour of the work, to the epic qualities in literature. But, on the other side of the coin, one is just as likely to listen to three of the most massive intellects in Europe happily discussing the merits of *The Wallet of Kai-Lung*.

When you meet the younger rank-and-file of scientists, it often seems that they do not read at all. The prestige of the traditional culture is high enough for some of them to make a gallant shot at it. Oddly enough, the novelist whose name to them has become a token of esoteric literary excellence is that difficult highbrow Dickens. They approach him in a grim and dutiful spirit as though tackling *Finnegans Wake*, and feel a sense of achievement if they manage to read a book through. But most young technicians do not fly so high. When you ask them what they read – 'As a married man,' one says, 'I prefer the garden.' Another says: 'I always like just to use my books as tools.' (Difficult to resist speculating what kind of tool a book would make. A sort of hammer? A crude digging instrument?)

That, or something like it, is a measure of the incommunicability of the two cultures. On their side the scientists are losing a great deal. Some of that loss is inevitable: it must and would happen in any society at our technical level. But in this country we make it quite unnecessarily worse by our educational patterns. On the other side, how much does the traditional culture lose by the separation?

I am inclined to think, even more. Not only practically but also intellectually and morally. The intellectual loss is a little difficult to appraise. Most scientists would claim that you cannot comprehend the world unless you know the structure of science, in particular of physical science. In a sense, and a perfectly genuine sense, that is true. Not to have read *War and Peace* and *La Cousine Bette* and *La Chartreuse de Parme* is not to be educated; but so is not to have a glimmer of the Second Law of Thermodynamics. Yet that case ought not to be pressed too far. It is more justifiable to say that those without any scientific understanding miss a whole body of experience: they are rather like the tone deaf, from whom all musical experience is cut off and who have to get on without it. The intellectual invasions of science are, however, penetratingly deeper. Psychoanalysis once looked like a deep invasion, but that was a false alarm; cybernetics may turn out to be the real thing, driving down into the problems of will and cause and motive. If so, those who do not understand the method will not understand the depths of their own cultures.

But the greatest enrichment the scientific culture could give us is – though it does not originate like that – a moral one. Among scientists, deep-natured men know that the individual human condition is tragic; for all its triumphs and joys, the essence of it is loneliness and the end death. But what they will not admit is that, because the individual condition is tragic, therefore the social condition must be tragic, too. Because a man must die, that is no excuse for his dying before his time and after a servile life. The impulse behind the scientists drives them to limit the area of tragedy.

They have nothing but contempt for those representatives of the traditional culture who use a deep insight into man's fate to obscure the social truth – or to do something prettier than obscure the truth, just to hang on to a few perks. Dostoevsky sucking up to the Chancellor Pobedonostsev, who thought the only thing wrong with slavery was that there was not enough of it; the political decadence of the *avant garde* of 1914, with Ezra Pound finishing up broadcasting for the Fascists; Claudel agreeing sanctimoniously with the Marshal about the virtue in others' suffering; Faulkner giving sentimental reasons for treating Negroes as a different species. They are all symptoms of the deepest temptation of the clerks – which is to say: 'Because man's condition is tragic, everyone ought to stay in their place, with mine as it happens somewhere near the top.' From that particular temptation, made up of defeat, self-indulgence, and moral vanity, the scientific culture is almost totally immune.

It is that kind of moral health of the scientists which, in the last few years, the rest of us have needed most; and of which, because the two cultures scarcely touch, we have been most deprived.

The Menace of Beatlism

....

Paul Johnson

In February 1964, then future NS *editor Paul Johnson wrote an article attacking the Beatles and all they stood for. It became the most complained-about piece in the* Statesman's *history.*

Mr William Deedes is an Old Harrovian, a member of the cabinet and the minister in charge of the government's information services. Mr Deedes, it will be remembered, was one of those five ministers who interviewed Mr Profumo on that fateful night and were convinced by him that he had not slept with Miss Keeler. I remember thinking at the time: 'If Deedes can believe that, he'll believe anything.' And indeed he does! Listen to him on the subject of the Beatles:

> They herald a cultural movement among the young which may become part of the history of our time ... For those with eyes to see it, something important and heartening is happening here. The young are rejecting some of the sloppy standards of their elders ... they have discerned dimly that in a world of automation, declining craftsmanship and increased leisure, something of this kind is essential to restore the human instinct to excel at something and the human faculty of discrimination.

Incredible as it may seem, this was not an elaborate attempt at whimsy, but a serious address, delivered to the City of London Young Conservatives. Not a voice was raised to point out that the Emperor wasn't wearing a stitch. The Beatles phenomenon, in fact, illustrates one of my favourite maxims: that if something becomes big enough and popular enough – and especially commercially profitable enough – solemn men will not be lacking to invest it with virtues. So long as the Beatles were just another successful showbiz team, the pillars of society could afford to ignore them. But then came the shock announcement that they were earning £6,250,000 a year – and, almost simultaneously, they got the stamp of approval from America.

This was quite a different matter: at once they became not only part of the export trade but an electorally valuable property. Sir Alec Home promptly claimed credit for them, and was as promptly accused by Mr Wilson of political clothes-stealing. Conservative candidates have been officially advised to mention them whenever possible in their speeches. The Queen expressed concern about the length of Ringo's hair. Young diplomats at our Washington embassy fought for their autographs.

The growing public approval of anti-culture is itself, I think, a reflection of the new cult of youth. Bewildered by a rapidly changing society, excessively fearful of becoming out of date, our leaders are increasingly turning to young people as guides and mentors. If youth likes jazz, then it must be good, and clever men must rationalise this preference in intellectually respectable language. Indeed, the supreme crime, in politics and culture alike, is not to be 'with it'.

Before I am denounced as a reactionary fuddy-duddy, let us pause an instant and see exactly what we mean by this 'youth'. Both TV channels now run weekly programmes in which popular records are played to teenagers and judged. While the music is performed, the cameras linger savagely over the faces of the audience. What a bottomless chasm of vacuity they reveal! The huge faces, bloated with cheap confectionery and smeared with chain-store makeup, the open, sagging mouths and glazed eyes, the broken stiletto heels: here is a generation enslaved by a commercial machine. Behind this image of 'youth', there are, evidently, some shrewd older folk at work.

And what of the 'culture' which is served up to these pitiable victims? According to Mr Deedes, 'the aim of the Beatles and their rivals is first class of its kind. Failure to attain it is spotted and criticised ruthlessly by their many highly-discriminating critics.' I wonder if Mr Deedes has ever taken the trouble to listen to any of this music? On the Saturday TV shows, the merits of the new records are discussed by panels of 'experts', many of whom seem barely more literate or articulate than the moronic ranks facing them.

*

The teenager comes not to hear but to participate in a ritual, a collective grovelling to gods who are blind and empty. 'Throughout the performance,' wrote one observer, 'it was impossible to hear anything above the squealing except the beat of Ringo's drums.' Here, indeed, is 'a new cultural movement': music which not only cannot be heard but does not need to be heard.

If the Beatles and their like were in fact what the youth of Britain wanted, one might well despair. I refuse to believe it – and so will any other intelligent person who casts his or her mind back far enough. What were we doing at 16? I remember reading the whole of Shakespeare and Marlowe, writing poems and plays and stories. At 16, I and my friends heard our first performance of Beethoven's Ninth Symphony; I can remember the excitement even today. We would not have wasted 30 seconds of our precious time on the Beatles and their ilk.

Are teenagers different today? Of course not. Those who flock round the Beatles, who scream themselves into hysteria, are the least fortunate of their generation, the dull, the idle, the failures: their existence, in such large numbers, far from being a cause for ministerial congratulation, is a fearful indictment of our education system, which in 10 years of schooling can scarcely raise them to literacy. What Mr Deedes fails to perceive is that the core of the teenage group – the boys and girls who will be the real leaders and creators of society tomorrow – never go near a pop concert. They are, to put it simply, too busy. They are educating themselves. They are in the process of inheriting the culture which, despite Beatlism or any other mass-produced mental opiate, will continue to shape our civilisation. To use Mr Deedes's own phrase, they are indeed 'rejecting some of the sloppy standards of their elders'. Of course, if many of these elders in responsible positions surrender to the Gadarene Complex and seek to elevate the worst things in our society into the best, their task will be made more difficult. But I believe that, despite the antics of cabinet ministers with election nerves, they will succeed.

The rise and fall of Default Man

Grayson Perry

Paddle your canoe up the River Thames and you will come round the bend and see a forest of huge totems jutting into the sky. Great shiny monoliths in various phallic shapes, they are the wondrous cultural artefacts of a remarkable tribe. We all know someone from this powerful tribe but we very rarely, if ever, ascribe their power to the fact that they have a particular tribal identity.

I think this tribe, a small minority of our native population, needs closer examination. In the UK, its members probably make up about 10 per cent of the population; globally, probably less than 1 per cent. In a phrase used more often in association with Operation Yewtree, they are among us and hide in plain sight.

They dominate the upper echelons of our society, imposing, unconsciously or otherwise, their values and preferences on the rest of the population. With their colourful textile phalluses hanging round their necks, they make up an overwhelming majority in government, in boardrooms and also in the media.

They are, of course, white, middle-class, heterosexual men, usually middle-aged. And every component of that description has historically played a part in making this tribe a group that punches far, far above its weight. I have struggled to find a name for this identity that will trip off the tongue, or that doesn't clutter the page with unpronounceable acronyms such as WMCMAHM. 'The White Blob' was a strong contender but in the end I opted to call him Default Man. I like the word 'default', for not only does it mean 'the result of not making an active choice', but two of its synonyms are 'failure to pay' and 'evasion', which seems incredibly appropriate, considering the group I wish to talk about.

Today, in politically correct twenty-first-century Britain, you might think things would have changed but somehow the Great White Male has thrived and continues to colonise the high-status, high-earning, high-power roles (93 per cent of executive directors in the UK are white men; 77 per cent of parliament is male). The Great White Male's combination of good education, manners, charm, confidence and sexual attractiveness (or 'money', as I like to call it) means he has a strong grip on the keys to power. Of course, the main reason he has those qualities in the first place is what he is, not what he has achieved. John Scalzi, in his blog Whatever, thought that being a straight white male was like playing the computer game called *Life* with the difficulty setting on 'Easy'. If you are a Default Man you look like power.

I must confess that I qualify in many ways to be a Default Man myself but I feel that by coming from a working-class background and being an artist and a transvestite, I have enough cultural distance from the towers of power. I have space to turn round and get a fairly good look at the edifice.

In the course of making my documentary series about identity, *Who Are You?*, for Channel 4, the identity I found hardest to talk about, the most elusive, was Default Man's. Somehow, his world-view, his take on society, now so overlaps with the dominant narrative that it is like a Death Star hiding behind the moon. We cannot unpick his thoughts and feelings from the 'proper, right-thinking' attitudes of our society. It is like in the past, when people who spoke in cut-glass, RP, BBC tones would insist they did not have an accent, only northerners and poor people had one of those. We live and breathe in a Default Male world: no wonder he succeeds, for much of our society operates on his terms.

Chris Huhne (60, Westminster, PPE Magdalen, self-destructively heterosexual), the Default Man we chose to interview for our series, pooh-poohed any suggestion when asked if he benefited from membership or if he represented this group. Lone Default Man will never admit to, or be fully aware of, the tribal advantages of his identity. They are, naturally, full subscribers to that glorious capitalist project, they are *individuals*!

This adherence to being individuals is the nub of the matter. Being 'individual' means that if they achieve something good, it is down to their own efforts. They got the job because they are brilliant, not because they are a Default Man, and they are also presumed more competent by other Default Men. If they do something bad it is also down to the individual and not to do with their gender, race or class.

If a Default Man commits a crime it is not because fraud or sexual harassment, say, are endemic in his tribe (coughs), it is because he is a wrong 'un. If a Default Man gets emotional it is because he is a 'passionate' individual, whereas if he were a woman it would often be blamed on her sex.

When we talk of identity, we often think of groups such as black Muslim lesbians in wheelchairs. This is because identity only seems to become an issue when it is challenged or under threat. Our classic Default Man is rarely under existential threat; consequently, his identity remains unexamined. It ambles along blithely, never having to stand up for its rights or to defend its homeland.

When talking about identity groups, the word 'community' often crops up. The working class, gay people, black people or Muslims are always represented by a 'community leader'. We rarely, if ever, hear of the white middle-class community. 'Communities' are defined in the eye of Default Man. Community seems to be a euphemism for the vulnerable lower orders. Community is 'other'. Communities usually seem to be embattled, separate from society. 'Society' is what Default Man belongs to.

In news stories such as the alleged 'Trojan Horse' plot in Birmingham schools and the recent child-abuse scandal in Rotherham, the central involvement of an ethnic or faith 'community' skews the attitudes of police, social services and the media. The Muslim or Pakistani heritage of those accused becomes the focus. I'm not saying that faith and ethnic groups don't have their particular problems but the recipe for such trouble is made up of more than one spicy, foreign ingredient. I would say it involves more than a few handfuls of common-or-garden education/class issues, poor mental health and, of course, the essential ingredient in nearly all nasty or violent problems, men. Yeah, men – bit like them Default Men but without suits on.

In her essay 'Visual Pleasure and Narrative Cinema', published in 1975, Laura Mulvey coined the term 'the male gaze'. She was writing about how the gaze of the movie camera reflected the heterosexual male viewpoint of the directors (a viewpoint very much still with us, considering that only 9 per cent of the top 250 Hollywood films in 2012 were directed by women and only 2 per cent of the cinematographers were female).

The Default Male gaze does not just dominate cinema, it looks down on society like the eye on Sauron's tower in *The Lord of the Rings*. Every other identity group is 'othered' by it. It is the gaze of the expensively nondescript corporate leader watching consumers adorn themselves with his company's products the better to get his attention.

Default Man feels he is the reference point from which all other values and cultures are judged. Default Man is the zero longitude of identities.

He has forged a society very much in his own image, to the point where now much of what other groups think and feel is the same. They take on the attitudes of Default Man because they are the attitudes of our elders, our education, our government, our media. If Default Men approve of something it must be good, and if they disapprove it must be bad, so people end up hating themselves, because their internalised Default Man is berating them for being female, gay, black, silly or wild.

I often hear women approvingly describe themselves or other women as feisty. Feisty, I feel, has sexist implications, as if standing up for yourself was exceptional in a woman. It sounds like a word that a raffish Lothario would use about a difficult conquest.

I once gave a talk on kinky sex and during the questions afterwards a gay woman floated an interesting thought: 'Is the legalising of gay marriage an attempt to neutralise the otherness of homosexuals?' she asked. Was the subversive alternative being neutered by allowing gays to marry and ape a hetero lifestyle? Many gay people might have enjoyed their dangerous outsider status. Had Default Man implanted a desire to be just like him?

Is the fact that we think like Default Man the reason why a black female Doctor Who has not happened, that it might seem 'wrong' or clunky? In my experience, when I go to the doctor I am more likely to see a non-white woman than a Default Man.

It is difficult to tweezer out the effect of Default Man on our culture, so ingrained is it after centuries of their rules. A friend was once on a flight from Egypt. As it came in to land at Heathrow he looked down at the rows of mock-Tudor stockbroker-belt houses in west London. Pointing them out, he said to the Egyptian man sitting next to him: 'Oh well, back to boring old England.' The Egyptian replied, 'Ah, but to me this is very exotic.' And he was right. To much of the world the Default Englishman is a funny foreign folk icon, with his bowler hat, his Savile

Row suit and Hugh Grant accent, living like Reggie Perrin in one of those polite suburban semis. All the same, his tribal costume and rituals have probably clothed and informed the global power elite more than any other culture. Leaders wear his clothes, talk his language and subscribe to some version of his model of how society 'should be.'

When I was at art college in the late Seventies/early Eighties, one of the slogans the feminists used was: 'Objectivity is Male Subjectivity.' This brilliantly encapsulates how male power nestles in our very language, exerting influence at the most fundamental level. Men, especially Default Men, have put forward their biased, highly emotional views as somehow 'rational', more considered, more 'calm down, dear'. Women and 'exotic' minorities are framed as 'passionate' or 'emotional' as if they, the Default Men, had this unique ability to somehow look round the side of that most interior lens, the lens that is always distorted by our feelings. Default Man somehow had a dispassionate, empirical, objective vision of the world as a birthright, and everyone else was at the mercy of turbulent, uncontrolled feelings. That, of course, explained why the 'others' often held views that were at such odds with their supposedly cool, analytic vision of the world.

Recently, footage of the UN spokesman Chris Gunness breaking down in tears as he spoke of the horrors occurring in Gaza went viral. It was newsworthy because reporters and such spokespeople are supposed to be dispassionate and impartial. To show such feelings was to be 'unprofessional'. And lo! The inherited mental health issues of Default Man are cast as a necessity for serious employment.

I think Default Man should be made aware of the costs and increasing obsolescence of this trait, celebrated as 'a stiff upper lip'. This habit of denying, recasting or suppressing emotion may give him the veneer of 'professionalism' but, as David Hume put it: 'Reason is a slave of the passions.' To be unaware of or unwilling to examine feelings means those feelings have free rein to influence behaviour unconsciously. Unchecked, they can motivate Default Man covertly, unacknowledged, often wreaking havoc. Even if rooted in long-past events in the deep unconscious, these emotions still fester, churning in the dark at the bottom of the well. Who knows what unconscious, screwed-up 'personal journeys' are being played out on the nation by emotionally illiterate Default Men?

Being male and middle class and being from a generation that still valued the stiff upper lip means our Default Man is an ideal candidate for low emotional awareness. He sits in a gender/class/age nexus marked 'Unexploded Emotional Time Bomb'.

These people have been in charge of our world for a long time.

Things may be changing.

Women are often stereotyped as the emotional ones, and men as rational. But, after the 2008 crash, the picture looked different, as Hanna Rosin wrote in an article in the *Atlantic* titled 'The End of Men':

> Researchers have started looking into the relationship between testosterone and excessive risk, and wondering if groups of men, in some basic hormonal way, spur each other to make reckless decisions. The picture emerging is a mirror image of the traditional gender map: men and markets on the side of the irrational and overemotional, and women on the side of the cool and level-headed.

Over the centuries, empirical, clear thinking has become branded with the image of Default Men. They were the ones granted the opportunity, the education, the leisure, the power to put their thoughts out into the world. In people's minds, what do professors look like? What do judges look like? What do leaders look like? The very aesthetic of seriousness has been monopolised by Default Man. Practically every person on the globe who wants to be taken seriously in politics, business and the media dresses up in some way like a Default Man, in a grey, western, two-piece business suit. Not for nothing is it referred to as 'power dressing'. We've all seen those photo ops of world leaders: colour and pattern shriek out as anachronistic. Consequently, many women have adopted this armour of the unremarkable. Angela Merkel, the most powerful woman in the world, wears a predictable unfussy, feminised version of the male look. Hillary Clinton has adopted a similar style. Some businesswomen describe this need to tone down their feminine appearance as 'taking on the third gender'.

Peter Jones on *Dragons' Den* was once referred to as 'eccentric' for wearing brightly coloured stripy socks. So rigid is the Default Man look that men's suit fashions pivot on tiny changes of detail at a glacial pace. US politicians wear such a narrow version of the Default Man look that you rarely see one wearing a tie that is not plain or striped.

One tactic that men use to disguise their subjectively restricted clothing choices is the justification of spurious function. As if they need a watch that splits lap times and works 300 feet underwater, or a Himalayan mountaineer's jacket for a walk in the park. The rufty-tufty army/hunter camouflage pattern is now to boys as pink is to girls. Curiously, I think the real function of the sober business suit is not to look smart but as camouflage. A person in a grey suit is invisible, in the way burglars often wear hi-vis jackets to pass as unremarkable 'workmen'. The business suit is the uniform of those who do the looking, the appraising. It rebuffs comment by its sheer ubiquity. Many office workers loathe dress-down Fridays because they can no longer hide behind a suit. They might have to expose something of their messy selves through their 'casual' clothes. Modern, overprofessionalised politicians, having spent too long in the besuited tribal compound, find casual dress very difficult to get right convincingly. David Cameron, while ruining Converse basketball shoes for the rest of us, never seemed to me as if he belonged in a pair.

When I am out and about in an eye-catching frock, men often remark to me, 'Oh, I wish I could dress like you and did not have to wear a boring suit.' *Have* to! The male role is heavily policed from birth, by parents, peers and bosses. Politicians in particular are harshly kept in line by a media that seems to uphold more bizarrely rigid standards of conformity than those held by any citizen. Each component of the Default Male role – his gender, his class, his age and his sexuality – confines him to an ever narrower set of behaviours, until riding a bicycle or growing a beard, having messy hair or enjoying a pint are seen as ker-azy eccentricity. The fashionable members' club Shoreditch House, the kind of place where 'creatives' with two iPhones and three bicycles hang out, has a 'No Suits' rule. How much of this is a pseudo-rebellious pose and how much is in recognition of the pernicious effect of the overgrown schoolboy's uniform, I do not know.

I dwell on the suit because I feel it exemplifies how the upholders of Default Male values hide in plain sight. Imagine if, by democratic decree, the business suit was banned, like certain items of Islamic dress have been banned in some countries. Default Men would flounder and complain that they were not being treated with 'respect'.

The most pervasive aspect of the Default Man identity is that it masquerades very efficiently as 'normal' – and 'normal', along with 'natural', is a dangerous word, often at the root of hateful prejudice. As Sherrie Bourg Carter, author of *High-Octane Women*, writes:

> Women in today's workforce ... are experiencing a much more camouflaged foe – second-generation gender biases ... 'work cultures and practices that appear neutral and natural on their face', yet they reflect masculine values and life situations of men.

Personally, working in the arts, I do not often encounter Default Man en masse, but when I do it is a shock. I occasionally get invited to formal dinners in the City of London and on arrival, I am met, in my lurid cocktail dress, with a sea of dinner jackets; perhaps harshly, my expectations of a satisfying conversation drop. I feel rude mentioning the black-clad elephant in the room. I sense that I am the anthropologist allowed in to the tribal ritual.

Of course, this weird minority, these curiously dominant white males, are anything but normal. 'Normal', as Carl Jung said, 'is the ideal aim for the unsuccessful.' They like to keep their abnormal power low-key: the higher the power, the duller the suit and tie, a Mercedes rather than a Rolls, just another old man chatting casually to prime ministers at the wedding of a tabloid editor.

Revolution is happening. I am loath to use the R word because bearded young men usually characterise it as sudden and violent. But that is just another unhelpful cliché. I feel real revolutions happen thoughtfully in peacetime. A move away from the dominance of Default Man is happening, but way too slowly. Such changes in society seem to happen at a pace set by incremental shifts in the animal spirits of the population. I have heard many of the 'rational' (i.e. male) arguments against quotas and positive discrimination but I feel it is a necessary fudge to enable just change to happen in the foreseeable future. At the present rate of change it will take more than a hundred years before the UK parliament is 50 per cent female.

The outcry against positive discrimination is the wail of someone who is having their privilege taken away. For talented black, female and working-class people to take their just place in the limited seats of power, some of those Default Men are going to have to give up their seats.

Perhaps Default Man needs to step down from some of his most celebrated roles. I'd happily watch a gay black James Bond and an all-female *Top Gear*, *QI* or *Have I Got News for You*. Jeremy Paxman should have been replaced by a woman on *Newsnight*. More importantly, we need a quota of MPs who (shock) have not been to university but have worked on the shop floor of key industries; have had life experiences that reflect their constituents'; who actually represent the country rather than just a narrow idea of what a politician looks like. The ridiculousness of objections to quotas would become clear if you were to suggest that, instead of calling it affirmative action, we adopted 'Proportionate Default Man Quotas' for government and business. We are wasting talent. Women make up a majority of graduates in such relevant fields as law.

Default Man seems to be the embodiment of George Bernard Shaw's unreasonable man: 'The reasonable man adapts himself to the world; the unreasonable one persists in trying to make the world adapt to himself. Therefore all progress depends on the unreasonable man.'

Default Man's days may be numbered; a lot of his habits are seen at best as old-fashioned or quaint and at worst as redundant, dangerous or criminal. He carries a raft of unhelpful habits and attitudes gifted to him from history – adrenalin addiction, a need for certainty, snobbery, emotional constipation and an overdeveloped sense of entitlement – which have often proved disastrous for society and can also stop poor Default Man from leading a fulfilling life.

Earlier this year, at the Being A Man festival at the Southbank Centre in London, I gave a talk on masculinity called: 'Men, Sit Down for your Rights!'. A jokey title, yes, but one making a serious point: that perhaps, if men were to loosen their grip on power, there might be some benefits for them. The straitjacket of the Default Man identity is not necessarily one happily donned by all members of the tribe: many struggle with the bad fit of being leader, provider, status hunter, sexual predator, respectable and dignified symbol of straight achievement. Maybe the 'invisible weightless backpack' that the US feminist Peggy McIntosh uses to describe white privilege, full of 'special provisions, maps, passports, codebooks, visas, clothes, tools and blank checks', does weigh rather a lot after all.

General election clerihews

Craig Brown

David Cameron
Is inclined to stammer on
Non-doms; but on 'zero hours'
He positively cowers.

Ed Miliband
Is a silly brand:
Hell, yeah! I couldn't feel sorrier
For that Unhappy Warrior.

Natalie Bennett
Insists, again, 'It
'Is all about basically – cough – what I would say is that –
'What we're talking about is what we're – cough – still looking at.'

Nick Clegg
Has been taken down a peg.
Today, you can't be too quick
To snap: 'I disagree with Nick.'

As Nicola Sturgeon
Began to burgeon
Things went topsy-turvy
For Jim Murphy.

Nigel Farage
Faced with a barrage
Of abuse, says 'Frankly, I'd ban it'
To the voters of Thanet.

George Osborne
Was born
To rule; and with a touch of lard he
Styles his hair like Oliver Hardy.

Krishnan Guru-Murthy
Seems a little curt; he
Never recovered from his beano
With Quentin Tarantino.

David Dimbleby
Remains nimble – he
Displays consummate ease
Saying, 'Next question, please!'

Jon Snow
Is full of get up and go,
But I'd avoid setting eyes
On those ties.

Evan Davis
Knows the way to behave is
Not to act so
Cross as Paxo.

Peter Hennessy
Is a bit of a menace; he
Has done more to bore me than
Any other historian.

Vince Cable
Is exceptionally able
But a book I won't be reading twice is
The Storm: the World Economic Crisis.

Chuka Umunna
Hums 'Una Paloma
Blanca', and radiates bonhomie
While discussing the economy.

Tony Blair
Talks a lot of hot air;
Or is calling for party unity
An investment opportunity?

Liam Fox
Remains tox-
ic; but to his credit he
Stays in touch with Adam Werritty.

Alastair Campbell
Springs back, like a bramble,
Reaching for Weapons of Mass Destruction
Whenever there's a ruction.

Chris Huhne
Is over the moon:
'Within a year or two
'I hope to be known as "Chris Who"?'

Harriet Harman
Would make a rotten barman:
As you were shooting the breeze
She'd call: 'Time, gentlemen, please!'

Eric Pickles
Is a martyr to tickles –
The redistribution of riches
Has him in stitches.

John Bercow
Is a bit of a jerk; oh,
And nor am I pally
With Sally.

Ed Balls
Mauls, brawls,
Bawls, galls and caterwauls;
But then palls.

Jacob Rees-Mogg
Looks on agog:
'Things have gone speedily downhill
'Since the Great Reform Bill.'

Grant Shapps
Is the discreetest of chaps:
He's seldom seen
Wearing the name-tag 'Michael Green'.

Russell Brand
Says: 'Why bother to stand
'When I can make a bigger stink as
'One of the World's Four Most Influential Thinkers?'

'Let's talk about genre'

Neil Gaiman and Kazuo Ishiguro

Neil Gaiman's New York Times *review of Kazuo Ishiguro's latest novel began a debate about the borders between fantasy and literary fiction. For a special issue guest-edited by Neil Gaiman and Amanda Palmer, the* New Statesman *brought the pair together to discuss genre snobbery and the evolution of stories.*

Neil Gaiman: Let's talk about genre. Why does it matter? Your book *The Buried Giant* – which was published not as a fantasy novel, although it contains an awful lot of elements that would be familiar to readers of fantasy – seemed to stir people up from both sides of the literary divide. The fantasy people, in the shape of Ursula Le Guin (although she later retracted it) said, 'This is fantasy, and your refusal to put on the mantle of fantasy is evidence of an author slumming it.' And then Michiko Kakutani in the *New York Times* reviewed it with utter bafflement. Meanwhile, readers and a lot of reviewers had no trouble figuring out what kind of book it is and enjoyed it hugely.

Kazuo Ishiguro: I felt like I'd stepped into some larger discussion that had been going on for some time. I expected some of my usual readers to say, 'What's this? There are ogres in it…' but I didn't anticipate this bigger debate. Why are people so preoccupied? What is genre in the first place? Who invented it? Why am I perceived to have crossed a kind of boundary?

NG: I think if you were a novelist writing in 1920 or 1930, you would simply be perceived as having written another novel. When Dickens published *A Christmas Carol* nobody went, 'Ah, this respectable social novelist has suddenly become a fantasy novelist: look, there are ghosts and magic.'

KI: Is it possible that what we think of as genre boundaries are things that have been invented fairly recently by the publishing industry? I can see there's a case for saying there are certain patterns, and you can divide up stories according to these patterns, perhaps usefully. But I get worried when readers and writers take these boundaries too seriously, and think that something strange happens when you cross them, and that you should think very carefully before doing so.

NG: I love the idea of genres as places that you don't necessarily want to go unless you're a native, because the people there will stare at you askance and say things like, 'Head over the wall to Science Fiction, mate, you'll be happier there ...'

KI: ... or, 'Come over here if you want but you're going to have to abide by our rules.'

NG: I think that there's a huge difference between, for example, a novel with spies in it and a spy novel; or a novel with cowboys in it and a cowboy novel. I have a mad theory that I started evolving when I read a book called *Hard Core* by Linda Williams, a film professor in California. It was one of the first books analysing hardcore pornography as a film genre.

She said that in order to make sense of it, you need to think of musicals, because the plot in a musical exists to stop all of the songs from happening at once, and to get you from song to song. You need the song where the heroine pines for what she does not have, you need the songs where the whole chorus is doing something rousing and upbeat, and you need the song when the lovers get together and, after all the vicissitudes, triumph.

I thought, 'That's actually a way to view all literary genres,' because there are things that people who like a genre are looking for in their fiction: the things that titillate, the things that satisfy. If it was a cowboy novel, we'd need the fight in the saloon; we'd need the bad guy to come riding into town and the good guy to be waiting for him. A novel that happens to be set in the Old West doesn't actually need to deliver any of those things – though it would leave readers of genre cowboy fiction feeling peculiarly disappointed, because they have not got the moments of specific satisfaction.

KI: So we have to distinguish between something that's part of the essence of the genre and things that are merely characteristic of it. Gunfights are characteristic of a western, but may not be essential to making the story arresting.

NG: Yes. One of the things that fascinated me about *The Buried Giant* is there are several places in it where people fight with sharp blades, and people are killed, and in each case it happens at the speed that it would have happened in real life and ends as abruptly and, often, unsatisfyingly: the character falls to the grass with what looks like a red snake slipping away from him, you suddenly realise, 'Oh, this is blood,' and you're thinking, 'This is not how a reader of fantasy expecting a good swordfight would have expected this swordfight to go.'

KI: If I was aware of genre at all during the fight scenes, I was thinking of samurai films and westerns. In samurai movies mortal enemies stare at each other for a long time, then there's one flash of violence and it's over.

What do you reckon would have happened if I'd been a writer steeped in fantasy? Would I have had people talking while bashing swords?

NG: You'd definitely have flashing blades. One of the pulp fantasy genres of the Thirties was 'Sword and Sorcery': there'd be mighty feuding warriors with large blades, talking, clashing, grunting … you would have got a solid half-page out of it, partly because the writers were paid by the word.

KI: When I first came to Britain at the age of five, one of the things that shocked me about western culture was the fight scenes in things like *Zorro*. I was already steeped in the samurai tradition – where all their skill and experience comes down to a single moment that separates winner from loser, life from death. The whole samurai tradition is about that: from pulp manga to art movies by Kurosawa. That was part of the magic and tension of a swordfight, as far as I was concerned. Then I saw people like Basil Rathbone as the Sheriff of Nottingham versus Errol Flynn as Robin Hood and they'd be having long, extended conversations while clicking their swords, and the hand that didn't have the sword in it would be doing this kind of floppy thing in the air, and the idea seemed to be to edge your opponent over a precipice while engaging him in some sort of long, expository conversation about the plot.

NG: What we're talking about here is jumping from one literary-slash-genre tradition to another.

KI: I'm very fond of westerns, particularly the later westerns. From the Fifties onwards, the gunfights become much more meditative and deliberate. There's a much bigger silent pause before the people facing each other draw their guns. The idea of the one-on-one showdown – which doesn't really make much sense when you think about it in terms of practical combat: it's much better to sneak up behind someone and shoot them in the back – became a genre tradition, that honourable guys, even bad guys, would prefer to face their enemy that way. *The Iliad* is fascinating on this. Its stand-offs are almost bizarre. There's supposed to be this huge, wild battle going on on the plains outside Troy, and yet in this mayhem one warrior faces another and they start a conversation: they say, 'Oh, and who are you? Tell me about your ancestry.' They swap stories about their grandfather, and one of them will say, 'You know, my dad met your dad when he was travelling, and he gave him a very nice goblet.' So a strange bubble develops around the two combatants. And then they fight, or sometimes they discover they rather like each other and decide not to. Things like the final confrontation between Hector and Achilles are definitely on the side of Kurosawa, not Errol Flynn.

But let me come back to the theory about pornography and the musical. So, you liked this idea?

NG: I loved the idea, because it seems to me that subject matter doesn't determine genre. Genres only start existing when there's enough of them to form a sort of critical mass in a bookshop, and even that can go away. A bookstore worker in America was telling me that he'd worked in Borders when they decided to get rid of their horror section, because people weren't coming into it. So his job was to take the novels and decide which ones were going to go and live in Science Fiction and Fantasy and which ones were going to Thrillers.

KI: Does that mean horror has disappeared as a genre?

NG: It definitely faded away as a bookshop category, which then meant that a lot of people who had been making their living as horror writers had to decide what they were, because their sales were diminishing. In fact, a lot of novels that are currently being published as thrillers are books that probably would have been published as horror 20 years ago.

KI: I don't have a problem with marketing categories, but I don't think they're helpful to anybody apart from publishers and bookshops.

NG: What was the reaction to *Never Let Me Go*? I think at that point the last thing anybody was expecting from you was a science-fiction novel, and that – although it was a novel about people – was quite uncompromisingly a science-fiction novel.

KI: I felt that there wasn't such an issue about science fiction as there has been this time about fantasy. Sci-fi ideas have been used in all kinds of fiction, and there's always been this tradition of what you could call *Nineteen Eighty-Four* science fiction: Orwell, H. G. Wells and so on.

Even so, it probably wouldn't have occurred to me to use the science-fiction dimension for *Never Let Me Go* ten or 15 years earlier. I actually tried to write that same story twice in the Nineties but I just couldn't find a way to make it work. And it was only the third time I tried, around 2001, that this idea came to me: if I made them clones, who were being harvested for organ donation, the story would work.

Before that, in a more realist setting, I was really struggling: how can I get young people to go through the experience of old people, how can I contrive this situation? I was coming up with not very good ideas, like they've all got a disease, or they came across nuclear materials and so they were doomed to a shorter lifespan.

Some time in the Nineties I felt a change of climate in the mainstream literary world. There was a younger generation of writers emerging who I really respected: David Mitchell was one of them. Or my friend Alex Garland, who's 15 or 16 years younger than me, who became famous for *The Beach* – he was showing me the screenplays he was writing, one of which was *28 Days Later*, which became the renowned zombie movie, and then he wrote *Sunshine*, about a manned expedition to the sun. Alex told me about graphic novels. He said I had to read Alan Moore and Frank Miller and all these people. So from the Nineties onwards, I sensed that there was a whole generation of people emerging who had a very different attitude to sci-fi, and that there was a new force of energy and inspiration because of that. I may have had the crusty prejudices of somebody of my generation but I felt liberated by these younger writers. Now I feel fairly free to use almost anything. People in the sci-fi community were very nice about *Never Let Me Go*. And by and large I've rather enjoyed my inadvertent trespassing into the fantasy genre, too, although I wasn't even thinking about *The Buried Giant* as a fantasy – I just wanted to have ogres in there!

NG: What fascinates me is that at the time when Tolkien was writing *The Lord of the Rings* it wasn't regarded as in the fantasy genre, either: the first part was reviewed in *The Times* by W. H. Auden. It was a novel, and that it had ogres and orcs and giant spiders and magical rings and elves was simply what happened in this novel. Back then these books tended to be produced in exactly the same way as you produced *The Buried Giant*, in that you'd written other things, and now you wanted to do a book in which, for the novel to work, you needed a dragon breathing magical mist over the world; you needed it to occur in a post-Arthurian world; you needed your monsters and your ogres and your pixies. There were people like Hope Mirrlees – who wrote modernist poetry and profoundly realistic fiction and who was one of the Bloomsbury set, but produced a wonderful novel called *Lud-in-the-Mist* – and Sylvia Townsend Warner, who wrote books like *Kingdoms of Elfin*. And these were simply accepted as part of mainstream literature.

KI: So what happened? Why have we got this kind of wall around fantasy now, and a sense of stigma about it?

NG: I think it came from the enormous commercial success in the Sixties, when the hippie world embraced *The Lord of the Rings* and it became an international publishing phenomenon. At Pan/Ballantine, the adult fantasy imprint, they basically just went through the archives of books that had been published in the previous 150, 200 years and looked for things that felt like *The Lord of the Rings*. And then you had people like Terry Brooks, who wrote a book called *The Sword of Shannara*, which was essentially a *Lord of the Rings* clone by somebody not nearly as good, but it sold very well. By the time fantasy had its own area in the bookshop, it was deemed inferior to mimetic, realistic fiction. I think reviewers and editors did not know how to speak fantasy; were not familiar with the language, did not recognise it. I was fascinated by the way that Terry Pratchett would, on the one hand, have people like A. S. Byatt going, 'These are real books, they're saying important things and they are beautifully crafted', and on the other he would still not get any real recognition. I remember Terry saying to me at some point, 'You know, you can do all you want, but you put in one fucking dragon and they call you a fantasy writer.'

KI: Maybe there's a dimension we're not really tackling. Is there something about books – as opposed to films and TV – that's inextricably linked with a sense of class? Do you remember *Educating Rita*?

NG: Of course.

KI: What happens there is, when a working-class girl wants to 'better herself', she goes to college and studies literature. That's what separates her from her class roots. She can't relate to her family any more, but she seems to be equipped in some kind of way to move into the middle-class world. There's always been that aspect to books. I've been very aware that is part of why some people want to read my work: they think it's prestigious to be seen to be holding a book by a literary author in their hand. If they are trying to make their way up the class ladder, it's not enough just to make a lot of money: you've also got to be able to converse well about culture, read certain kinds of authors and go to certain kinds of plays. I'm always very uneasy about that.

NG: So we're actually talking about reading for pleasure as opposed to reading for improvement. The Victorian idea of Improving Literature – people who want to somehow improve themselves or their mind; you can look at their bookshelves and know who they are – and the people who just read because they want to go into the story.

KI: I don't have a problem, necessarily, about reading for improvement. I often choose a book because I think I'm going to enjoy it, but I think also it's going to improve me in some sense. But when you ask yourself, 'Is this going to improve me?' what are you really asking? I think I probably do turn to books for some sort of spiritual and intellectual nourishment: I think I'm going to learn something about the world, about people. But if by 'improving', we mean it would help me go up the class ladder, then it's not what reading and writing should be about. Books are serving the same function as certain brands of cars or jewellery, in just denoting social position. That kind of motivation attaches itself to reading in a way that probably doesn't attach itself to film.

Many of the great classics that are studied by film scholars are sci-fi: Fritz Lang's *Metropolis*, Tarkovsky's *Solaris*, Kubrick's *2001*. They don't seem to have suffered from the kind of genre stigmatisation their equivalents would have done in book form.

NG: I remember as a boy reading an essay by C. S. Lewis in which he writes about the way that people use the term 'escapism' – the way literature is looked down on when it's being used as escapism – and Lewis says that this is very strange, because actually there's only one class of people who don't like escape, and that's jailers: people who want to keep you where you are. I've never had anything against escapist literature, because I figure that escape is a good thing: going to a different place, learning things, and coming back with tools you might not have known.

I was book-reviewing a lot in the early Eighties, and it seemed for a while like all young adult books were the same book: about some kid who lived in slightly squalid circumstances, with an older sibling who was a bad example, and the protagonist would have a bad time and then run into a teacher or adult who would inspire them to get their life back on track. It was depressing. The wonderful thing about J. K. Rowling was that suddenly the idea that you can write books for kids that go off into weird and wonderful places – and actually make reading fun – is one of the reasons why children's books went from being a minor area of the bookshop to a huge force in British publishing.

When I started writing *Coraline*, in 1991, and showed it to my editor, he explained that what I was writing was unpublishable. He wasn't wrong. His name was Richard Evans; he was a very smart man, with good instincts. When he explained why writing a book intended for children and adults that was functionally horror fiction for children was unpublishable, I believed him.

KI: The objection was what, exactly? That it was too scary?

NG: It was too scary, it was very obviously aimed at both children and adults, it was weird, fantastic horror fiction, and they didn't have a way of publishing it. They knew which librarians bought what and how things got reviewed, and this was simply not something that they could have sold. It wasn't until much later, when I was in a world in which the Lemony Snicket books had happened, and Philip Pullman and Rowling were being read, and the idea of crossover books aimed at both children and adults existed, that it was published.

KI: Perhaps things that deviated from realism were treated with great suspicion. But *Coraline* seems to be self-evidently a book that confronts all kinds of very real things. It's about a child learning to make distinctions between certain kinds of parental love, to distinguish between a love that is based on somebody's need and fulfilling somebody's need, and what is actually genuine parental love, which may not at first glance look particularly demonstrative. I don't see how anybody can mistake it for a kind of escapism: you're not just taking children on some sort of strange, enjoyable ride.

NG: I think the rules are crumbling and I think the barriers are breaking. I love the idea also that sometimes, if you're actually going to write realistic fiction, you're going to have to include fantasy. For example, having friends who are very religious and who live in worlds in which God cares about them, and their dead ones are watching them from heaven – these are normal, sane, sensible, twenty-first-century people, but if one were to write about their world, you would need to write in terms of something that would be recognisable as either magical realism or, possibly, fantasy.

KI: My guiding principle when writing *The Buried Giant* was that I'd stay within the parameters of what somebody in a primitive, pre-scientific society could rationally believe. So if you don't have a scientific explanation for why somebody dear to you has got ill, it seems to me perfectly sensible to go for an explanation that went something like, 'A pixie came in the night and gave my dear wife this illness, and I only wish I'd done something about it, because I heard something moving around that night and I was just a bit tired and I thought, well, it's a rat or something ...'

If it was within the imaginative world of the people of that time, I'd allow it literally, in my fictional world, but I wouldn't allow a flying saucer or a Tardis, because that was outside their realm.

NG: We're getting a lot of confluence now. Looking at people like Michael Chabon, David Mitchell, Emily St John Mandel, writers who are just willing to go and explore. They grew up in a world where science fiction and fantasy were around; they grew up in a world of good children's books.

KI: Yes, it's almost become the norm, now, for new writers to think in terms of dystopian fiction or sci-fi.

NG: It's a good way to go. I don't think there's a human being on the planet who has not, in some way in the last 15, 20 years, encountered the phenomenon of future shock that Alvin Toffler described: the idea that it's all moving a bit fast, that things are changing, that the world that our parents and grandparents knew is not the world we are living in now. If you're in that environment, then science fiction is a kind of natural way of talking about it, and particularly dystopian science fiction, which always begins when a writer looks around, sees something they don't like and thinks, 'But if this goes on, then ...'

KI: I think it's interesting that the word 'dystopian' has become so popular now. There's something reassuring when I read that word, because it's saying it's some sort of dark, logical extension of the world that we know; it's going to be a commentary on our world. And so that the fear of irrelevance isn't there. If I sense that a writer is just weaving some sort of self-referential alternative world, that will not tell me anything emotionally or intellectually about the one I live in, I would lose patience and say, 'I can't be bothered to go there; why do I want to go there?' Do you have any sympathy with that?

NG: I am like you in that way. But I could extend this idea that escapism is simply good as a thing to include things like Mills & Boon novels, things that bring joy to people, a joy that will never be reviewed in literary pages, because it is simply – you know – the equivalent of eating an ice cream. I think that always gets viewed with suspicion, like the Victorian triple-decker novels that Miss Prism was writing in *The Importance of Being Earnest*, or the commentary in the *Lady Chatterley* case: 'Would you let your servant read these?' – the idea that if servants are going to read things, they should read improving literature, not things that are simply distractions.

I'm not arguing that no book is better than another, I'm just saying that books have different purposes. Fundamentally, I'm all for the democracy of books, and for the idea that at least some of the hierarchy of books is artificial. There was a science-fiction writer named Theodore Sturgeon writing in the Forties and Fifties, who coined Sturgeon's law. He said, 'Well, 90 per cent of science fiction is crap, but then 90 per cent of everything is crap,' which is always a useful thing to remember.

KI: I would like to see things breaking down a lot more. I suppose my essential position is that I'm against any kind of imagination police, whether they're coming from marketing reasons or from class snobbery.

But maybe the stigma against fantasy is something much wider than in the fiction world. Since industrial times began, it's sort of true to say that children have been allowed a sanctioned world where fantasy and imagination is deemed to be fine, in fact, almost desirable. But then when they get to a certain age, they have to start getting prepared to be units of the labour force. And so, society has to start getting the fantasy element out of the children, so that they can become factory workers, soldiers, white-collar workers, whatever, because it's seen to be not useful to the overall economic enterprise to have children growing up maintaining that fantasy element. You don't want people who are too dreamy or who are imagining things: you want them to accept this is the nitty-gritty of real life, that they've just got to get on with it.

I'm not suggesting we're necessarily being manipulated by some sinister government or anything; it's just there in society. Parents will naturally discourage children once they get to a certain age from continuing with the fantasy element in their lives; schools will, too. It becomes taboo in the society at large.

Maybe the reason it's been loosening up, and the stigma is going away to some extent in the last 25 years or so, is that the nature of our capitalist enterprise has changed. We're no longer factory workers, white-collar workers, soldiers, and so on. And with the advent of blue-sky thinking, the new tech industries that have led the way in the last two decades seem to require some kind of imagination. Perhaps people are beginning to think there is some economic use in actually allowing us to indulge in what was once deemed childish fantasy. I sound like some sort of Seventies sociology professor, but I feel there's something in this.

NG: You know, I was in China in 2007, and it was the first ever state-sponsored, Party-approved science-fiction convention. They brought in some people from the west and I was one of them, and I was talking to a number of the older science-fiction writers in China, who told me about how science fiction was not just looked down on, but seen as suspicious and counter-revolutionary, because you could write a story set in a giant ant colony in the future, when people were becoming ants, but nobody was quite sure: was this really a commentary on the state? As such, it was very, very dodgy.

I took aside one of the Party organisers, and said, 'OK. Why are you now in 2007 endorsing a science-fiction convention?' And his reply was that the Party had been concerned that while China historically has been a culture of magical and radical invention, right now, they weren't inventing things. They were making things incredibly well but they weren't inventing. And they'd gone to America and interviewed the people at Google and Apple and Microsoft, and talked to the inventors, and discovered that in each case, when young, they'd read science fiction. That was why the Chinese had decided that they were going to officially now approve of science fiction and fantasy.

KI: That is so interesting.

NG: Which actually articulates your theory exactly. It's about the economy and the workforce of a society in which the act of imagining is as important as the act of toiling. We have machines that can toil, but we don't have machines that can imagine.

KI: Have you ever done an event at a Microsoft campus or Google?

NG: I have. I've done Google and I've done Microsoft. Google was like going to a magical party held by nice people – it was a few years ago; I don't know if they're still quite as enthusiastic and filled with sweeties and so forth now. Whereas I turned up on the Microsoft campus and had half an hour of trying to persuade the person on the front desk that my name was not something else that also had an N and a G in it, and I was not here to give a lecture on cyber-security, and eventually managed to find some people who were in a room where they had been waiting for me for 45 minutes, and apparently cellphones didn't work very well, so they hadn't been able to get our message. It was a strange kind of contrast.

KI: But the interesting thing is that you were invited to the Microsoft campus. Indeed, I was there last month. It is seen to be good for the company, and I suppose in a wider sense it's good for the economy.

Moving on from the genre question, I'd be interested to ask you about these fascinating relationships which recur in your work, between somebody who has a normal human lifespan, and an immortal or very long-lived being. Do you know why you're drawn to that relationship?

NG: There are things I can point at that probably set me off, the first of which was probably watching *Doctor Who* as a very small boy, and starting to realise that this man in this blue box was going to be functionally immortal, but his friends were going to be left behind in time. And also pets. You get pets and your lifespans do not match. I remember realising that as a very small boy, and thinking it was absolutely tragic. You know, my mouse has just died of old age and he's three.

The human lifespan seems incredibly short and frustrating, and for me, one of the best things about being a reader, let alone a writer, is being able to read ancient Greek stories, ancient Egyptian stories, Norse stories – to be able to feel like one is getting the long view. Stories are long-lived organisms. They're bigger and older than we are. And the frustrating thing about having 60 years or 80 years or, if medical science gets fancy, 120 years, is that actually 1,000 years would be really interesting. You want to step back and go, 'Where do you get this view?' and where we get it from is passing on stories, and handing down knowledge and experience.

You sit there reading Pepys, and just for a minute, you kind of get to be 350, 400 years older than you are. I've always loved the idea of making things longer, changing perspective. And part of looking at things in the long term is also, I think, in a weird way, worry about the future.

KI: There's an interesting emotional tension that comes because of the mismatch of lifespans in your work, because an event that might be tragic for one of us may not be so for the long-lived being. There's an episode of *Doctor Who* that you wrote, called *Doctor's Wife*, and one of the most haunting things about that was a passage where Rory and Amy are lost in some kind of weird time vortex thing. Rory ages enormously, he's waiting like 70 years, while Amy is running around on the other side of the door ... And she keeps getting visions of him grown really, really old and he's been waiting for her, whereas for her, it's just been like 20 seconds, and he's saying, 'Where were you, where were you?' Eventually he turns into just a pile of remains, human remains, and all you see is an angry, bitter piece of graffiti scrawled up on the wall, maybe in blood, for all we know. His love has turned to hate, because he just waited and waited for her.

Recently I've been interested in the difference between personal memory and societal memory, and I'm tempted almost to personify these two things. A society, a nation, goes on and on, for centuries: it can turn Nazi for a while and cause mayhem. But then the next generation comes along and says, you know, 'We're not going to make that mistake again.' Whereas an individual who happens to live through the Nazi era in Germany, that's his whole life.

NG: If you're going to try and tell one of those stories, then the urge comes to start figuring out a way that you can have a conversation between somebody who can see the big picture, or is the big picture, and somebody who is in some way a brick in the wall. One of the most beautiful things about fiction is that you can have those conversations if you need them.

KI: In those cases being able to resort to fantasy opens things up enormously. I've often done this, even if it doesn't look so obvious, even if there aren't things that look like mythical creatures. Creating an incredibly stuffy English butler in *The Remains of the Day*, I was very aware that I was taking something that I recognised to be a very small, negative set of impulses in myself – the fear of getting hurt in love, or that urge to just say, 'I don't want to figure out the political implications or the moral implications of my job, I'm just going to get on with my tiny patch'; those kinds of little urges we all recognise in ourselves – taking those and exaggerating them, and turning them into a kind of monstrous manifestation. The butler doesn't look like a conventional monster, but I always thought that he was a kind of monster.

NG: I love the idea of Stevens as a monster!

KI: I'm reminded of something Lettie says in *The Ocean at the End of the Lane*: 'Monsters come in all shapes and sizes. Some of them are things people are scared of. Some of them are things that look like things people used to be scared of a long time ago. Sometimes monsters are things people should be scared of, but they aren't.' I thought that last category was really interesting. What are the monsters that stand for things that we should be afraid of but we aren't?

NG: I think it's very easy to not be afraid of slow things, and not be afraid of things that apparently have your best interests at heart, and sometimes not to be afraid of things that mask themselves in efficiency and humanity. I was reading the memoirs of Rudolf Höss, commandant of Auschwitz, and his letters home are filled with talking about how his men were working hard, who was doing well, how they got an extra trainload of people in, and: 'By the way, give little Willy the present I sent and the chocolate, and I hope you enjoyed the schnapps.' And it was so horribly human.

It is the monstrosity that waits there inside normality, that waits in humanity. I wish that all monsters could be serial killers, could be crazed, could be dangerous, but the problem is that they're not. Some of them are, horrifyingly, people who in their own head have somehow got to the point where they think they're doing a good job, doing the right thing. But they're still monsters.

KI: You wonder about Boko Haram, these people who shoot buses full of children, who believe girls shouldn't be educated and so on. Do they actually believe that they're doing good?

NG: The tragedy for me of something even like 9/11 is that I do not believe that the people piloting those planes were going, 'I am an evil person doing an evil thing.' I think they were going, 'I am doing what God wants, I am doing God's will; I am doing good, look at me striking against evil.'

KI: I wanted to ask you a bit more about stories being very long-lived beings. You've said that some stories actually adapt and survive as society changes around them.

NG: My favourite example of a story that mutates is 'Cinderella'. The story may well have begun in China, where actually they care a lot more about foot size than they do in the west. But it reaches France, and you have a story about a girl whose dead mother gives her these fancy fur slippers, fur being *'vair'*, but somewhere in the retelling the V-A-I-R becomes V-E-R-R-E, and they become glass slippers. The homonym happens, and now you have glass slippers, which make no sense. You didn't really have the technology in medieval France to make glass slippers; wearing them would be stupid, they would cut your feet, they would break. Yet, suddenly, you have an image that that story then coagulates around. And now 'Cinderella' just spreads and spreads – it has a huge advantage over all the other stories about girls who are sort of dirty and sit by the fire and magic things happen to them. 'Cinderella' is the one that survived.

KI: Do you think that if stories are left in the hands of professional storytelling institutions, like film studios and publishing houses, they are less likely to mutate in an honest way? Do you think the commercialisation of storytelling could actually be interfering in the natural development and growth of this kind of long-lived being?

NG: What a lovely idea! Where stories are concerned, I tend to be very Darwinian. Because I look at something like 'Sleeping Beauty'. Disney retold 'Sleeping Beauty'; one can assume that its 'Sleeping Beauty' reached more people than any other version has. And yet, if people tell the story you won't get the Disney version where she meets the prince that morning, you'll get a tower of thorns growing up and a hundred years passing before a prince turns up. It feels like a much better version.

I think that there's definitely the battery farming of stories out there, but I don't think they take over: they simply indulge our craving.

KI: Is fan fiction today an example of stories starting to mutate? Now you have this phenomenon, which involves both professional writers – P. D. James writing a sequel to *Pride and Prejudice*, or Sebastian Faulks writing another James Bond – and amateurs making up things around their favourite books, and writing prequels and sequels.

NG: It's not a new phenomenon. I love the fact that, you know, in the early versions of *King Lear*, the story had a happy ending. Shakespeare turned it into a tragedy, and through the eighteenth and nineteenth centuries they kept trying to give it a happy ending again. But people kept going back to the one that Shakespeare created. You could definitely view Shakespeare as fan fiction, in his own way. I've only ever written, as far as I know, one book that did the thing that happens when people online get hold of it and start writing their own fiction, which was *Good Omens*, which I did with Terry Pratchett. It's a 100,000-word book; there's probably a million words of fiction out there by now, written by people who were inspired by characters in the book.

KI: What do you feel about that?

NG: Mostly I feel happy about it. But I think the happiest and proudest of people would have been, in those terms, the Stan Lees and the Jack Kirbys, the people who created characters in comics. Kirby was the artist, but also the creating, driving force behind the Fantastic Four, Iron Man, Captain America, the Hulk, the X-Men, in the early Sixties. These guys created characters about whom people are forever inventing, spinning off, and there's something very wonderful about that.

KI: Yes, there is. I'm often asked what my attitude is to film, theatrical, radio adaptations of my novels. It's very nice to have my story go out there, and if it's in a different form, I want the thing to mutate slightly. I don't want it to be an exact translation of my novel. I want it to be slightly different, because in a very vain kind of way, as a storyteller, I want my story to become like public property, so that it gains the status where people feel they can actually change it around and use it to express different things.

NG: Yes, the moment that you have a live actor portraying a character, something exciting is happening; it's different, and if it's really happening in front of you live, then, again, you're seeing something that's new.

So I do love it when people grab my stuff and take it and do things with it. I love copyright – I love the fact that I can feed myself and feed my children with the stuff I make up. On the other hand, copyright length right now is life plus 75 years, and I don't know that I want to be in control of what I've created for 75 years after I've died! I don't know that I want to be feeding my great-grandchildren. I feel like they should be able to look after themselves, and not necessarily put limits on what I've created, if there's something that would do better in the cultural dialogue. I loved Les Klinger's legal case, establishing that the Conan Doyle Estate had basically been running a shakedown operation for the last 20, 30 years, where they've been getting people to pay money to license Sherlock Holmes when Holmes was out of copyright.

KI: I didn't know about that, actually. Since Sherlock Holmes went out of copyright, certainly, he has started to mutate and evolve in a very energetic way. I don't know if it would have been possible, for instance, to have the Cumberbatch modernised series, had it been under copyright. And Holmes is a very interesting example, I think, of a figure who's mutated over the years and evolved. I think if you did a big study of *Doctor Who*, you'd see that the essential story has actually changed to serve the different climates of the times. It's clear that the Daleks started off as Nazis and the Cybermen were communists. But my daughter was saying that, for their generation, the Cybermen represent the people being turned into mindless wage slaves in the twenty-first-century workplace. Now the fear of the communist takeover of the world has receded, the Cybermen can become almost the opposite – something that represents a unit of the rampant capitalist culture.

I wonder if *Doctor Who* will turn out to be one of these creatures who live for a long, long time, as a story that will be a hundred-year-old being, a 300-year-old being. I love this idea of yours of stories being long-lived beings because it seems to have implications for what our ambitions should be, as people who sit at home and write them.

NG: I know that when I create a story, I never know what's going to work. Sometimes I will do something that I think was just a bit of fun, and people will love it and it catches fire, and sometimes I will work very hard on something that I think people will love, and it just fades: it never quite finds its people.

KI: Even if something doesn't catch fire at the time, you may find it catches fire further down the line, in 20 years' time, or 30 years' time. That has happened, often.

NG: Exactly. There's a beautiful essay by A. A. Milne where he says, 'I want to draw your attention to a completely forgotten book that none of you have ever heard about that is one of the best books in the world, and it's by Kenneth Grahame. And you've all heard of him, because he wrote *Dream Days* and *The Golden Age*' – two popular books – 'but he also wrote a book called *The Wind in the Willows*, which none of you have heard of.'

KI: Aha. Stories are interesting in that way. They sometimes just emerge, after some mysterious kind of hibernation period. You can never tell what is going to be one of these long-lived creatures and what isn't. It would be interesting to think, if stories are creatures, whether some of them are actually deceitful creatures. Some of them would be deeply sly and untrustworthy, and some of them would be very uplifting.

NG: There would definitely be bad ones. But how would we know? How would we ever find out?

9 OCTOBER 2015

'I was killed when I was 27': The curious afterlife of Terence Trent D'Arby

Kate Mossman

Imagine this. You're 25 years old and your debut album of perfectly polished soul-rock-pop-funk sells one million copies in the first three days of release. It delivers three Top Ten hits, winning you numerous platinum gongs and a Grammy Award, and parachutes you right into the arena of the 1980s megastars you idolise. You drive the music press into a frenzy: they say you combine the voice of Sam Cooke and the moves of James Brown with the louche beauty of Jimi Hendrix. You are mentored by Springsteen, Leonard Cohen and Pete Townshend; you spend hours on the phone with Prince and sing on Brian Wilson albums. You even meet your hero Muhammad Ali, whose attitude you've ingested, saying: 'Tell people long enough and loud enough you're the greatest and eventually they'll believe you.' In case anyone is in any doubt about just how important you are, you draw a parallel between your destiny and that of Martin Luther King.

Early one morning, at the end of one of your six-hour, joss-stick-infused overnight interviews, a journalist asks you what happens if your follow-up album isn't as successful as your first. For once, you are lost for words. 'That's like asking me what I would do if my dick fell off ...'

The man who slips into the hotel lobby in Milan looks like a fashion district local – one scarf over his dreadlocks, another curled round his neck – but there's an inward energy about him, like one of those fragile celebrities who doesn't want to be noticed but cannot help it: it's all there in the cut of the trousers and size of the blue-bottle shades.

I've been given instructions for my meeting with Sananda Maitreya. 1. Please don't mention the name 'Terence Trent D'Arby', as it is painful for him. 2. Please don't make any comparisons with Prince regarding his name change, which occurred in 1995 after a series of dreams. 3. Please don't ask him things like, 'What songs do you think would make a good single from your new album, *Rise of the Zugebrian Time Lords*?'

The hotel is next to Milan's cathedral, the Duomo, where Maitreya (formerly Darby) proposed to his Italian wife, the architect and former television presenter Francesca Francone, some years ago during a Catholic Mass. We go to the sixth floor and find that nothing is quite right up there: the room is too hot; he orders a whiskey and Coke and can't find a bottle opener; we find one and it doesn't work. Finally, he takes a long, reassuring slug and declares, 'I feel like I'm going on a date when I've been married 25 years. I don't know how to do this any more.'

He says softly: 'One thing about Italians is you can't let them in your head. They're inquisitive. The English and Germans are a dog tribe; the Italians are cats. They're very helpful, but it's in their own rhythm, their own way, and it can drive you crazy.'

It's an odd start to an interview, but even as a young man Terence Trent D'Arby liked to discourse on a broad range of subjects. An American who rejected his homeland, D'Arby was living in Britain through what he refers to today as 'the Thatcher Revolution'; he was a strange, exotic bird, dropped down in the streets of London, cruising around on a motorbike in the video for his hit song 'Sign Your Name' and appearing frequently on the Channel 4 show *The Tube* (he had a year-long affair with its host, Paula Yates). Today, his accent is New York, but back then it was English; the apostrophe he adopted was a mark of his rapid self-elevation. He was all things to all people, and once began a *Q Magazine* interview deconstructing the defeat of Neil Kinnock in the 1987 election.

'Oh my God, I can't believe you thought I was a socialist,' he says now. 'I was nothing more than an opportunist. Any socialist tendencies I may have had were cured when I got my first tax bill. All artists are socialists until they see another artist with a bigger house than theirs.'

D'Arby had cut his teeth in a German funk band while stationed in Frankfurt with Elvis Presley's old regiment; and like that other army boy, Hendrix, he came to fame in a London that wanted his music more than the country he came from. The producer Martyn Ware – a founder member of Heaven 17 and the Human League – worked with him on his debut LP, *Introducing the Hardline According to Terence Trent D'Arby*, which also included the hit songs 'Wishing Well' and 'If You Let Me Stay'. He describes D'Arby as 'a box of fireworks going off in every direction. I have never met anyone so driven.' Ware would arrive at the studio in the morning and find D'Arby already sitting there in the dark, analysing live recordings of Sam Cooke: 'It was like he was studying at university to be a classic soul singer.'

Out in the world, his preternatural confidence was magnetic. 'He was *the* world's most beautiful man,' Ware says. 'I used to walk around Soho with him and women would literally stop and stare – he looked like a god because he's got that boxer's body, and he was a bit androgynous, too. Even the men fancied him.' (D'Arby once said he had sex more often than he washed his hair.)

To the music press, he posed a dilemma. As a pop star he was so perfect, Charles Shaar Murray wrote in 1988, he was 'like something invented by three rock critics on the 'phone'. They called him two things: a genius, and a wanker. To make things more confusing, the very same people calling him a genius were the people calling him a wanker. Worse still, D'Arby worshipped these people. While living in Germany he had devoured the *NME* and *Melody Maker*. 'I had an intellectual crush on Nick Kent, Charles Shaar Murray and Julie,' he says today – 'Julie Burchill. But she is so reactionary now.' He knew that British rock hacks thought American artists were boring to interview so he set out to be different.

Terence Trent D'Arby's follow-up album, 1989's *Neither Fish Nor Flesh*, was not the triumph he had predicted. It was an experimental psych-soul project featuring tribal drums, surf rock guitar and cosmic libretto: 'To an outside world I *will* not be defined!' Early in its inception, D'Arby's old team received a Dear John letter saying that he felt like this was his moment: he wanted to produce, master and engineer the project himself. He is credited as playing, among other things, kazoo, saxophone, sitar and timpani on the record. He invited Martyn Ware to hear the album when it was finished (in another darkened studio session, which D'Arby himself did not attend). 'And although I thought it was very brave,' Ware tells me, 'I just couldn't hear the singles.' The album stiffed – spectacularly, for its time – selling just 300,000 copies (the debut sold over nine million). It brought about a downfall straight out of a Greek tragedy. In music lore, its creator disappeared from the face of the earth on 23 October 1989, the moment the record was released. The truth is slightly different: he soldiered on valiantly for a few years, did a naked cover shoot for *Q* in 1993 and his third album, *Symphony Or Damn*, produced four top 20 singles in the UK, among them 'Delicate' and 'Let Her Down Easy'. But all this is irrelevant, because no one believes that Terence Trent D'Arby died in 1989 more than Terence Trent D'Arby himself.

'It felt like I was going to join the 27 Club,' he says quietly, referring to the rock'n'roll heaven inhabited by Jim Morrison, Janis Joplin, Kurt Cobain and all the others who died at that unfortunate age. 'And psychologically I did, because that is exactly the age I was when I was killed.'

His speech has an automatic quality and there is very little eye contact. You don't interact with him, you lob questions over the top of what he's saying and hope that he might catch them.

'The bottom line is, we're all pretty much sleepwalking,' he says. 'The most difficult thing artists have to deal with is the crushing difference between what they know they can do with their dream being supported, and the reality they have to navigate with the business.'

Over the years he has blamed his former record company, Sony, for the failure of his career, saying it refused to promote *Neither Fish Nor Flesh*. He drew parallels with George Michael, who fought a long battle with Sony in the same era, claiming it wished to keep him in a situation of 'creative slavery' when he wanted to branch out with his sound. But George Michael is still with us. I'm curious to know whether, with hindsight and a change of identity, Sananda Maitreya finds that his feelings about the causes of his career failure have changed. 'The good news is, most record company people are motivated by the same reason most of us are: greed,' he says. 'So, no, when you look back at it, it didn't make much sense for management not to want my second record to succeed.'

The alternative reasons he gives are a surprise. 'I came around at a time when myself, Michael Jackson, Prince, Madonna and George Michael, we were considered kind of dangerous,' he says. 'To the system, to the establishment, you become a rival politician.'

The establishment's urge to end his career was so great, he says, that there were debates about him in the House of Lords. His real nemesis was not the Thatcher administration, but 'the 800lb gorilla in the room, Michael, Master Jackson', who saw him as a threat and, having bought up the Beatles catalogue in 1985, held 'more power than the Pope' within the industry.

Every few minutes in our long conversation, Maitreya cuts away from dark realms of government plots and talks more candidly about the business. 'It's only a matter of time before a cheaper model of you comes along,' he explains. 'Record companies say, "Hey, if you like *this* asshole, you're going to like *this* asshole – plus we're making a higher margin on this asshole." They don't tell you that while you're getting smarter, commanding more for yourself, you're putting an egg-timer on your career.'

As a young man he once observed, 'This industry doesn't like too many black faces around at one time. If someone puts me on the cover of a magazine, they ain't going to be putting another black face on the cover for a while because it wouldn't make commercial sense and that's the way of the world.' Already selling millions to a white yuppie audience, D'Arby could afford to be philosophical about genre pigeonholing but the digs at his rivals abounded. He claimed that black artists before him – Lionel Richie, Luther Vandross, Michael Jackson – had emasculated themselves to get into the charts. He would be Jerry Lee Lewis, he once declared, rather wonderfully: 'the embodiment of the white man gone bad.'

Today he does not name the new, cheaper-to-run assholes who came up when the industry had 'successfully killed my primary image', so I draw his attention to a poem on his website, from 2002.

> *For Lenny K.*
> *Fear not, Your girls are safe!*
> *I've got an italian girlfriend now*
> *And my leash is pretty short*
> *Ps Also let me say to you now how*
> *proud I am of you.*
> *You took care of the tribes necessary*

> *business and moved it forward*
> *And kept the light on.*
> *I know it wasn't easy. Bless you!*

I ask him whether this poem was dedicated to Lenny Kravitz, who achieved success the year Terence died and was also, like him, a sexy black rock star who'd grown up listening to the Stones.

He says he can't remember writing the poem, but then concedes: 'At one point I thought they would give Lenny my social security number as well. I think my greatest envy of him was that he actually did have a tremendous amount of support from his record company while I was always fucking arguing with mine.

'Much of what I wanted to do was moved over to him while I was going through my mortification period.'

In August, at a festival in Sweden, Kravitz's leather trousers split on stage and the unfortunate incident went viral. He was revealed to be wearing no underpants, and a cock ring. I ask Maitreya whether he saw the internet clip.

'No,' he says, and for the first time a spark dances in his eye. 'Choreographed for sure. The only thing I could think to do with a cock ring now is keep my house keys on it.'

In hindsight, it's impossible to imagine a *Game of Thrones* playing out in the late 1980s and early 1990s between a handful of black male rock stars – D'Arby, Kravitz, Seal, Michael Jackson and Prince. Yet Jackson, paranoid about everyone, indeed felt threatened by D'Arby; he was upset when his lawyer, John Branca, took D'Arby on as a client, and urged him to drop him.

'The hero factory is there to produce pop idols,' Maitreya says. 'We're fools, we wear the fools' hats. Our job is to be publicly flogged and beaten when it's time to do that. The price of fame is: when we need to crucify you, you need to be available to us. We'll give you a good burial, make some nice T-shirts. Each of them pays their own price. You don't just come through unscathed.'

Did he hold on to his publishing rights? Does he still get royalties?

'Yeah. I wasn't a total idiot.'

In January 2009 Lady Gaga told the world, '... I've always been famous, you just didn't know it.' The press enjoyed her nuclear sense of self-belief and the postmodern, almost academic way she talked about her music, borrowing a limb from all her heroes and setting herself alongside them. Five years later, Gaga was declared dead by various publications – but not before she had rendered Madonna irrelevant. In 1988, Terence Trent D'Arby declared he'd be as big as Madge, too. 'The worst thing she could possibly do is not to have died young like Marilyn,' he says. 'How considerate of Marilyn to have died, so we didn't have to deal with the reality of the fact that even our goddesses get older.'

In the afterglow of his first album's success, he declared he would finally break America – and shortly afterwards he turned up on the cover of *Rolling Stone*. But every long profile of him began with enthusiastic speculation about his inevitable fall. 'He created this monster,' Ware says. 'It started off as a giggle, an ironic thing. He understood the business of star-building, and he became his own experiment. Then he fell out with journalists who were extremely eager to pull him down.'

Before he joined the army, D'Arby studied journalism for a year at the University of Florida. He records our interview and emails me afterwards. I'm half expecting him to retract some of the things he has said, but he's just improving a few of his quotes. The old self-belief is still there but these days it is shot through with pain. Where does it come from? Can he explain, now Terence is dead and buried?

He has never told anyone this, he says, but on the night of 8 December 1980 he dreamed that he met John Lennon on the street in New York and extended his hand, and felt Lennon 'basically walk into' him. When he awoke he heard that Lennon had been killed. 'From the age of 18 onwards, I had a different confidence about what was meant to happen to my life. I can only say this with all relative humility: I saw myself as a Beatle.'

A few years ago, Sananda Maitreya's wife told him his attitude was that of a typical New Yorker. 'I thought about it, and I said, "Actually, that's right, you know," because New Yorkers have a chip on their shoulder, too.'

He was born in Manhattan in 1962 to a gospel singer and counsellor, Frances Howard, and raised by her and the man he now refers to as his stepfather, Bishop James Benjamin Darby. Pop music was banned from the household: hearing Michael Jackson's voice floating from a neighbour's yard was 'like my first kiss'. The family moved from New York to DeLand in northern Florida, where his stepfather became pastor of the city's Church of Our Lord Jesus Christ and chairman of the Pentecostal international board of evangelists. Terry Darby, as he was known, was a successful pupil – he became managing editor of the school paper and sang in a student chorus called the Sound of the Seventies – but he got into fights. He had problems with black kids and with white kids ('Fuck the both of you – I'm green,' is how he once put it) and suffered his first fall from grace when, during one scuffle, he stabbed someone with his afro hair pick. Boxing was an outlet for his anger – he won the prestigious Golden Gloves prize in Orlando at 17 and caught the attention of army coaches. His parents persuaded him to go to university instead but he was frustrated there, particularly by his lack of success with women. He dropped out and joined the army but soon got fed up of taking instructions from people he considered less intelligent. After amassing a number of reprimands he was discharged at 21.

Maitreya tells me today that he was an illegitimate child, raised with five legitimate children. 'The circumstances of my birth were very embarrassing to my mother,' he says. 'My biological father was a married man, so basically, in any event, it was already a messy situation.'

I ask him if this biological father was white (he has often drawn attention to his light skin). '... or an alien, or both. Point is, I came into the world in a very compromising situation, and because of my mother's religious upbringing abortion was out of the question.'

He tells me that his mother 'made it very, very clear that Jesus was the most important thing in her life, and she did what she could not to project the fact that I was an embarrassment to her. I spent most of my life unconsciously competing with Jesus for my mother's attention. Which is kind of tough, because first of all, I couldn't see him, except for pictures, and second of all he wasn't really there, and it's tough to compete with somebody who's invisible.'

Does he still talk to her? She can be seen on YouTube, singing gospel under the name Mother Frances Darby.

'I'm not sure she's even the same woman,' he says, vaguely. And then, as he has been given to doing throughout his career, he pulls his experience – and probably that of many other pop stars – into focus for a moment. 'If you have a chip on your shoulder, use it,' he says. 'In Latin, fame means hunger, and I'm hungry. Not a hundred people in my generation could have done what I did, and the difference between us is that they got from their environment what they needed. There was no need for them to mount some huge, fucking life-destroying campaign to show the world, "Look, I am worthy of my mother's attention".'

Did he have a nervous breakdown?

'Of course I had a breakdown,' he says. 'It was clearly a breakdown, and all you can do is surrender and try to not put too many pills into your body. You could say, clearly this guy had some sort of bipolar crisis.'

And where was he when this breakdown happened?

'I was living in great fabulous fucking mansions in Sunset Boulevard on my own,' he says, sounding suddenly weary, and tapping my tape recorder. 'Are you sure this thing is on?'

Maitreya says he has inherited 'a degree of family madness, some male schizophrenia issues', from his Scots-Irish bloodline. He talks about the connection between madness and creativity, comparing the management of demons to the delicate power balance involved in a man having successful dominance over a wolf. Yet the cast of characters in attendance during his breakdown – which occurred after he moved to Los Angeles in the mid-1990s, feeling alienated by the British press – appears to have been more mundane.

'I can remember getting up in the middle of the night and sleepwalking to the bathroom, taking a piss, and having a quiet inner voice saying, "Don't worry. Some day, you're going to change both the music and the business",' he says. 'I do believe that Master Lennon, being an angel of the Lord, is available to a lot of people in inspiring circumstances. I believe the same about Elvis, the same with Master Michael, even though he was a huge nemesis in that lifetime. Since his death, he definitely knows he owes me some karma.'

It was angels who named him Sananda, he says, in dreams during his depression. 'Then, later, I realised I think I need a second name, because I didn't want to piss Madonna off, you know!'

*

The singular ambition that burned *Neither Fish Nor Flesh* to cinders has only intensified over time. Sananda Maitreya puts out a new album every two years on his independent label, Treehouse. They usually feature two dozen compositions; his puntastic titles include *Nigor Mortis* and 'Neutered and Spade'. Each project is the fruit of finally having the space to 'completely regurgitate all the stuff that went into my becoming an artist in the first place'. For several years there has been talk of a film about his life, he says, but he is struggling to get involved because he can see three or four different ways of telling the story.

The new project, *Rise of the Zugebrian Time Lords*, is a retro-futuristic concept album spread over two discs of 'bipolar' excess. Maitreya's decision to start with a Beatles song, 'You're Going To Lose That Girl', should come as no surprise. The energy of the project is almost exhausting. Instruments – he plays them all – form a noisy zoo of woodwind, blues guitar and a loose, jangly piano spooked by the spirit of Carole King. What is this record? A Broadway musical for one? A fantastic exercise in rock'n'roll hubris? An aural exploration of mental health issues?

Surprisingly, he doesn't want to talk about it. I press him about the lyrics to 'Giraffe', a likeable, child-friendly melody that contains the lines: 'Giraffe / can I have your autograph? / Please sign it to Sananda'. When I suggest that it sounds like a song from *Sesame Street* he brightens. For the past five years he has been listening almost exclusively to children's music with his two sons, aged three and five. Joe Raposo, who wrote many of the programme's best-loved songs, including 'It's Not Easy Being Green', is one of his favourite composers. His husky voice swells into a perfect, sparkly croon: *Can you tell me how to get – how to get to Sesame Street!* 'You know,' he says, 'I think Elvis Costello was also influenced by some of Raposo's stuff. You're not supposed to say that, as an angry young writer, "Oh yeah, I listen to *Sesame Street*," but I can hear certain devices of his that sound like that whole *Electric Company* style of songwriting.'

His boys love 'Giraffe', but he can't be around while they are listening to it; his wife later tells me she has to wait until he's out of the house to play it to them. He talks touchingly about love being 'something you have to work on – it doesn't just come to you'. As a young man, he scythed his way through women, partly because of his mother issues, he thinks: then one day he decided to stop, 'because you're only going to wind up looking for the same thing anyway'.

He can't listen to anyone else's pop music these days. His only comfortable relationship is with 'Master Beethoven', who presumably is dead enough not to offer any painful competition. But clearly the man who makes a double album and then can't play it again is living daily with bigger enemies than 'Lenny Cockring Kravitz' (as he calls him in his follow-up email) or the ghost of Master Jackson. Across the record there are hints of the cinnamon-voiced psychedelic wonders that could emerge from the pen of Sananda Maitreya, were he to allow a producer or A&R team to get their hands on his work. 'His voice is even better than it was at the time,' says Martyn Ware, who still receives each new project in the post from his old charge. 'But he has no sub-editor.'

'Tell me about your new album' is usually the most boring prompt in the rock'n'roll interview. The second – 'How has being a father changed you?' (Maitreya also has a grown daughter from a previous relationship) – yields similarly surprising results. 'Anything else at this point in life is a bonus, because I've already done the most important thing, simply to have passed my genes on to some other bitches,' Maitreya says, showing me a picture of two small boys who look just like him, only with blond, curly hair and blue eyes.

'I'm very confident that my first son is my biological father and it gives me the chance to have finally a relationship with him. My first son is also a continuation of the life that I left behind.'

His first son might be Terence Trent D'Arby? Does that not worry him?

'Preferably they'll both want to follow their mother and be architects,' he says.

As the afternoon draws to a close he talks again of bloodlines. Originally all the world was black, he tells me: 'Bitches looked like me! Didn't look like you!' His own white, 'land-owning, slave-owning blood' is another reason Providence gave him his assignment, he says.

And once we're back on to that, something clicks down in him again. We're on to Jonah and the Whale, 'being spat out unceremoniously after three days', and thence, without pause, to vampires. For a moment, he becomes agitated when he realises that the brown cotton scarf that was covering his dreads has disappeared. It's true enough: one minute I was looking at it and the next it wasn't there. So much magic has been talked in this room today that I think, for a moment, that Sananda Maitreya's headscarf might have vanished into thin air and I'll have to tell someone about it afterwards. We search and find it down the back of his seat.

'What was I saying?'

I want to tell him not to re-join his mystical thread. He was so much happier talking about Elvis Costello. But we're back to the industry, and death. The irony is, the industry he was raised in is dead and buried, too.

'And in killing the messengers they killed a whole generation,' Maitreya says. 'Like Maestro Thom Yorke: they alienated him, and he was providing the answers they needed.'

Surely the point is that you're free now?

'Yeah, well, free is relative,' he says. 'The moment we're met with too much freedom, we shit our pants.'

The closing of the liberal mind

John Gray

All that seemed solid in liberalism is melting into air. In Europe the EU struggled for over seven years to reach a trade deal with Canada, one of the most 'European' countries in the world; at the same time, banking crises are festering in Italy and Germany and the continuing migrant crisis continues to strengthen far-right parties. In Britain Jeremy Corbyn's strengthened hold over Labour following an ill-considered attempt to unseat him has reinforced a transformation in the party that reaches well beyond his position as leader. At a global level, Vladimir Putin is redrawing the geopolitical map with his escalating intervention in Syria, while the chief threat to the repressive regime Xi Jinping is building in China appears to be a neo-Maoist movement that harks back to one of the worst tyrannies in history. A liberal order that seemed to be spreading across the globe after the end of the Cold War is fading from memory.

Faced with this shift, liberal opinion-formers have oscillated between insistent denial and apocalyptic foreboding. Though the EU is barely capable of any action, raddled remnants of the old regime – Ed Miliband, Clegg, Mandelson, 'the master' himself – have surfaced to demand that Brexit be fudged and, in effect, reversed. Even as the US election hangs in the balance, many are clinging to the belief that a liberal status quo can be restored. But Trump's presidential campaign has already demolished a bipartisan consensus on free trade, and if he wins, a party system to which his Republican opponents and Hillary Clinton both belonged will be history. Dreading this outcome and suspecting it may yet come to pass, liberals rail against voters who reject their enlightened leadership. Suddenly, the folly of the masses has replaced the wisdom of crowds as the dominant theme in polite discourse. Few ask what in the ruling liberalism could produce such a debacle.

The liberal pageant is fading, yet liberals find it hard to get by without believing they are on what they like to think is the right side of history.

The trouble is that they can only envision the future as a continuation of the recent past. This is so whether their liberalism comes from the right or the left. Whether they are George Osborne's City-based 'liberal mainstream', or Thatcherite think tanks, baffled and seething because Brexit hasn't taken us closer to a free-market utopia, or egalitarian social democrats who favour redistribution or 'predistribution', an entire generation is finding its view of the world melting away under the impact of events.

Today's liberals differ widely about how the wealth and opportunities of a market economy should be shared. What none of them question is the type of market globalisation that has developed over the past three decades. Writing in *Tribune* in 1943 after reviewing a batch of 'progressive' books, George Orwell observed: 'I was struck by the automatic way in which people go on repeating certain phrases that were fashionable before 1914. Two great favourites are "the abolition of distance" and "the disappearance of frontiers".' More than 70 years later, the same empty formulae are again being repeated. At present, the liberal mind can function only to the extent that it shuts out reality.

It is not surprising that there is talk of entering a post-liberal moment. The idea has the merit of grasping that the liberal retreat is not a revolt of the ignorant masses against enlightened elites; it is mostly the result of the follies of liberals themselves. But the revulsion against liberalism is not all of one piece. There is a world of difference between the May government inching its way towards a more intelligent way of living with globalisation and Trump's dream of globalisation in one country. The creeping advance of anti-liberal forces across the European continent is something else again.

Accepting that this is a post-liberal moment does not imply that we should give up on values of freedom and toleration. Quite the contrary: the task at hand is securing the survival of a liberal way of life. But the greatest obstacle to that end, larger even than the hostility of avowed enemies of liberalism, is a liberal ideology that sees state power as the chief threat to freedom. Liberal societies have a future only if the Hobbesian protective role of the state is firmly reasserted. Balancing the claims of liberty against those of security will never be easy. There are many conflicting freedoms, among which political choices must be made. Without security, however, freedom itself is soon lost.

*

Nothing illustrates the decay of liberalism more vividly than the metamorphosis of the Labour Party. There has been a tendency to interpret Corbyn's rise as a reversion to the Trotskyite entryism of the early 1980s. Some in the party – possibly including the shadow chancellor, John McDonnell – may see their role in terms of converting Labour to some type of neo-Marxism. That does not explain why so many of Labour's new members seem to want to bury the party in the form in which it has existed throughout its history.

Something like a blueprint for the shift of power in the party was set out in Ralph Miliband's *Parliamentary Socialism*, first published in 1961. Miliband's attack on the Parliamentary Labour Party (PLP) anticipated the Corbynite strategy with uncanny prescience. Cautioning his comrades on the left who wanted to use Labour as a vehicle for socialism, Miliband wrote in a 1972 postscript to the book:

> The kind of political changes at the top which a good many socialists hope to see one day brought about in the Labour Party, and which would signify a major ideological shift to the left, would presumably, given the nature of the political system, have to be engineered from within the ranks of the Parliamentary Labour Party. But to say this is surely also to indicate how unrealistic that hope is. It is unrealistic because it ignores the perennial weakness of the parliamentary left. That weakness is not accidental but structural ... There have been some exceptions: a few Labour MPs have, so to speak, slipped through the net. But they have remained isolated and often pathetic figures, bitterly at odds not only with their leaders but with that large and permanent majority of the Parliamentary Labour Party which entirely shares its leader's orthodox modes of thought.

Ralph Miliband condemned the PLP as an obstacle to fundamental change and looked to a mass movement outside Labour's core structures. But history has proved more fertile than his imagination. In a strangely poetic turn of events, an anti-parliamentary party of a kind he believed Labour could never become was brought into being, more than 40 years later, when, by changing the membership rules, Ed Miliband created a historic opening for one of its most isolated and insignificant figures. Promoted by moderates as a modernising move, on a par with Tony Blair's revision of Clause Four, this accidental reform has altered Labour structurally and irreversibly. Corbyn's rise to power could not have occurred if the party's moderates had not been so devoid of new thinking. They realised that Ed Miliband's social-democratic moment had failed to arrive and knew that Labour faced an uphill task in becoming electable again. But all they had to offer were empty slogans that reeked of the past. As a result, Labour has become unelectable in any foreseeable future.

Anyone who imagines the party's electoral fortunes could be revived by a new leader – a charismatic figure from across the water, perhaps – has not taken the measure of the change that has taken place. Although parts of Labour remain outside Corbyn's control, including much of local government – most importantly, Sadiq Khan's London – the chief power base of any future leader of the party will be the mass movement that Corbyn has built. Realigning Labour with the electorate can only be done against the opposition of most of the party membership. In these conditions a campaign of the sort Neil Kinnock waged against Militant is no longer feasible. Internecine warfare will continue and may intensify, but Labour's moderate tendency has no chance of regaining control.

In one sense, Corbyn's Labour is the practical realisation of Ralph Miliband's dream. Yet it is not a party Miliband would recognise easily. Labour has become not a retro-Trotskyite sect, but a contemporary expression of formless discontent. Trotsky was a vain and pitiless figure, who crushed a workers' rising in Kronstadt in 1921 and rejected criticism of the practice of hostage-taking that he implemented during the Russian Civil War as 'Quaker-vegetarian chatter'. But, even at his worst, Trotsky could not have proposed anything as inane and intrinsically absurd as retaining Trident submarine patrols while removing the missiles' nuclear warheads, as Corbyn did in January.

The party Corbyn has created is not easily defined. Aside from the anti-Semitism that is a strand of its make-up, it has no coherent ideology. The legacy of Marxism is notable for its absence. There is no analysis of changing class structures or any systematic critique of the present condition of capitalism. Such policies as have been floated have been plucked from a blue sky, without any attempt to connect them with earthbound facts. The consensus-seeking values of core Labour voters are dismissed as symptoms of backwardness. As for the concerns about job security and immigration that produced large majorities in favour of Brexit in what used to be safe Labour areas, the Corbynite view seems to be that these are retrograde attitudes that only show how badly working people need re-education.

Corbyn's refusal to specify any upper limit to immigration at the last party conference in Liverpool illustrated his detachment from electoral realities. But far from being a debilitating weakness – as it would be if Labour were still a conventional political party – this rejection of realistic thinking is the principal source of his strength in the new kind of party he has created. From being a broad-based institution that defended the interests of working people, Labour has morphed into a vehicle for an alienated fringe of the middle class that finds psychological comfort in belonging in an anti-capitalist protest movement. While a dwindling rump of trade union barons continues to act as power-broker, Labour's northern fortresses are crumbling.

The defining feature of Corbynite Labour is not an anachronistic utopian socialism, but a very modern kind of liberal narcissism. Looking two or three general elections ahead, the party could well reach a membership of over a million even as it struggled to elect a hundred MPs. The party's role would then be one of permanent opposition, without the privileges that go with being an alternative government.

The claim that what has emerged from Corbyn's takeover of the Labour Party is an inchoate and extreme type of liberalism may seem perverse. He and his followers never cease to inveigh against neoliberal economics – a blanket term that seems to include every market economy in the world – even as they show a consistent bias in favour of tyrannies in their protests against military action, their anti-war campaigns focusing solely as they do on the policies of Western governments. It might seem that Labour under Corbyn has abandoned liberal values altogether, and there are some who talk of a new left-fascism.

Yet this is too easy an analysis of the change that has taken place. Corbyn's Labour is no more crypto-fascist than it is Trotskyite. In some respects – such as his support for unlimited freedom of movement for people – it embodies a hyperbolic version of the liberalism of the most recent generation. In others, it expresses what liberalism has now become. There have always been many liberalisms, but the mutation in liberal thinking over the past few decades has been deep and radical. From being a philosophy that aimed to give a theoretical rationale to a way of life based on the practice of toleration, it has become a mindset that defines itself by enmity to that way of life.

Corbyn's 'inclusive' attitude towards Hamas, Hezbollah and the IRA fits in with a left-liberal world-view that supports anti-colonial struggles in a general embrace of identity politics. Fashionable nonsense about cultural appropriation may not matter much, as it has been largely confined to increasingly marginal universities. However, it expresses what has come to be seen as a liberal principle: the right of everyone to assert what they take to be their identity – particularly if it can be represented as that of an oppressed minority – by whatever means are judged necessary. If free speech stands in the way, the practice must be discarded. It terrorism is required, so be it. This represents a fundamental shift in liberal thinking.

The overriding importance given to rights – a selective reading of them, at any rate – is one of the marks of the new liberalism. In one form or another, doctrines of human rights have been around for centuries, and a conception of universal rights was embodied in the UN Declaration of 1948. But rights became central and primary in liberal thought only in the 1970s with the rise of the legalist philosophies of John Rawls and Ronald Dworkin, which held that freedom can be codified into a fixed system of interlocking liberties that can be interpreted by judges. On the libertarian right, Friedrich Hayek proposed something similar with his constitutional proposals for limiting democracy.

Protecting liberty is not just a matter of curbing government, however. Rolling back the state in the economy and society can have the effect of leaving people less free – a fact that was recognised by liberal thinkers of an earlier generation. Maynard Keynes understood that free trade allowed consumers a wide range of choices. He also understood that freedom of choice is devalued when livelihoods face being rapidly destroyed on a large scale, and partly for that reason he refused to treat free trade as a sacrosanct dogma. He never imagined freedom could be reduced to a list of rights.

The move to rights-based liberalism has had damaging effects in many areas of policy. A militant ideology of human rights played a part in some of the worst foreign policy disasters of recent times. The ruinous military adventures of the Blair-Cameron era did not fail because there was not enough post-invasion planning. They failed, first, because in overthrowing the despotisms of Saddam Hussein and Muammar al-Gaddafi they destroyed the state in both Iraq and Libya, leaving zones of anarchy in which jihadist forces could operate freely. More fundamentally, they failed because human rights cannot be imposed on societies that have never known them and where most people may not want them.

Any suggestion that liberal values are not humanly universal will provoke spasms of righteous indignation. Liberals cannot help believing that all human beings secretly yearn to become as they imagine themselves to be. But this is faith, not fact. The belief that liberal values are universally revered is not founded in empirical observation. They are far from secure even in parts of continental Europe where they were seen as unshakeable only a few years ago. In much of the world they are barely recognised.

That liberal values belong in a particular way of life was the central theme of the essays collected in my book *Post-Liberalism* (1993). Modern liberalism is a late growth from Jewish and Christian monotheism. It is from these religious traditions – more than anything in Greek philosophy – that liberal values of toleration and freedom have sprung. If these values were held to be universal, it was because they were believed to be ordained by God. Most liberals nowadays are secular in outlook, yet they continue to believe that their values are humanly universal.

It has never been clear why this should be so. A common response conjures up Enlightenment values against the demon of relativism, somehow forgetting that modern relativism emerged from the Enlightenment. Others invoke cod-theories in social science which claim that only liberal societies can be modern. Francis Fukuyama's thesis is the best known, but they all assert that globalisation is producing a worldwide middle class that is demanding political freedom, as the European bourgeoisie is supposed to have done in the nineteenth and twentieth centuries.

In fact, the European middle classes threw in their lot with authoritarian regimes as often as they supported freedom and democracy, and the same is true at a global level today. Much of the middle class in Russia appears wedded to a combination of consumerism and nationalism, and in China most seem to want nothing more than rising living standards and freedom in their private lives. In the United States, on the other hand, unchecked globalisation is destroying the middle classes.

If the liberalism that has prevailed over the past generation was a falsifiable theory it would long since have been abandoned. There is no detectable connection between advancing globalisation and the spread of liberal values. Liberals resist this because it empties their lives of significance. For them, liberalism is a surrogate religion, providing the sustaining illusion that their values express the meaning of history.

These may seem arguments far removed from everyday politics, but they have important practical implications. Liberal societies cannot depend on history for their survival. They need to defend themselves, and here the cult of rights needs deflating. Human rights may have value as symbolic barriers against the worst evils, such as genocide, slavery and torture. Where they are not backed by state power, however, human rights mean nothing: less than nothing, in fact, if they encourage people to believe they will be protected when (as in Srebrenica and now in Aleppo) the power to protect them is lacking. Human rights cannot serve as a template for world order. When they are used to promote evangelical military campaigns they endanger the way of life they were meant to protect.

Popular revulsion against established elites has produced some curious responses. There is constant talk about reason being junked in an emotional rejection of experts, as was supposed to have happened in this year's EU referendum campaign. Yet the record hardly justifies any strong claims on behalf of those who claim special insight into economics or politics. Much of what has passed for expert knowledge consists of speculative or discredited theories, such as the sub-Keynesian ideas that support quantitative easing as a permanent regime and the notion that globalisation benefits everybody in the long run. When rattled liberals talk of the triumph of emotion over reason, what they mean is that voters are ignoring the intellectual detritus that has guided their leaders and are responding instead to facts and their own experiences.

What British voters are not doing is repudiating the society in which they live. For some critics of liberalism, what is needed is a rejection of individualism in economics and culture. This is the message of John Milbank and Adrian Pabst in *The Politics of Virtue.* The book promotes a neo-medievalist vision of organic community that would be familiar to Hilaire Belloc and G. K. Chesterton, whom Milbank and Pabst cite approvingly. Post-liberalism of this kind is, in my view, a dead end in politics. Most people in Britain do not want to live in organic communities. They are not nostalgic for an imaginary past, and show little fondness for the claustrophobic intimacy of unchanging, homogeneous neighbourhoods. They want what Thomas Hobbes called commodious living – in other words, the amenities of modern economy – without the chronic insecurity that is produced by unfettered market forces. Rather than rejecting market individualism, they are demanding that it be constrained. They would like to inhabit a common culture but are happy for it to contain diverse beliefs and lifestyles.

A post-liberal society is one in which freedom and toleration are protected under the shelter of a strong state. In economic terms, this entails discarding the notion that the primary purpose of government is to advance globalisation. In future, governments will succeed or fail by how well they can deliver prosperity while managing the social disruption that globalisation produces. Obviously it will be a delicate balancing act. There is a risk that deglobalisation will spiral out of control. New technologies will disrupt settled patterns of working and living whatever governments may do. Popular demands cannot be met in full, but parties that do not curb the market in the interests of social cohesion are consigning themselves to the memory hole. The type of globalisation that has developed over the past decades is not politically sustainable.

To expect liberals to comprehend this situation would be unreasonable. For them, it is not only the liberal order that is melting away, but any sense of their own place in history. From being the vanguard of human progress, they find themselves powerless spectators of events. But they insist that the solution to the crisis of liberalism is clear. What is needed is more of the same: a stronger infusion of idealism; an unyielding determination to renew the liberal projects of the past. The notion that any of these projects needs to be revised or abandoned – global free trade, say, or the free movement of labour across national borders – is unthinkable. The only thing wrong with past policies, they will say, is that they were not liberal enough.

Adamant certainty mixed with self-admiring angst has long defined the liberal mind and does so now. Yet beneath this, a different mood can be detected. All that really remains of liberalism is fear of the future. Faced with the world they thought they knew fading into air, many liberals may be tempted to retreat into the imaginary worlds envisioned by left-leaning non-governmental organisations, or conjured up in academic seminars. This amounts to giving up the political struggle, and it may be that, despite themselves, those who embodied the ruling liberalism are coming to realise that their day is done.

The Rest
of Life

Hop-picking

George Orwell

'A holiday with pay.' 'Keep yourself all the time you're down there, pay your fare both ways and come back five quid in pocket.' I quote the words of two experienced hop-pickers, who had been down into Kent almost every season since they were children, and ought to have known better. For as a matter of fact hop-picking is far from being a holiday, and, as far as wages go, no worse employment exists.

I do not mean by this that hop-picking is a disagreeable job in itself. It entails long hours, but it is healthy, outdoor work, and any able-bodied person can do it. The process is extremely simple. The vines, long climbing plants with the hops clustering on them in bunches like grapes, are trained up poles or over wires; all the picker has to do is to tear them down and strip the hops into a bin, keeping them as clean as possible from leaves. The spiny stems cut the palms of one's hands to pieces, and in the early morning, before the cuts have reopened, it is painful work; one has trouble too with the plant-lice which infest the hops and crawl down one's neck, but beyond that there are no annoyances. One can talk and smoke as one works, and on hot days there is no pleasanter place than the shady lanes of hops, with their bitter scent – an unutterably refreshing scent, like a wind blowing from oceans of cool beer. It would be almost ideal if one could earn a living at it.

Unfortunately, the rate of payment is so low that it is quite impossible for a picker to earn a pound a week, or even, in a wet year like 1931, fifteen shillings. Hop-picking is done on the piece-work system, the pickers being paid at so much a bushel. At the farm where I worked this year, as at most farms in Kent, the tally was six bushels to the shilling – that is, we were paid twopence for each bushel we picked. Now, a good vine yields about half a bushel of hops, and a good picker can strip a vine in ten or fifteen minutes; it follows that an expert picker might, given perfect conditions, earn thirty shillings in a sixty-hour week. But, for a number of reasons, these perfect conditions do not exist. To begin with, hops vary enormously in quality. On some vines they are as large as small pears, on others no bigger than hazel nuts; the bad vines take as long to strip as the good ones – longer, as a rule, for their lower shoots are more tangled – and often five of them will not yield a bushel. Again, there are frequent delays in the work, either in changing from field to field, or on account of rain; an hour or two is wasted in this manner every day, and the pickers are paid no compensation for lost time. And, lastly, the greatest cause of loss, there is unfair measurement. The hops are measured in bushel baskets of standard size, but it must be remembered that hops are not like apples or potatoes, of which one can say that a bushel is a bushel and there is an end of it. They are soft things as compressible as sponges, and it is quite easy for the measurer to crush a bushel of them into a quart if he chooses.

As the hop-pickers often sing –

> *When he comes to measure,*
> *He never knows where to stop;*
> *Ay, ay, get in the bin,*
> *And take the bloody lot!*

From the bin the hops are put into pokes, which are supposed when full to weigh a hundredweight, and are normally carried by one man. But it often needs two men to handle a full poke, when the measurer has been 'taking them heavy'.

With these working conditions a friend and myself earned, this September, about nine shillings a week each. We were new to the job, but the experienced pickers did little better. The best pickers in our gang, and among the best in the whole camp, were a family of gypsies, five adults and a child; these people, spending ten hours a day in the hop-field, earned just ten pounds between them in three weeks. Leaving the child out of account (though as a matter of fact all the children in the hop-field work) this was an average of thirteen and fourpence a week each. There were various farms nearby where the tally was eight or nine bushels to the shilling, and where even twelve shillings a week would have been hard to earn.

Besides these starvation wages, the hop-picker has to put up with rules which reduce him practically to a slave. One rule, for instance, empowers a farmer to sack his employees on any pretext whatever, and in doing so to confiscate a quarter of their earnings; and the picker's earnings are also docked if he resigns his job. It is no wonder that itinerant agricultural labourers, most of whom are in work ten months of the year, travel 'on the toby' and sleep in the casual ward between jobs.

As to the hop-pickers' living accommodation, there is now a whole tribe of Government officials to supervise it, so presumably it is better than it used to be. But what it can have been like in the old days is hard to imagine, for even now the ordinary hop-picker's hut is worse than a stable. (I say this advisedly: on our farm the best quarters, specially set apart for married people, were stables.) My friend and I, with two others, slept in a tin hut ten feet across, with two unglazed windows and half a dozen other apertures to let in the wind and rain, and no furniture save a heap of straw: the latrine was two hundred yards away, and the water tap the same distance. Some of these huts had to be shared by eight men – but that, at any rate, mitigated the cold, which can be bitter on September nights when one has no bedding but a disused sack. And, of course, there were all the normal discomforts of camp life; not serious hardships, but enough to make sure that when we were not working or sleeping we were either fetching water or trying to coax a fire out of wet sticks.

I think it will be agreed that these are thoroughly bad conditions of pay and treatment. Yet the curious thing is that there is no lack of pickers, and what is more, the same people return to the hop-fields year after year. What keeps the business going is probably the fact that the Cockneys rather enjoy the trip to the country, in spite of the bad pay and in spite of the discomfort. When the season is over the pickers are heartily glad – glad to be back in London, where you do not have to sleep on straw, and you can put a penny in the gas instead of hunting the firewood, and Woolworth's is round the corner – but still, hop-picking is in the category of things that are great fun when they are over. It figures in the pickers' mind as a holiday, though they are working hard all the time and out of pocket at the end. And besides this there is the piece-work system, which disguises the low rate of payment; for 'six bushels a shilling' sounds much more than 'fifteen shillings a week.'

And there is the tradition of the good times ten years ago, when hops were dear and the farmers could pay sixpence a bushel; this keeps alive the tales about 'coming home five quid in pocket'. At any rate, whatever the cause, there is no difficulty in getting people to do the work, so perhaps one ought not to complain too loudly about the conditions in the hop-fields. But if one sets pay and treatment against work done, then a hop-picker is appreciably worse off than a sandwich-man.

Twenty-Four Hours in Metroland

Graham Greene

The little town always had an air of grit about it, as one came in under the echoing tin railway arch associated with shabby prams and Sunday walks, unwilling returns to Evensong – grit beside the watercress beds and on the panes of the station's private entrance which the local lord had not used for generations. Neither country nor city, a dormitory district – there are things which go on in dormitories ...

Sunday evening, and the bells jangling in the town; small groups of youths hovered round the traffic lights, while the Irish servant girls crept out of back doors in the early dark. 'Romans', the elderly lady called them. You couldn't keep them in at night – they would arrive with the milk in a stranger's car from Watford, slipping out in stockinged feet from the villas above the valley. The youths – smarmed and scented hair and bitten cigarettes – greeted them in the dark with careless roughness. There were so many fishes in the sea ... sexual experience had come to them too early and too easily. The London, Midland and Scottish Line waited for everyone.

Up on the hillside the beech trees were in glorious and incredible decay: little green boxes for litter put up by the National Trust had a dainty and doyly effect; and in the inn the radio played continuously. You couldn't escape it: with your soup a dramatised account of the battle of Mons, and with the joint a Methodist church service. Four one-armed men dined together, arranging their seats so that their arms shouldn't clash.

In the morning, mist lay heavy on the Chilterns. Boards marking desirable building lots dripped on short grass where the sheep were washed out. The skeletons of harrows lay unburied on the wet stubble. With visibility shut down to fifty yards you got no sense of a world, of simultaneous existences: each thing was self-contained like an image of private significance, standing for something else – Metroland, loneliness. The door of the Plough Inn chimed when you pushed it, ivory balls clicked and a bystander said, 'They do this at the Crown, Margate' – England's heart beating out in bagatelle towards her eastern extremity; the landlady had a weak heart, and dared not serve food these days in case she went off just like that in the rush. In a small front garden before a red villa a young girl knelt in the damp with an expression abashed and secretive while she sawed through the limbs of a bush, and a woman's angry voice called 'Judy, Judy', and a dog barked in the poultry farm across the way. A cigarette fumed into ash with no one in sight, only a little shut red door marked Ker Even; 'the leading Cairn Terrier Farm' was noisy on the crest of the down, the dogs like the radio, never ceasing – how does life go on?

At the newsagent's in the market town below the Chiltern ridge there was a shrewd game on sale, very popular locally, called 'Monopoly', played with dice and counters – 'The object of owning property is to collect rent … Rentals are greatly increased by the erection of houses and hotels … Players may land in jail.' The soil exacted no service and no love: among the beechwoods a new house was for sale. It had only been lived in a month: the woods and commons were held out by wire. The owners, married last December, were divorced this summer. Neither wanted the house. A handyman swept up the leaves – a losing fight – and lamented the waste. 'Four coats of paint in every room … I was going to make a pond in that dell – and I was just getting the kitchen garden straight – you can see for yourself.'

Kick these hills and they bleed white. The mist is like an exhalation of the chalk. Beechwoods and gorse and the savage Metro heart behind the Whipsnade wire: elephants turning and turning behind glass on little aesthetic circular platforms like exhibits in a 'modern' shop window, behind them dripping firs as alien as themselves; ostriches suddenly visible at thirty yards, like snakeheads rising out of heaps of dung. A wolf wailing invisibly in the mist, the sun setting at 4.30, the traffic lights out in the High Street and the Irish maids putting the door on the latch. In an hour or two the commuters return to sleep in their Siberian dormitory – an acre of land, a desirable residence for as long as the marriage lasts, no roots, no responsibility for the child on the line. 'The object of owning property …'

Am I a Jew?

Bernard Levin

Well, now. I have a Jewish name, but there is many a Gentile Isaacs, so why not a Levin? I have a Jewish nose, though oddly enough, I cannot see its Jewishness in a mirror, only in a photograph. In any case, it is a meaningless test. The good Dr Morris Fishbein, who in the course of his researches into this subject undoubtedly measured more noses than any man has measured before or since, concluded that there was no such thing as a 'Jewish' nose, or that if there was, it was possessed by so many undoubted Aryans that there was no way of ensuring that the Jews would win – or lose – by a nose.

There are more persuasive, though still superficial, arguments. I like Jewish food, Jewish jokes, hold some traditionally Jewish beliefs, such as the respect for learning. (I can remember to this day the shock of incredulity I had at school when a non-Jewish friend told me that he had had a great struggle to be allowed to take up his scholarship. His uneducated father's attitude – more common then than now – had been that 'What was good enough for me is good enough for my son.' This attitude was absolutely inconceivable in a Jewish home.)

None of this will provide any real evidence, though. I was brought up on Jewish food, and the fact that I enjoy it is only an index to the strength of early environmental influence. Jewish jokes appeal to me because of their underlying gallows-humour, which I like because I am at heart a melancholic. I still laugh when my sister tells the story of *kreplach*, not because the *goyim* can't understand it, but because of its Thurberesque suggestion of the frailty of human happiness and the prevalence of unreason.

Of course, I am begging the question. I know perfectly well that I am a Jew; what I am really inquiring into is what this means to me. Let us start with religion. I rejected Judaism more or less as soon as I was old enough to have any understanding of what religion was about. All religions have their obsessions with form, ritual, observance. I don't know whether I feel further from Judaism than from most religions because its particular observances – the dietary laws, for instance – seem to me sillier today than their equivalent in, say, Roman Catholicism; or whether the savage monotheism of Jehovah (or Nobodaddy) repels me. I think that there are parts of the Pentateuch that are about as nasty as anything I have ever read anywhere, but you might also say the same thing about St Paul.

Of course, one would have to be very dull of spirit not to find beautiful and fine some aspects of Judaism. A well-ordered Seder (the Passover-eve family service) is a very remarkable experience – but to me largely aesthetic. I have an uncontrollable revulsion at the sight of someone lighting a cigarette from a candle (some Jews who have long rejected Judaism feel sick at the sight of someone putting a pat of butter on a steak), because I was brought up to look upon a candle as a holy thing. I no longer believe consciously that it is a holy thing, but I do believe that it is a beautiful one and its use to light a cigarette seems to me vulgar and belittling. Such objective religious sympathies as I have are with the quietist faiths, like Buddhism, on the one hand, and with a straightforward message of salvation like Christianity, on the other. I am unable in fact to accept any of them, but can imagine myself a convert to several faiths; not Judaism, however.

Race, then. Aha. First, I accept what biology and anthropology tell me about race and its attendant oceans of nonsense. There are no innate superiorities or inferiorities; even if there were, there is no such thing as a separate Jewish race, though there may be a race of Semites. (The Jews in modern times have found their greatest antagonists in the Germans and the Arabs; with the former they have many of their most deeply ingrained characteristics in common, and with the latter their very race.) There's something in this more than natural, if psychology could find it out. Besides, suppose there was a Jewish race, and I was of it; what would follow from that? There is a Negro race; membership of it implies that you are black, but need imply nothing else. So you may be a nice Jew or a nasty one, a clever or a foolish, a generous or a mean, a clubbable or a solitary. I can list my qualities and defects; more meaningfully, I can get a candid friend to do so. I can give myself marks down the list; but for the life of me I cannot see that, whatever the total, it adds up to anything I have in common with Mr Jack Solomons or Mr Ewen Montagu QC.

Which brings me to the only point at which there can any longer be room for doubt. The concept of race is too completely exploded to provide a fair test. Let us think not of race, but of psychology and characteristics. *Have* I anything in common with Mr Solomons or Mr Montagu? If so, what? And if I have not – which is what I believe – have I entirely dissolved any meaning in my own life, indeed any objective meaning at all, for the word Jew?

There is an interesting paragraph on this point by Bernard Berenson, though it seems to me to demonstrate the opposite of what he was arguing.

> A Jew is the product of being cooped up in a ghetto for over 1,200 years. His conditioning from within and without, the outer pressure driving more and more to defensive extremes, the inner clutching to rites, to practices, to values making for union and for safety, the struggle for food and survival, the lust for pre-eminence and power: all have ended in producing the Jew, regardless of what racial elements originally constituted him.

Precisely; then the Jew is nothing but a conditioned reflex to a conditioned stimulus (who could have thought the behaviourists could help us here?). And although the idea seems capable of bearing the weight of a considerable structure of generalisation, it falls down as soon as you look at Israel. If a hardy, martial, fair-haired and blue-eyed people are now the heirs of Zion, surely the case for environment is proved? When Herzl's trumpet finally felled the walls of the ghetto, Jewry won her greatest victory. Why, Israel even has her own anti-Semitism, in the discrimination of the Ashkenazim against their culturally more backward brethren from the East. Perhaps it will go like this, then. While the Jews of the Diaspora become more completely assimilated – the rate of intermarriage continues to grow, generation by generation – Israel will become more and more remote from any of the traditional concepts of Jewishness. She is still heavily influenced by theocracy; but the ultimately inevitable *Kulturkampf* must break the rabbinical power and turn Israel into a modern secular state.

This may mean that the last test of the *Déracinés* will become their attitude to Israel. I think I can clear myself here, even after the severest Positive Vetting. My attitude to Israel – admiration for the incredible achievements, hope that it will continue, combined with the strongest condemnation of her crime against her original Arab population and the campaign of lies waged ever since on the subject – does not mark me off in any way from a Gentile of similar political outlook. And the other obvious crude test – one's attitude to the Final Solution – I claim to pass with marks above the average, insisting that the slaughter of Russians by Stalin in not much smaller numbers and for no less wicked and senseless reasons should be equally condemned.

And I cannot see that there are any valuable babies that I risk emptying out with the bath-water of my rejection of any concept of Jewishness. I can admire Spinoza or Disraeli or Menuhin just as much without my judgement being affected by any thought of their origins, and I have the additional advantage of being able to despise Ilya Ehrenburg without any reservations.

Has it come to this? Has an idea so old and tenacious, so provocative of generosity and malice, good and evil, responsible for such prodigious outpourings of words and deeds ceased to have any meaning at all? For me, it has. Yet I must face the last logical barrier, the same in effect as the first logical barrier that surrounds Christianity. How can such an idea have survived and conquered half the world, if it is not true? Similarly, how can Jewry have survived, how indeed can she have continued to attract the attention of anti-Semitism, if there is no such thing?

Only here am I conscious of any logical weakness in my position. For to an anti-Semite I could not bring myself to deny that I am a Jew, and I would not only not dream of changing my name, but think the less of the Courtenay-Cohens and Lipschitz-Logans for doing so. Yet time will surely take care of this problem, too (plus the fact that the antis have now got somebody else to pick on; not even Dr Fishbein can measure away the Negro's blackness). The world now has no excuse for not knowing what anti-Semitism can lead to, and actually does, on the whole, show signs of amending its attitude accordingly.

And now it is the others who will be increasingly exposed as illogical. If you do not consider yourself Jewish enough to go to Israel, and not Judaistic enough to go to the synagogue, what is left but a vague necessity to belong? And this will disappear, or at any rate be dispersed, with further inter-marriage and assimilation; so, of course, will the superficialities attributable to upbringing and environment.

The proprietor of my favourite Jewish restaurant tells me that a high, and growing, proportion of his customers are not Jewish. For my part, I reserve the right to go on laughing at the story of the *kreplach* while not particularly caring for the *kreplach* themselves.

Goose-Stepping

Julian Barnes

When the early results came through on Day One of the Moscow Olympics, we learned that Russia had won a gold medal in the free pistol shooting. Well, they would, wouldn't they, my viewing companions sneered back at the set in unison. As these morally tatty Games proceed, it's going to become harder and harder to avoid lapsing into a state of self-pitying international paranoia. Take the case of Danny Nightingale, our gold-medal hope in the modern pentathlon. He randomly selects a Russian horse for the show jumping leg, and rides it more or less impeccably round the ring, except that the daft commie nag chooses to drop its rear hooves into precisely as many fences as there are onion domes on St Basil's. Explanation? Quite obviously, a subcutaneous KGB electrode implanted in the haunches of every horse, and a belted figure high up in the stands 'whispering' into his sleeve.

'Moscow 80 = Berlin 36' declared a chalk slogan near my home for the length of half a shower. Not really; but you'd think, wouldn't you, that the Russians would be keen to avoid providing for worldwide transmission too many images which evoked those earlier propaganda Games? At the opening ceremony, the Olympic flag was trooped by 'eight unknown sportsmen' (i.e. eight really not very good sportsmen) in pale blue lightweight suits and white gloves; they goose-stepped round the stadium to Beethoven's Ninth Symphony, legs sabre-dancing out and free arms flung vigorously across opposite shoulders. (Of course, the goose-step is commonplace in Eastern Europe, and doesn't have fascist connections over there; but even so, it's nothing if not martial, and looks very odd on a sportsman, however unknown.)

This queasy image had no sooner appeared than it was amplified. Behind the eight Daks stormtroopers came 22 additional high-kickers, though looking a little more Austin Reed in their blue blazers and white slacks. White gloves again – though this time they were designed to protect the strutters' hands against 'accidents' from the rear ends of the white doves they carried aloft on their straightened right arms. A dove of peace on the end of a Nazi salute: was it the year's strangest image?

Lord Killanin made a tactful speech, and the only children left in Moscow duly bombarded him with gladioli as if he were Barry Humphries. Brezhnev, speaking from a panelled bus shelter, was allowed (by Olympic tradition) only one sentence in which to open the Games; but who can monitor Russian punctuation – and the result was something so long it might have been scripted by Bernard Levin. The British athletes stayed away, and the team's *chef de mission* paraded with an Olympic flag, which the Soviet TV producer craftily excised from the picture. As a result, the Russian viewer was free to conclude that the British had become so enfeebled and ricketstricken a race after a year of Mrs Thatcher that all they could raise for the Games was a single middle-aged pole-vaulter.

One wondered what the average Muscovite in the stadium made of it: or rather, the average, sanitised, with-dissidence-removed Muscovite. Most of them, of course, couldn't see much anyway because they had to keep on holding up coloured cards to construct a kaleidoscope of insincere slogans ('O Sport Thou Art Peace', etc.). Why is this form of stadium entertainment so popular behind the Iron Curtain and so antipathetic to us? Is it perhaps because it seems to us to emphasise the antishness of the participants; whereas it seems to them to prove that expressions of the popular will can be both located and pungently conveyed? But what must it feel like to be a chap with a placard, turning it over by command, never seeing the result of your endeavours, and constantly blocking out the sun? It must be a bit like singing in the chorus of the *Messiah* while wearing earplugs. Perhaps one of the card-bearers who made Jimmy Hill's face for the opening credits of *Match of the Day* will write and elucidate.

The Olympics began – doubtless not intentionally – just as Gay Pride Week was ending. BBC2 acknowledged the occasion with an *Inside Story* on *Coming Out*: a useful programme at a time when there seems to be a certain mild backlash against gays. Not just among Leviticans like Sir John Junor either: a lot of heterosexuals who supported gay lib as a principle now seem less pleased with it in practice. To some, gay couples are acceptable as long as they keep house plants and do French knitting in the long winter evenings; but if they jump about on the streets, dress in leather, and (my God) *look* gay, then they're held to be overstepping the mark. *We* didn't intend for you to behave like *that* when we legalised you, is the patronising implication.

What 'that' may involve was occasionally made explicit in this programme: 'You then have to get across,' murmured a Hammersmith press officer, softly, 'that you enjoy sodomy ... it's very pleasant, very OK.' One felt the soft shuffle of tightening sphincters all across the country; but it was bravely said. At the moment, homosexuality is legal rather as prostitution is legal, and scarcely more socially acceptable; so, as *Inside Story* made clear, all the old reality of being homosexual – of guilty suicides, shamed and bitter parents, arbitrary job dismissals – continues unabated. Gay pride is only partly about being proud to be gay; it's also about relief at surviving as such.

Russell Harty's new chat show, *Sorl Baht Booooks* (as the title song has it), will soon presumably be retitled *Sorl Baht Sex*. Last week the Lip discussed boffing with the parents of Louise 'Test Tube' Brown and with a benign Christopher Isherwood. As a relief between these two serious bits, Robert Morley was paid to plug his son Sheridan's new anthology. Memo to Russell: I've just written a book, and my dad's free any time.

Notes from a maternity ward

Angela Carter

Towards the end of the 38th week, I grow bored with saying 'Fine',
when asked at the antenatal clinic how I'm doing. So I try a little
joke. It backfires. God, how it backfires. 'How do you feel?' 'A bit
apprehensive,' I say. 'Not so much about the birth itself as about the
next 20 or 30 years.' The consultant, an unreconstructed Thatcher
clone – that is, she looks like Thatcher minus the peroxide and the
schlap – turns on me a face costive with high moral seriousness. 'You
have done the right thing in not having an abortion,' she says. 'But
there is still time. It you have any doubts at all, I urge you to seriously
discuss adoption with your husband – I know he's only a common-
law husband, of course.'

I'm overwhelmed by incredulity. Had I ever mentioned abortion in
connection with this incipient cherub? Are my *compañero* and I not
the Darby and Joan of our circle? Should I say we just got hitched?
What business is it of hers, anyway? I lapse into outraged silence.
Later, I will weep with fury, but, if I do so now, who can tell how she
will misinterpret that. I seethe. Who does she think she is; or I am?
And if she delivers this kind of unsolicited advice to the white middle
class – to a member of it who has given her occupation as 'journalist',
to boot – then what manner of abuse does she feel free to dish out to
the black proletariat? How come she's lived so long? And why don't
I punch her in the nose? I'll tell you why. Because she's chosen to
insult me when I'm flat on my back, dress pulled up, knickers down,
vulnerable, helpless, undignified.

I would publish her name to the four winds, and gladly. But the hell
of it is, she turns out to be a good doctor, as far as the mechanics
are concerned. Callous and insensitive perhaps; but quick to spot a
malfunction. A gift not to be sneezed at. And, furthermore, a woman
so straitjacketed by self-righteousness I doubt she'd ever understand

why I want to crucify her. After all, her concern was only for what was best for the baby. And hadn't I virtually said I didn't want him? When she sees me, all pale and proud, on the ward after he's born – he chuckling in a glass box like a very expensive orchid – she's as nice as pie. Well done, she says.

'She'. Note how this consultant is female. I'm lying in at the embattled South London Hospital for Women, the last place I expected to be insulted. But there you go. Here, women treat women and she's the only one of them who treated me like a piece of shit.

I haven't been in hospital for 30 years, so I can't comment on the decline in the standards of the NHS; the floors aren't polished until they turn into lethal ice-rinks any more, which is no bad thing. The food has certainly improved, in comparison with the early Fifties. The sheer wonder of the NHS remains; that they will do the best they can for us, that we are not at the mercy of a free-market economy, that the lovely nurses smile as if they meant it and hug you when you are sad.

Inevitably, this particular hospital is scheduled for the axe. No amount of special pleading on behalf of women whose religion specifies they be treated by doctors of the same sex seems likely to save it: it is due to close down next April, its various wards – it's a general hospital – distributed around other local hospitals. The staff seems scarcely able to believe that some miracle won't save the place. If the Minister of Health turns into a woman tomorrow, there might be a chance, especially if (s)he then converted to Islam.

It is a rather elegant, red-brick building convenient for Clapham South Tube station (the Northern Line). It overlooks green and pleasant Clapham Common. It is, obviously, very well equipped; only needs a coat or two of paint and a few vases of plastic flowers to be fit for – who? The young woman in the bed next to me made a shrewd guess as to what would happen to the building once the NHS moved out. 'They'll sell it to bloody Bupa, won't they,' she opined.

The midwife shows me how to put the baby to the nipple. 'Look deep into his eyes,' she says. 'It helps with the bonding.' Good grief! Aren't we allowed any choice in the matter, he and I? Can't I learn to love him for himself, and vice versa, rather than trust to Mother Nature's psychophysiological double bind? And what of his relationship with his father, who has no breasts? Besides, it's very difficult to look him in the eye. He fastens on the nipple with the furtive avidity of a secret tippler hitting the British sherry, glancing backwards to make sure nobody else gets there first. When he strikes oil, he instantly becomes comatose. Am I supposed to poke him into consciousness: 'Hey, baby, don't nod off, we're supposed to be bonding.' More like bondage. Constrained affection; what resentment it will breed, in time. It's all part of the mystification in which the process of childbirth is so richly shrouded. For he is doomed to love us, at least for a significant initial period, because we are his parents. The same goes for us. That is life. That's the hell of it.

Somebody gave us an American publication called *Giving Birth*. A collection of photographs of mothers and fathers sharing the experience. (Where's the lesbian couple? Discrimination!) The parents look ecstatic; radiant; touchingly, comically startled and so on. Lots of shots of little heads poking out of vulvas. Also quotes from participants: 'I felt I had to be very focused. It was almost like meditation,' says one mother. It is compiled by somebody called Mary Motley Kalergis, another name on my post-partural hit-list. (Isn't one allowed a year's justifiable homicide after the event?) The photographs are all in black and white, please note. And, indeed, colour film would have made souvenir snaps of the finale of my own *accouchement* look like stills from a Hammer horror film. While what was going on next door, an emergency Caesarean, well, that certainly wasn't like meditation, not half it wasn't! This truly nauseating book is designed to mystify. It is about as kitsch as a fluffy blue bunny, and as much to do with the realities of parturition as a fluffy blue bunny has to do with a real live baby.

OK, OK. So this notebook has submerged under a sea of baby shit. Mao Zedong called a pig 'a manure factory on four legs'. A baby is much the same, except it remains stationary. Some people suggest you chuck boiled disposables on the compost heap. There are a few other suggestions for utilising the formidable quantities of ordure produced by the average baby and heedlessly thrown away every day. To say nothing of the valuable amounts of methane they emit. At the end of *War and Peace*, Tolstoy has Natasha ankle-deep in baby shit; impossible not to read something vindictive into that, although he does make Pierre soil his hands, too.

Anyway, there is nothing wrong with baby shit. The TV news gobs out fresh horrors into the living room every evening; insulted by the specific urgencies of the neonate, that appalling dichotomy – the one between our lives as we live them and the way that forces outside ourselves shape them for us – seems less desperate than usual. Under the circumstances, a mercy.

The bugger, bugged

Hugh Grant

When I broke down in my midlife crisis car in remotest Kent just before Christmas, a battered white van pulled up on the far carriageway. To help, I thought. But when the driver got out he started taking pictures with a long-lens camera. He came closer to get better shots and I swore at him. Then he offered me a lift the last few miles to my destination. I suspected his motives and swore at him some more. (I'm not entirely sympathetic towards paparazzi.) Then I realised I couldn't get a taxi and was late. So I had to accept the lift.

He turned out to be an ex-*News of the World* journalist and paparazzo, now running a pub in Dover. He still kept his camera in the car's glove box for just this kind of happy accident. More than that, he was Paul McMullan, one of two ex-*NoW* hacks who had blown the whistle on the extent of the paper's phone-hacking, particularly under its former editor Andy Coulson. This was interesting, as I had been a victim – a fact he confirmed as we drove along.

He also had an unusual defence of the practice: that phone-hacking was a price you had to pay for living in a free society. I asked how that worked, but we ran out of time, and next thing we had arrived and he was asking me if I would pose for a photo with him, 'not for publication, just for the wall of the pub'.

I agreed and the picture duly appeared in the *Mail on Sunday* that weekend with his creative version of the encounter. He had asked me to drop into his pub some time. So when Jemima [Khan] asked me to write a piece for this paper, it occurred to me it might be interesting to take him up on his invitation.

I wanted to hear more about phone-hacking and the whole business of tabloid journalism. It occurred to me just to interview him straight, as he has, after all, been a whistle-blower. But then I thought I might get more, and it might be more fun, if I secretly taped him, the bugger bugged, as it were. Here are some excerpts from our conversation.

Me: So, how's the whistle-blowing going?

Him: I'm trying to get a book published. I sent it off to a publisher who immediately accepted it and then it got legal and they said, 'This is never going to get published.'

Me: Why? Because it accuses too many people of crime?

Him: Yes, as I said to the parliamentary commission, Coulson knew all about it and regularly ordered it … He [Coulson] rose quickly to the top; he wanted to cover his tracks all the time. So he wouldn't just write a story about a celeb who'd done something. He'd want to make sure they could never sue, so he wanted us to hear the celeb like you on tape saying, 'Hello, darling, we had lovely sex last night.' So that's on tape and so we can publish … Historically, the way it went was, in the early days of mobiles, we all had analogue mobiles and that was an absolute joy. You know, you just … sat outside Buckingham Palace with a £59 scanner you bought at Argos and get Prince Charles and everything he said.

Me: Is that how the Squidgy tapes [of Diana's phone conversations] came out? Which was put down to radio hams, but was in fact …

Him: Paps in the back of a van, yes … I mean, politicians were dropping like flies in the Nineties because it was so easy to get stuff on them. And, obviously, less easy to justify is celebrities. But yes.

Me: It wasn't just the *News of the World*. It was, you know – the *Mail*?

Him: Oh absolutely, yeah. When I went freelance in 2004 the biggest payers – you'd have thought it would be the *NoW*, but actually it was the *Daily Mail*. If I take a good picture, the first person I go to is – such as in your case – the *Mail on Sunday*. Did you see that story? The picture of you, breaking down … I ought to thank you for that. I got £3,000. Whooo!

Me: But would they [the *Mail*] buy a phone-hacked story?

Him: For about four or five years they've absolutely been cleaner than clean. And before that they weren't. They were as dirty as anyone … They had the most money.

Me: So everyone knew? Would Rebekah Wade have known all this stuff was going on?

Him: You're not taping, are you?

Me: [*slightly shrill voice*] No.

Him: Well, yeah. Clearly she ... took over the job of [a journalist] who had a scanner who was trying to sell it to members of his own department. But it wasn't a big crime. [*Ed*: Rebekah Brooks was cleared of phone-hacking charges following her trial in 2014.]

It started off as fun – you know, it wasn't against the law, so why wouldn't you? And it was only because the MPs who were fiddling their expenses and being generally corrupt kept getting caught so much they changed the law in 2001 to make it illegal to buy and sell a digital scanner. So all we were left with was – you know – finding a blag to get your mobile [records] out of someone at Vodafone.

Me: So they all knew? Wade probably knew all about it all?

Him: [...] Cameron must have known – that's the bigger scandal. He had to jump into bed with Murdoch as everyone had, starting with Thatcher in the Seventies ... Tony Blair ... Maggie openly courted Murdoch. So when Cameron, when it came his turn to go to Murdoch via Rebekah Wade ... Cameron went horse riding regularly with Rebekah. I know, because as well as doorstepping celebrities, I've also doorstepped my ex-boss by hiding in the bushes, waiting for her to come past with Cameron on a horse ... before the election to show that Murdoch was backing Cameron.

Me: What happened to that story?

Him: The *Guardian* paid for me to do it and I stepped in it and missed them. They'd gone past – not as good as having a picture.

Me: Do you think Murdoch knew about phone-hacking?

Him: Errr, possibly not. He's a funny bloke given that he owns the *Sun* and the Screws ... quite puritanical. Sorry to talk about Divine Brown, but when that came out ... Murdoch was furious: 'What are you putting that on our front page for? You're bringing down the tone of our papers.' [*Indicating himself*] That's what we do over here.

Me: Well, it's also because it was his film I was about to come out in. It was a Fox film. [*A pause here while we chat to other customers, and then –*]

Him: So anyway, I was sent to do a feature on *Moulin Rouge!* at Cannes, which was a great send anyway. Basically my brief was to see who Nicole Kidman was shagging – what she was doing, poking through her bins and get some stuff on her. So Murdoch's paying her five million quid to big up the French and at the same time paying me £5.50 to fuck her up … So all hail the master. We're just pawns in his game. How perverse is that?

Me: Wow. You reckon he never knew about it?

Him: [*pause*] I don't even think he really worried himself too much about it.

Me: What's his son called?

Him: James. They're all mates together. They all go horse riding. You've got Jeremy Clarkson lives here [in Oxfordshire]. Cameron lives here, and Rebekah Wade is married to Brooks's son [the former racehorse trainer Charlie Brooks]. Cameron gets dressed up as the Stig to go to Clarkson's 50th birthday party [*Ed*: it was actually to record a video message for the party]. Is that demeaning for a prime minister?

So basically, Cameron is very much in debt to Rebekah Wade for helping him not quite win the election … So that was my submission to parliament – that Cameron's either a liar or an idiot.

Me: But don't you think that all these prime ministers deliberately try to get the police to drag their feet about investigating the whole [phone-hacking] thing because they don't want to upset Murdoch?

Him: Yeah. You also work a lot with policemen as well … One of the early stories was [*and here he names a much-loved TV actress in her sixties*] used to be a street walker – whether or not she was, but that's the tip.

Me and Chum: MLTVA?!

Me: I can't believe it. Oh no!

Chum: Really??

Him: Yeah. Well, not now …

Chum: Oh, it'd be so much better if it was now.

Him: So I asked a copper to get his hands on the phone files, but because it's only a caution it's not there any more. So that's the tip

... it's a policeman ringing up a tabloid reporter and asking him for ten grand because this girl had been cautioned right at the start of his career. And then I ask another policemen to check the records ... That's happening regularly. So the police don't particularly want to investigate.

Me: Do you think they're going to have to now?

Him: I mean – 20 per cent of the Met has taken backhanders from tabloid hacks. So why would they want to open up that can of worms? ... And what's wrong with that? It doesn't hurt anyone particularly. I mean, it could hurt someone's career – but isn't that the dance with the devil you have to play?

Me: Well, I suppose the fact that they're dragging their feet while investigating a mass of phone-hacking – which is a crime – some people would think is a bit depressing.

Him: But then – should it be a crime? I mean, scanning never used to be a crime. You're transmitting your thoughts and your voice over the airwaves. How can you not expect someone to stick up an aerial and listen in?

Me: So if someone was on a landline and you had a way of tapping in ... do you think that should be illegal?

Him: I'd have to say quite possibly, yeah. I'd say that should be illegal.

Me: But a mobile phone – a digital phone ... you'd say it'd be all right to tap that?

Him: I'm not sure about that. So we went from a point where anyone could listen in to anything. Like you, me, journalists could listen in to corrupt politicians, and this is why we have a reasonably fair society and a not particularly corrupt or criminal prime minister, whereas other countries have Gaddafi. Do you think it's right the only person with a decent digital scanner these days is the government? Are you comfortable that the only people who can listen in to you now are – is it MI5 or MI6?

Me: I'd rather no one listened in. And I might not be alone there. You probably wouldn't want people listening to your conversations.

Him: I'm not interesting enough for anyone to want to listen in.

Me: Ah ... I think that was one of the questions asked last week at one of the parliamentary committees. They asked Yates [John Yates, acting deputy commissioner, Metropolitan Police] if it was true he thought the *NoW* had been hacking the phones of friends and family of those girls who were murdered ... the Soham murder and the Milly girl [Milly Dowler].

Him: Yeah. Yeah. It's more than likely. Yeah ... It was quite routine. Yeah – friends and family is something that's not as easy to justify as the other things.

Me: But celebrities you would justify because they're rich?

Him: Yeah. I mean, if you don't like it, you've just got to get off the stage. It'll do wonders.

Me: So I should have given up acting?

Him: If you live off your image, you can't really complain about someone ...

Me: I live off my acting. Which is different to living off your image.

Him: You're still presenting yourself to the public. And if the public didn't know you ...

Me: They don't give a shit. I got arrested with a hooker and they still came to my films. They don't give a fuck about your public image. They just care about whether you're in an entertaining film or not.

Him: That's true ... I have terrible difficulty with him [*points to pap shot of Johnny Depp*]. I was in Venice and he was a nightmare to do because he walks around looking like Michael Jackson. And the punchline was ... after leading everyone a merry dance the film was shot on an open balcony – I mean, it was like – he was standing there in public.

Me: And you don't see the difference between the two situations?

Chum: He was actually working at this time? As opposed to having his own private time?

Him: You can't hide all the time.

Me: So you're saying, if you're Johnny Depp or me, you don't deserve to have a private life?

Him: You make so much more money. You know, most people in Dover take home about £200 and struggle.

Me: So how much do you think the families of the Milly and Soham girls make?

Him: OK, so there are examples that are poor and you can't justify – and that's one of them.

Me: I tell you the thing I still don't get – if you think it was all right to do all that stuff, why blow the whistle on it?

Him: Errm ... Right. That's interesting. I actually blew the whistle when a friend of mine at the *Guardian* kept hassling me for an interview. I said, 'Well if you put the name of the Castle [his pub] on the front page, I'll do anything you like.' So that's how it started.

Me: Have you been leant on by the *NoW*, News International, since you blew the whistle?

Him: No, they've kept their distance. I mean, there's people who have much better records – my records are non-existent. There are people who actually have tapes and transcripts they did for Andy Coulson.

Me: And where are these tapes and transcripts? Do you think they've been destroyed?

Him: No, I'm sure they're saving them till they retire.

Me: So did you personally ever listen to my voice messages?

Him No, I didn't personally ever listen to your voice messages. I did quite a lot of stories on you, though. You were a very good earner at times.

Those are the highlights. As I drove home past the white cliffs, I thought it was interesting – apart from the fact that Paul hates people like me, and I hate people like him, we got on quite well. And, absurdly, I felt a bit guilty for recording him. And he does have a very nice pub. The Castle Inn, Dover, for the record. There are rooms available, too. He asked me if I'd like to sample the honeymoon suite some time: 'I can guarantee your privacy.'

Christopher Hitchens: The last interview

Richard Dawkins

This was Christopher Hitchens's last interview, and it was published in the New Statesman *the day after his death in December 2011. As the news travelled around the globe, the piece became a media sensation.*

Richard Dawkins: I've been reading some of your recent collections of essays – I'm astounded by your sheer erudition. You seem to have read absolutely everything.

Christopher Hitchens: It may strike some people as being broad but it's possibly at the cost of being a bit shallow. I became a journalist because one didn't have to specialise. I remember once going to an evening with Umberto Eco talking to Susan Sontag and the definition of the word 'polymath' came up. Eco said it was his ambition to be a polymath; Sontag challenged him and said the definition of a polymath is someone who's interested in everything and nothing else. I was encouraged to read widely – to flit and sip, as Bertie [Wooster] puts it – and I think I've got good memory retention. I retain what's interesting to me, but I don't have a lot of strategic depth. A lot of reviewers have said, to the point of embarrassing me, that I'm in the class of Edmund Wilson or even George Orwell. It really does remind me that I'm not. But it's something to have had the comparison made.

RD: As an Orwell scholar, you must have a particular view of North Korea, Stalin, the Soviet Union, and you must get irritated – perhaps even more than I do – by the constant refrain we hear: 'Stalin was an atheist.'

CH: We don't know for sure that he was. Hitler definitely wasn't. There is a possibility that Himmler was. There's no mandate in atheism for any particular kind of politics, anyway.

RD: The people who did Hitler's dirty work were almost all religious.

CH: I'm afraid the SS's relationship with the Catholic Church is something the Church still has to deal with and does not deny.

RD: Can you talk a bit about that – the relationship of Nazism with the Catholic Church?

CH: The way I put it is this: if you're writing about the history of the 1930s and the rise of totalitarianism, you can take out the word 'fascist', if you want, for Italy, Portugal, Spain, Czechoslovakia and Austria, and replace it with 'extreme-right Catholic party'. Almost all of those regimes were in place with the help of the Vatican and with understandings from the Holy See. It's not denied. These understandings quite often persisted after the Second World War was over and extended to comparable regimes in Argentina and elsewhere.

RD: But there were individual priests who did good things.

CH: Not very many. You would know their names if there were more of them. When it comes to National Socialism, there's no question there's a mutation, a big one – the Nazis wanted their own form of worship. Just as they thought they were a separate race, they wanted their own religion. They dug out the Norse gods, all kinds of extraordinary myths and legends from the old sagas. They wanted to control the churches. They were willing to make a deal with them. The first deal Hitler made with the Catholic Church was the *Konkordat*. The Church agreed to dissolve its political party and he got control over German education. Celebrations of his birthday were actually by order from the pulpit. When Hitler survived an assassination attempt, prayers were said, and so forth. There's another example. You swore on Almighty God that you would never break your oath to the Führer. This is not even secular, let alone atheist.

RD: There was also grace before meals, personally thanking Adolf Hitler.

CH: I believe there was. Certainly, you can hear the oath being taken – there are recordings of it – but this, Richard, is a red herring. It's not even secular. They're changing the subject.

RD: But it comes up over and over again.

CH: You mentioned North Korea. It is, in every sense, a theocratic state. It's almost supernatural, in that the births of the Kim family are considered to be mysterious and accompanied by happenings. It's a necrocracy or mausolocracy, but there's no possible way you could say it's a secular state, let alone an atheist one. Attempts to found new religions should attract our scorn just as much as the alliances with the old ones do. All they're saying is that you can't claim Hitler was distinctively or specifically Christian: 'Maybe if he had gone on much longer, he would have de-Christianised a bit more.' This is all a complete fog of nonsense. It's bad history and it's bad propaganda.

RD: And bad logic, because there's no connection between atheism and doing horrible things, whereas there easily can be a connection in the case of religion, as we see with modern Islam.

CH: To the extent that they are new religions – Stalin worship and Kim Il-sungism – we, like all atheists, regard them with horror.

RD: You debated with Tony Blair. I'm not sure I watched that. I love listening to you [but] I can't bear listening to ... Well, I mustn't say that. I think he did come over as rather nice on that evening. What was your impression?

CH: You can only have one aim per debate. I had two in debating with Tony Blair. The first one was to get him to admit that it was not done – the stuff we complain of – in only the *name* of religion. The authority is in the *text*. Second, I wanted to get him to admit, if possible, that giving money to a charity or organising a charity does not vindicate a cause. I got him to the first one and I admired his honesty. He was asked by the interlocutor, 'There is no mandate in atheism for any particular kind of politics' at about half-time: 'Which of Christopher's points strikes you as the best?' He said: 'I have to admit, he's made his case, he's right. This stuff, there is authority for it in the canonical texts, in Islam, Judaism.' At that point, I'm ready to fold – I've done what I want for the evening. We did debate whether Catholic charities and so on were a good thing and I said: 'They are but they don't prove any point and some of them are only making up for damage done.' For example, the Church had better spend a lot of money doing repair work on its AIDS policy in Africa, [to make up for preaching] that condoms don't prevent disease or, in some cases, that they spread it. It is iniquitous. It has led to a lot of people dying, horribly. Also, I've never looked at some of the ground operations of these charities – apart from Mother Teresa – but they do involve a lot of proselytising. They're not just giving out free stuff. They're doing work to recruit.

RD: And Mother Teresa was one of the worst offenders?

CH: She preached that poverty was a gift from God. And she believed that women should not be given control over the reproductive cycle. Mother Teresa spent her whole life making sure that the one cure for poverty we know is sound was not implemented. So Tony Blair knows this but he doesn't have an answer. If I say, 'Your Church preaches against the one cure for poverty,' he doesn't deny it, but he doesn't affirm it either. But remember, I did start with a text and I asked him to comment on it first, but he never did. Cardinal Newman said he would rather the whole world and everyone in it be condemned for ever to eternal torture than one sinner go unrebuked for the stealing of a sixpence. It's right there in the centre of the *Apologia*. The man whose canonisation Tony had been campaigning for. You put these discrepancies in front of him and he's like all the others. He keeps two sets of books. And this is also, even in an honest person, shady.

RD: It's like two minds, really.

CH: I think we all do it a bit.

RD: Do we?

CH: We're all great self-persuaders.

RD: But do we hold such extreme contradictions in our heads?

CH: We like to think our colleagues would point them out. No one's pointed out to me in reviewing my God book *God Is Not Great* that there's a flat discrepancy between the affirmation he makes on page X and the affirmation he makes on page Y.

RD: But they do accuse you of being a contrarian, which you've called yourself …

CH: Well, no, I haven't. I've disowned it but I am a bit saddled with it.

RD: I've always been very suspicious of the left-right dimension in politics. It's astonishing how much traction the left-right continuum [has] … If you know what someone thinks about the death penalty or abortion, then you generally know what they think about everything else. But you clearly break that rule.

CH: I have one consistency, which is [being] against the totalitarian – on the left and on the right. The totalitarian, to me, is the enemy – the one that's absolute, the one that wants control over the inside of your head, not just your actions and your taxes. And the origins of that are theocratic, obviously. The beginning of that is the idea that there is a supreme leader, or infallible pope, or a chief rabbi, or whatever, who can ventriloquise the divine and tell us what to do. There have been some thinkers – Orwell is pre-eminent – who understood that, unfortunately, there is innate in humans a strong tendency to worship, to become abject. So we're not just fighting the dictators. We're criticising our fellow humans for surrendering and saying, '[If] you offer me bliss, of course I'm going to give up some of my mental freedom for that.' We say it's a false bargain: you'll get nothing. You're a fool.

RD: One of my main beefs with religion is the way they label children as a 'Catholic child' or a 'Muslim child'. I've become a bit of a bore about it.

CH: You must never be afraid of that charge, any more than stridency. If I was strident, it doesn't matter – I was a jobbing hack, I bang my drum. You have a discipline in which you are very distinguished. You've educated a lot of people; nobody denies that, not even your worst enemies. You see your discipline being attacked and defamed and attempts made to drive it out. If you go on about something, the worst thing the English will say about you, as we both know – as we can say of them, by the way – is that they're boring.

RD: Indeed. Only this morning, I was sent a copy of [advice from] a British government web site, called something like 'The Responsibilities of Parents'. One of these responsibilities was 'determine the child's religion'. Literally, determine. It means establish, cause ... I couldn't ask for a clearer illustration, because, sometimes, when I make my complaint about this, I'm told nobody actually does label children 'Catholic' or 'Muslim'.

CH: Well, the government does. It's borrowed, as far as I can see, in part from British imperial policy – you classify your new subjects according to their faith. You can be an Ottoman citizen but you're a Jewish one or an Armenian Christian one. And some of these faiths tell their children that the children of other faiths are going to hell.

RD: I would call it mental child abuse.

CH: I can't find a way, as a libertarian, of saying that people can't raise their children, as they say, according to their rights. But the child has rights and society does, too. Now, it would be very hard to say that you can't tell your child that they are lucky and they have joined the one true faith. I don't see how you stop it. I only think the rest of society should look at it with a bit of disapproval, which it doesn't.

RD: There is a tendency among liberals to feel that religion should be off the table.

CH: Or even that there's anti-religious racism, which I think is a terrible limitation.

RD: Do you think America is in danger of becoming a theocracy?

CH: No, I don't. The people who we mean when we talk about that – maybe the extreme Protestant evangelicals – I think they may be the most overrated threat in the country. They've been defeated everywhere. Why is this? In the 1920s, they had a string of victories. They banned the sale, manufacture and distribution and consumption of alcohol. They made it the constitution. They'll never recover from [the failure of] Prohibition. It was their biggest defeat. They'll never recover from the Scopes trial. Every time they've tried [to introduce the teaching of creationism], the local school board or the parents or the courts have thrown it out. They try to make a free speech question out of it but they will fail with that, also. People don't want to come from the town or the state or the country that gets laughed at.

RD: Yes.

CH: And if they passed an ordinance saying there will be prayer in school every morning from now on, one of two things would happen: it would be overthrown in no time by all the courts, with barrels of laughter heaped over it, or people would say: 'Very well, we're starting with Hindu prayer on Monday.' They would regret it so bitterly that there are days when I wish they would have their own way for a short time.

RD: Oh, that's very cheering.

CH: I'm a bit more worried about the extreme, reactionary nature of the papacy now. But that again doesn't seem to command very big allegiance among the American congregation. They are disobedient on contraception, flagrantly; on divorce; on gay marriage, to an extraordinary degree that I wouldn't have predicted; and they're only holding firm on abortion, which, in my opinion, is actually a very strong moral question and shouldn't be decided lightly. I feel very squeamish about it. I believe that the unborn child is a real concept, in other words. So, really, the only threat from religious force in America is the same as it is in many other countries – from outside. And it's jihad-ism, some of it home-grown, but some of that is so weak and so self-discrediting.

RD: It's more of a problem in Britain.

CH: And many other European countries, where its alleged root causes are being allowed slightly too friendly an interrogation, I think. Make that much too friendly.

RD: Some of our friends are so worried about Islam that they're prepared to lend support to Christianity as a kind of bulwark against it.

CH: I know many Muslims who, in leaving the faith, have opted to go … to Christianity or via it to non-belief. Some of them say it's the personality of Jesus of Nazareth. The mild and meek one, as compared to the rather farouche, physical, martial, rather greedy …

RD: Warlord.

CH: … Muhammad. I can see that that might have an effect.

RD: Do you ever worry that if we win and, so to speak, destroy Christianity, that vacuum would be filled by Islam?

CH: No, in a funny way, I don't worry that we'll win. All that we can do is make absolutely sure that people know there's a much more wonderful and interesting and beautiful alternative. Christianity has defeated itself in that it has become a cultural thing. There really aren't believing Christians in the way there were generations ago.

RD: Certainly in Europe that's true – but in America?

CH: There are revivals, of course, but I think there's a very long-running tendency in the developed world and in large areas elsewhere for people to see the virtue of secularism, the separation of church and state, because they've tried the alternatives …

RD: If you look at religiosity across the world you find that religiosity tends to correlate with poverty and with various other indices of social deprivation.

CH: Yes. That's also what it feeds on. But I don't want to condescend about that. I know a lot of very educated, very prosperous, very thoughtful people who believe.

RD: I'm often asked why it is that this republic [of America], founded in secularism, is so much more religious than those western European countries that have an official state religion, like Scandinavia and Britain.

CH: [Alexis] de Tocqueville has it exactly right. If you want a church in America, you have to build it by the sweat of your own brow and many have. That's why they're attached to them. The Jews – not all of them – remarkably abandoned their religion very soon after arriving from the shtetl.

RD: Are you saying that most Jews have abandoned their religion?

CH: Increasingly in America. When you came to escape religious persecution and you didn't want to replicate it, that's a strong memory. The Jews very quickly secularised. American Jews must be the most secular force on the planet now.

RD: While not being religious, they often still observe the Sabbath and that kind of thing.

CH: There's got to be something cultural. I go to Passover every year. Sometimes, even I have a Seder, because I want my child to know that she does come very distantly from another tradition. It would explain if she met her great-grandfather why he spoke Yiddish. And then there is manifest destiny. People feel America is just so lucky. It's between two oceans, filled with minerals, wealth, beauty. It does seem providential to many people.

RD: Promised land, city on a hill.

CH: All that and the desire for another Eden. Some secular utopians came with the same idea. Thomas Paine and others all thought of America as a great new start for the species.

RD: I've heard another theory that, America being a country of immigrants, people coming from Europe, where they left their extended family and left their support system, were alone and they needed something.

CH: The reason why most of my friends are non-believers is not particularly that they were engaged in the arguments you and I have been having, but they were made indifferent by compulsory religion at school.

RD: They got bored by it.

CH: They'd had enough of it. They took from it occasionally whatever they needed – if you needed to get married, you knew where to go. Generally speaking, the British people are benignly indifferent to religion.

RD: Can you say anything about Christmas?

CH: Yes. There was going to be a winter solstice holiday for sure. The dominant religion was going to take it over and that would have happened without Dickens and without others.

RD: The Christmas tree comes from Prince Albert; the shepherds and the wise men are all made up.

CH: Cyrenius wasn't governor of Syria, all of that. Increasingly, it's secularised itself. This 'Hap-py Holidays' – I don't particularly like that, either.

RD: Horrible, isn't it? 'Happy holiday season.'

CH: I prefer our stuff about the cosmos.

The day after this interview, I was honoured to present an award to Christopher Hitchens in the presence of a large audience in Texas that gave him a standing ovation, first as he entered the hall and again at the end of his deeply moving speech. My speech ended with a tribute, in which I said that every day he demonstrates the falsehood of the lie that there are no atheists in foxholes: 'Hitch is in a foxhole, and he is dealing with it with a courage, an honesty and a dignity that any of us would be, and should be, proud to muster.'

Random acts of senseless generosity: In praise of pessimism

Will Self

The last time I remember going out with my mother it was to Hampstead Heath. We drove there in my car, then walked arm in arm along the terrace in front of Kenwood House. As if elliptically commenting on our own halting progress my mother said: 'The good thing about being a pessimist is that you're never really wrong-footed; even before you've put one foot in front of the other you suspect that you're likely to trip up, and that makes adversity much easier to deal with.'

She died three weeks later, lying in a bed in the Royal Ear Hospital. Not, you understand, that there was anything in particular wrong with her hearing; rather, despite the cancer that had metastasised from lymph to liver to brain, she remained highly attuned to the vapidity of yeasayers.

Indeed, I imagine the last thing she heard – and silently dismissed – before she slid into the coal-hole of inexistence was some well-meaning health professional or other, telling her it was all going to be all right.

That was a quarter-century ago, but my mother's valedictory wisdom has stayed with me, informing my life, refining an epicurean attitude to personal life and a stoical one towards public events. For those who would dismiss pessimism out of hand, seeing it as a negative and self-fulfilling prophecy, let's lay our jokers on the table right now: in respect of which of the major social and political developments of the past 25 years would optimism have been an appropriate attitude to take? My mother would have had to hang on only a few months in order to prop herself up in bed, or possibly lie supine, while I read aloud to her Francis Fukuyama's essay in the *National Interest* 'The End of History?'. How she would have snorted derisively at Fukuyama's assertion that the end of the Cold War would be followed by the worldwide dissemination of benign western liberal democracy.

Of course, in 1989, the immiseration of the former Soviet Union was just a gleam in wannabe oligarchs' eyes and the rise of Putin's Potemkin democracy lay some way ahead. The US was about to disengage itself from a range of proxy wars across the globe, in order to reinvest its peace dividend in the prosecution of a brand new range of hegemonic interventions.

A decade had already passed since the Camp David accords that were to have ushered in a peaceful era – but there was no sign of a lasting peace in the Middle East then and there certainly isn't now. Indeed, US support of the Israeli state's expansionist territorial aims remains to this day the festering pressure sore on the posterior of international relations. Mum, a Jew who believed passionately in justice for the Palestinian people, wouldn't have been in the least bit surprised about this.

Nor, I imagine, would she have kept her sunny side uppermost as the western coalition's air forces vaporised the retreating Iraqi conscript army at the end of the first Gulf war. An optimist, of necessity, believes in a future typified by knowns, because if – in the rousing chorus of the Blair government's accession anthem of 1997 – 'things can only get better', then this must be in comparison with what already obtains. The pessimist, by contrast, is fully attuned to Donald Rumsfeld's unknown unknowns: the black swans that swoop down out of a clear blue sky to annihilate thousands of New York office workers. The pessimist does not sanction foreign wars on the basis that democracy can issue forth from the barrel of a gun – which is not to say that pessimists don't believe in the need to defend democratic values. Indeed, the chief paradox of whatever still obtains in the way of British greatness is that it derives from Churchillian pessimism: while the appeasers were optimistically waving their brollies, Winnie was scrying the storm clouds of the Nazi blitzkrieg. It was when optimism got the better of him – believing in the continuation of British rule in India – that Churchill's Pollyanna intransigence contributed to the deaths of up to three million Bengalis in the 1943 famine.

No, in foreign affairs a healthy dose of pessimism – if by this is meant a willingness to accept that things may be for the worst in a less-than-perfect world – is definitely indicated. But domestically the optimism (if you can call it that) of the Thatcher–Blair neoliberal consensus hardly seems to have been borne out. Abed in the late 1980s, receiving cancer treatment that may have been less advanced than that of today, but which nonetheless was administered free and on demand with no caveats, my moribund mother would have undoubtedly been right in taking a gloomy view of the sell-off of our public assets.

As we shiver our way through an interminable winter, facing both fuel poverty in individual households and collective energy insecurity after having bartered our oil reserves for a mess of banker's pottage, the much-vaunted efficiency of the market seems like just another optimistic mirage. Food banks opening at the rate of two a week, sickness benefit claimants about to be struck off by private contractors without any recourse to justice – these are developments that wouldn't have fazed her.

She regarded the auto-cannibalistic tendencies of capitalism not from a theoretical perspective, but with the weary eyes of an American child of the Depression era. She had witnessed her own father keep the family afloat by organising fire sales for bust department stores.

Indeed, what are speculative bubbles if not the purest example of optimism run wild? The same sort of loony thinking that once invested in perpetual motion machines leads the contemporary credulous to believe that financial wizardry can conjure something out of nothing. The same glad-eyed and groundless enthusiasm for the Good News that the Redeemer's arrival is imminent also leads people to believe that economies can continue to grow for all eternity, spawning more goods for more clap-happy consumers. I'm by no means the most eminent Cassandra to have pointed out that there's a worm in the Enlightenment's apple of knowledge; this distinction belongs to my *New Statesman* colleague John Gray. But, by contrast with him, I retain the same ideals as I always did: a belief that an egalitarian and essentially socialistic society is worth striving for.

Is this a paradox? I think not. Moreover, I also hold that a healthy streak of pessimism is pretty much mandated by such idealism. Let me explain. For every instance of a pessimistic forecast being fulfilled that I've set out above, the optimist can probably instance a counter-example. So be it. But the optimist also thinks that it is her willingness to entertain a better future that acts as a psychic midwife to its birth. How, the optimist argues, can you be bothered to struggle for a state of affairs that you regard as at best unlikely, and quite possibly altogether unattainable? The answer lies in the appreciation that the political and the personal are linked not instrumentally, but existentially. Subscribing to an ideology, whether it bases its appeal in the reasonable prolegomena of a Rousseau-inflected state-of-nature, or one of the instinctive and Hobbesian variety, nonetheless involves the individual in an act of deferral of the form: not now, but given such-and-such, then.

It is this 'such-and-such' that forms the basis of all institutionalised appeals to political action: the communist utopia is forestalled quite as much as the thousand-year Reich; both retreat in advance of the measured tramping of the mobilised masses. At a less dramatic level, politicians in our highly imperfect (but still vaguely operable) representative democracies exhort us with their manifesto promises of jam tomorrow and seek to remind us of the jam we spread on yesterday's bread. It's no wonder that electorates that are gummed up within the mechanisms of internet commerce find such appeals increasingly difficult to hear above the whine of their computers. After all, this is the most compelling contemporary paradigm of gratification: push the button to receive jam by express 24-hour delivery; and if you sign up for repeat deliveries, you can indeed have tomorrow's jam today.

It is this consumerist ethic – if it can be so glorified – that has eaten away at any remaining semblance of altruism, its chomping in synchrony with the optimistic belief in the power of the market to unite mouths efficiently with jam. And this also explains why all political parties and charitable organisations now aspire to the form of commercial enterprises, complete with marketing departments and tax breaks for donations. Implicit in all of these activities, whether ostensibly dedicated to social welfare or to capital aggregation, is a utilitarian calculus. The nature of the good – or goods – may be disputed, but the conviction remains that it can be factually accounted for and numerically arrived at.

Yet to live a full life is not to cede such a large percentage of it to a purely statistical perspective; such a life – to borrow the title of Céline's novel – is merely death on the instalment plan. And it is the optimist, paradoxically, who enforces such a life on the generality of humankind with her plea that we look to a better future.

I have, as you have probably realised, a good deal of sympathy for that apocalyptic tendency that led Spanish anarchists to burn the town hall records and string up the priest. But I don't think we have to resort to such excesses in order to reclaim the primacy of the here, the now and the individual over the insistent compulsions of the there, the then and the collective. All that's necessary is to expect the worst but live hopefully, if by 'living hopefully' is meant to invest the present in the raiment of all the idealism any of us could wish for – to practise, in the telling phrase of Basho, the Japanese Zen poet, 'random acts of senseless generosity'.

We do not arrive at any idea of what is best for the collective unless we are prepared to seize the day and practise it on our own behalf. Most mature individuals understand what this means in respect of themselves – it's just all those feckless others that they don't trust to act appropriately. And so, by one means or another, they seek to organise society in such a way as to corral the human kine and herd them towards pastures new. But really, the sweet-smelling grass is beneath our hoofs right now: what is required is that we take pleasure in what is available to us. I said above that my pessimism resulted in an epicureanism when it came to personal life. Unfortunately, in our gastro-fixated culture, the epicurean is associated with fancy concoctions of wheatgrass, rather than the stuff growing close to hand. We need to redress this balance and understand that once the basic necessities of life are accounted for, all the rest can be creative and even wilful.

The optimist can never embrace this perspective, driven as she is by an inchoate need that can always be shaped by others so as to tantalise her. The optimist – again, paradoxically – lives in fear of a future that she endeavours, futilely, to control. The optimists can never be that most desirable of things: a meliorist, because every setback is necessarily a disaster. For the pessimist, it's simply a matter of shit happens, but until it does, make hay.

But if I may end, as I began, on a personal note (rightly so, given the tenor of what I've had to say), while I have maintained a pessimistic cast of mind for the past quarter-century, there are many areas of my life in which my pessimism has been unwarranted – none more so than in respect of the *New Statesman*. In 1988 my career as a contributor was in distinct abeyance; 25 years on it's going strong, and long may it and this vehicle for it continue.

14 AUGUST 2015

There won't be blood

Suzanne Moore

Something in me has died. Not an actual thing. I know what that feels like. I have had a dead foetus inside me and been told to go home and wait to miscarry 'naturally'. This is different. Another kind of ending. The bits that made me a woman of some description ... they are still there, but they have no useful function. No more ovulation. No more bleeding. No more babies. No more contraception. No more wondering. No more tampon tax. The curse is lifted.

I want a medal, a paper hat, a prize; some kind of public recognition or a rite of passage at least, involving fire-eating, chanting and mescalin. Instead I find that no one wants me even to talk about it. 'It' being the menopause. 'My womb is a tomb' doesn't seem to work well as a conversation starter.

'Can I have some sort of certificate?' I ask my poor GP.

'It doesn't really work like that.'

'When can I say it's over, that I'm done?'

She sighs. I like her and I feel if she could she would give me more than a wry smile.

No one really asks me how I am getting on with the old 'change of life'. Especially not men. They probably think that would be rude and I would bite their heads off and they would probably be right. I don't really have the mood swings that some talk about. I have just the one mood. Rage. I am enraged as soon as I wake up, enraged by the news, enraged by how the world is, enraged when I can't sleep, and I can never sleep.

Some women cry. A lot. My friend cried because she saw a baby: 'A baby at the bus stop. I cried at the bus stop.' She repeats the story several times until the bus stop is more significant to me than the baby. This is the hormonal horror that awaits. Weeping on buses. *She is fully gone*, I think to myself. A few years older than me, and constantly fanning herself. An evening with her is a trial, as the heating has to be switched on and off several times. Her thermostat has packed up. Her actual thermostat, the one in her house. It's all the fiddling.

It is somehow reassuring to know most of my women friends are even more deranged than me. They talk of herbs and potions from hippie shops, black cohosh and sage tea, which is revolting. But some of the sisterhood around this time of life is what my kids would call 'judgy'. There are right ways and wrong ways to do it. The natural and the unnatural. That is what being a woman is, I decide. Doing it the wrong way. I am further incensed.

'Are you having hot flushes?' my doctor asked at one point.

'I don't know.'

'Then you are not,' she says. 'You would know if you were. You are in the perimenopause.' She doesn't have time to explain the perimenopause. I suspect it's because she can't. It can go on for ten years, apparently. Ten years?!

It's just as well I am handling everything so well. I end my relationship because it's bad and I end it badly because there is no other way. A process of shedding starts. Some hoard and hold on. This is not for me. Some intuition tells me that freedom will demand letting go.

At the time, I didn't see these feelings as menopausal. But now I do. This deep sense of time passing, through one's flesh, of not wanting more of the same, a sense of coming into the present and only the present, understanding that time is valuable and time has passed: these come through knowing that parts of my life are over. I can no longer create life – and I have created three – so now I must create my own. This self-creation is either selfish or absolutely necessary to survive. Yes, I can jump out of a plane, get a new 'hobby', rush around in a flurry of activities involving Zumba and watercolours … but why would I? The manic overachievement of the menopausal feels a lot like denial.

Read the medical books. Look at the fashion spreads. Women dry up. Youth is moist, wet, dewy. Old women are husks with coarsened skin and thinning vaginal walls and the cause of this curse is hormonal: oestrogen. We no longer produce enough of it. The ovaries stop their egg production. The average age for the menopause is 51 but it can come much earlier. Chemotherapy will bring it on. IVF treatment induces it; this is the fresh hell.

Some sail through it. I asked a brilliant 80-year-old I met smoking at a party about it. 'Honey,' she said, 'I was too damn busy to notice.' That generation was tougher than mine in every way. Some of our angst is cultural. To put it into perspective, historically a lot of women just died before they got to this age. We are the lucky ones.

Having lost enough friends along the way, I know this but I can't avoid the questions: what does it mean to be a woman who, having served her purpose – reproduction – may have another kind of life? We may not define ourselves by our reproductive organs, whether we have children or not, but we are defined by them. Whatever your opinion about your role, your sex, your gender, your identity, your biology, your destiny, something is physically happening. If one enters 'womanhood' with menstruation, now you are exiting it. A predator whose bones are thinning is a woman to be feared. A woman whose ovaries no longer do what they should do is somehow ungendered and possibly disgusting.

The sanctioned discussions around the menopause are fairly limited, mostly to 'ageing'. The physicality is rarely mentioned. Instead we ask: 'Can we have more older women on TV?' 'Can a grandmother be a president?' 'Can mutton be a lamb shish?' Well, yes, obviously, if these are the parameters of the debate.

Inevitably, then we see pictures of women who look good for their age. Helen Mirren, Carine Roitfeld and the other one. You know, some other one who is still desirable. I want to scream. It is their *job* to look good. This is not the job of most women, although we are increasingly groomed to think it is, to define ourselves purely physically. The advice comes thick and heavy as we try to stop being thick and heavy. It is relentless and relentlessly boring. Exercise and everything in moderation. Another part of me dies.

The menopause is not sexy. We get it. We don't get it. It might be ultra-sexy, actually. Hormones are druggy and – rather like in pregnancy – some women find their libido shoots up; for others, it declines and they express relief. We are all different but the truism remains that our bodies, battle-scarred as they may be, are now somewhere we ought to feel at home. To not feel at home is the source of terror. To feel the fear of where this all might be heading.

Simone de Beauvoir could barely look at herself in the mirror, her own ageing was so horrific to her. For some, the cloak of invisibility of middle age is worn with aplomb; for others, it is a shroud. The worrying about libido, too much, too little, is real. If you want to depress yourself, google 'clitoral atrophy'. Although I am not a doctor, the solution seems to be: use it or lose it.

The lack of information around the menopause is one of the things that has shocked me most. It is a mystery to many well-informed women. The perimenopause, for instance, is an all-purpose diagnosis for all kinds of ills. Many women are told they are 'peri' with no idea what this means. Erratic bleeding, insomnia, itching, vaginal dryness, memory lapse and vasomotor disturbance are just a few of the symptoms that could make you 'peri'. You are post-menopausal when you haven't had a period for over a year.

The lack of definition bothered me. The female body can be a mess, so I simply decided to have it – the menopause – one cold November weekend a few years ago. I took to my bed, decided that my time was over and nested in a cloud of self-pity. By the Monday I was bored and went out and saw a great gig. These are a good menopausal activity, as they occur in dark spaces and no one cares if you perspire.

But I am not surprised so many women end up utterly depressed. If the menopause is seen as basically a disease, as lack, then women's bodily chemistry must be rebalanced with hormone replacement therapy or antidepressants. Lately I am seeing that a lot. Middle-aged women are now on selective serotonin reuptake inhibitors (SSRIs) for what are basically the symptoms of menopause. The encroaching darkness must be kept at bay. Having seen women go from crawling around on all fours to functioning well on HRT, I know it can help. But why is there so little discussion about long-term medicating of the female body?

Despite my melodrama, in truth, I hardly suffered at all. Why would I? I never had terrible periods: indeed, I used to see PMT in others as a form of attention-seeking. But when menopausal insomnia hit me I felt unable to function.

'Can you not fall asleep, or do you keep waking?' the doctor asked. 'Both.'

More blood tests. Too much cortisol. 'It's the stress hormone. Your body is somehow trying to kick-start your ovaries. It will try anything.'

'I hate my ovaries,' I wailed. The doctor prescribed me tricyclics, the old-fashioned kind of antidepressants, just to use at night. Immediately I trebled the dose. When Michael Jackson died, my first thought was to wonder what sleeping medication he was on. Can I get that? That is what insomnia does.

As the drugs didn't work, I was offered the sleep clinic. Off I trotted weekly to cognitive behavioural therapy, the NHS's new bargain-basement cure-all. The first thing I was told by a shrink was that I must stop referring to our therapy as 'The Insomniac Club' or, indeed, referring to myself as an insomniac. My thinking needed reframing.

Again, no one wanted me to use the word 'menopause' but they pushed me to learn something called 'sleep hygiene'. When I described physical feelings of insomnia that were decidedly menopausal, that I could actually feel descending on me, they talked about turning off my laptop. This did not help. Mostly I didn't understand why I was having group therapy with a perfectly nice but unemployed man who couldn't sleep at night because he slept all day; a wired and scratchy young woman who was always shivering; a very angry man who claimed not to have slept for ten years; and a shy emo who did sleep, but was troubled by the idea of seasonal affective disorder.

But the reason I was there summed up for me what is wrong with our attitudes to the menopause. A psychiatrist had assessed me over the phone.

One of the questions he asked was: 'Do you have dark thoughts?'

'Yes.'

'What kind of thing?'

'I just think about how I will die and everyone I know will die and how dying is when everything you hold dear is taken away from you bit by bit.'

'Do you have those thoughts often?'

'Yes, often. I always have had. But now a lot.'

To me, this is normal. The NHS clearly does not have a tick box labelled 'existentialism'. Somehow over the phone I had been assessed as mildly suicidal. Nothing happened. I just got a letter telling me as much, which is ... cheerful, first thing in the morning. The thing is, I'm not in the least suicidal – but menopause is something to do with death and yet no one wants you to say this out loud. No one at all.

To deny the connection to death is a lie. Your body is not returning to a previous state. The death may be metaphorical, as you are not dying, unless your body was only ever there for childbearing. Are women who have not had children lesser women? Are we only defined by motherhood and fuckability? No, of course not. We are more than that. That's what we tell ourselves. But what is this *more*? How do we reproduce ourselves for ourselves? If you have a moment. If you are not looking after children and parents. If you can be bothered.

Maybe that's why so much cheery advice on looking younger (it's not happening) or getting a pet or internet dating can be grating. And inane. A further denial of loss. I've never met a woman who misses having periods, but I know many who felt a form of mourning in middle age. The mourning is unvoiced and unsure because one of the things women learn very young is that putting yourself at the centre of things is unbecoming. The flood of feelings about life, death, ageing, sex and the whole damn shebang is easier to push away, to belittle, than to confront.

This may also explain the constant uplift of some of the blogs on the subject. At least women do exchange information online, and because most of us are so clueless this is useful. I knew far more as a teenager about what menstruation was than I knew about the menopause as a fiftysomething. While information is scant, the drive to be happy is so manic that it is near hysteria.

My favourite advice was on the value for menopausal symptoms of a nice, hot bath with Taoist oils (no idea). There was a picture of an antique bathtub and an inspirational quote – 'There must be quite a few things that a hot bath won't cure, but I don't know many of them,' from Sylvia Plath. *The* Sylvia Plath. That well-known life coach.

Is a jaunty sense of humour a response to fear? Germaine Greer may have been right when she said that what women 'are afraid of losing is not femininity, which can always be faked and probably is always fake, but femaleness'. If by femaleness she means the ability to reproduce – certainly not a defining part of every woman's life – then the return to the individual that existed before menstruation raises interesting questions. Her view may be seen as unfashionable essentialism, or rather we may begin to see the menopause as a form of transitioning. For it is a time of transition. Undoubtedly. Is a woman who is free of her 'sexual and reproductive destiny' less of a woman? If so, someone needs to explain what a woman is exactly and why she may not now become more of herself.

In the early 1990s the menopause and what it meant were explored by feminists such as Greer and Gail Sheehy, who stood at opposite ends of the spectrum. For Sheehy, the menopause was something that women as health consumers would lobby around, breaking the last great taboo. HRT would stop osteoporosis and heart attacks, and women could embrace a second adulthood in ways men couldn't. Some medics described women low in oestrogen as 'the walking dead' and Sheey's 1991 book *The Silent Passage* is a call to arms to demand intervention.

Since then, debates about HRT and breast cancer have raged and the standard dosage of HRT has come down.

The theory is that sexless cronehood can thus be swerved. The practice turns out to be different. The sexed-up older woman, the 'cougar', honed and toned, botoxed and HRTed up to the nines, is still a figure of fun, for men and for other women. We do not like the bodies of older women even when they are our own. And every pleasure-giving thing from sunlight to gin is said to age us faster. The menopausal woman must decide whether she will go with thinning bones or a higher risk of breast cancer – and for many it is no choice at all, as they feel so terrible. We still have to function.

The production (and politics) of oestrogen is incredibly complicated both within our bodies and without. Too much of it is bad for us. Too little of it is bad for us. This was brought home to me when I was in a hospital with yet another friend with a tumour in her breast. 'It's because I smoked, isn't it?' she said to the consultant.

'No. We see every type of breast cancer here and the only things that all the women have in common is that they have breasts and produce oestrogen.'

Not all cancers are related to oestrogen but some are. It is produced in the female body, mainly through the ovaries, but also the liver and the adrenal glands. A few of the things that make us produce too much of it and are therefore dangerous are excess fat, too many carbohydrates, alcohol, meat and perfume – basically what I would call the finer things in life. Then there's all the excess oestrogen in the environment from plastics, pesticides and from women who are leaking it out all over the shop because they are on the Pill.

At this point, if you are sensible, you may make an informed choice about a healthy diet and exercise to get through menopausal symptoms. Cortisol – the likely cause of my insomnia – is related to insulin production, so I can vouch that if you cut out all sugar and alcohol your mood will level out, your cravings will stop and your night sweats will ease. After three weeks of this, however, I felt such a life wasn't really worth living.

Upping your calcium is a good idea. Women swap hard-won tips such as 'tahini is a great source of calcium' but it's all a bit reminiscent of that time when you've just had a baby and you go out and people assume that all you want to talk about is babies, when it's the last thing you want to do. Except this time it's even worse, because you're talking about seeds. Still, you are now in the zone of bone scans and mammograms, with bowel cancer tests to look forward to.

I was called in for a smear. While the cold metal was still inside, the nurse said casually: 'Well, you won't be needing these so often. Cervical cancer is a young woman's disease.' As I was putting my knickers back on she pulled back the curtain to hand me a leaflet on pelvic floor exercises.

This was one of the better days.

As always, for the rich, there is something better and more 'natural'. The common or garden kind of HRT is made from hormones extracted from the urine of pregnant horses. Private doctors prescribe BHRT instead: bio-identical hormone replacement therapy. Bio-identicals are said to be natural. They are made not from horse piss but from Mexican yams, which, let's face it, sounds a lot nicer. And somehow more feminine.

Bio-identicals are prescribed in carpeted offices and individual doses after a series of tests. Those who take them swear by them. As so often, though, a lot of sense goes out of the window when people start talking about drugs versus naturally occurring chemicals, Big Pharma versus ... private 'BHRT' medication.

It's a minefield of wishful thinking. This is an argument about giving women synthetic hormones rather than the naturally occurring versions that some of their advocates insist are not drugs. This is patently rubbish: if something is stopping your hot flushes and depression and keeping your skin smooth and all the things that BHRT claims, then it's a drug. Perhaps BHRT is a better drug and the way it is prescribed is better than the random handing-out of normal HRT by stressed-out GPs. Perhaps it is a better way, but to argue for access to these better drugs, or more information, we would have to think politically about the menopause and it is hard to be political about things that embarrass us.

Indeed, we may begin to question why this stage of life must be dealt with by chemicals at all. Are women to spend most of their lives ingesting hormones to stop them getting pregnant, and then the rest of it ingesting others to mimic the effects of oestrogen? For this is what we are doing.

Is the answer to every woman struggling with aches, pains and questions about her very being simply HRT or SSRIs? It can certainly feel like that. At one stage I dabbled with HRT. I can't remember why. It was a locum and I think he wanted to get me and my dark thoughts out of his surgery. For nine days I took the pills, waiting to feel something. But there was nothing. On the tenth day I woke in the night with what I can only describe as labour pains and with puddles of blood everywhere. My 'femaleness' had returned with a vengeance and it was so horrible, I had to stop myself dialling 999 and telling them I was Carrie.

HRT may be a godsend for some, but there is something very odd in tricking the female body into thinking it is still capable of reproduction when it is not, just in order to remain lubricated and shiny. Those with partners now have no excuse for twin beds or relief from 'conjugal duties'. With Viagra and HRT and the ideology that sex is compulsory for health and happiness, we can all go on for ever and ever. The time when women could call it a day or no longer need to scratch that itch is gone. For some, there is joy in no longer fearing pregnancy; for others, sex is one less chore they have to perform. Or it may be that many older women renounce sex because men have renounced them for a younger model and it's easier to pretend it's a choice.

Lubrication is important in so many ways. *Use* lube for sure. But know that you no longer have to *be* it. All those years when femininity was enacted as social lubrication have gone. You don't have enough time left to go round making everyone else feel comfortable. Let them sort themselves out. What does return – or never left but I can only now admit to – is what I can only describe as the delightful cockiness of adolescence.

Alongside this is the rage. The rage I felt so intensely is so obviously a rage against the dying of the light that I am suspicious of New Age stuff that seeks to pacify it. Holding on to this rage and not caring what people think of it is powerful.

What helps is paying attention to yourself – and I don't mean exfoliation regimes, I mean attention to your interior self, because the outside is going to decline whatever you do. Listen to your psyche beginning to grasp what it does not want to let itself know: that it is not immortal. Listen and learn, for this is the place creative thought comes from. Creation is always to imagine something living beyond yourself out there in the world. This urge surely is not reducible to femaleness or reproduction. So this time of loss may be a time of gain if you allow it.

Pleasure is still possible because at this time, thankfully, most of us start needing glasses. We can no longer see all the flaws that young girls with luminous skins search for on themselves with eyes like microscopes. The light may indeed be dying but we all need a dimmer switch at hand.

As we start to exit 'womanhood' we need again to redefine it. The curse. The change. These old words come up as some seek a power grab in the realm of the spiritual, too often the substitute for real power. Serenity can't possibly be a bad goal, though I don't see so many middle-aged men seeking it. Instead, I prefer Angela Davis's take on the serenity prayer: 'I'm no longer accepting the things I cannot change. I'm changing the things I cannot accept.'

Menopause makes us impatient. This is good. Women my age won't just melt away and we won't become invisible. It's a fight for sure, but then it always is. Womanhood and femaleness, born or made, is nomadic. That place we call home shifts so much over the course of a lifetime. In this movement lies some knowledge that may scare us as much as it may set us free.

'The change' can be medicated, but what the menopause does is tell us explicitly that although parts of us are now 'done', there is more to do and it's now or never. Accepting this can feel bloody awful sometimes and whatever gets you through the night may indeed be worth having. Unquestioningly dulling all these feelings associated with menopause exacts another price, too. Natural is not better than unnatural yet surely by 50 or so women should be able to make informed choices that can only happen when we discuss exactly what those choices are. Too few do. Doctors who are trained to prescribe HRT do not know quite how and when to take women off it. There is withdrawal, and there is no soft landing for so many. HRT is not a cure for menopause but a ploy to delay it and the devastating symptoms often return. Except now you are in your sixties, not your fifties. Many seem unclear about this.

For me, some clarity comes after and even during the heat daze. It just does. One day I am in an office and a guy says to me: 'You're on fire lately, Suzanne.'

'Wow!' I think. 'What a sensitive sort of man is this man, knowing about my fluctuating hormones. How does he know that I'm currently what one of my friends describes as "sweaty and mental"?'

Normally when women are given a compliment we demur. But there's no need any longer.

'You are right!' I say. 'I am actually on fire!'

He looks slightly worried. He backs away. He clearly thinks I am mad, so I decide to leave the building and go to the revolving door.

It whirls round as I push the door harder, as I am now on the way to the next place. Everything changes. Inside and outside. All the time. How did I ever think life was anything but this?

This. Now.

I am 'in the moment', as they say.

The door jams. I have pushed it too hard. We are all stuck. Now a young woman trying to come into the building starts tutting that I am making her late. I burst out laughing to myself and I don't care who sees me cackling.

Then the door starts moving again and through I go.

The Good Daughter

Janice Turner

In Tate Britain is a painting by the Victorian artist George Elgar Hicks of a woman ministering tenderly to her invalid father. It is called *Comfort of Old Age*. The work is the final panel of Hicks's triptych *Woman's Mission*. The first part, *Guide of Childhood*, in which the same figure teaches her little boy to walk, has been lost. But the second panel also hangs at the Tate in London: *Companion of Manhood* shows our heroine consoling her husband after ghastly news.

Hicks depicted 'woman' in her three guises – mother, wife, daughter – and in her ideal state, the selfless provider of guidance, solace and care. Her life has meaning only in so far as it nourishes and facilitates the lives of others, principally men.

Domestic and emotional labour, we call it now. Feminists have long campaigned both for this to be acknowledged as real work and for men to do their share. Women cannot reach their potential at the office, notes Facebook's Sheryl Sandberg in her book *Lean In*, until men pull their weight at home. But this has always been the toughest, messiest fight, because it is about domestic harmony, varying standards of personal hygiene, nagging, sulking and love. Besides, there is an enduring sense, little changed since Hicks's day, that not only are women better at caring duties, but it is their natural lot.

I have spent a long time in the first two panels of the triptych: a partner/wife for 30 years, a mother for 21. (My two sons are grown and pretty much gone.) And I have seen, in the course of my adult life, enormous progress in those two domains. Men no longer assume that wives will dump their careers to follow them on foreign postings, for instance, or that mothers cannot work. According to research by the Office for National Statistics, women still do 40 per cent more household chores than men but, growing up, I never saw a man make dinner, let alone push a pram. Marriages are increasingly equal partnerships and each generation of fathers is more engaged.

Now I have reached the third panel, the trickiest bit of the triptych. My 93-year-old mother is 200 miles away in Doncaster, and since my father died, five years ago, she has been living alone. She is – I must stress – admirable, independent, uncomplaining and tough. A stoic. Someone who doesn't mourn her every lost faculty but relishes what she can still do. Yet almost everyone she ever knew is dead, and I am her only child: her principal Comfort of Old Age.

For a long time, the landscape was a series of plateaus and small dips. Her little house acquired rails, walking frames, adaptations; she wears an emergency pendant. But until she broke her hip four years ago, she wouldn't even have a cleaner. ('I don't want strangers in my house.') She managed. Just. But since Christmas the terrain has shifted. A persistent infection, two collapses, three ambulance rides, tachycardia (in which your heart beats to the point of explosion), but then, after three weeks, back home. Finally I persuaded her to have carers – nice, kindly, expensive – for an hour five times a week. (She demanded days off.) A slightly lower plateau.

Then, a few weeks ago, a neighbour called to say that my ma's curtains were still closed at 4pm. She was found dehydrated, hallucinating. (She hadn't pressed her emergency button; it was a non-carer day.) I hurriedly packed my bag for God knows how long, then scrambled north to sit by her bedside believing, for the third time this year, that I was watching her die.

For three weeks, on and off, I slept alone in my teenage single bed, in the house where I grew up, weeping every time I opened a cupboard to see her cake tins or Easter eggs for her grandsons. That week, I read a news report about how having children makes people live two years longer. Of course! As her daughter, I was her advocate, hassling doctors for information, visiting, reassuring, making sure she was fed, washing her soiled clothes (even long-stay units won't do laundry), trying to figure out what to do next. God help the childless! Really, who will speak for them?

Finally, having wrestled her into (almost) daily care – she is very stubborn – I returned to London to find a letter. I am a *Times* columnist and write a weekly notebook slot, occasionally featuring my mother. I am used to harsh reader critiques of my life. But this, I must say, stung. It was from a man who lives in Cheshire (he had supplied his name and address), and he wanted me to know what a terrible person I am. 'I have been puzzled when reading your column over the past months how you have been able to leave your mother – whose serious health issues you have used as copy ... to holiday in Mexico, East Anglia and Norway.' I was 'selfish and self-regarding', and I should be ashamed.

He was not the first. Online posters often chide me for maternal neglect, and otherwise kind letters sometimes conclude: 'But I do think your mother should move in with you.' Anyway, my egregious Mexican holiday had been long delayed by her illness and although she was well when I left, I was braced to fly back at any moment. The Norway trip was to visit my son on his 21st birthday. No matter. How dare I have a life.

I was reminded of when my children were young and I was a magazine editor. The guilt-tripping, the moral judgement: the looks from full-time mothers, the pursed lips from older relatives. Why bother having kids if you work full-time? Back then, I was 'selfish and self-regarding', too. My husband, who worked vastly longer hours, was blameless.

So let me warn you that just when you're free from being judged as a mother, you'll be judged as a daughter. It is the last chance for reactionary types who resent women's career success, or just their freedom to live how they choose, to have a dig. Look at this selfish bitch, weekending in East Anglia when she should be a Comfort of Old Age.

When we say someone is a Good Dad, it means he turns up to football matches and parents' evenings, gives sensible advice, isn't a derelict alcoholic or a deserter. I know many fathers do much, much more. But that is the bar to Good Dadhood. It is pretty low. To qualify as a Good Mother, however, a woman must basically subsume her entire existence into her children and household and may only work part-time, if at all.

So, what is a Good Daughter? A US report showed in 2014 that daughters were twice as likely as sons to care for their elderly parents. In a survey of 26,000 older Americans, Angelina Grigoryeva, a sociologist at Princeton University, discovered that daughters provide as much care as they can manage, while sons do as little as they can get away with. If they have sisters or even wives, men are likely to leave it to them. I can find no equivalent UK study, but I'd bet the same is true here.

I know many sons who help out with ageing parents: Sunday care-home visits or a spot of DIY. Some do the truly grim stuff, such as washing and toileting a frail, dementia-patient father. And all sons – unless they are estranged, or cruel, or in prison – are Good Sons. Being a Good Daughter is a much tougher gig. However often I go north, sort out bills, buy new ironing boards, listen to my mother's worries, take her shopping, organise her Christmas presents and stay awake worrying, it won't be enough. A friend visits her disabled mother every day, despite her family and career, sorts out wheelchairs and carers, runs errands. Her three brothers drop by for ten minutes once a fortnight: so busy, so important! Yet my friend's care is a given, and her brothers are 'marvellous'. A truly Good Daughter would quit her job, have her old mother move in and tend to her alone.

The truth is I don't want to be a full-time carer, any more than I wanted to be a full-time mother. And I don't want to live with my ma any more than she wants to live with me. Now that I've served out my motherhood years, I want to do other things with my life besides looking after people. Is that a shocking admission? Men wouldn't give it a second thought.

Yet politicians of left and right are always telling us that the solution to our screwed-up social-care system is the family. To socialists, the 'care industry' is further evidence of marketisation and the profit motive taking over the personal sphere. Jeremy Hunt, the Health Secretary, has said that he favours the 'Asian model' and the care minister David Mowat said recently that we must care for our parents as unquestioningly as we do our children. In practice, these all amount to the same thing: women, chiefly daughters and daughters-in-law, toiling away unpaid.

After Christmas, while my mother *was* living with me, frail and recuperating from her infection, I hired a private carer so that I could work. This lovely woman was boundlessly kind, calm, patient, unfazed: I am none of these things. Ask me to fix the car, get sense from a doctor, shout at the council: I'm Action Daughter, at your service. But expect me to sit still in a room making nice for hours and I am crap. In Hicks's Woman's Mission, I have failed.

A *Times* reader chastised me for hiring help: 'Well, I'd expect to look after my own mother myself.' And I was reminded once more of early motherhood, when I employed a nanny. Yes, a nanny, not a childminder or a nursery. I know the word makes left-wing men crazy: you cold, rich, privileged cow. That nanny, funnily enough, allowed both my husband and me to work, but it was me who got the rap.

Even hiring a cleaner is 'problematic'. A good feminist shouldn't expect a poorer woman to clear up after her, I hear. To which I reply: my mother was a cleaner for thirty years and her meagre wages paid for my new shoes. When a couple hire a cleaner, it is nearly always to compensate for the shortfall in male domestic labour, yet it is the woman, again, who has somehow failed.

In the third part of the triptych, paid help for elderly parents is even more of a dereliction of female duty. My mother's next-door neighbour has cared for her invalid father, unaided, for 20 years; a friend has remodelled her house to accommodate her elderly parents. Across Britain are millions of people who care for relatives with little respite. When I say that a private carer now visits my mother, I do so with shame because, most days, this is the only company she receives. A nice lady called Sue helps with her jigsaw puzzle, chats to her, does some light housework and fetches her shopping. But what she is paying for is a surrogate me.

It tears up my heart. Yet it is complicated. What if you live far from your home town: should you be expected to return? My unmarried aunt came back after an interesting single life to live with my grandmother until her death. Her siblings didn't thank her for this sacrifice. Indeed, without the status of marriage, she was treated with disdain.

Last month, as a Nigerian health assistant helped Ma to the hospital bathroom, I remarked that she lives alone. '*Why?*' came the horrified response. In her culture, this made no sense. But northern European society has evolved an individualism that often transcends notions of family and duty. This applies to the old and offspring alike.

Largely our elderly do not want, Asian-style, to be infantilised by their children, or bossed around by their daughters-in-law. (The claim that Indian parents are 'revered' is undermined by rampant elder abuse.) My ma wants to watch *Corrie*, eat quiche, not feel she is in the way. 'I like to please myself,' is her refrain. Her home of almost 50 years is her carapace: her central fear is of being too ill to stay. Despite the much-discussed return of 'multigenerational living', the most popular British solution is the 'granny annex', where an old person maintains autonomy behind her own front door.

Moreover, members of the baby-boomer generation recoil at living with their parents. We spent our teenage years trying to escape. What if your upbringing featured divorce, personality clashes, arguments, abuse? What if, like me, you left your working-class culture for a completely different life – what if you have little in common? Or your widowed father now expects you to run around after him like a skivvy, just as he did your mum? You can reject your roots for your entire adulthood, then your parents' frailty yanks you home.

Now those Guide of Childhood years seem simple and golden, although the parallels are striking. From stair gates to stairlifts; from pushchairs to wheelchairs; the incontinence provision; the helplessness. But raising children is largely a cheerful, upward trajectory. Elderly care is an uneven descent, via those dips and plateaus, towards some hidden crevasse. There is no compensatory boasting, showing cute snaps on your phone. You learn not to mention geriatric travails. People look uncomfortable or bored: too grim.

But, just as a child shows you the world anew – look, a spider, a leaf, the sea, Christmas! – through clear, unjaded eyes, older people reveal what truly matters in the end. A reader remarked that it was probably best that my mother, at 93, now died. I replied that she gets more joy in M&S than some get from a Caribbean cruise. With age, the world distils down to elemental pleasures: seeing a grandchild, a piece of cake, a sunny day, the warmth of a hand. When my father was very close to death and when recently my ma was at her sickest, both still managed to utter the words 'I love you'. Just as when a frightened child cries for you in the night, you are utterly irreplaceable, needed.

And it will be your turn soon, when your parents are old. We are living longer, often fading out in medically preserved decrepitude over many years. I can't understand why both as individuals and as a society we refuse to plan. Well, actually I can. It's horrible. As my mother always says: 'When it happens, it happens.'

Yet there is so much we could do. Come up with a cross-party agreement on how to fund social care through the tax system. Invest money and imagination in ways that old people can remain in their home, rather than slash home help. Develop friendship schemes and clubs, so the lonely aren't so dependent on faraway children. Enable the old to use the internet: few are online, though no one would benefit from it more. Rip up the care-home model in which the elderly are objects in a chair: let people be their full human selves until the end.

Above all, we must redraw that final panel of the triptych. Don't judge daughters more harshly than sons. Don't let men slink away from their fair share. Don't wield the family as a glib solution. Instead, acknowledge that it is hard, heart-rending work, being a Comfort of Old Age.

8 DECEMBER 2017

On the Tube, I saw the father I'd never met – and was happy to find that I had nothing to say to him

Stephen Bush

Being from a single-parent family is hereditary. In my case, I got it from my father, who left my mother before I was born. Like most hereditary conditions, from time to time, you'll find yourself discussing it in circumstances you can't control and in a manner that makes you mildly uncomfortable.

In my case, well-meaning people ask what my father does, which leaves me with the unlovely choice between honesty, which makes the questioner feel awkward, and lying, which is hard to keep up for long.

Honesty is particularly fraught, because an eccentric minority always believes that the polite response to 'I don't know, we've never met' is to ask, 'Why not?' and inquire whether I ever *wanted* to meet him.

Quite why this is considered appropriate conversation at a social event has never been clear to me. My father left because he wasn't, at that time, interested in having either a long-term relationship or a child. We haven't spoken since because I haven't wanted to make contact, and neither has he.

Before the era of Facebook, Twitter and LinkedIn, I might have wanted to meet him – to find out what he looked like, if nothing else. But thanks to Google Chrome's 'Incognito' mode, I have been able to ascertain the most important detail, which is that both sides of my family boast full heads of hair well into their fifties but that, sadly, what we retain in volume we do not match in colour.

I've learned to enjoy the upsides of having an absent father. One is that you don't have flaws like everyone else, merely kinks that the missing parent would have ironed out had he stuck around. Over the years, I've blamed him for: being bad at football, not having a girlfriend, being bad at ballet, being bad at DIY, not having written a novel, not knowing what I wanted to do after university, being short tempered and not doing my tax return on time.

The other upside is having one member of your family who can't ring up to complain about how they've been treated. My mum can phone, email and even tweet if she doesn't like something I've said. If my dad wants to complain, he has to fork over 18 years of unpaid child support plus interest first, which is a considerable deterrent.

Freed from the chains of journalistic accuracy, I have used my father as a creative device to write about cuts to tax credits, the presidency of Barack Obama, the correct way to cook pasta and the merits of *Harry Potter*. Which is not quite as valuable as child support, but it is considerably more versatile.

That said, I've never written anything about my father that isn't true. It's just that how I feel about him, on any given day, is a reflection of what's going on inside my head rather than a comment on a real, living person. Which is why it was something of a shock when I recently met the real, living person who is my father at Blackfriars Underground Station in London.

Well, 'met' is perhaps putting it too strongly. The *New Statesman* office is near Blackfriars and I work in parliament at Westminster, so I spend a lot of time on the Tube. On one trip from the office to Westminster, I saw someone who looked eerily familiar. If you've ever spent five minutes staring at someone, trying to work out which wedding you saw them at, only to realise you've been eyeballing a weatherman, you'll know the feeling: I stared at him for a few moments trying to work out if he had something to do with Brexit, before clocking that I'd seen his face on LinkedIn.

Then, just as you do when you realise that a terrified semi-famous person is wondering why a stranger is peering intently at them, I looked at my feet and walked past the man who had no idea that I was his son.

Why did I do that? Why didn't I take what is – let's face it – probably the only chance I'll have to talk to my father? Because in that moment, I realised I had nothing I really wanted to say to him.

And the reason for this is: I'm happy. Happy in work, in love, and surrounded by my real family: a complicated network of friends, in-laws and the mother who stuck around. I couldn't honestly have said I was angry with him, or I wished that he hadn't left, because I'm happy with how my life worked out in the end.

But I don't want to absolve him. He couldn't know, close to 30 years ago, that the child he was walking out on would have the good fortune to be born into a country about to experience close to two decades of uninterrupted, low-inflation growth, most of that presided over by a Labour government firmly committed to improving the condition of the poor. (One of Gordon Brown's forgotten achievements is that even after the financial crisis, child poverty continued to fall, because tackling it remained the government's central mission.)

My father couldn't know that I would benefit from investment in schools, museums and fantastic teachers, and the world's best mother. But I did, which means that while a number of people – the taxpayer, society, my mum – have a legitimate grievance against my father, I don't, not really. It worked out OK.

The dispiriting truth is that it might be different today: child poverty has increased every year for the past three years, even during periods of economic growth. Changes to the child maintenance regime have made it even harder to force absent parents to pay up, while the botched introduction of Universal Credit makes it more difficult for single parents in work to stay out of poverty.

And so I walked away from the man who was – or might have been – my father thinking this: I need to spend less time writing about an imaginary, lost parent, and more time writing about how much harder it is to be a kid like me today.

Wounded healer

Phil Whitaker

It was dark by the time I got to Linda's. I'd been her GP for seven years but this was the first time I'd been asked to visit her at home. I retrieved my bag from the boot, put my hood up against the wintry drizzle, and made my way across the sward that separated her house from the road. My shoes swished through the wet, uncut grass. On summer evenings, children from some of the other old Somerset miners' cottages would be out playing; their own private rec. Tonight it was deserted.

Trevor answered my knock.

'She's through here,' he said, ushering me into the warmth of the small hallway.

Linda was sagged in a sofa that had been squeezed against one entire wall of the compact living room. In the time it took to greet her, I noticed that her skin was sallow, even allowing for the artificial light. And every now and then, one of her arms or legs would jerk involuntarily. She managed a weak smile, but her eyes were dull and distracted – preoccupied by something more vital than social niceties.

I perched beside her, my hand reaching for her wrist. Cool. Pulse fast and thready.

'What's been going on?' I asked. The message left with reception suggested she'd contracted a stomach bug, but Linda was far more unwell than that.

Trevor was standing in the doorway, half-in and half-out of the room. He gave me the bare bones. Linda had been home from hospital just a few weeks, and was having terrible trouble with her stoma – the opening in her abdominal wall where her bowel now discharged following her recent surgery. It was continuously pouring out high volumes of liquid stool despite the drugs intended to counter this. Linda and Trevor found it hard to keep up with the frequent bag changes, day and night. The past few days she'd been feeling very nauseous, and yesterday the vomiting had begun.

I clicked open my bag while Trevor was speaking and took out my sphygmomano-meter, not voicing the question uppermost in my mind: why take so long to call? The meter showed Linda's blood pressure to be half what you might expect for a woman in her mid-sixties. While I was measuring it, a couple more jerks animated her limbs, as though she were being tugged by an impatient puppeteer.

'I'm really sorry, Linda,' I said, 'but I'm going to have to readmit you.'

She'd let Trevor do the talking until this point, but now she let out a groan. 'No, please,' she said. 'I'll be all right.'

I explained that she wouldn't; I said I thought her kidneys had shut down as a result of dehydration. Now that vomiting had set in she was on a one-way street. 'If you don't go back in, you're not going to make it.'

'I can't,' she said. 'I just can't face it.'

'Come on, Lin.' Trevor's voice had a trace of suppressed panic. 'It'll be all right. It won't be for long.'

Still Linda shook her head. What should have been a routine, if substantial, operation to remove a bowel tumour had been beset by complications. She'd ended up staying in hospital for near enough two months, lurching from one crisis to another: return visits to theatre to deal with post-operative infection; severe pneumonia and sepsis; in and out of high dependency and ITU; needles and drips and surgical drains; to say nothing of her radically altered body image and the indignities of a malfunctioning stoma. She'd been battered until she'd long passed the point of caring, and then she'd been battered some more. Finally making it home had been a watershed, an end to the whole torrid saga.

Now I understood the delay in seeking help: she was afraid. You might think that if a doctor told someone they were dying, and that going to hospital offered them a chance of life, they would jump at it. You might think that someone like Linda, who had gone through so much to try to be cured of cancer, wouldn't throw it all away at the 11th hour. You might be wrong.

The language of cancer echoes that of war: fights and battles, bravery and resistance. But, like soldiers, patients can develop shell shock. The strength of their reactions can be overwhelming, making re-engagement with the enemy impossible. Sometimes surrender seems the only thing to do.

I remember the words he said, and the way he said them. I must have been about 13. My mum and my brother and sister were out. It was just Dad and me at home.

He came and found me. Or maybe he just came across me. For some reason, I think I was sitting at the bottom of our stairs. I may well have been: it's where the phone was in our house back then, so I might have just finished chatting to a friend. Wherever I was, what burns bright in my mind are his words, and the catch in his voice: 'Phil. I think the cancer's come back.'

He'd been to the loo, he said. But instead of a normal bowel motion, there had been a mess of bloody diarrhoea. Looking back these 38 years later, I understand that he would have been terrified. I can see why he would have felt suddenly, awfully alone. Why he had to tell someone, whoever was around. That need would have been overwhelmingly urgent – the need to have someone connect with him, understand his fear, touch him and tell him they were sorry and that they loved him and that they were sure it was going to be all right. But at the age of 13 I didn't understand any of that. All I saw was my father, panic-stricken. I didn't really know what cancer was. Nor did I know what it would mean if it had come back. I think it probably scared me, seeing him like that. Maybe, in the blinkered egocentricity of adolescence, it repulsed me a little.

I don't remember touching him. I certainly didn't tell him I was sorry and that I loved him. I didn't know what he needed, not back then. I didn't know what to do.

Ever since modern medicine conquered many of the dreaded infectious diseases such as pneumonia, smallpox and diphtheria, which used to end so many lives prematurely, cancer has become our most feared adversary. By the time primary tumours announce themselves by causing symptoms, it is often too late to effect a cure. Whether we know it or not, by then the patient is often in the unyielding grip of an aggressive disease that will not be eradicated. By then, hidden deposits called metastases are often seeded elsewhere in the body, silently beginning their work of destruction.

For a long time, surgery was the only weapon doctors possessed with which to fight back. Cancers would be cut out; occasionally that proved effective, but much more commonly the disease would soon recur. Wider, more radical excisions were developed in the hope of clearing tumours once and for all. Recurrence still proved a problem, and those patients who did survive paid a heavy price in terms of the mutilation caused by the surgical cure.

The development of radiotherapy in the early twentieth century, and chemotherapy in the 1950s, expanded the therapeutic arsenal and enabled less drastic surgery to be performed. These treatments certainly improved outcomes, but survival rates for many tumours remained fairly poor. And the balance between treating the cancer and poisoning the patient is perilously fine. Unlike infectious disease, where antibiotics target cellular mechanisms unique to the foreign microbe, cancer is comprised of our own cells turned insurgent. Both radiation and chemotherapy drugs kill cancer cells, but they kill our normal tissues, too.

Gradually, as the discipline of oncology advanced and different tumour types and stages became systematically classified, it became clear that the defining characteristic of cancers that proved ultimately to be cured was how early they were caught. The way round having to wage such a blitzkrieg on the patient's body must be to detect tumours earlier, well before they had announced their presence by causing symptoms, and well before the process of metastasis had occurred. The hunt for effective screening tests was joined.

Where screening has been possible it has improved cure rates. But it has also generated some surprising findings, which have demonstrated that cancer is a far more complex process than we have hitherto realised. Mammography, for example, picks up many more tumours than would be expected from what we know of breast cancer incidence. The inescapable conclusion: by no means all cancers detected by screening will actually go on to become the life-threatening disease we so fear. Estimates vary widely, but most doctors now accept that of every three tumours detected by mammography, only two would have gone on to present as cancer.

Such 'overdiagnosis' is a feature of all tests that seek to detect cancer early. Until we have a better understanding of how to identify which screen-detected tumours can safely be left alone, we have no choice but to subject significant numbers of patients to aggressive curative treatment who may not actually need it. But the phenomenon of overdiagnosis may also offer valuable insights into the factors that enable tumours to cause clinical disease. It seems likely that our immune systems are able to counter or contain many tumours – many of us are walking around with cancers that we don't know about, which will never do us harm. Only once a cancer has acquired the capacity to evade immune system control – or when some other illness, adverse life-event, or medical treatment causes the immune system itself to become suppressed – only then does the disease we have traditionally thought of as 'cancer' begin to take hold.

Dad's was a testicular tumour. He noticed it when I was about 20 months old. Because of its superficial location, men often find an untoward scrotal lump at an early stage, whereas cancers developing deep within the body are frequently advanced by the time anyone is aware that they are there. He was swiftly admitted to hospital, where an operation removed the affected testicle along with the primary tumour.

The patient in the bed next to Dad when he was recovering from surgery was dying from an advanced bowel cancer. The memory of his wasted, jaundiced body; the pain he was in; the vomiting and the loss of dignity and control, haunted my father. As did the memory of the bloody diarrhoea that poured out of him. Within the five years prior to his own diagnosis, Dad had lost both his parents to different forms of the disease. It must have felt to him as if cancer was everywhere around, inexorably destroying anyone it touched. And now it had come for him, too.

By the time of Dad's diagnosis, radiotherapy had become well established as an adjunctive treatment. Testicular cancers are usually exquisitely sensitive to radiation. After he'd got over his operation, Dad underwent a series of irradiations of the abdomen – a field encompassing the regional lymph nodes to which testicular tumours commonly spread, the aim being to mop up any metastases that may have broken away from the primary tumour and seeded elsewhere.

He had every prospect of being cured. But no one could tell him if he had been. Treatment over, he spent year after year living with the knowledge that, any day, some symptom or sign might manifest to mean that his cancer had recurred.

Vince was angry with me. A few months before, he had consulted me about a niggling ache just below his ribcage. He worked in sales and spent hours behind the wheel – the discomfort was very recent and only came on when doing long stints of driving. I couldn't find anything to worry about when I examined him, and he being just 40, there was unlikely to be anything much going on. So I suggested we give it a bit of time to see if it would settle down. We left it that he would come back two or three weeks later if it showed no sign of resolving.

I was away on leave so it was a colleague of mine, Simon, to whom he returned. Simon wasn't too concerned either, but given that things hadn't settled spontaneously, he did what I would have done and arranged an ultrasound scan just to be sure. It identified a tumour on the right kidney.

The NHS moves fast when cancer is found: Vince was swept up by the system. A CT scan showed that the cancer had already spread. Although the primary tumour was due to be removed surgically, and subsequent chemotherapy would knock back the secondary deposits, the urologists had told Vince that a cure was not going to be possible.

Now Vince had come for a follow-up. He kept his gaze averted for much of the consultation, rarely meeting my eyes. I told him how sorry I was to hear the news. I sorted out certification to take him out of work while treatment proceeded. I made some tentative enquiries as to how he was coping. His replies were curt, bitter. The air between us crackled with undischarged electricity. I knew what was going on: he believed that if I had arranged the ultrasound the first time he came, the cancer would have been caught earlier and a cure might still have been possible.

I would have liked the chance to explain. To tell him how many patients we see with vague symptoms that don't appear to have any underlying cause. How so often these resolve without intervention, and prove to have been nothing more than a muscular ache, or a bit of bowel irritability.

Time is what we use: if there's nothing definitely wrong on first presentation, the passage of a few weeks will often see the symptoms settle down. And for those rare patients like Vince, where a nebulous discomfort proves to have been the first indication of serious trouble, a couple of weeks' delay in diagnosis won't have made any difference to the outlook. His tumour will have been growing for years; the metastases now visible on a CT scan will have long since occurred.

I wanted to explain all this, but I couldn't force it on him – to do so would have been self-indulgent, me justifying myself. It had to be him to raise the subject – him to tell me outright that he thought I had let him down. In a way, I was surprised that he had chosen to come back to me, that he didn't continue the journey with Simon. I assumed it was because he wanted to have it out with me.

It was when I asked how things were at home that the grief came. Vince said he had three young children whom he would now never see grow up. And his wife. How was she going to cope when he'd gone, trying to help with the kids' devastation while struggling with bereavement of her own? I sat and listened, my heart going out to him. There was nothing I could do to make it better; he just needed someone to hear and understand. He talked about memory boxes, about recording videos of himself for the children's futures. The ideas sounded puny when set against the monstrous juggernaut bearing down on him – when what he was screaming for inside was not to have to face it at all. But they were things for him to cling to, concrete tasks he could set himself so that he could feel he wasn't going to be completely erased from his family once he had gone.

It was a long consultation, and gradually the pent-up charge in the air seemed to dissipate. We ended with a firm handshake and meeting each other's eye. I wished him good luck with the operation, and encouraged him to make contact once he'd been discharged. After he'd left, I spent a few minutes alone before calling the next patient through. Maybe Vince hadn't been angry with me at all – anger is such a common emotion when we're faced with life-threatening news. Perhaps it was my own sense of guilt at not getting the diagnosis when he first came – even though I knew it would have made no difference – and I was assuming the anger I was detecting was directed not at his situation, but at me.

Actually, I knew it was – Simon had forewarned me as much. But I think it was the fact that I had sat and listened and allowed him to express his fears that had changed things between us. We had connected in his shock and grief.

My dad was even younger than Vince, just 35, when his testicular tumour came to light. He also had three young children and a wife. There was the fear he would have felt for all our futures. The hope he would have clung to that the doctors' pronouncements of the possibility of complete cure would somehow come true. The anxiety of those early years, living under the constant threat of recurrence. He was often tense during my younger childhood, unable to cope with the noise and mayhem caused by us kids. He used to retreat to his bedroom; I could hear the relaxation tape playing in there, the soothing voice of the therapist encouraging him to clench then let go of the various muscle groups around his body in turn. I didn't know what it was all about, not back then. I just hated the way he would blow up when things overwhelmed him, and I viewed his fragility with faint disdain.

It was to be David's last Christmas – he and his now grown-up children all knew. Grandchildren were mustered from different parts of the country, their parents warning them that Grandad wouldn't look like he used to. What had started as a tiny skin cancer overlying his jaw had come back again and again. Increasingly radical and disfiguring operations, radiotherapy and skin grafting had been deployed, but still new islands of tumour would erupt. The surgeons and oncologists had recently declared that there was nothing further they could do.

Some of the cancers were now open craters and sores; David's battle-scarred face was permanently half-hidden beneath sanitising dressings. He had maybe a few months before the disease would cause some fatal event to occur. The whole clan assembled to enjoy – and to gift him – one last family Christmas. Handmade cards were crafted; his eldest grandchild practised how to play his favourite carol on the guitar. Memories were made; memories were shared. Then the family dispersed again, back to the lives they had to run, braced for what they knew would shortly come.

It was Peter, his eldest son, who tracked down the clinical trial.

The power of the internet. French doctors, seeking to recruit patients just like David: those with end-stage squamous-cell skin cancer for whom no further conventional treatment was possible. The patients couldn't be too far gone, though; they had to be fit enough to travel and to undergo experimental treatment. Thankfully, at the time Peter discovered the trial, David was still within this narrow window. A month or two later and he would have been too ill.

So, trips on the Eurostar every three weeks. After the first few treatments, David's tumours started to regress. Another four cycles and all open wounds had fully healed; tumour deposits in the lungs previously visible on scans had shrunk considerably. Bandages and dressings were discarded. Precious energy had in part returned. There is going to be at least one more Christmas for David and his family, maybe more. How many, no one can say. This is the forefront of medicine, finding out how much time these new drugs might buy. Or if, conceivably, they might even be cures.

I qualified nigh-on three decades ago, and most of my career has spanned an era in which surgery, radiotherapy, chemotherapy and some hormone manipulations were the only tools we had with which to battle cancer. Now, we're on the cusp of a new generation of treatments. The field of molecular biology has been gradually revealing the mechanisms by which tumours spread and grow – how they generate new blood vessels, for example, to feed each metastasis, a process known as angiogenesis. And, crucially, we are also beginning to understand the tricks that cancers employ to evade immune system control.

The drug that has transformed David's prognosis is a form of immunotherapy – a broad term for treatments that restore or enhance the ability of the immune system to attack cancer cells. He has responded spectacularly; his immune system has wasted no time in bringing his tumours back under control.

There is fevered activity worldwide to exploit the power of immunotherapy. Drugs like the one David has been receiving interrupt the processes by which malignant cells fool the immune system into leaving them alone. Others, once bound to the surface of tumour cells, act as beacons, attracting white blood cells to attack. Still others, spliced to conventional chemotherapy drugs, can deliver lethal doses right to the heart of a cancer, while minimising exposure for the patients' own healthy cells.

Some immunotherapy drugs have passed clinical trials and are now deployed in routine practice. They are very expensive at present, and their use is generally reserved for when conventional treatment has failed. Over time, though, the costs will come down, enabling more widespread use. They're not without side effects, and many are effective in only a limited range of cancers, but for the first time since I qualified there is a whole new class of treatments to bring to bear on our ancient foe.

Dad was wrong. There was a flurry of appointments with the gastroenterologists, but the bloody diarrhoea that he had feared indicated his cancer had returned proved to be something else entirely: colitis, an inflammatory condition of the bowel, possibly a late complication of the radiotherapy that had helped to save his life in the late 1960s.

He survived to see his children grow up and become a computer programmer, a teacher and a doctor. Grandchildren were born. He kept working as a civil servant for a number of years, but the combined toll of his physical and psychological traumas eventually led to early retirement. Freed from the stresses of commuting and work, he went on to enjoy perhaps the best period of health he had known for decades. Even the colitis miraculously resolved.

I was a partner in a practice by the time new difficulties arose. The skin over the bottom of his back – in the area of his old radiotherapy field – started to break down and refused to heal despite a plastic surgeon's best efforts at grafting. Then a routine blood test picked up a problem with his liver. An ultrasound scan found extensive metastases. A biopsy revealed an aggressive, poorly differentiated cancer that might have arisen originally from squamous skin cells. It's a long-recognised problem with radiotherapy: some 35 years after treatment, the radiation that once saved a life can prove to have caused a new cancer to form.

Vince surprised me by being on something of a high. He actually sounded excited, filling me in on events at the hospital. With his primary kidney tumour removed by the urological surgeons, he had been sent to the oncologists for further treatment. And the news they had given him was far better than he had originally feared. His standard chemotherapy regime was going to be augmented with a relatively new drug that should block angiogenesis, starving his metastases of a blood supply. The oncologist had hinted at other hopes to latch on to; should this fail to control his cancer, there was the possibility of using immunotherapy. There are ongoing clinical trials which might bring promising drugs on stream in the coming years.

Vince had been on the internet, reading about the kinds of agents currently in the pipeline. He can see a future mapping out in which his current treatment buys him sufficient time for new therapies to come along. Each time his cancer develops mutations to get round the effects of one drug, there may be another available to bring it back under control. Perhaps, in time, there might even prove to be a cure. The prognosis is still guarded, Vince told me, but the oncologist has been talking in terms of years. I smiled back, infected by his upbeat tone. He can see himself being around to enjoy family life for a long while yet.

Vince shook my hand again when he came to leave. His grip felt strong. All thought of the few weeks' delay in arranging that first ultrasound scan had been set aside. The spectacular advances of the new era have given Vince a big dose of that most precious of medicines: hope.

I finally found a form of words to help Linda, slumped and traumatised and utterly exhausted on that sofa in her cramped old miners' cottage. I talked about how she had been tackling an assault course – perhaps the worst assault course in the world – and how she had surmounted what she'd thought would be the final obstacle and made it home. But just as she'd turned the last corner, expecting to see the finishing line, there proved to be one more sheer wall in her path.

And yet... on the other side of that, there was the finish line. I don't imagine that was solely what decided her; Trevor's increasingly desperate encouragement will have carried more weight. But that picture of a gruelling assault course made her feel understood and gave her a mental image with which to summon the courage for one last push.

On admission, her kidneys were indeed seen to be in acute failure. As a result, a salt called potassium had accumulated in her bloodstream to dangerously high levels. This could have sent her heart into a fatal rhythm disturbance at any moment. But with careful fluid and insulin therapy in hospital, her kidneys were revived and the dangerous potassium excess brought back to normal. She was back home with Trevor within a matter of days.

Her stoma was reversed by a further operation the following year, but that failed to resolve the high-output bowel that had caused her such problems. She's seen any number of specialists, trying to find an answer to the intractable diarrhoea and faecal incontinence that subsequently ensued. Finally, and very much as a last resort, a consultant at the continence clinic recommended she try a probiotic dietary supplement used to help patients with inflammatory bowel disease. It isn't perfect, but it has improved things to the point where she's now able to get out and about without the fear of soiling herself if she can't immediately get to a loo.

It's now more than five years since her original surgery for the bowel tumour, long enough for us to be reasonably confident that she's been cured. Even in the worst case, should the cancer rear its head again there are now both conventional chemotherapy and newer agents that can be used.

We've just marked the 15th anniversary of Dad's death. He saw an oncologist with the result of the liver biopsy, who said he could give him some generic chemotherapy that had about a 20 per cent chance of buying him a few more months, albeit any extra time gained would be marred by the side effects of treatment. Bravely, after weighing the pros and cons, he decided it wasn't worth it. He returned home and prepared to die.

I was no longer that ignorant 13-year-old boy. I told him I loved him more than once, and touched on the things about him that I admired – what a great job he'd done as a father to us in spite of everything he'd been through. Our relationship had never been entirely easy; the health problems he'd endured had made it so. I didn't say goodbye in the way I would have liked. But at least I knew what to do.

We gathered the family for one last Christmas, all his grandchildren too. He was still in reasonably good shape – it would be some months before the cancer overwhelmed him. Memories were made; memories were shared. I knew he dreaded what was to come, that he was haunted by the memories of that wasted man dying in the bed next to his, 35 years before.

We were all still down there shortly after New Year. I went from our rented holiday cottage to be with him when his GP came round for a review. After his doctor had gone, he wanted to sleep – he'd had very little the night before. Mum and I stayed talking in the sitting room for a while, then I decided it was time to head back to rejoin my brood.

I'd left my coat on the hook on the back of his bedroom door, so I crept in quietly so as not to disturb him. I glanced across to see if he was stirring, and instantly recognised that he had gone. A heart attack, probably, while he was fast asleep; he wouldn't have known a thing. He had been spared the drawn-out death he had so long dreaded. And I was on hand to break the news and to support Mum.

It is such a truism that it has become a cliché: the wounded healer. The child, exposed to serious health problems in his or her family, growing up to enter the caring professions, the unconscious driving us as adults to try to put right everything that in childhood was so wrong.

Reading an update article on the new generation of cancer treatments by a world-renowned professor of oncology in London, I was not surprised to find that he, too, had a father who had suffered from cancer. It had inspired him to enter the field, and set him on the course of his life's work. His particular interest is in cancer vaccines – using extracts from tumours to create inoculations that will stimulate a vigorous immune response when injected back into the patient: a different form of immunotherapy.

Elsewhere, researchers are attempting to exploit nanoparticle technology as a way of infiltrating chemotherapy drugs directly into cancer cells, sparing normal tissues from toxic side effects. The burgeoning field of DNA editing – making precise changes to the genes that orchestrate cell biology – is helping scientists to investigate cancer mutations under laboratory conditions. It's a long way off, but one day this technology may offer the prospect of repairing or neutralising key genetic changes that give cancers their malignant potential.

I wonder sometimes if I haven't failed to find the right vocation. The branch of medicine I went into – general practice – has little to do with curing cancer. Detecting it amid the myriad symptoms patients come to talk to us about – yes. Ensuring that those who prove to have the disease get referred to the surgeons and oncologists who will try to save their lives – yes. But should I not have spent my career researching, or wielding the scalpel, or prescribing the radiation and drugs that might actually save life?

I play my part. And an important role is being able to listen, to come alongside, to hear and absorb people's terror and fear, and where possible impart a dose of hope. Somewhere inside me remains that 13-year-old boy sitting at the bottom of the stairs, just him and his Dad home alone; the father terrified by the bloody diarrhoea that seemed to herald the end of everything; the boy without the first idea of what he should do.

Time travel on a winter's woodland walk

Helen Macdonald

I try to walk in a wood for a few hours before nightfall on every New Year's Day. I've walked woods in low sun, deep snow, rain, and in dank mist that clings to the skin and seems more water than air. I've walked blocks of scruffy adolescent pines, ancient lowland forests, beechwoods, farm copses, made my way down muddy paths through stands of alder and birch. Sometimes I'm with family or friends. Most often I'm on my own. I'm not sure exactly when my New Year walks began, but over the years they've become as familiar a winter tradition as overcooking the turkey or spending too much money on my Christmas tree.

There's a special phenomenology to walking in woods in winter. On windless days there's a deep hush that makes the sound of a stick breaking underfoot resemble a pistol shot. It's a quietness that fosters an acute sensitivity to small sounds that earlier in the year would be buried under a riot of birdsong. The rustle of a vole in dead bracken at my feet, the dry scratches of a blackbird turning over dead leaves in search of spiders.

Now the trees are leafless, wildlife is more visible, but so am I. I'm often met by the alarm calls of jays, nuthatches, robins, grey squirrels; harsh noises designed to inform me that they know I am there. Being sworn at by woodland creatures is disquieting, but at the same time oddly comforting. Modern cultures of nature appreciation so often assume the natural world lives apart from us, is something to watch and observe merely, as if through thick plate glass. These alarm calls remind me that we have consequential presence, that animals we like to watch are also creatures with their own needs, desires, emotions, lives.

A winter wood reveals the bones of the landscape it grows upon, the geographical contours of slopes, gullies and hollows. Its trees become exercises in pattern recognition, each species possessing its own texture of bark, its own angles and arrangements of branches and twigs. After the leaves have fallen, winter lets light and weather into the wood, and low trunks newly exposed to sunlight turn green with algae as winter days lengthen towards spring.

Because life is less obvious in a winter wood, where it does subsist – as bright stars of moss, or fungal fruiting bodies enduring winter frosts with antifreeze-packed cells – it demands attention. One year, I was held spellbound for a long moment by a cloud of winter flies in a patch of weak sun in the middle of a woodland ride, intensely aware of their fragility, their momentary purchase on this world.

The lack of obvious life in winter inevitably reminds me of the limits of my perception. Most of the life here is either too small for me to see, or exists underground. Beneath my feet, an intricate network of mycorrhizal fungal threads link plant roots to each other and the soil. They not only grant trees access to crucial nutrients, but give them a means of communicating with each other.

It's easy for us to think of trees as immutable, venerable presences against which we can measure the span of our lives, our own small histories. But trees grow, leaves fall, winters grip the ground. That woods are places of constant change was something that took a long time for me to understand. As a child I assumed that the woods near my home would stay the same forever. Today, many of the paths I used to walk are blocked with thickets of birch trees, though my memories of those routes live on.

Summer forests give me little sense of time past or times to come, for they're a buzzing, glittering, shifting profusion of life. Everything seems manifested; there's no clear sense of potentiality. But forests in winter are very different. To me they evoke time with sometimes astonishing force. Winter days always move fast towards darkness, and when the wind is bitter I'm always thinking of what it will be like in an hour or so, in the warm back at home. Above me are last year's bird nests, built to hold long-fledged broods, and around me signs of life obscured in summer by dense growths of ground vegetation: deer-nibbled saplings, fox earths, tufts of badger hair on bare, low thorns.

And always, while my feet are treading on last year's leaves, those of next spring are already furled in buds on the tips of winter twigs.

After a light covering of snow, the prints of woodland mammals and birds are things you can read to rewind time. Pheasant tracks end with an imprint of wings, each indent of a primary feather furred with frost, recording the moment the bird took off from the ground the previous evening to fly to roost. In a Wiltshire wood that seemed utterly devoid of animal life, I once followed the prints of a brown hare right across the snow to a pool of dark water, saw the place where it drank, and from the spacing of the prints of each padded foot, saw how fast or slow it had travelled on its way.

So often we think of mindfulness, of existing purely in the present moment, as a spiritual goal. But winter woods teach me something else: the importance of thinking about the passage of time, and about different senses of scale. They can show you the last five hours, the last five days, the last five centuries, all at once. They're wood and soil and rotting leaves, but they are also places where different time frames coexist. In them, potentiality crackles in the winter air. And that is the deepest reason why I'm drawn to them on the first day of each new year. It's a day to think about the passing of time and one's place in the world, and there is no better place to do it than a wood in winter.

The Peak

....

Edward Docx

I

The Man

For a moment, the world is as it used to be – unconfined, uncurtailed, alive with human teeming: coronavirus-free. The early light of a mid-April morning is already at the window. Sun-shot images flit through his mind: he's playing somewhere in a rock pool by the sea with his two children; his wife is laughing. Then the half dreams fade and, already, he can sense anxiety seeping through some defensive wall in the back of his mind, pooling and mingling with the rising self-doubt. This is the peak, they say: today, tomorrow, soon.

Normally – the word seems to have to stretch itself further and further back in time – normally, Jim Down would kiss his wife and get up and head into work. But today he's on the night shift at the hospital so he has to stay in bed, stop his mind racing, try to sleep. He needs to rest. The shifts have gone up from nine hours to 12. And they are relentless. How many days has he been doing this? He's lost count. The world of medicine – his world, our world, the only world – has never been like this. There is no relevant history, no textbooks and no studies. Nothing is peer-reviewed or follow-the-procedure. The virus is obscure, monolithic, alien. They are fighting blind. Hand to hand. Bed to bed. He tries to sleep. But there's a voice from his dreams that persists in his waking: Jo's voice. 'Are you sure,' Jo asks? 'Will it be OK? Are you sure?' But he's not sure. And so what is he going to say to Jo?

Jim Down is 49. He is slim, fit, fair and 6ft 1in with dark blue inkwell eyes in which other people write their stories while he listens – patiently. He has disconcertingly boyish looks and an old-school English demeanour – that odd mixture of determination and diffidence, confidence and anxiety, can-do courage and better-safe-than-sorry. He looks like the kind of man that Roger Bannister might have asked to set pace for him when he ran the sub-four-minute mile: two metronomically dependable laps without detectable fuss or falter before quietly standing aside to clap the other man home.

He's also the doctor that you might have seen on the BBC evening news a few times. The first time in 2006 when he came out to announce the death of Alexander Litvinenko after the defector's polonium poisoning by Russian spies. The second time on the main segment of the evening news on 6 April when Fergus Walsh, the BBC's health correspondent – suited-up in plastic, visor and gloves – was briefly allowed to enter the Covid-19 wards of University College Hospital (UCH) in central London. Jim's voice is muffled behind the mask and visor but the whole country heard it cracking when he spoke: 'I think it's very hard on the families,' he said, 'my kids are at home, my wife is home schooling. It's easy for me, I've got a job and I am busy all day. They don't really know what it's like here – whether we are bringing home the virus – and they've been amazing. They just let me do what I need to do and I'm just incredibly grateful to them.'

Jim's wife is the actress, Patricia Potter. Coincidentally, she played a doctor, Diane Lloyd, in the BBC series *Holby City*. They were married in 2007. And the twins were born in 2009 – a boy and a girl.

Jim's father was a doctor. His father's father was a doctor. His mother's father was a doctor. His own training began 33 years ago when he was 16 and he chose the A-levels that would lead to his studying medicine. Then five years at Bristol University medical school. Then a year as a house doctor, intern junior; qualified but unregistered. Then a couple of years in Exeter training as an anaesthetist. Until, finally, he came to London to start his real apprenticeship: seven truly intense years of dual training in anaesthetics and intensive care. He chose the former because it is a highly sensitive minute-by-minute discipline and then took the unusual step of adding intensive care because it seemed to him to be the extreme end of all disease processes. Now, he is one of the consultants in charge of critical care – the Intensive Care Unit (ICU) – at the pre-eminent University College Hospital.

Tonight, that will mean he will lead as many as 75 hospital staff through the toughest night of their professional lives. He's not sure of the number of patients yet but the count is rising. The expectation is somewhere between 60 and 80 – depending on admissions, on deaths. He strongly resists the idea that his whole life has been in preparation for this moment. Instead, he insists he is just a doctor doing his job surrounded by some truly exceptional colleagues. Everything is collaborative. He's not a leader, let alone a hero. He dislikes even the word. He would much rather talk about the people he has been working alongside – how he's witnessed them rising to the challenges and working in conditions unlike anything they have previously known. He lists fellow doctors and nurses and porters and physios and pharmacists and ward clerks until he is forced to move on. He doesn't want to be formally interviewed, he says, and he doesn't want to be quoted. All he wants is to let the general public know what that night in April – the peak – was really like for the health workers who dealt with it. Medically, psychologically, from the inside. Because little has changed, he says, and right now they are preparing for a second surge this winter.

The truth is that Jim Down is one of the doctors with the most hands-on experience of Covid-19 in the country. He won't allow superlatives. But if you fell ill with the disease and you could ask for anyone, then you could do no better than ask for Jim.

Today, though, too-early awake, all he wants to do is get up and help home school his children, play with them, make their breakfast, talk. The weather has been unseasonably warm and it's going to be another beautiful day. Good Friday. He wishes he was religious. But he knows only too well that it takes more than three days to bring people back from the dead. And that nobody rises alone. Each of the patients he sees in the ICU will have two dozen of the very best healthcare professionals looking after them at one time or another – all day and all night. A constant vigil. Every minute. Often for weeks.

The peak is coming. He shuts his eyes and tries to slip the knots of consciousness. In his half-sleep, he hears the sound of coughing and the wheeze of the machines. The peak, the trough, the test.

II

The hospital

University College Hospital is a teaching hospital founded in 1834 in the north of the centre of London – near Euston station. Jim loves the place in the way a teacher loves the school at which they gave of their best – not just the buildings, but the atmosphere, the rooms, the rituals, the canteens, the meetings, the people. He drives into work because he lost the key to his bike on the first day of wearing the PPE – personal protective equipment; putting the gear on is easy enough but taking it off when every surface carries potential infection is an awkward and elaborate unpeeling fraught with layers of anxiety. An anxiety that attacks the quintessence of being human – touching, breathing, embracing.

London looks at its most attractive in the lower angle of the evening light. He has noticed that everywhere the cherry trees are blooming more intensely than ever – ivory, pink and pale rose – as if in urgent counterpoint to all the sickness. Like the birdsong. Like the weather. But crossing the city seems surreal. Everything is familiar; everything is unfamiliar. The dissonance between the emptiness of the streets and the hitherto routine footfall of millions affects him in ways he cannot process. Likewise, listening to the news as he drives is almost hallucinatory. Not the details of the broadcast – which often seem distant and irrelevant compared to the intimate reality of his daily combat with Covid-19 – but the astonishing fact that every guest and every item on the show is focused entirely on his job. There's nothing else. And it's the same on every single news programme – it's all about medicine, the virus, the lives saved, the lives lost; the work he and his colleagues are doing. And it sounds as mad and dystopian to him as it does to everyone else.

He catches the government minister saying they are expecting the peak to be over soon with a note of – what? – enthusiasm in his voice. He listens with ears precisely cognisant of the truth. The truth that they were too slow to lockdown; that the government had due warning but was sluggish and facetiously contrarian; that preparation was poor; that weeks were lost; that lives were lost; that some of the other hospitals have already fallen over and sent their patients to UCH; that many are woefully short of the protective equipment they need. He turns the radio off. He has noticed that these wider truths become more and more irrelevant the closer he gets to the hospital itself. The objective becomes subjective each time he steps over the threshold. The numbers become names. He ceases to care about the politics, the statistics, the arguments and to care instead for the patient in front of him. Over at St Thomas' Hospital, one of the other great London teaching hospitals, the patient in front of his opposite number this weekend is the Prime Minister.

He parks in the space donated by a member of the public and walks towards the hospital. He thinks about the calls he has to make. Jo and her husband, David, have somehow got to him. He knows what it is: it's the way Jo asks the question, 'Are you sure?' Not in a nasty or even passive-aggressive way; but because this seems a reasonable question to ask a doctor. But the problem is nobody knows anything about the disease. The problem is that nobody is sure.

On Tottenham Court Road, he feels another surge of anxiety. He wonders if he should go to live in a nearby hotel to protect his family at least. He knows for certain of nine fellow staff members who have the virus; he was sat in airless rooms with them for weeks. There is fear circulating. He's never experienced the medical community like this. The rumour mill – yes; but, also, the daily reporting of the actual deaths of fellow doctors and nurses and health workers. And they see every age and every type of person with Covid-19. A 29-year-old died two weeks previously – no underlying health issues. He has read some journalism that is cavalier and fatuous and he is concerned that the wider public has not grasped how terrifying this illness becomes. Of all the deaths he has seen in the ICU, these are the worst. The struggle for breath. The sudden inexplicable deteriorations. No loved ones present. Too many people are dying face down and alone surrounded by the muffled murmur of strangers dressed in visors and plastic.

He treats his anxiety by hurrying inside the hospital. Peak or no peak: they will all do their best for each and every patient. And, once inside, he feels the instant relief of purpose, work and focused colleagues. Something truly remarkable has happened at UCH. Something life-affirming in its way. A complete and serious transformation at incredible speed. They are as ready as they will ever be. He heads towards the lifts. For the first time since he awoke this morning, he feels pride and resolve flooding back.

They knew what was coming. One of UCH's top professors – Mervyn Singer – called European friends and colleagues in Italy back in February and early March. Their chief executive Marcel Levi – who is also a professor and front-line clinician, born in Holland – had spent a long time working in Perugia. So the community of European doctors communed and medical staff learned everything there was to know first-hand and in as much detail as their fellow professionals could give. The lackadaisical UK government seemed to be ignoring the advice so the medics ignored the government. By early March, all the senior staff were coming in additionally on their Saturday nights to go through plans, protocols and detailed preparation.

They got as far ahead as they could. They ensured they had the equipment they would need – and, crucially, lots of oxygen. They converted eight out of the 12 operating theatres into Covid-19 wards. They changed a stroke unit into a 28-bed high dependency ward – solely for Covid-19 patients. They had their normal ICU units optimised for Covid-19 to deal with whatever the peak turned out to be.

Meanwhile, 35 consultant anaesthetists became intensivists – adding to the normal 18. Seventy or so doctors from all over the hospital were enlisted to help – surgeons, gynaecologists, dentists, urologists, paediatricians, trainees and neurosurgeons. They went from 180 nurses to nearly 350. From nine physios to 45. Five intensivists came over from Great Ormond Street along with ten specialist intensive care nurses.

Jim's pass bleeps him into the ward. Tonight, he thinks, UCH is totally focused. If you trained for anything in medicine, then tonight you trained for Covid-19. Apart from babies being born, this hospital is doing nothing else.

III

The Intensive Care Unit

He goes into the consultants' office. This is the handover. Normally (that word again), he would be being briefed by one person about maybe 15 patients, but now there are four consultants briefing him on just short of 70 patients – all with Covid-19. He will be the sole lead on the night shift. The smaller London hospitals are sending more patients – struggling for PPE; not enough oxygen; no capacity. The other doctors – his friends – highlight two cases they have that they think need his immediate attention. He's struck afresh by their calm, their rigour. The challenge is that all the patients need immediate attention. Continually. Everywhere, in every bed, life is held tenuously. He goes to put on his PPE as fast as he safely can.

He is careful to remain outwardly assured but he walks at double speed on the ward. He takes one look at the two patients – Andrew and Beth – and he makes the decision: they both need to come down to the ICU. This is the first of roughly 200 decisions he will make on the shift tonight. They are both in CPAP (Continuous Positive Airway Pressure) oxygen masks and there are serious risks with moving them – if anything goes wrong in the lifts, where there is no life support, they will die. But they have to be taken down. They need to be intubated – the inserting of a tube down the trachea so that a ventilator supplies oxygen to the patient directly to the lungs.

He lets his eyes travel around his assembled colleagues. They all know the same thing: that Beth is a nurse and that she was working in a Covid-19 hospital, as they are all doing now. He says he will lead Beth's intubation himself.

Now the night starts to move at speed. He makes his way through the wards. The beds come at him. Curtain after curtain. Patient after patient. So many so seriously sick. He is grateful to be surrounded by so much competence. He confers with his colleagues as he goes – trying to hear and be heard through his visor without raising his voice. If he were to never stop, eat, go to the toilet, or do anything else, he would have roughly ten minutes per patient. He has to go faster than he has ever gone before. He has to go slower than he has ever gone before.

At every bed, he checks the date of the patient's symptoms. The date of intubation. Are they on antibiotics? Should they be? Is there a secondary bacterial infection with which antibiotics might help? Or is this just what Covid-19 looks like? In which case – will the antibiotics be useless and even harmful? And which antibiotics? Or could there be a secondary fungal infection? Nobody knows the answers to any of these questions.

Should he thin the blood? There's lots of talk about high rates of blood clots forming in the legs and breaking off to the lungs – but what about the risks of bleeding, especially in the brain? Is the ventilator set optimally? Should he lighten the sedation and allow them to 'breathe up' and interact with the ventilator or will that perpetuate the inflammation and make things worse? Or should he keep them deeply sedated and fully ventilated which means they'll be so much weaker and delirious from all the sedatives – and is that worse? Nobody knows the answers to these questions either.

Should he give fluids to help the kidneys – or keep them dry to help the lungs? Why do so many get kidney failure? Should he give steroids? Why has this patient got worse all of a sudden? Why is this patient improving? Nobody in any hospital knows the answers to any of these questions. All they can do is learn fast and maintain total vigilance.

There are so many patients. Doctors eddy and mill around the beds. He thinks: the nurses are working at a level that no human being can sustain. He thinks: this is what courage looks like – raw and unmediated.

Already, 60 minutes in, the PPE has become nightmarish to work inside: hot, claustrophobic, disorientating and alienating. He can feel – physically feel – the strain that everyone is under. They all have to put their names and their roles on their chests because they can't recognise one another. Everyone suffers from the crushing headaches. Inside the visors, they can no longer hear one another clearly above the whirr and beep of the life-support machines, the alarms, the dialysis pumps, the computers, the treatment systems, the air conditioners.

Normally, they pop in and out of the bays, passing on medical or patient information; but instead, every conversation has become cumbersome and strained. They have to use walkie-talkies to communicate with fellow staff outside the ward every time they need something, because they can't take the PPE off and then put it back on. And they are tearing through supplies.

The psychology is – if anything – worse. Normally, the ICU would be a balancing act between those recovering from elective surgery and those arriving from Accident and Emergency. Normally, he'd be doing a nine-hour shift with a group of people – all of whom he knew and who knew each other. Normally, the unit would comprise patients who have the full scope of acute conditions: pancreatitis, accident trauma, meningitis, sepsis, brain haemorrhages, drug overdoses, suicide attempts. Normally, there would be a whole history of medicine and experience to deal with each and every one. Normally, there's a route to recovery.

But not now. Now, everyone is ill with the same new disease. And there's no cure. This is as crushing mentally as the PPE is claustrophobic physically. Bed after bed of immobile human beings lying faceless on their fronts. Machines keeping them alive. This is the vision of the virus. Like something too dark even for Philip K. Dick or William Blake. He tells himself again to remember to recognise that none of the people are working in their normal environment or doing their normal job.

There is something, too, about the fact that Covid-19 is in the atmosphere, in the very air, that makes it worse. Even as they work, the staff are all dealing with the fear of actually dying themselves. And this is not a vague fear such as the public might suffer; but a fear born of watching their fellow professionals being wheeled in – here, now – because here comes stricken Beth, the nurse, through the ward.

At least she has made it down, he thinks.

IV

The Procedure

The medical staff gather at Beth's bed. Jim Down lets his eyes go round his colleagues again. There is a surgeon doing a junior's job. Two more doctors who did not choose a career in intensive care. An ICU nurse. A dental surgeon. A nurse who was brought in from paediatrics at short notice. His fellow anaesthetist, Mike. They all wear the stress differently. In the last few days, he has witnessed every human reaction – from tears and breakdown all the way through to the counterproductive fortitude of staff who refuse to rest. Now though, he can sense the unease somehow coming through the plastic gowns they're all wearing. He checks the monitors. Even in normal times, intubation is a serious procedure. With Covid-19, it becomes much, much more difficult.

Normally, he would hold a mask over the patient and give them roughly three litres of pure oxygen into the lungs. This would buy him some time. The oxygen saturated in the patient's blood would stay at a good level – hopefully above 90 per cent – for maybe five minutes simply by using the three litres they had already inhaled. He would then put the drugs in. Put the patient to sleep. Paralyse them. All the time, he would watch the readings of the oxygen saturation in the blood – the 'sats' level as they call it. He would insert the tube past the vocal cords and into the trachea. Any drop in the patient's levels of oxygen in the blood would come back up to 97 per cent – optimum – as soon as he had got the tube in.

But the problem is that Covid-19 patients are already on pure oxygen from the mask; he cannot turn it up any higher. Beth has all the oxygen possible; he can't get any more into her lungs. Worse, when they take Beth's mask off, he knows that she will immediately start to turn blue. Covid-19 patients cannot last more than a minute without full oxygen support. The oxygen in her blood will immediately start to drop. And when it hits 90 per cent, it begins to drop even faster, the rate of descent accelerating. The whole procedure, therefore, which would normally take five minutes, has to be done in less than one.

He is the team leader. He needs to keep the atmosphere calm. He has done this operation himself many times but it's important that there are as many anaesthetists as possible capable of doing it in the time. And Mike is one of the best.

He checks everyone is ready and gives the signal. The pressure is intense. All the alarms go off immediately. Beth's blood oxygen saturation level drops – 80 per cent, 75 per cent. Mike has the metal blade over her tongue so that he can access the trachea. But, involuntarily, Beth is coughing. Aerosol Covid-19 straight onto Mike's visor. Outwardly, Jim is still calm. Sats at 65, he says, quietly. But inside, he is screaming – get on with it, get on with it, get the tube in. Every moment could be a catastrophe. Mike's hands are steady. Jim watches him manoeuvre the tube – delicately, deftly – with total concentration and precision. Sats at 55 per cent, he says. They don't have the option to abort because this is Covid-19 and Beth won't make it back on the mask. They have less than ten seconds before her heart stops. Mike gets the tube in. Jim hooks up the machine. She's at 50 per cent. But they're in.

Normally, the sats would now climb but, this being Covid-19, the oxygen in Beth's blood is rising far too slowly. Jim thanks Mike and gives the immediate instruction for the team to get her on her front. The back of the lungs are usually more inflamed with the disease; the front are usually in very slightly better shape. He can see one of the doctors blinking back sweat – resisting the overwhelming temptation to wipe his eyes. He thinks that despite all the organ and blood support it comes down to something very basic: on her front, Beth might live: on her back, she will die.

The team goes into the preparation. Each time they turn patients, it is difficult and dangerous. There are all the airway tubes. There are the lines in for all the drug infusions into the neck. There are the lines into the arteries. There's the catheter. The dialysis lines. They lose or twist anything and Beth will crash. And, of course, Beth is unconscious so the risk of injury is increased. Are her eyes covered and protected? Is she ready? Yes. They look at one another through their visors. Ready, steady, he says as loud as he can. And turn.

Beth is on her front. The oxygen begins to crawl back up. He checks his watch – he's running late. He has to get out and call patients' relatives. He can't keep them waiting. For each of them, Jim Down knows, his call is vital, their lifeline.

V

The Relatives

Normally, the relatives would be here, of course, and he'd speak to them in person. Normally, they'd be sat around the beds bringing all manner of gifts; doing what human beings do in love and solidarity to cheer and comfort one another. But now they are in a particular state of absent agony: unable to visit, unable even to speak to their fathers and mothers, sons and daughters. Cut off. Anxious. Locked down at home and listening to the death count climb every afternoon.

He takes off his PPE – slowly, quickly – and walks to the nurses' station where the phones are set up. There is a team of volunteer hospital staff who field all the calls. They make lists of relatives. They check everyone has been called back. They help with the video calls. Their work is tireless and means everything to the relatives ringing in. He is chary of the phrase 'unsung heroes' – but in any case, he says, there are not choirs enough in Britain. They give him the numbers. He wishes the hospital had time to find an area a little less public for these conversations. But nothing is ideal and all he can do is lean away from the other staff and into the receiver.

Normally, one of these calls would be a psychological ordeal for any doctor. Jim Down is experienced, of course, but there's nothing that really prepares you for talking to someone about how close to death their mother is, their father, their son, daughter, sister, brother. Tonight he has four calls to make. Three now. One later. He is relieved the call to Jo will be in the morning – at around 6am – after he has again checked on David. He takes a breath. He is pleased at least to be out of the PPE. He makes a conscious effort to take account of how important each word he says is to the person with whom he will speak. Each call has to take as long as it takes. But he has no time. More patients are being admitted. And he's needed urgently in the theatre as soon as he can get back there.

He picks up the phone and listens to a daughter crying for her mother. She wants so badly to come in to see her mum, she doesn't care if she gets it. The second call is overseas. He can hear the agony in the son's voice – the self-recriminations: he should have flown back at Christmas, but he didn't know, he didn't know. On the third call, he has to tell a young woman that her dad is deteriorating; that the prognosis is not good; that at 77 it is likely that the machines are torturing her father; that the route back is very hard now. He has to be honest – he says that there's only a very small chance that her dad will make it. She asks him what he can do? Is there anything – anything in the world –

that can save her dad? He can't think of any way to answer her question except with a promise: I'll do everything, he says, that I would do for my own dad.

VI

The Virus

Sometime in the dead of the night, Jim Down is on his way towards theatre where there are three patients in urgent need of his attention simultaneously. It must be 2am or 3am. These are the hours where the night seems both to shrink and to stretch and to open before him like a void or a black passageway leading deeper into absence – or darkness, he's not sure.

He thinks about the virus as he walks. There are WhatsApp messages all the time from the international medical community, research papers shared, but it's too soon for meaningful data. He reads what he can whenever he can – lifts, queues, awake when he should be asleep – and he is moved by a sense of the collective: human beings everywhere questing for the same information all over the world. Science, medicine, the effort to understand the workings of reality. Everything else comes second now: art, sport, economics; the posturing of politicians; the phoney proclamations of religion. Something has been proven, he thinks, something profound in the communal psychology about where we place our true reliance. Perhaps the clapping is a sign of this. What he and his colleagues would like most of all, though, is proper funding and a trustworthy government.

The virus. Most people he sees have had the fever – a three- to four-day illness – and then a sickening second bout around day six or seven. This is where they start to worsen – nobody knows why some and not others. Genetics? Their body's inflammatory response? In any case, the breathlessness has usually become acute by the time they are in front of him and their tissues are starting to be deprived of oxygen: hypoxia. On the chest X-rays, there are infiltrates – the typical shadowing of both lungs that looks somehow medieval, he always thinks, like they're fighting something they don't understand. Which they are and which they don't.

There are often the classic blood signs: a drop in lymphocytes, the white blood cells involved in the protection against disease; and all the markers of inflammation are up. Some people come back after being on CPAP, rally, recover. Others struggle. When they have to intubate, they attempt to ventilate the lungs gently – it has to be precise, careful. Human lungs are highly sensitive. Too hard and the inflammation gets worse. They dialyse the kidneys. The machines take over. Sometimes the inflammation settles down. Sometimes the blood markers settle. Sometimes the patient starts the long and difficult journey back.

But, sometimes, the oxygen levels stay stubbornly low. Patients fall into acute respiratory distress syndrome. And now mechanical ventilation becomes even more difficult as the machine tries to get oxygen in without injuring the lungs or causing abnormal pockets of air to form between the lung and chest wall. The lungs become fibrotic – stiffer – and it becomes harder to get the carbon dioxide out. The patient dies slowly of hypoxia.

He passes bay after bay. The hospital is at full stretch. He has never seen a night so busy. As he's crossing the walkway between buildings in the hospital, he catches sight of the night sky. All week, a huge and sickly pale moon has been lumbering across the heavens – as full and as close as it ever comes to the Earth. The supermoon, they say. The perigee. The peak. Easter 2020. His fervent hope is that this time will come to be known as the worst few days of the virus in the United Kingdom. They need to keep the numbers down. There is no other medicine possible in these conditions. If the infection rate climbs, then you risk lives and you shut down the hospitals for all the other emergencies. Many people die. Simple as that.

He enters the last bay in the converted operating theatre and pulls back the curtain. He stands a moment in the semi-darkness. The very air seems crushed in here, as if the night itself is struggling to breathe. Life has shrunk and shrivelled to almost nothing – the heaving of machines. He has the momentary feeling that this is the very centre of the disease; the inner chamber where the virus sits enthroned, preening and sneering, malign, intelligent.

The nurse, Maria, is alone. Through his visor he can see the stretched contours of her face. From her body language, he intuits that something is seriously wrong. She is one of the very best he has ever worked alongside – buoyant, funny, rebarbative and resilient beyond any measure the hospital has yet conjured. They have laughed together, worked together, dealt with all manner of triumph and tragedy, life and death. She gives better than she gets. She's a leader and an example and would consider herself neither. She is the nurse he would choose to look after his own children.

She's been here all night. He stands beside her. She would normally have said something by now. She is checking lines in. Working at three times her usual speed. He asks about adding some enoximone, another infusion for the heart. But something is wrong. And when she looks at him again, he can see what it is: she is furious. Her eyes are narrow and molten hot with fierce accusation. She stands back from the patients and rounds on him.

I cannot do this, she says. I cannot do this for five patients at the same time. You need to sort something out, Jim, because this isn't working.

He stands still and listens. Keeps his eyes steady. Nods. He's screwed up. He's come marching in and merely added to her workload. The nurses cannot do any more. His heart goes out to her. He has never seen her like this. The truth is that the people who watch the patients are the nurses. Hour after hour into the night – an unceasing vigil – all the time, acutely hypersensitive to every change, imagined or otherwise. Yes, he thinks, the public should know: it is the nurses who truly contend with this disease – close up and physically, with their hands and with their eyes.

Normally, Maria would have one patient to care for. Normally, she would have one night-plan per patient to administer. This means drawing up the drugs, giving the drugs (all of them dangerous), running complex machinery – the ventilators, the disposable parts of the dialysis machines, dealing with a whole host of infusions for sedation, monitoring blood pressure and heart output; managing the needs of feeding, bowels, urine, mouth care, eyes. But tonight Maria has five patients to care for and she's trying to deliver a level of care to each and every one of them that would make her proud. Not even proud: just what is right. And that level of care is not possible.

There are other nurses who are willing to help but they're not trained. You can't become an expert in a week. ICU nurses are highly specialised and in very short supply. He is well aware that every hospital in London is desperate for them. That's why all the new Nightingale wards worry him. You can build the beds. You can even get the equipment. But there are only so many doctors and nurses who are trained in intensive care. And so many of the nurses are from overseas and from the European Union. He wishes the nation could see what he sees. Why would a government seek to alienate its own nurses? What kind of men would knowingly turn a nation against so many of the people who care for its sick?

He feels a reciprocal charge of anger. The heat and claustrophobia in here are intense. OK, he says. You are completely right. We need a plan for now and we need a plan for how we're going to relieve nurses of some of this work. Maria calms. Yes, she says. Yes.

Three out of the five patients are in trouble now. Not because of anything Maria has or hasn't done but because everywhere tonight, patients are suddenly collapsing, because that's how Covid-19 works. He makes another decision. Normally, they can do everything in parallel. But now they are going to have to work in sequence. Who first? Another decision. Frank first.

Frank is in the deepest trouble. Let's simplify things, he says. Let's simplify the heart drugs. Let's go to adrenaline. Deal with that problem. Yes, Maria says. They pick up a walkie-talkie so they can order up what they need. Right – now let's get the dialysis up and running. They work together. But as they do so, a junior arrives and tells him that Patti's carbon dioxide is climbing behind them. He has to go over to Patti immediately. His mouth is dry. He needs water. He can't use a stethoscope for fear of infections. He has to use his experience, do everything by feel, look at the ventilator. He changes the filter and alters the setting.

More alarms. The third patient is crashing – Louis. Alarms going crazy. He switches beds again. Everything is hard to assess with Louis because he is on his front. He scans all the equipment, his eyes like blisters. The virus is here in the room – a presence. He can feel it. In the air. In the throats of the patients. On their PPE. Maria is beside him. There are no more ICU nurses free and there are no more ICU consultants. Everything that happens now happens because he and Maria manage it. Life or death again.

Ten minutes later, he's greatly relieved to be joined by one of his anaesthetic consultant colleagues. More nurses arrive. Another doctor. They all work together. Deep in the physical lives of their patients: their throats, their kidneys, their lungs, their hearts, their blood, their excretions, fighting the virus, moment by moment, alarm by alarm, staving off death as it comes at them again and again, now here, now there. This is the true meaning of the peak.

They stabilise all three in turn. He hates having to choose but this time it has been OK. He stands back. For a second, his mind travels from the asphyxiating crucible of this operating theatre and he thinks about how far human beings have come – through all of human history until now. And here they stand: half a dozen men and women in semi-darkness, swathed in blue plastic, blue gloves on their hands, masks, visors, surrounded by more human beings who lie all-but-dead on beds around them – tubes into their lungs and veins and organs. Here they stand, working to sustain life itself, which is the only miracle he truly believes in. When it comes right down to it, there is no greater sanctity than life, and no greater religion than reality. He looks up and tries to convey some warmth of fellow feeling merely through the movement of his eyes.

Maria smiles back. We're going to get these bastards back to their families alive, she says, and they can bloody well take care of them.

VII

This is Jim Down

The sun is rising. Easter Saturday. Someone comes over and says that the nurses have got a tablet to David, Jo's husband – and would he mind doing the call back on the ward all together? He had forgotten about Jo. The emergencies have been relentless. But this is good news, he thinks, because it might be easier if David is on the call so that Jo can see and hear her husband's condition for herself. He's made the decision to intubate David. He can't delay any longer. He had been dreading telling Jo this on the phone – all her questions that he could not answer.

Perhaps it's the night, perhaps it's because he is roughly Jim's age, perhaps it's because Jo is roughly his wife's age, perhaps it's because David and Jo also have two children the same age as his own, but Jim is affected as soon as he arrives at David's bed. The nurses have put a tablet in a clear freezer-storage bag and David is struggling to talk to his wife, Jo, on the screen through the smothering effect of the plastic and in between desperate gasps from the CPAP mask.

What affects Jim is not just what David is saying but also the way that he is saying it. Only around 50 per cent of patients who are intubated survive, and David somehow knows this. Jim can tell that David is therefore trying to say that he loves his wife without upsetting her – without sounding like he thinks he's going to die. He's trying to say his last words without them sounding like his last words.

'You know that I love you.' David's voice is hoarse, his breath perilously short. 'You have everything you need to be OK. You know that I love you. You know that I love you. Tell the children I love them every single day. Promise me. Tell them every day.'

'I love you, too, David,' Jo replies. And Jim can tell that she is valiantly trying to give her husband courage and reassurance in return – also without sounding as though she, too, is afraid he's going to die. 'And when this is over,' she says, 'we're going to take the kids and show them where we got married. I love you so much, David. And I know you are going to get through this.'

Three things he has come to understand. Human beings are capable of breathtaking dignity. Human beings are capable of breathtaking compassion. And, in the face of death, all human beings want to hear and to say the same thing: 'I love you.'

That's all there was, or is, or could ever be to say. It makes no difference, of course, to the virus, to science, to the swollen moon or the rising sun. But it makes all the difference in the world to human beings.

'I love you very much David,' Jo says – she waves at the camera and now Jim can tell that it's costing her everything she has not to cry. 'You're the love of my life.'

One of the nurses has turned away. Jim has forgotten for a moment that he is in charge of this man's care. He forces himself to grip his own emotions and then leans forward so that he appears in the camera line and so that Jo can see him. And he says the only thing he can think of to say.

'Hello Jo, this is Jim Down. I am David's doctor. We spoke on the phone. Don't you worry: we'll take good care of David. We'll take very good care of him.'

With the exception of the main protagonist, the names have been changed in this piece.

Short Stories

'darktime'

Kate Atkinson

*And in that day they shall roar against them like the roaring of the sea:
and if one look unto the land, behold darkness and sorrow, and the
light is darkened in the heavens thereof.*

Isaiah 5:30

In the beginning was the Void. Then came the Word and with the Word the World began.

Then one day, to everyone's surprise, the Void returned and Darkness rolled over the land.

Tuesday 15 May 2012, to be precise. On Mountain Standard Time in Cochise County it was 6am and Phil Beckett was still asleep. He usually beat the sun to rising but not today and when he woke a few minutes later, feeling thick-headed and grouchy, he remembered with regret the booze he'd drunk the previous evening. He'd thrown a barbecue in the backyard to celebrate the arrival of his first grandchild – a boy (a bonus, but he knew he couldn't say that to either his daughter or his wife). 'Preston', he was called. Odd kind of name, in Phil's opinion. He'd hoped for 'Philip'. He usually stuck to beer but last night he had wetted the baby's head with an 18-year-old single-barrel bourbon he'd been saving for this very occasion. His daughter, Melissa, his only child, was an ambitious attorney with a law firm in Tucson and the 'occasion' had been a long time coming.

Thanks to last night's Elijah Craig, he rolled out of bed like a much older man. His wife had been on Cuba libres all night and was still asleep. She wasn't a drinker by nature and Phil didn't much want to be around when she woke. He shambled into the kitchen and switched on the Keurig Elite their son-in-law had bought them for their wedding anniversary last month. Phil preferred the old aluminium stove-top pot but it seemed to have disappeared. The Keurig's convenient, his wife said, and Blake would be upset if he thought we didn't use it. How would he know? Phil asked. Blake had been to the Double Diamond exactly three times in five years. He has a hidden camera or something?

He drank his coffee on the porch. The morning was hotter than usual. And quieter. He looked out over his land and thanked God for His bounty in giving his grandfather this little corner of south-east Arizona. Phil ran a four thousand deeded acre spread, the best watered in the county, three hundred head of cattle out there, prime beef on the hoof. And not one of them was making a sound this morning.

He looked for the big skinny tom that he admired and disliked in equal measure. It usually came out to greet Phil as soon as it heard him moving about, slinking out of the barn where it slept at night. If Phil was feeling benevolent he shared the cream from his coffee with it. No cat this morning. No birds either. The dog was here, though, ambling out of the house with the same hungover gait as Phil instead of bounding around enthusiastically. Mitch, a retriever-cross, a big puppy-dog really, not a rancher's dog. Phil rubbed the top of its head with his knuckles. Sure is quiet this morning, he said to the dog. He was spooked by the sound of his own voice. He glanced up and felt weirdly relieved to see a buzzard high in the sky, revolving slowly on a lazy thermal.

Come on, buddy, he said to Mitch, draining his coffee cup. Let's go for a drive.

The dog liked sitting up front in the cab of the heavy-duty Silverado with its head out the window, grinning like a dope as its ears fluttered in the breeze. This morning, however, it sat up straight, scouting through the windshield as if it were riding shotgun in Indian country.

They followed the dirt track up to the ridge, from where there was a good view of the creek and the low pasture below. It took a moment for Phil to understand. What the heck? he said, glancing over at Mitch as if the dog might confirm what he was looking at. The dog's ears twitched but otherwise it remained impassive.

The cattle were lying on the ground – forty or so of them – as if they had been pushed over by a giant hand. When he was a boy Phil had played with an old wooden Noah's Ark that had been his father's and he had an unexpected memory of the pleasure he had taken in lining up all the animals and then knocking them over, like dominoes, all the way from elephant down to cat. The smaller species – mice, insects – were lost long before Phil was born. He wondered if the Noah's Ark was still in the attic and if 'Preston' would like it.

He crashed the Silverado into reverse and accelerated back down the track and across the rough terrain towards the pasture. When he clambered out of the cab he could feel his heart jittery in his chest.

He counted thirty-eight. All dead. He grabbed for his cell, dialled Ken Traub over at the Double E. Ken answered immediately, said he was standing in the middle of a corral of twenty yearling steers. All dead.

Next, Phil tried Shane Hollander at the Bar K. He was a strict Lutheran, Phil had never heard him swear, but today he surprised him by answering the phone, saying, What the fuck, Phil?

Dead cattle? Phil said.

No, Phil. Dead people. Dead people everywhere. All dead.

One p.m. on the other side of the world. Greenwich Mean Time in the Waitrose on Morningside Road where Genevieve was sheltering from the rain that had suddenly turned heavy and winterish for May. Since being made redundant from an architectural practice three months ago she found herself lingering, loitering even, in places that she would normally have speeded through.

She was reflecting on the whiteness, some might say pastiness, of the well-fed faces around her. Not at all like the Chesser Asda where she usually shopped and which, as well as being a haven for the tired, the poor and the huddled masses, was also, unlike Waitrose, populated with people of every nationality and colour.

But not green, Gus said. Or blue, or red or purple or –

Enough, Genevieve said. He was a very literal child. He was six, in school. She had lied to get him into his (good) primary, said they lived with her mother in the Grange. (You're moving back in with me? Genevieve's mother said, keeping her face admirably neutral.) Now, with all this time on her hands, Genevieve found herself frequenting the school's catchment area – shops, cafés, the library – mildly paranoid that anonymous authority figures were spying on her, trying to catch her out in the lie. (They are, Genevieve's mother said.)

As an economy measure, she had recently sold her car, so here she was, taking refuge from the lunchtime rain in a clean, well-lighted place where it was reassuring (or possibly not) to know that there were so many different brands of balsamic vinegar in the world, something not apparent in the Chesser Asda.

Genevieve picked up a 'mini' watermelon, hefty and round like a cannonball, before wandering aimlessly over to the flower-stand where she plucked a slender sheaf of gladioli from a galvanised bucket. She should probably get a basket even though both items seemed too unwieldy to be confined to one. She would not normally have bought either watermelon or gladioli. She wasn't even sure she wanted them (and, more to the point, could she afford them?). Fetching a basket would be a commitment. She began to experience the usual kind of low-grade existential angst she associated these days with decision-making.

From her post at the flower-stand, Genevieve had a clear view of the supermarket's glass entrance doors. It was still raining heavily. Should she make a run for it? She could hardly stay in Waitrose all afternoon. (Or could she?) She watched as the automatic doors, obedient to an invisible will, swished politely apart to admit a middle-aged woman, the hearty, outdoors type, suitably dressed, top-to-toe, for the rain. Beyond the woman, Genevieve could see an elderly man, stooped and crooked, who was snailing heroically towards the doors. He was what her mother would have called 'dapper' – good tweed overcoat, a cap on his head, a cane in one hand, an umbrella held awkwardly aloft in the other. He was once a little boy like Gus. Bruised knees, filthy hands (always), a stoic yet hopeful demeanour. Small on the outside, vast on the inside. Gus would one day be an old man like him. Genevieve's heart came suddenly untethered.

A draught of damp air from the open doors made her shiver. The chill brought with it an odd animal-like premonition. She was still holding the watermelon in one hand and the gladioli like a spear, as if she were about to pike something, in the other. Fruit and flowers, offerings at the temple. She returned the flowers to the galvanised bucket and watched as the old man stopped to close his umbrella, shaking the rain off it. The doors closed again before he reached them.

*

And then the world went dark. Completely, as if someone had flicked the switch on the sun. Pulled the plug, too, for there were none of the tiny jewels of coloured light, the humming and thrumming, that indicated electronic life. Smoke alarms and cash registers, freezers, fridges and sprinklers, were all lifeless. No emergency lights, nothing glowing with faint comfort. No daylight coming in through the automatic doors either. Dark inside and out. For a moment Genevieve had the Damascene thought that she had been struck blind.

She groped in her bag for her iPhone. Also dead.

After what seemed like a long silence, as complete and absolute as the darkness, people began to voice their bafflement. A quiet, poignant *Hello?* from somewhere near her right shoulder. *Who turned the lights out then?* from a would-be joker and then the voice of a small child, inquisitive rather than frightened, but nonetheless distressing to Genevieve, saying, *Mummy?*

Is there anyone there? someone asked, as though they were partaking in a seance. A hand brushed Genevieve's hair and she was reminded of the ghost train at the seaside of her childhood. It was as if they were playing a sombre game of blind man's buff, governed by rules of extreme bourgeois rectitude. A raised managerial voice advised everyone to keep calm, although as far as Genevieve could tell no one was panicking. Someone bumped against her *(Sorry, sorry)*, knocking the watermelon from her hands. Genevieve heard it land with a thud and roll away, a planet discarded by a careless child-god.

She was not the only one, it seemed, who thought they had suddenly lost their sight. *Blind?* someone said, as if trying out the word for size. Genevieve thought of *The Day of the Triffids*. It seemed improbable. What was more likely – an invasion from outer space by killer alien plants or a total eclipse of the sun and its electronic cohorts? But then surely eclipses were foreseen, charted events, not sudden biblical calamities?

The 'pulse'. She had read about it in a newspaper a few months ago. It was something to do with solar flares. An increase in sunspot activity was due and was going to cause geomagnetic storms, knocking out satellite communications and causing blackouts on earth. 'Catastrophe' and 'chaos' were predicted across the globe (it was an article in the *Daily Mail*, she remembered now). She wished that she had paid more attention. She wasn't sure what a geomagnetic storm was but it certainly didn't *sound* good.

But then, just as suddenly as it had been turned off, the power was snapped on again. People blinked at the sudden assault on their retinas from the overhead lights and looked about in confusion as if they were expecting something to have changed during their unexpected daytime journey into night. Everything was just as it had been. Daylight had returned outside. A blink, that was all. The universe blinked.

Waitrose rebooted itself and the air was filled once more with the low whining and buzzing noises of robotic insect life as the big fridges and the cash registers came back to life. The automatic doors began dutifully opening and closing again. Several people headed straight for the outside but the majority of customers, after some hesitation, recommenced shopping. A babel of mobile-phone ringtones started to fill the air. Genevieve supposed everyone wanted to share their own experience of the dark. Once they would have written laborious letters and the event would be forgotten by the time the letter was delivered into another hand. Her iPhone vibrated in her own hand. It was Genevieve's mother asking if she was all right. Yes, she said. (Was she?)

Look outside, Genevieve's mother said.

The customers who had already left Waitrose were still standing in a little huddle near the doors, looking aghast. Genevieve saw the dapper old man, lying supine on the concrete, his cap tilted rakishly, a peaceful expression on his face, even though the hard rain was falling steadily on it. She hurried towards him, crouching down and feeling for a pulse. None. Standing up, she found herself next to the woman who was dressed so well for the rain.

Has someone phoned for an ambulance? Genevieve asked and the woman who was dressed for rain (but who would never leave her house again, no matter the weather) simply lifted her arm and pointed like a mute seer at the length of Morningside Road. That was when Genevieve realised that the crowd's distress was not on account of the dapper old man but for a much wider horror.

Everywhere that she looked there were people lying on the ground – as though they had been struck by a narcoleptic spell. The *Big Issue* seller who hung around the entrance to Waitrose was curled up like a baby next to the ranks of wire trolleys. A young woman who was sprawled in the middle of the pelican crossing was still grasping the handle of a pushchair. The baby inside the pushchair looked – like the dapper old man – as if it were taking a much-needed nap. The old Romanian beggar woman who sat every day outside the hospice shop had keeled over, her hand still outstretched for coins. One man and his dog were bedded down on the pavement together. It was a new Pompeii.

Cars had crashed into each other, others were slewed across the road, passengers and drivers lying insensible, half in and out of the doors. A bus standing at a nearby stop had opened to admit passengers into its belly. Everyone inside the bus looked as though they had fallen asleep in their seat. The people waiting in the queue had dropped where they stood in a tidy fashion. The bus driver remained at the bridge, piloting a ghost bus, his head lolling forward as if he were taking forty winks while waiting for his tardy passengers to board. The automatic doors kept trying to close but were foiled by the inert body of a woman draped across the platform, her bus pass still clutched in her hand.

No one was waking up. No one was climbing to their feet and shaking their head in bewilderment at the sudden enchantment that had overtaken them. They were dead, Genevieve thought. All of them. Dead.

From what? Gas? A terrorist attack (in Morningside?). An acoustic device – the kind they had on ships to repel pirates (again – Morningside?). Or had they all simply drunk the Kool-Aid, obedient to some bizarre order, while Genevieve was debating whether to buy a watermelon?

But – not everyone was dead. No one who had been locked in Waitrose was dead, for example, and when Genevieve looked around she could see people in cars, in shops, on buses, who were definitely alive. People who had stayed inside. Behind closed doors. Whereas everyone who had been *outside* –

Jesus Christ – the school playground! *Gus.* Genevieve reeled from the thought as if she taken a physical blow, staggered, and almost tripped over the body of the dapper old man. She set off at a run, pushing her way past the living and dodging the dead with the adroitness of the counties hockey player she had once been.

*

So, Genevieve said tentatively, not wishing to rekindle any alarming memories. What happened at school?

The little kids were scared, Gus said.

You're a little kid.

He made a face. Not really.

Thank God for the rain, which had meant that the whole school had spent their lunchtime indoors. There were a few peripheral casualties. The crossing-man on duty, a classroom assistant. Genevieve had to skirt the body of the deputy head lying just outside the school gates. A smoker, paying the price of her habit.

I'm never letting you out of my sight again, she said to Gus.

Never?

Never.

He shrugged. OK.

Glancing out of the window, Genevieve saw a sparrow land on the bird table in the shared garden of the block of flats. It began to peck nervously at the toast crumbs that one of Genevieve's elderly neighbours put out each morning. It was the first bird that Genevieve had seen all day. The elderly neighbour herself was spreadeagled on the path. Her fat ginger cat who spent most of his day asleep inside was sniffing the old lady's body with greedy curiosity. Burying the dead was going to be a problem, Genevieve thought.

What? Gus said.

Nothing.

Now wash your hands.

On the television, newsreaders and pundits were wallowing in the apocalypse. It had been worldwide and had lasted exactly five minutes. A cataclysmic event more overwhelming in its awfulness than anything previously experienced on the planet – half a million Krakatoas, a hundred thousand Hiroshimas.

The commentators were talking in Cretan terms – *The end of civilisation as we know it.* The greatest disaster since the dinosaurs were wiped out. The Black Death had killed a third of the world's population but it had taken only people (only!) but the Dark (as it was apparently now called) seemed indiscriminate in its choice of prey.

Billions of farm animals in the fields had gone but the battery hens and the veal calves survived. Children in playgrounds and streets all laid out but the worst kind of paedophiles and murderers in jail were spared. Diamond miners survived, trawlermen died. Swaths of the poor were scythed down – workers in the fields, the homeless, the drunks and the whores on the street.

In the great shanty towns of Karachi, Lagos and Cape Town, corpses were scooped up by bulldozers. Two-thirds of the population of Africa wiped out. All the animals of the Serengeti, of the Antarctic, of the Malaysian rainforests.

Planes plummeted like game birds from the sky, although some miraculously survived, coasting silently through the blackout before regaining power. Cyclists, dog walkers, cricket teams, sunbathers, tourists on the Grand Canal. Princess Anne. The Prime Minister. All gone. In the Far East, moving into night at the time of the disaster, there were slightly fewer casualties although it seemed that all it took was an open window – a crack – for the Dark to get in.

The population of New Zealand fared best, not so the forty million sheep that lived there.

There were myriad theories. In order of popularity these were: a shock-and-awe alien attack; a new kind of plague; a cull by God; a hole in the space-time continuum (this, of course, would evolve into the Void theory); an increase in the earth's magnetism – or a sudden decrease; a poisonous miasma emanating from Venus; the revenge of Gaia. 'A terrible harrowing,' the Archbishop of York said, and was condemned for being overly biblical.

Across the globe people rioted and looted and stockpiled. As you would. Genevieve thought of all the useful things she might have bought in Waitrose when she had the opportunity. The shelves would be cleared now, even the balsamic vinegar would have been snatched.

Not only the birds but also the bees survived. No one understood why, but they were grateful (pollination and so on). Many scientists, shut away in their labs, had also survived and would soon be set to work on the reason for the illogical staying power of the birds and bees (no one foresaw what a problem they would become).

The plump, newly elevated Deputy Prime Minister appeared on television, basking in the seriousness of his position. He exhorted everyone to stay calm and not panic. He sounded like a supermarket manager. The spirit of the Blitz was invoked. Genevieve turned the television off.

Will it happen again? Gus asked.

I hope not, Genevieve said.

But it did. At 1.05 p.m. the following day the universe blinked once more. A lot of the casualties were people who were burying the dead from the first time.

It lasted for five minutes and came five minutes later every day. Like clockwork. People were thankful for this regularity. *You can set your watch by it*, but at the same time, as it were, the implications of this machine-like precision were disturbing.

The people who remained adapted. Dying embers of church congregations were fanned into life as many turned to religion. Others sank into apathy. Genevieve's mother said she wished she'd had shares in one of the artificial meat corporations.

Genevieve wondered what they would do if one day the Dark came and didn't go away again.

Phil Beckett never did make sense of what happened to his daughter and grandson. Five years after the first Dark, when anyone with any sense knew to the exact second when it was coming, knew to take all necessary precautions, she broke down on I-8.

Every couple of miles along the interstate there were billboards saying 'Avoid the Void!' and 'Don't Let the Dark In!'. Did she not *see* them? She was so smart. Why had she been so dumb?

She was found on the hard shoulder, Preston by her side, holding her hand. He'd just started elementary school. They had got out of the car and had started walking – in eighty-five degree heat. Why? Why hadn't she just waited for a breakdown truck? A passing motorist saw them running back to the car but the Dark overtook them.

That was three months ago. His wife had turned to God and pills. Phil had given up on God, didn't believe in pills.

Blake came round all the time. He hadn't had a job since the first Dark. Phil felt a coldness towards him that was maybe unfair. Maybe not.

They had been doing OK. After the cattle went, Phil had transformed the Double Diamond into a dude ranch. *We never take you out in the Dark*. That all stopped with Melissa's death. The horses were up for sale now.

Midday. The Dark was due at twenty past the hour.

Going out to settle the horses, Phil shouted to his wife.

The horses were always skittish beforehand. His wife was watching TV in the living room, reruns of crap – *The Bold and the Beautiful, All My Children* – shows that were cancelled years ago. His wife didn't reply.

Come on, Phil said to the dog.

A shadow passed over them. One of the giant flocks of Arizona grasshopper-sparrows flying overhead. Once on the most endangered list, a darned nuisance now.

In the barn, Phil checked the windows, searched everywhere for cracks and pinholes, all the time talking soothingly to the horses. At 12.18 he stepped outside and shut the door behind him, leaving the dog inside with the horses, but Mitch started scratching at the door, whining sadly. His wife treated Mitch with amiable indifference. Phil tried to put himself inside the dog's head. What would Mitch want? Pretty much the same as he wanted himself, he guessed.

Come on then, buddy, Phil said, opening the barn door, shutting it carefully again after Mitch came out.

The dog stood sentinel by his side, waiting patiently for whatever was going to happen. Phil put out his hand and rubbed the dog's head. His watch was slow and the Dark surprised them both when it came.

'Then Later, His Ghost'

Sarah Hall

The wind was coming from the east when he woke. The windows on that side of the house boxed and clattered in their frames, even behind the stormboards, and the corrugated metal sheet over the coop in the garden was creaking and hawing, as though it might rip out of its rivets and fly off. The wind bellowed. All the structures it hit or ran through sang and moaned. December 23rd. The morning was dark, or it was still night. He lay unmoving beneath the blankets, feet cold in his boots, his chest sore from breathing unheated air. The fire had gone out; the wood had burned too high with the pull up the chimney, or the flames had been extinguished by gusts. It was hard keeping it in overnight. Coal was much better; it burned hotter and longer, but it was hard to find and too heavy to carry.

He pulled the blankets over his face. *Get up*, he thought. If he didn't get up it would be the beginning of the end. People who stayed inside got into trouble. No one was going to help them. Part of him understood – who wanted to die outside, tossed about like a piece of litter, stripped of clothing by the hands of the wind, then lodged somewhere, dirt blowing dunes over your corpse? Crawling into a calm little shelter was preferable.

Something hard clattered along the roof, scuttling over the slates, and was borne away. There was a great *ooming* sound above, almost oceanic, the top of the sky heaving and breaking. Whatever had been kept in check by the old Gulf Stream was now able to push back, unfurl and lash around. A bully of a wind. No wonder people had once created aerial gods, fiends of the air or the mountaintops. Even he took it personally, sometimes – yelling uselessly at the force, his voice tiny and whipped away. Not often though, it didn't really help. When it came from the east a lot of the remaining house roofs went, and whole walls could topple – another reason not to stay inside too much. You had to be alert to the collapses. He turned on his side and shivered as the cold crept down his neck. The sofa he was lying on felt damp. The cushion he was using as a pillow smelled of wet mortar. He didn't usually sleep in this room, but Helene was now in his.

Another sizeable object crashed past the house, splintering against the gable and flying off in separate pieces. He'd heard the wind shifting and strengthening during the night, though he was used to sleeping with the sound percussing his dreams. He couldn't remember the last still day, the trees standing upright and placid, the air itself seeming to vanish, to not exist. Stillness seemed like a childhood myth, like the glory of August hay-timing, or Father Christmas. Last night he'd slept restlessly; his dreams were turbulent – wars, animals stampeding, Helene being swept away. After a night like that it was hard to get up. Other days he almost liked the climate. He liked being one of the only ones left in the town, the impetus; he liked letting go of the ropes strung between buildings and jumping so his coat could sail him several feet forward, flying like a spectre.

Get up, he thought. And then, because it was proving difficult, he thought, *Buffalo*. He pictured the buffalo. It was enormous and black-brown. It had a giant head and the shoulders of a weightlifter, a tapered back end, small, upturned horns. It looked permanently, structurally braced. He sat up, moved the blankets away, and then stood. He found the torch next to the sofa and switched it on. The cold made him feel older and stiffer. He moved around and lifted his legs gymnastically to get his blood moving. He did some lunges. There was a portable gas stove in the corner of the room and he set the torch next to it, ignited the ring, boiled water and made tea. He drank the tea black. There were no smuts in the grate. Perhaps he'd leave the fire a day to save fuel – the temperature was about four or five degrees, he guessed, manageable. So long as Helene was warm enough.

He took the torch and moved through the building, to the room where she slept. It was warm. She slept with the little tilly lamp on. She didn't like the dark. Her fire was still glowing orange. She was sound asleep. She was lying on her side and her belly mound was vast under her jumper. He picked up the cast-off blanket from the floor and draped it back over her. She didn't move. She seemed peaceful, though her eyes were moving rapidly behind her eyelids. The wind was quieter this side of the house, the leeside. It whistled and whined as it slipstreamed away. Little skitters of soot came down the chimney and sparks rose from the cradle. He looked at Helene sleeping. Her hair was cut quite short, like his, but hers curled and was black. When they were open her eyes were extremely pretty, gold-coloured, gold to green. He imagined climbing on to the bed next to her and putting his arm over her shoulder. Sometimes when he was checking on her she woke up and looked at him. Mostly she knew he was just checking, bringing her tea, or some food, or more wood for the fire. But sometimes she looked afraid. He knew she worried about the baby coming; that frightened him too. He was practical, and he'd found a medical book, but still. Helene was very quiet mostly. She'd done well, he thought, lasting it out, but she didn't seem to think so. He thought probably she hadn't developed any methods to help, like picturing the buffalo, and he worried about her. She was probably thirty, or thirty-five. She'd been an English teacher, though not his; she liked sardines in tomato sauce, which was good because he had lots of tins. She was very polite and always thanked him for the food. *That's all right,* he'd say, and sometimes he'd almost add, Miss. She never said anything about what had happened to her, or the baby, but he could guess. No one would choose that now. He had found her in the Catholic cathedral, what was left of it. There were two dead bodies nearby, both men; they looked freshly dead when he uncovered their faces. She was looking up at the circular hole where the rose window had been. She wasn't praying or crying.

He left some tea for her in a metal cup with a lid, and some sardines, and went back to his room. He did a stock check. He did this every day, unnecessarily, but it made him feel calmer. Calor gas bottles, food, clothes, batteries, duct tape, painkillers, knives, rope. The cans were piled in such a way that he could count them by tens. This house still had water, a slow trickling stream that was often tinted and tasted earthy. He still hadn't worked out if it had its own well. But it made life easier – he didn't have to rig up a rainwater funnel. He'd been collecting packets of baby formula too, but when he'd showed Helene she'd just looked sad.

There was a box with more delicate things inside, frivolous things, he sometimes thought, other times, precious. Photographs – of his mother, and his little brother in school football strip – his passport, though it was useless now, and the pages he'd been collecting for Helene. She loved reading, and he didn't have much to read in the house. He'd been hunting for the play for a month or two and it was a very difficult task. So many books had been destroyed. Once the buildings were breeched nothing paper lasted; it warped and rotted, the ink smudged. Sometimes just a paragraph, or a line, was all he could hope for. *So dear the love my people bore me, nor set a mark so bloody on the business: but with fairer colours painted their foul ends. In few, they hurried us aboard a bark, bore us some leagues to sea, where they'd prepared a rotten carcass of a boat, not rigg'd ...*

The town's library had been demolished in the first big storms. No wonder: it had been built in the Sixties, part of the civic centre. The older the building, the longer it lasted, generally: people had gotten very bad at construction, he thought, or lazy. He was good at salvaging. He was good at it because he was good at moving around outside. He wasn't timid, but he never took anything for granted. He wore the rucksack strapped tight to his body, like a packed parachute, taped up his arms and legs, tested the ropes, and always looked in every direction for airborne debris. He never assumed it was safe.

He took a tin of sockeye salmon out of the stack, opened it and ate it cold. Ulcers starred his tongue. He probably needed some fruit, but he'd rather give the fruit to Helene. He was hungry and he ate too fast. In winter having two meals was important – breakfast and dinner – even if they were small. This was the fourth winter. Last Christmas he hadn't really celebrated because he was by himself, but having Helene made things nicer. He scraped the last flakes out of the tin with his nail and ate them. He drank the oil, which made him gag. He saved the tin – while they were still greasy they were good for making flour and water dumplings over the fire, though the dumplings tasted fishy. As well as the surprise gift, he'd been planning their Christmas meal. He'd had a tin of smoked pheasant pâté for two years, too much of a boon to eat by himself. There was a jar of redcurrant. A jar of boiled potatoes. And a tin of actual Christmas pudding. They would have it all warmed. Two courses. He even had a miniature whisky with which to set fire to the pudding.

He went to the back of the house, peered through a gap in the stormboards and watched the dawn struggling to arrive. Daylight usually meant the wind eased slightly, but not today. The light was pulsing, murky yellow aurorae. There were the usual items speeding past on the current – rags, bits of tree, transmuted unknowable things. Sometimes he was amazed there were enough objects left to loosen and scatter about. Sometimes he wondered whether these were just the same million shoes and bottles and cartons in flight, circling the globe endlessly, like tides of scrap. The clouds passed fat and fast overhead, and were sucked into a vortex on the horizon, disappearing into nothing. There was sleetish rain, travelling horizontally, almost too quickly to see. It was a bad idea to go out today – too big a wind. His rule was nothing more than a ninety, or what he gauged to be a ninety. But he wanted to find the last few pages.

He went back to his room and got ready. He put on hefty waterproof trousers and jacket. He cleaned and put on the goggles. He pulled the hood of the jacket up, yanked the toggles and tied them tightly. He taped the neck. He taped his cuffs and his ankles, his knees and his elbows. He put on gloves but left them untaped so he could take them off if he found any more books; he would need his fingers to be nimble, to flick through and tear out. It might mean he would lose one glove, or both, but he'd risk it. When he was done he felt almost airtight, like some kind of diver, *a storm-diver*, he thought. But it was better not to get too heroic. For a while he'd worn a helmet, but it had made him feel too bulky, too heavy, not adapted. He weighted the rucksack down with the red stone – he didn't like to think of it as his lucky stone, because he wasn't superstitious, but secretly he did think it was lucky. It was egg-shaped, banded with pink and white – some kind of polished gneiss. It had been in the geology lab at school and he'd later found it, looking through the wreckage. It sat in the bottom of the rucksack like a ballast, leaving enough room for anything that he discovered on his excursions and wanted to bring back. He had plastic wrapping for anything delicate. He was good at discerning what was useful and what was not; he hadn't brought back many useless things, though the temptation was to save beautiful items, or money. His mother had always joked his birthdays were easy – as a kid he didn't need many toys, field comforts, or gadgets. His mother had died in the flu pandemic. So had his little brother.

There were two doors to the house – one on the north side and one on the west. He stood by the west door and thought, *Buffalo*. He opened the door and felt the draw of air, then opened it wider and moved into the alcove behind the storm door. The storm door opened inwards and could be locked either side. He moved the bolt, forced himself out into the buffeting air, planted his feet and fastened it behind him. Either side of the house, the wind tore past, conveying junk, going about its demolition. Behind him, the house felt solid. It'd been a good choice – a squat, single-storey longbarn on the low-lying outskirts of town, with shutters and big outer doors. He'd modified it a bit, nailing, building break-walls. The coop in the garden was more hopeful than practical. This was his fifth house. The first – his mother's, a white Thirties semi – had gone down as easily as straw, along with the rest of the row. The brick terraces had proved more durable, he'd lived in two, but they were high-ceilinged; once the big windows and roofs gave out they were easy for the wind to dismantle. Before the barn he'd been sharing with a man called Craig in a rank bunker near the market, a sort of utility storage. It was a horrible, rat-like existence – dark, desperate, scavenging. Craig was much older than him, but wasn't clever or good at planning. Things had turned bad. He got out as soon as he could and wasn't sorry. A lighthouse would have been best, round, aerodynamic, deep-sunk into rock, made to withstand batterings. But the coast was impossible – the surges were terrifying. Before everything had gone down he'd seen news footage; he couldn't quite believe the towering swells. He had nightmares about those waves reaching inland.

He inched along the barn wall, towards the open. He'd planned a route through town. He would keep to the west side of streets wherever he could, for protection, but that meant being in the path of anything collapsing. In the past he'd outrun avalanching walls, he'd been picked up and flung against hard surfaces and rubble heaps, his collarbone and his wrist had been fractured. There were only so many near misses. He would need to judge the soundness of structures, only venture inside a building if the risks seemed low. He would go into the Golden Triangle – some of the big Victorian houses there were still holding and they were more likely to have what he was looking for. At the corner of the house he knelt, tensed his neck and shoulder muscles and put his head out into the rushing wind. The force was immense. He checked for large oncoming objects, then began to crawl along the ground. Staying low reduced the possibility of being knocked over, or decapitated. What had once been the longbarn's garden was now stripped bald of grass. Clods of earth tumbled past him. The wind shunted his backside and slid him forward. He flattened out and moved like a lizard, towards the farm buildings and the first rope. He had different techniques, depending on the situation. Sometimes he crawled miles. Sometimes he crouched like an ape and lumbered. Other times he made dashes, if there were intermittent blasts, cannonballing the lulls, but he could get caught out doing that. Sometimes it was better to walk into the wind head on, sometimes leaning back against it and digging your heels in was best.

It had been a while since he'd been out in anything as strong. It was terrifying and exhilarating. The fury bent him over when he tried to stand, so he stayed low, a creature of stealth and avoidance. He clung to the cord that ran between the buildings. He'd tested the bindings only a few days ago, but still he gave a good yank to make sure it hadn't begun to untether. This rope he'd put up himself, and he trusted it. A lot of the ones in town he'd redone too. He traversed it slowly while the wind bore between the buildings. After the farm, there was a dangerous open stretch. *The Huff*, he called it, because the weather always seemed filthy-tempered there. It had been a famous racecourse. Then the town started properly: its suburbs, its alleys and piles of stone. Once it was a town of magnificent trees. Plane trees, beeches, oaks. The big avenues had been lined by them, their leaves on fire in autumn, raining pollen in spring. Now they were mostly gone – uprooted and dying. There was a lot of firewood to haul away, though. He hardly ever saw anyone else taking it. He could probably count on one hand the number of people he saw in a month. Occasionally, a big armoured vehicle passed through, military – its windows covered in metal grilles. The soldiers never came out. A lot of people had gone west because it was supposed to be milder, there was supposed to be more protection and organisation. He'd never wanted to leave. He didn't believe it anyway.

When he got to *The Huff* he almost changed his mind and went back. The air above was thick with dirt, a great sweeping cloud of it. Every few moments something rattled, fluttered or spun past, bounced off the ground and was lobbed upwards. On tamer days he'd sledged across the stretch on a big metal tray, putting his heels down to slow the contraption and flinging himself sideways to get off. Today, no larks, he'd be lucky not to break his neck. Crossing it would mean agreeing with the wind rather than fighting it, becoming one of many hurled items, colliding with others, abraded, like a pellet in a shaker. It was too wide a tract of land to rope; he had to go without moorings.

There was no let-up, so he gave himself a moment or two to prepare and then he let go of the farm walls and began to crawl across. He tried to move his limbs quickly to keep up with the thrust of the current, but it was too strong. Within moments the wind had taken him, lifting his back end and tossing him over. He felt the red stone slam into his spine. He started tobogganing, feet first. He tucked his head in, rolled on his side, brought his knees up and felt himself scraping along. The ground was hard and bumpy and vibrated his bones. He put his hands down and felt debris filling his cuffs. Something sharp caught his anklebone and stung. *Shit*, he thought, *shitshitshit*. He went with it, there was nothing he could do, and after a while managed to slow himself and regain some control. But still he was propelled. He hoofed his boots down and tried to brake. He was nearly at the edge of the racecourse, where the old, outer flint wall of the town began. The wind shoved him hard again and he went tumbling forward. His shoulder and knee hit the pointed stones. He lay for a moment, dazed and brunted against the structure, dirt pattering around him. It was hard to breathe. The air tasted of soil.

He spat, turned his head. When he opened his eyes one pane of the goggles was cracked, splitting his view. He was all right, but he had to move. He crawled along the boundary wall, around trolleys and piles of swept rubbish. His knee throbbed. A superbruise. At the first gap he went through. He sat up, leant against the sharp flint and caught his breath. He cleaned his goggles, emptied his gloves. *Reckless idiot*, he thought. *Don't fuck it up.* He did want to live – moments like this reminded him. Moments like this made him feel more real than he ever had before. He became more skilful because of them. He evolved.

The boundary wall was twelve feet thick. Whoever had built it had meant business. Sections had been restored when he was a kid. It was holding up well. He looked at the town. Something catastrophic had passed over; that's how it looked now. Razed. Roofs and upper floors were gone; cars were parked on their backs, their windscreens smashed. The big storms had left domino rubble in every direction, scattered fans of bricks and tiles, bouquets of splintered wood. Old maps meant nothing. New streets had been made, buildings rearranged. He had to keep relearning its form as its composition shifted.

He got up, crouched low, surveyed the route and limped off. It was a mile to the Golden Triangle. He saw no one. He kept to the safer routes and used the secure ropes when he had to, hauling himself hand over hand. He squinted through the broken goggles, seeing an odd spider-like creature in front of him, but he didn't take them off – the last thing he needed was to be blinded. The ruins were depressing, but he occasionally saw miraculous things in them. An animal, though they were rare. There were no birds, not even distressed gulls; nothing could cope in the torrid air. The rats had done OK, anything living below ground level. Cats and dogs were few, and always emaciated and wretched. There was no food, nothing growing, not much to kill. People's survival instincts were worse, he often thought, but they could at least use can openers. Two years ago he'd seen a stag. It was standing on the football field in front of him, reddish, six points on each antler. It was standing perfectly still, like something from the middle of a forest, and it didn't panic or run. It was standing as if it had always stood there, as if tree after tree had been stripped away around it, until the forest was gone and there was nothing left to shield it.

He'd seen awful things too. A man sliced in half by a flying glass pane, his entrails worming from his stomach. Craig's broken skull. The good things had to be held in the mind, and remembered, and celebrated. That was why he had to get the pages for Helene and why they would have a nice Christmas.

He made his way slowly through the town, forcing his body against the blast. He kept leeside wherever he could and watched for flying timber and rockslides. He crossed the little park at the edge of the Golden Triangle. There were stumps where the central pavilion had stood. The trees lying on the ground were scoured bare. Sleet had begun to gather along their trunks. He hoped it wouldn't turn to snow and lie; it was hard enough keeping his footing. When he got to the Victorian district he was surprised to see smoke leaking from one of the heaps. He made his way over, cautiously, but it was just a random fire burning along a beam, some stray electrical spark, perhaps, or friction. Two rows away the houses were in better shape. Some only had holes in the roofs and lopped-off chimneys. The windows were mostly out. He could hop through the bays if the lintels were safe.

He always called out to make sure they were empty first. It wasn't really etiquette. It wasn't really robbing. It was retrieval of what had been abandoned. He'd been in some of them before, checking for food, batteries, essentials. They had been lovely places once, owned by doctors and lawyers, he imagined. There were remnants – cast-iron fireplaces, painted tiles; even some crescents of stained glass hanging on above the door frames. Damp and fungus and lichen grew inside the walls. He tried a couple, searching through the downstairs rooms – he never went upstairs if he could help it, it was too dangerous. The wind moaned through the rooms, shifting wet curtains and making the peeling wallpaper flicker. There were pulpy masses on the shelves, rotting covers, the sour smell of macerating paper.

He stepped among the detritus, broken glass and broken furniture, digging through piles, tossing collapsed volumes aside. He'd been dreaming about finding a complete works – that would really be something special – bound in plastic perhaps, unviolated. But, like Bibles, they were the first to go, their pages wafer-thin and frail. He'd studied the play in school, not with any particular enjoyment. He could remember bits of it, the parts he'd had to read out. *As wicked dew as e'er my mother brush'd with raven's feather from unwholesome fen drop on you both! A south-west blow on ye …* Perhaps Helene had taught it. Reading it again might help her, if she could begin to think differently. She could read it while she nursed the baby. She could think about the good things that remained. All he needed were the last two acts. He'd found sections of the rest, dried the pages, sorted the scenes and put them in order, as best he could. There'd been some extensive gluing – it wasn't an attractive gift, by any stretch.

After ten or eleven houses he was starting to lose hope and worry about the daylight. The wind was not letting up: if anything it was gaining power. There had been a couple of worryingly big bangs nearby, something shattering. He went back out on to the street and made his way further into the Golden Triangle. There was a big house further along, free-standing, walled. It had upper bays as well as lower. A vicarage, maybe. Part of the roof was gone. The gate was padlocked but the frame had come away from the post and he forced his way through the gap. In the garden the plant pots and urns were smashed apart but one of the small fruit trees was still standing, defiantly, petrified black globes hanging from its lower branches. He went through the lower window, down a hallway. He knew, even before he got to the big room at the back of the house, that he was going to find what he was looking for. Fortune favours the brave, he thought. He forced a swollen door into a parlour. The walls had once been red but were now darker, browny, like blood that had dried. There was a fireplace, heaped full of clinker and charred wood, pieces of chimney brick and sleeving. There was a man sitting in a chair, a corpse. His eyelids were shrinking back; some wisps of hair left on his head. The skin was yellow and tight and retreating off the bone. A blanket was wrapped around his shoulders. There was no bad smell. He didn't look too closely.

He went to the shelves. There were rows and rows of hardbacks. He could even read the titles on some of the spines. There was a collection of Shakespeares, mottled, mould blooming along them, but readable. He found it in the middle. He took off his gloves and opened it carefully; the edges of the paper were moist, stuck, and they tore slightly when moved, but it held together. He flicked gently to the end. *I'll deliver all; and promise you calm seas, auspicious gales and sail so expeditious that shall catch your royal fleet far off.*

He smiled. He took off his rucksack, wrapped the book in a plastic bag and a towel and put it inside one of the small compartments. He put the rucksack back on, clicked the straps across his chest, drew them tight, and put on his gloves. It would be a good house to go through for other things, but he didn't want to get caught out and not be able to get across town and over *The Huff* to the longbarn. He didn't want to leave Helene alone longer than he had to. She might be having the baby. He would come back, after Christmas, and search properly.

He closed the door on the dead man. On the way out he saw his reflection in the dusty, cracked hall mirror. The hood was drawn tightly around his head; he was earless and bug-eyed, like an alien. The metallic tape around his neck looked like grey scales. His face was filthy and covered with cuts. He put out his sore tongue. Suppose he wasn't really human any more, he thought. Suppose he was a kind of demon, made in this place. How would he know? But he felt human; he remembered feeling human. His knee hurt. And he could use a can opener. And he liked Christmas. He turned away from the mirror and climbed back out of the window. Snow was driving past on the wind.

'The Christmas Story'

Ali Smith

It was the middle of October and the leaves on the trees still green; it was a weekend, it was the Saturday, we'd woken up late. I came downstairs in my pyjamas and went to the front room to get some oranges to make the orange juice. I opened the door. The front room was full of children.

This was a bit of a shock, since we don't actually have any children, and there were quite a lot of them, all about eight or nine years old, overfilling the two seats and the couch. A child with its back to me was halfway up the bookcase balancing one smallshoed foot on the second bookshelf and the other on the arm of the couch, stretching across the front of the picture of the boats as if straightening the picture. The others were all sitting quiet, good as gold. Several were watching the off television as if any moment it'd turn itself on and they didn't want to miss that.

I backed out of the doorway and closed the door. I stood outside it for a moment. I opened it again. They were all still there. The one who'd been up on the bookcase was now lying on her front along the back of the couch, chin on hands, watching the blank television like the others. Draped along the top of the frame of the boat picture there was a thick silver-looking ribbon of, what was it? It looked synthetic. It glinted in the autumn sun. I closed the door again.

I went upstairs.

Full of *what?* you said.

I think one of them is putting up Christmas decorations, I said.

You pulled on a dressing gown. I went round the bedroom finding clothes to put on. We both went downstairs, opened the door and stood in the doorway.

Whose are they? I said.

You brightened next to me. You crossed the room.

Hi everyone, you said.

Hi-i! the children sang back.

I looked round the room. All the pictures on our walls now had tinsel topping their frames. There was tinsel stuck with Sellotape round the light switch. You stood at the coffee table and switched the TV on with the remote.

Yeah, the girl in the hacking jacket said from under her riding helmet.

Thank you very much, the girl in the pink tutu said.

There were those two, the one in the pony-riding clothes and the ballet one, and there were a boy and a girl dressed in peculiar Robin Hood costumes with great exaggerated jagged hems on their clothes, like they were wearing cartoon rags. There was a girlish boy or maybe it was a boyish girl, hard to tell, in jeans and a little suede waistcoat with an apple-shaped piece of suede for a pocket. There was the child who'd first been up at the picture-rail. She was wearing something like Beatles *Sgt Pepper* clothes and she was perched up on the back of the couch now cutting bits out of folded white cardboard with our kitchen scissors. A snow of little white triangles fell away from the blades and down behind the cushions.

The air in the room smelled high and sweet. I leaned a little against the open door and the door resisted. There was possibly another one, or maybe more than one, there behind it.

A rough-looking boy pushed a demure-looking girl. The girl pushed him back twice as hard. One of the other children told them to stop it. I gesticulated at you. You stepped back over and through them and across the room and we left them settling down round the John Wayne film, the one where he's old and has the eyepatch on.

I shut the door. We stood on the other side of it in the hall for a bit, not speaking. We could hear John Wayne behind it. *I never shot nobody I didn't have to.*

Through in the kitchen I sat down at the table. You hoisted yourself up on to the unit and sat with your legs dangling down over the doors.

What's going on? I said.

No idea, you said.

You said it sheepishly. You kicked your legs against the doors.

Doesn't that film have a scene in it with a snakepit? I said.

He takes on the girl even though she's a bit of a schoolmarm, you said. Then he rides down the hill at the bad guys with both his hands in the air. Remember? He puts his reins in his mouth and rides right at them down the slope. He reloads his rifle as he goes, he sort of tosses it in the air and reloads it at full gallop – it's amazing. Remember?

No, I said. How did they get in? Shouldn't we be phoning the police or the council or someone?

Look, you said. Listen. You know that book.

What book? I said.

The one I was reading last week, you said. The week before. The one where I kept asking you to listen to the bits I was reading out and you kept getting annoyed.

The boring self-help psychology one? I said.

The book you told me was drivel, you said.

The one called *Release Your Inner Child?* I said.

You jumped down off the unit. All the things in the kitchen shook.

I'll be back in a minute, you said. I'm just going to teach them how to use the remote. In case they don't like the snakes.

Won't they know already? Aren't kids these days all, like, born already technologically savvy?

The kitchen door closed. I'd said the word savvy to an empty room.

They were still there at lunchtime. By lunchtime I'd heard through the wall, several times, a song whose words were about keeping your spirits up if you're lost in the woods. By lunchtime, when I knocked on my own front-room door as if I was a stranger in someone else's house, and opened it and went in, you were sitting in front of the fireplace. You were surrounded by children.

It was kind of lovely.

But then I noticed that the front-room big light had a lot of cardboard snowflakes hanging off a snarl of bright red thread wound round its flex.

They couldn't have reached to do that. You must have helped them.

You noticed me, finally.

Are they going to need lunch? I said.

Do you guys need lunch? you said to the room.

No thank you! they chorused, polite and old-fashioned.

When you stood up and came over to me they formed a semi-circle round the lit television. They were amusing themselves by flicking channels. It was as if they'd never seen channels flicking before. It was as if they'd never seen so many channels. They kept exclaiming in amazement. They seemed particularly to like the commercials. When the commercial breaks ended and the programmes started again they flicked channels expressly to find more commercials, and every time the single commercial which mentioned Christmas came on, the one about sofas, the whole room shimmered with excitement.

They can't *all* be your inner children, I said. (I said it quietly. I didn't want to offend them.) I mean, *that* one's quite like you. But the others?

I pointed at the two in the Robin Hood clothes.

Babes in the Wood, you said. Panto I got taken to when I was about ten, at the local theatre, and it had that man from *Basil Brush* in it as The Storyteller or The Woodcutter, and someone from, you know, those sisters, as his wife, the Nolan Sisters. She was such a good singer.

The panto children burst into song.

In the wood, in the wood, things don't look like they're so good
When you can't see the wood for the trees.
Never fear, never fear, cause with me beside you here
Being lost in the woods is a breeze.

I went seven times, you whispered. It made me want to be an actor. Made my mother furious.

Don't even think about moping, the children sang. *For wherever we happen to roam.*

You started to hum along. Then you joined in. You knew the words.

Together we'll keep ourselves hoping. Till we hope ourselves all the way home.

I pointed at the girl in the tutu then the girl in the pony clothes. They were in a huddle on the floor in front of the fireplace with a couple of others, taking little wooden figures out of a weather-beaten cardboard box and placing them round a tiny empty crib on the hearth.

You shrugged.

What can I say? you said. I was a versatile child.

I pointed at the one wearing the bright military-looking jacket, the one who'd been doing the decorating. She had a tall hat on now with a little peaked cap. She'd taken the riding crop off the pony girl and was spinning it expertly in the air well above the height of the hat.

Were you in some kind of brass band as well? I said.

No, you said, I've no idea who she is. Oh, but wait. I know. I know who she might be. Caitlin was a champion baton twirler, I think she used to –

Caitlin? I said. As in Caitlin your ex?

She had a drawerful of medals, you said, she'd won them all by the age of eleven, and one day she showed me –

You're carrying your ex's inner child around with you? I said.

She was good, you said. She was still good even in her thirties. One day when we were first together she actually got out her baton and we went out into her driveway and she –

And now she's here in my house? I said.

Our house, you said. No, but listen, she was really good. She did this show right there in the driveway and all the neighbours came out of their houses and clapped.

You noticed the look on my face.

Well, I can hardly ask her to go, can I? you said. And she seems quite important to the group dynamics. And I mean, I don't even know that she's actually Caitlin's. What if she's mine, too? What if, say, something in *her* childhood simply appealed to something in *my* –

Not just her, I said. I need you to make them all leave.

Your face fell. Then you looked straight at me and gave the slightest shake of your head.

No? I said.

You stood with your shoulders helpless and your eyes defiant.

The children were all now ignoring the TV and making cooing noises round the boy who'd earlier been having the pushing fight with the girl. Now he and that same girl were passing the little wooden baby Jesus between them, cupped from hand to hand like a baby mouse, a precious insect.

I pushed you out of the way, bent down and picked up the beaten-up old cardboard box. It had a few painted figures still left in the bottom of it, the three kings, it looked like, left till last. I marched out of the room. I rattled the kings against each other through the kitchen. I opened the back door. I went to the far end of the garden, held the box high in the air over the neighbours' fence, above the place where they keep their mulch pile. I turned it upside down. The kings fell out. Follow that star, why don't you? I said.

Then I dropped the empty box after them over the fence, too.

I came back up to the house. I stood in the front room. I looked right past you. I cleared my throat:

Right. Come on everybody. It's been lovely having you. Thank you for coming. But it's time you all left now.

No response.

Come on, I said as brightly as I could. Gather your stuff. Make sure you take everything you brought with you.

Nothing. Then the very slight smatter of a giggle.

Don't you hear me? I said.

Don't you hear me? one of them echoed behind me and the room ran with the under-laughter.

Time you all went! I said.

Time you all went! the one behind me repeated in a copy of my voice that was pure insolence.

The room erupted in anarchic squeals. We turned to look. She was dark and very small, neatly dressed in clean school clothes though it was a Saturday. She was sitting behind the door on what looked like a little black slab, like a reinforced box or case – the kind of case a musical instrument gets kept in.

You shook your head.

I've absolutely no idea where that one's come from, you said.

I woke up, turned over in bed, you snoring lightly next to me; it was an early Saturday morning in mid-October and the leaves outside still green. The temperature that day was 20 degrees and after we'd got up and had breakfast it was such a lovely autumn day we drove to the woods, the ones where we have a membership and can park the car in the special car park for nothing (well, for £25 annual membership paid in advance), and tramped around with all the other people in the unseasonal warm, and when we got back that night we sat in front of the television and watched the annual celebrities learning to dance and the annual real people, some of whom can sing and some of whom can't, make the annual sacrifice of themselves under Albert

Speer lighting, which is what you always say about *The X Factor*.

Then, in the middle of one of the ad breaks, my head filled with flute music.

Sumer is icumen in. Lhude sing cucuu, and I'd also played a version of Petula Clark's 'Downtown' on that flute at a Christmas school concert, and there was 'Snowbird', there was 'Go Tell It On the Mountain', there was 'In the Bleak Midwinter' but with a different tune from the usual one. I'd actually forgotten for all these years that I'd once learned the flute.

I turned down the sound on the TV.

Have you ever heard this version of 'In the Bleak Midwinter'? I said. I hummed it.

No, you said. It's pretty.

Then we turned the sound back up.

The weeks passed. On TV the Christmas commercials thickened themselves into stories. A geeky little girl wearing 1950s clothes but living in the present made biscuits for school with the help of a beautiful shopgirl. A small boy helped a CGI penguin find love. Some men on opposite sides in the trenches climbed over the mud, played football and slipped chocolate into each other's pockets. The adverts were for buying things in shops. (Gallipoli, Verdun, Ypres, Somme. A hundred and eighty thousand, seven hundred and fifty thousand, eight hundred and fifty thousand, a million.)

The autumn-winter schedule dramas passed, all just-post-First World War haircuts, rough sex scenes and acts of violence happening to women and girls, but it was all right, because when someone was rough like that you knew he was definitely a bad guy. Gillian Anderson, her face doleful, was changing out of a police uniform. She seemed to be taking a very long time to undo the buttons of her shirt. Perhaps it was a shirt with more than the usual number of buttons, or maybe police uniforms have more buttons than normal clothes. I went through to dry some cups in the kitchen and came back in again and she was still working her way down her front. A small boy was stolen and his parents stumbled brokenly about. Every episode got a little closer to the mystery and the taboo of what had actually happened to him. That story was very gripping. It was going to run almost all the way to Christmas.

Then it was Black Friday. All over the UK people rioted for half-price TVs. In the USA, where people were rioting about a lot more than TVs, armed police stood in a line waving their shields under the words SEASON'S GREETINGS strung across the road in tinsel the colour of fire.

(All that time, there at my side, I'd felt it, a slight pressure, size of a small clear self.)

You've had your time, a man was shouting on *Newsnight*. It's our time now. Your time's over.

I ignored him. I went back through to the kitchen and stared out into the darkness of the garden. The trees over our neighbours' fence would be bare and hung with rain tonight. The branches would be diamonded. But I couldn't see anything but myself in the electric reflection in the window.

(The kings were in the compost. They'd be deep in leaves. The paint on their turbans would be peeling, their faces maybe eaten. The gifts in their hands would have turned to paint-flaked wood.)

You came through.

What's the matter? you said.

Matter? I said. Nothing.

I went back through with you. We sat down on our sofa together to watch *Border Patrol* or whatever was up next.

'Robbie Brady's astonishing late goal takes its place in our personal histories'

Sally Rooney

Conor calls her from an alleyway, near a plastic skip. It's going to eat his phone credit if she picks up, and he expects himself, in light of this, to hope belatedly that she won't pick up, but he finds himself, regardless, hoping that she does. And she does. She says hello in a crisp, amused voice, as if this phone call is already part of an ongoing joke between them.

Were you watching that? he says.

Oh, I was watching. The atmosphere in the stadium looked like fun.

It was good, yeah.

I envied you slightly, says Helen. I've been here looking at the memes for the last hour.

Relaxing now, he leans against the alleyway wall. It's late but still warm out in Lille, a humid heat, and he's been drinking since the late afternoon.

Memes about the match? he says. Are there ones already?

Oh yeah, it's like simultaneous. It's actually very interesting in the sense – well, do you want to hear my opinions about memes or are you busy?

No, go on.

Are there roaming charges?

I have free calls, he lies, implausibly and without really deciding to.

On the other end of the line, Helen doesn't question the plausibility of Conor having free calls while in France, mainly because she doesn't really register what he's said, beyond the sense that he has given her permission to talk about what she was already thinking about before. She's sitting on her bed, her back against the headboard. She sat this way for the duration of the Ireland-Italy match, which she streamed online and watched alone, eating a bowl of instant ramen noodles with disposable chopsticks while the light in her window faded from a bluish-white to a whitish-grey and finally to dark.

It's interesting to watch an event being recycled as culture in real time, she says. You know, you're watching the process of cultural production while it takes place, rather than in retrospect. I don't know if that's unique.

Yeah, I get you. And, uh. Well, I'm drunk so I'm not going to be at my sharpest here, but I want to say, you know, the disintegration of the idea of authorship.

Totally. That's sharp, you're very sharp. You don't even sound drunk.

I think about memes a lot, he says.

Helen lifts her laptop off her lap and on to the empty part of the bed, as a gesture of commitment to the conversation.

But what's tricky about the point you're making, she says, is that it becomes very difficult to locate power. And to analyse operations of power, culturally. I guess we're used to doing that through the hegemonic figure of the author, or at least through some identifiable power structure like a movie studio or an ad company.

Yeah, and now it's just happening through like, spontaneous mass participation.

I guess you could argue online spaces are gendered and classed in particular ways but like, are they even?

Let's never forget gender, says Conor. Gender everywhere, I would suggest. Are you hearing a lot of noise on the line?

A group of fans have just vacated the bar next to him and flooded on to the street cheering. In the lights over the bar their jerseys have that cheap-looking nylon sheen. They're singing something to the tune of the 1979 Village People hit 'Go West'. Almost all the chants, for some reason, are sung to the tune of 'Go West', making the individual lyrics difficult to decipher in many cases, creative and redolent of spontaneous mass participation though they are.

A little bit now, she says. Are you somewhere busy? It was quiet before so I assumed you were back in the hostel.

No, still at the bar. With the, yeah – the legendary Irish fans.

That's you, you're a legendary Irish fan now. Are you wearing a jersey?

No, I'm kind of keeping my distance, he says. I'm trying not to sing too much or like, suck up to any cops or anything.

The sucking up to cops I must say is a global embarrassment.

French cops as well. The policemen of a country literally renowned for racism. But anyway, look, here we are.

Having said this, Conor realises that it sounded like an attempt to move the conversation on to some new destination. He can practically hear their sudden mutual awareness that he hasn't yet explained why he's calling her, that he has hollowed out a little well in the conversation now where this explanation should go, and yet he doesn't have one, or indeed anything further to say at all. He even considers hanging up, and emailing later to say the signal cut out.

He last saw Helen six weeks ago, at the beginning of May. He was visiting her in Cambridge for the weekend. After a long and tiresome day of travel and vague anxiety about currency, he arrived on Friday night. All day he'd been mentally converting sterling to euro in an attempt to keep track of how much money he was wasting on bus tickets and cups of coffee, and this minor but persistent cognitive effort had drained him and made him feel miserly and self-conscious. It was dark when he got off the bus. He remembers now the flat blue surface of the park beside the bus stop, picked out by streetlights, and the strange flavour of weather, the crisp quality of air, the cool winding-down of a day that might earlier have been warm. He saw Helen then, waiting in her little jacket and scarf, he was amused somehow by the sight of her, and he laughed and felt better.

They walked back to her apartment together, chatting about nothing really. He remembers the yellowish stone facade of her building while she rooted in her bag for the keys. Upstairs she made tea and laid out a little food. They talked until very late. Eventually, in her room, she undressed for bed. He sat on the sofa, where he had put his sleeping bag, and she was talking about something to do with her thesis, how much reading she had glanced at before and now had to do in earnest, and that it made her feel slightly fraudulent, and while she was saying this, she was standing at the wardrobe putting on her nightdress. She was partially, but it seemed not consciously, hidden by the wardrobe's open door. Still he could see her bare left shoulder, her slim white upper arm. She hung her blouse on a wire hanger, replaced it in the wardrobe, and without looking up said: are you watching me?

I'm looking in your direction generally, he said, but not 'watching' as such.

She laughed then and closed the wardrobe door. It was a black nightdress, longish, with shoulder straps.

I was listening to what you were saying, he said.

Oh, I know. I'm very sensitive to losing someone's attention.

He found this remark pleasantly cryptic at the time. Now on the phone he waits for Helen to say something, though it is by the unspoken rules of ordinary conversation obviously his 'turn' to speak, having just signalled that he has something to say.

Good match anyway, he says.

I wish I'd been there. Were you swept away on a tide of emotion?

I was swept a bit, yeah. I shed a tear.

She laughs. That's very sweet, she says. Did you really?

A tear came to my eye, I don't know if it was shed or not.

I was watching alone so I couldn't really experience the full range of emotions, she says. It's like when you go to see a film in the cinema, you laugh in places you wouldn't laugh if you were watching on your own. But it doesn't make the laughing false, you know. Being alone is just less enjoyable.

Are you lonely?

She pauses at this question, which is unusual to hear from Conor, and for the first time in the conversation, including the time when he earlier claimed to be drunk, she's struck by the possibility that he might actually be drunk.

I have to say, I don't like most English people very much, she says. So yeah, living in England, that becomes lonely. Maybe I'm just getting a bad impression of them with the referendum coming up.

Yeah, that looks rough. I think they will stay in, though.

I hope so. Either way it's brought out a lot of very ugly things.

I do feel for you having to live there, he says.

She, too, is thinking of the weekend he visited, the beautiful weather they had. On Saturday they woke up late, to a radiant blue sky powdered with tiny clouds. She made a pot of coffee, they ate toast and oranges. She tidied up the breakfast dishes while he showered, and she was comforted by the noise of the hot water tank and the rush of the taps. When he reappeared in the kitchen he was dressed, and she was still wearing her nightgown, with a cardigan wrapped over it. There was this moment of abrupt eye contact between them, which made her feel as if they hadn't really looked at one another since he arrived. Their eyes stilled the whole room. She thought about satirising this moment lightly to deprive it of its seriousness, maybe by doing something mock-flirtatious, but she couldn't rely on her flirting to seem comic to him rather than grotesque. Instead she turned away, flustered, and he just hovered there not saying anything.

It was a warm day out and Helen remembers what she wore: a flimsy white blouse, a pale ballet skirt, her flat shoes. She wasn't concerned, or doesn't remember being concerned, about her appearance in any real way, but she registered dimly that she would rather look bad than look as if she were trying to look good. They wandered around the Fitzwilliam Museum together in the afternoon, talking. After that they had lunch, and after lunch more coffee. Conor was telling some funny story about work and Helen laughed so much that she spilled coffee on her skirt, which pleased him. She knew that he relished her laughter. It seemed to give him some private, almost sheepish satisfaction, and while she laughed he would avert his eyes slightly, as if to look at her directly would be too much.

She's met a lot of very intelligent people in Cambridge, people who take a brittle pride in demonstrating how clever they are. She somewhat enjoys engaging them in conversation, little jousting exchanges, until the other party becomes defensive and irritable. But the enjoyment is ultimately feline, as if she's idly batting her interlocutor back and forth between her paws. There's something about their kind of intelligence which isn't lively or curious. Conor, who works in a call centre for a mobile service provider, is her ideal conversational partner, the person around whom she feels most clear-minded and least remote. They keep up with one another effortlessly in conversation, and maybe for this reason, or maybe out of a sincere and long-standing mutual affection, their discussions don't become competitive. Helen finds it philosophically sustaining that two people who agree on everything can still find so much to say to one another.

Most people are pretty liberal here, she says, and they're self-congratulatory about that. You can see they have a lot of contempt for normal people, who didn't go to Cambridge or don't have college degrees. And I think the contempt is actually part of what they congratulate themselves on.

Am I a normal person, to you?

Is that ... you're objecting to my use of the phrase 'normal people', or we're talking about our relationship?

He smiles. His eyes are tired and he closes them. The lids feel wet somehow. Well, I like to think I'm very special to you in some ways, he says. He can hear her laughing.

I am curious why you've called, she says. But I'm happy to be talking to you so I don't mind if there's no reason.

I'll be honest with you, I got carried away watching that match. The tide of emotion you were speaking about. And I felt an impulse to give you a ring. I wanted to tell you I love you, and all that.

For a few seconds he hears nothing at all. He can't tell what she's doing on the other end of the line. Then there's a faint noise like a laugh, and he realises it is a laugh.

I love you, too, she says. I was trying to think of something intelligent to say there about how we feel and express love through these communal cultural experiences like football, but then I thought, oh my god, shut up. I love you, too, I miss you.

He wipes at his eyes with the hand that isn't holding the phone. Her voice has a soft, wet quality to him, associated with the deepest consolation he has ever felt.

The weekend I stayed with you, I kind of thought something might happen, he says. But I don't know. Maybe it's good that it didn't. He swallows. I lied about having free calls, he adds. So I probably shouldn't stay on that long.

Oh, she says. Well, that's alright. Go and celebrate.

There's a final silence, in which they both feel the same nameless feeling, the same stirring impulse toward an unknown act, each in fact wanting the other to say again: I love you, I love you very much, but unable to say it again themselves. Despite this unexpected sense of irresolution, of something unfinished, they are each pleased at having managed to extract this new confession from the other, Helen thinking herself the more pleased because Conor said it first, and he thinking himself the more pleased because she didn't have the excuse of drunkenness. They say their goodbyes, distracted now. Conor slips his phone back into his pocket, stands up from the alleyway wall. On the main road a police car drives by, its siren revolving silently, and the fans cheer, for the police or for some other unrelated reason. Helen puts her phone on her bedside table with a soft clicking sound, glass on wood, and then pauses for a moment in stillness. She looks at the opposite wall as if a certain thought has only just now occurred to her. Absently she touches her hair, unwashed today. Then in one seemingly natural, thoughtless motion, she lifts her laptop back on to her crossed legs and taps the trackpad with two outstretched fingers to light the screen.

Poems

'Adlestrop'

Edward Thomas

The poet and essayist Edward Thomas's well-loved poem was first published in the New Statesman *in June 1917, shortly after his death at the Battle of Arras.*

Yes. I remember Adlestrop –
The name, because one afternoon
Of heat the express-train drew up there
Unwontedly. It was late June.

The steam hissed. Someone cleared his throat.
No one left and no one came
On the bare platform. What I saw
Was Adlestrop – only the name

And willows, willow-herb, and grass,
And meadowsweet, and haycocks dry,
No whit less still and lonely fair
Than the high cloudlets in the sky.

And for that minute a blackbird sang
Close by, and round him, mistier,
Farther and farther, all the birds
Of Oxfordshire and Gloucestershire.

'Easter, 1916'

W. B. Yeats

I have met them at close of day
Coming with vivid faces
From counter or desk among grey
Eighteenth-century houses.
I have passed with a nod of the head
Or polite meaningless words,
Or have lingered awhile and said
Polite meaningless words,
And thought before I had done
Of a mocking tale or a gibe
To please a companion
Around the fire at the club,
Being certain that they and I
But lived where motley is worn:
All changed, changed utterly:
A terrible beauty is born.

That woman's days were spent
In ignorant good will,
Her nights in argument
Until her voice grew shrill.
What voice more sweet than hers
When, young and beautiful,
She rode to harriers?
This man had kept a school
And rode our winged horse.
This other his helper and friend
Was coming into his force;

He might have won fame in the end,
So sensitive his nature seemed,
So daring and sweet his thought.
This other man I had dreamed
A drunken, vain-glorious lout.
He had done most bitter wrong
To some who are near my heart,
Yet I number him in the song;
He, too, has resigned his part
In the casual comedy;
He, too, has been changed in his turn,
Transformed utterly:
A terrible beauty is born.

Hearts with one purpose alone
Through summer and winter seem
Enchanted to a stone
To trouble the living stream.
The horse that comes from the road,
The rider, the birds that range
From cloud to tumbling cloud,
Minute by minute change;
A shadow of cloud on the stream
Changes minute by minute;
A horse-hoof slides on the brim,
And a horse plashes within it;
Where long-legged moor-hens dive,
And hens to moor-cocks call;
Minute by minute they live:
The stone's in the midst of all.

Too long a sacrifice
Can make a stone of the heart.
O when may it suffice?
That is Heaven's part, our part
To murmur name upon name,
As a mother names her child
When sleep at last has come

On limbs that had run wild.
What is it but nightfall?
No, no, not night but death;
Was it needless death after all?
For England may keep faith
For all that is done and said.
We know their dream; enough
To know they dreamed and are dead;
And what if excess of love
Bewildered them till they died?
I write it out in a verse –
MacDonagh and MacBride
And Connolly and Pearse
Now and in time to be,
Wherever green is worn,
Are changed, changed utterly:
A terrible beauty is born.

'Here'

Philip Larkin

Swerving east, from rich industrial shadows
And traffic all night north; swerving through fields
Too thin and thistled to be called meadows,
And now and then a harsh-named halt, that shields
Workmen at dawn; swerving to solitude
Of skies and scarecrows, haystacks, hares and pheasants,
And the widening river's slow presence,
The piled gold clouds, the shining gull-marked mud,

Gathers to the surprise of a large town:
Here domes and statues, spires and cranes cluster
Beside grain-scattered streets, barge-crowded water,
And residents from raw estates, brought down
The dead straight miles by stealing flat-faced trolleys,
Push through plate-glass swing doors to their desires –
Cheap suits, red kitchen-ware, sharp shoes, iced lollies,
Electric mixers, toasters, washers, driers –

A cut-price crowd, urban yet simple, dwelling
Where only salesman and relations come
Within a terminate and fishy-smelling
Pastoral of ships up streets, the slave museum,
Tattoo-shops, consulates, grim head-scarfed wives;
And out beyond its mortgaged half-built edges
Fast-shadowed wheat-fields, running high as hedges,
Isolate villages, where removed lives

Loneliness clarifies. Here silence stands
Like heat. Here leaves unnoticed thicken,
Hidden weeds flower, neglected waters quicken,

Luminously-peopled air ascends;
And past the poppies bluish neutral distance
Ends the land suddenly beyond a beach
Of shapes and shingle. Here is unfenced existence:
Facing the sun, untalkative, out of reach.

'Digging'

Seamus Heaney

Between my finger and my thumb
The squat pen rests; snug as a gun.

Beneath my window, a rich rasping sound
When the spade sinks clean into gravelly ground:
My father, digging. I look down

Till his straining rump among the flowerbeds
Bends low, comes up twenty years away
Stooping in rhythm through potato drills
Where he was digging.

The coarse boot nestled on the lug, the shaft
Against the inside-knee was levered firmly.
He rooted out tall tops, buried the bright edge deep
To scatter new potatoes that we picked
Loving their cool hardness in our hands.

By God, the old man could handle a spade;
Just like his old man.

My grandfather cut more peat in a day
Than any other man in Toner's bog.
Once I carried him milk in a bottle
Corked sloppily with paper. He straightened up
To drink it, then fell to right away
Nicking and slicing neatly, heaving sods
Over his shoulder, going down and down
For the good turf. Digging.

The cold smell of potato mould, the squelch and slap
Of soggy peat, the curt cuts of an edge
Through living roots awaken in my head.
But I've no spade to follow men like them.

Between my finger and my thumb
The squat pen rests.
I'll dig with it.

'Last letter'

Ted Hughes

What happened that night? Your final night.
Double, treble exposure
Over everything. Late afternoon, Friday,
My last sight of you alive.
Burning your letter to me, in the ashtray,
With that strange smile. Had I bungled your plan?
Had it surprised me sooner than you purposed?
Had I rushed it back to you too promptly?
One hour later – you would have been gone
Where I could not have traced you.
I would have turned from your locked red door
That nobody would open
Still holding your letter,
A thunderbolt that could not earth itself.
That would have been electric shock treatment
For me.
Repeated over and over, all weekend,
As often as I read it, or thought of it,
That would have remade my brains, and my life.
The treatment that you planned needed some time.
I cannot imagine
How I would have got through that weekend.
I cannot imagine. Had you plotted it all?

Your note reached me too soon – that same day,
Friday afternoon, posted in the morning.
The prevalent devils expedited it.
That was one more straw of ill-luck
Drawn against you by the Post-Office

And added to your load. I moved fast,
Through the snow-blue, February, London twilight.
Wept with relief when you opened the door.
A huddle of riddles in solution. Precocious tears
That failed to interpret to me, failed to divulge
Their real import. But what did you say
Over the smoking shards of that letter
So carefully annihilated, so calmly,
That let me release you, and leave you
To blow its ashes off your plan – off the ashtray
Against which you would lean for me to read
The Doctor's phone-number.
My escape
Had become such a hunted thing
Sleepless, hopeless, all its dreams exhausted,
Only wanting to be recaptured, only
Wanting to drop, out of its vacuum.
Two days of dangling nothing. Two days gratis.
Two days in no calendar, but stolen
From no world,
Beyond actuality, feeling, or name.

My love-life grabbed it. My numbed love-life
With its two mad needles,
Embroidering their rose, piercing and tugging
At their tapestry, their bloody tattoo
Somewhere behind my navel,
Treading that morass of emblazon,
Two mad needles, criss-crossing their stitches,
Selecting among my nerves
For their colours, refashioning me
Inside my own skin, each refashioning the other
With their self-caricatures,

Their obsessed in and out. Two women
Each with her needle.

That night
My dellarobbia Susan. I moved
With the circumspection
Of a flame in a fuse. My whole fury
Was an abandoned effort to blow up
The old globe where shadows bent over
My telltale track of ashes. I raced
From and from, face backwards, a film reversed,
Towards what? We went to Rugby St
Where you and I began.
Why did we go there? Of all places
Why did we go there? Perversity
In the artistry of our fate
Adjusted its refinements for you, for me
And for Susan. Solitaire
Played by the Minotaur of that maze
Even included Helen, in the ground-floor flat.
You had noted her – a girl for a story.
You never met her. Few ever met her,
Except across the ears and raving mask
Of her Alsatian. You had not even glimpsed her.
You had only recoiled
When her demented animal crashed its weight
Against her door, as we slipped through the hallway;
And heard it choking on infinite German hatred.

That Sunday night she eased her door open
Its few permitted inches.
Susan greeted the black eyes, the unhappy
Overweight, lovely face, that peeped out
Across the little chain. The door closed.
We heard her consoling her jailor
Inside her cell, its kennel, where, days later,
She gassed her ferocious kupo, and herself.

Susan and I spent that night
In our wedding bed. I had not seen it
Since we lay there on our wedding day.
I did not take her back to my own bed.
It had occurred to me, your weekend over,
You might appear – a surprise visitation.
Did you appear, to tap at my dark window?
So I stayed with Susan, hiding from you,
In our own wedding bed – the same from which
Within three years she would be taken to die
In that same hospital where, within twelve hours,
I would find you dead.
Monday morning
I drove her to work, in the City,
Then parked my van North of Euston Road
And returned to where my telephone waited.

What happened that night, inside your hours,
Is as unknown as if it never happened.
What accumulation of your whole life,
Like effort unconscious, like birth
Pushing through the membrane of each slow second
Into the next, happened
Only as if it could not happen,
As if it was not happening. How often
Did the phone ring there in my empty room,
You hearing the ring in your receiver –
At both ends the fading memory
Of a telephone ringing, in a brain
As if already dead. I count
How often you walked to the phone-booth
At the bottom of St George's terrace.
You are there whenever I look, just turning
Out of Fitzroy Road, crossing over
Between the heaped up banks of dirty sugar.
In your long black coat,
With your plait coiled up at the back of your hair

You walk unable to move, or wake, and are
Already nobody walking
Walking by the railings under Primrose Hill
Towards the phone booth that can never be reached.
Before midnight. After midnight. Again.
Again. Again. And, near dawn, again.

At what position of the hands on my watch-face
Did your last attempt,
Already deeply past
My being able to hear it, shake the pillow
Of that empty bed? A last time
Lightly touch at my books, and my papers?
By the time I got there my phone was asleep.
The pillow innocent. My room slept,
Already filled with the snowlit morning light.
I lit my fire. I had got out my papers.
And I had started to write when the telephone
Jerked awake, in a jabbering alarm,
Remembering everything. It recovered in my hand.
Then a voice like a selected weapon
Or a measured injection,
Coolly delivered its four words
Deep into my ear: 'Your wife is dead.'

'Passing-Bells'

Carol Ann Duffy

That moment when the soldier's soul
slipped through his wounds, seeped
through the staunching fingers of his friend
then, like a shadow, slid across a field
to vanish, vanish, into textless air ...
there would have been a bell in Perth,
Llandudno, Bradford, Winchester,
rung by a landlord in a sweating, singing pub
or by an altar-boy at Mass – in Stoke-on-Trent,
Leicester, Plymouth, Crewe, in Congresbury,
Littleworth – an ice-cream van jingling in a park;
a door pushed open to a jeweller's shop;
a songbird fluttering from a tinkling cat – in Ludlow,
Wolverhampton, Taunton, Hull – a parish church
chiming out the hour; the ringing end of school –
in Wigan, Caythorpe, Peterborough, Ipswich,
Inverness, King's Lynn, Malvern, Leeds –
a deskbell in a quiet, dark hotel; bellringers' practice
heard by Sunday cricketers; the first of midnight's bells
at Hogmanay – in Birkenhead, Motherwell, Rhyl –
there would have been a bell
in Chester, Fife, Bridgend, Wells, Somerton,
Newcastle, in city and in town and countryside –
the crowded late night bus; a child's bicycle;
the old, familiar, clanking cow-bells of the cattle.

'Men Talking'

Wendy Cope

Anecdotes and jokes,
On and on and on.
If you're with several blokes,
It's anecdotes and jokes.

If you were to die
Of boredom, there and then,
They'd notice, by and by,
If you were to die.

But it could take a while.
They're having so much fun.
You neither speak nor smile.
It could take a while.

'Emergency'

Simon Armitage

The four-pump petrol garage
finally closed,
its defeated owner
inhaling his ghost
in a disused quarry
by coupling the lips of his car exhaust
to the roots of his lungs
via a garden hose;

on the bulldozed forecourt
they threw up a tram-shed
for decommissioned emergency vehicles
where a skeleton workforce
service all manneration
of mothballed workhorses
for occasional call-outs
to sitcoms, period dramas and film sets.

And the actual fire station's
up for rent,
that chapel-shaped building
where they stabled the one engine,
spit-buffing and wire-woolling
the chrome fenders,
T-cutting the steel coachwork
to a flame red.

So what you see,
as the letting-agent puts it,
is what you get:
boot cupboard, functional kitchenette,
brass hooks – two still holding
a brace of yolk-yellow plastic helmets –
northlight roof-windows
and inspection pit.

The makeshift crew
were volunteer part-timers:
butchers, out-menders,
greasy perchers and hill-farmers
who'd pitch up in bloody aprons,
boiler suits or pyjamas
then venture forth,
fire-slaying on the tender.

Sometimes in dreams
my fire-fighting forefathers
appear, alien-like,
breathing from oxygen cylinders
through a sudden parting
of towering, black cumulonimbus
on fully telescoped
turntable ladders.

The bank's gone as well,
and also the post office,
though in the store-cum-off-licence
you can sign a gyro
with a string-and-sellotape-tethered
half-chewed biro
or deface a scratch-card
or sell a bullmastiff.

The horizon ablaze –
is it moor-fire or sundown?
In the local taproom
prescription jellies and tin-foil wraps
change hands under cover
of *Loot* magazine
and Tetley beer mats.
What is it we do now?

'The Hinds'

Kathleen Jamie

Walking in a waking dream
I watched nineteen deer
pour from ridge to glen-floor,
then each in turn leap,
leap the new-raised
peat-dark burn. This
was the distaff side;
hinds at their ease, alive
to lands held on long lease
in their animal minds,
and filing through a breached
never-mended dyke,
the herd flowed up over
heather-slopes to scree
where they stopped, and turned to stare,
the foremost with a queenly air
as though to say: *Aren't we*
the bonniest companie?
Come to me,
You'll be happy, but never go home.

'Driftwood Houses'

Clive James

The *ne plus ultra* of our lying down,
Skeleton riders see the planet peeled
Into their helmets by a knife of light.
Just so, I stare into the racing field
Of ice as I lie on my side and fight
To cough up muck. This bumpy slide downhill
Leads from my bed to where I'm bound to drown
At this rate. I get up and take a walk,
Lean on the balustrade and breathe my fill
At last. The wooden stairs down to the hall
Stop shaking. Enough said. To hear me talk
You'd think I found my fate sad. Hardly that:
All that has happened is I've hit the wall.
Disintegration is appropriate,

As once, on our French beach, I built, each year,
Among the rocks below the esplanade,
Houses from driftwood for our girls to roof
With towels so they could hide there in the shade
With ice creams that would melt more slowly. Proof
That nothing built can be for ever here
Lay in the way those frail and crooked frames
Were undone by a storm-enhanced high tide
And vanished. It was time, and anyhow
Our daughters were not short of other games
Which were all theirs, and not geared to my pride.
And here they come. They're gathering shells again.
And you in your straw hat, I see you now,
As I lie restless yet most blessed of men.

Acknowledgements

The idea for this book stemmed from a conversation I had with Alan Samson many years ago and I would like to thank him and his team at Weidenfeld & Nicolson, especially Simon Wright and Sarah Fortune, for their enthusiasm for this project. A collection of pieces by so many celebrated names could not have happened without the generous support of the writers themselves and of the agents and estates of the authors no longer with us: there are too many to name and thank individually but they all clearly subscribe to the adage that you can judge a person by the company they keep.

This book could not have happened without the help of my colleagues at the *New Statesman* whose commitment to presenting something of the magazine's extraordinarily rich heritage has been inspiring. I should like to thank, in particular, Michael Prodger for his wisdom and editorial judgement, Tom Gatti, Emily Bootle, Gerry Brakus, Mike Danson (owner of the *New Statesman*) and Ken Appiah, as well as all of those colleagues who worked on the special editions of the magazine showcasing our archive that we published to celebrate the *New Statesman*'s centenary in 2013.

Jason Cowley